D1461613

Books are to be returned on or before
the last date below.

PCCS Books — publishers of counselling, psychotherapy and critical psychology texts

CRITICAL PSYCHOLOGY DIVISION

Commissioning Editors: Craig Newnes and Guy Holmes

This is Madness
A critical look at psychiatry and the future of mental health services
Edited by **Craig Newnes, Guy Holmes** and **Cailzie Dunn**
ISBN 1898059 25 X , 1999

This is Madness Too
Critical perspectives on mental health services
Edited by **Craig Newnes, Guy Holmes** and **Cailzie Dunn**
ISBN 1898059 37 3, 2001

Personality as Art
Artistic approaches in psychology
Peter Chadwick
ISBN 1898059 35 7, 2001

Spirituality and Psychotherapy
Edited by **Simon King-Spooner** and **Craig Newnes**
ISBN 1898059 39 X, 2001

Beyond Help
A consumers' guide to psychology
Susan Hansen, Alec McHoul and **Mark Rapley**
ISBN 1898059 54 3, 2003

The Gene Illusion
Genetic research in psychiatry and psychology under the microscope
Jay Joseph
ISBN 1898059 47 0, 2003

Violence and Society
Making sense of madness and badness
Elie Godsi
ISBN 1898059 62 4, 2004

Beyond Prozac
Healing mental suffering
Dr Terry Lynch
ISBN 1898059 63 2, 2004

Power, Interest and Psychology
David Smail
ISBN 1898059 71 3, 2005

www.pccs-books.co.uk

Just War
Psychology and Terrorism

EDITOR

RON ROBERTS

PCCS Books
Ross-on-Wye

First published in 2007

PCCS BOOKS
2 Cropper Row
Alton Road
ROSS-ON-WYE
HR9 5LA
UK
Tel +44 (0)1989 763 900
contact@pccs-books.co.uk
www.pccs-books.co.uk

**Just War:
Psychology and Terrorism**

British Library Cataloguing in Publication Data.
A catalogue record for this book is available from the British Library.

ISBN 978 1 898 05992 9

Cover design by Old Dog Graphics
Cover image by Mario Minichiello

Printed by Cromwell Press, Trowbridge, UK

CONTENTS

For Majda

I believe that despite the enormous odds which exist, unflinching, unswerving, fierce intellectual determination, as citizens, to define the real truth of our lives and our societies is a crucial obligation which devolves upon us all. It is in fact mandatory.

Harold Pinter

The world economy is the most efficient expression of organized crime. The international bodies that control currency, trade, and credit practice international terrorism against poor countries, and against the poor of all countries, with a cold-blooded professionalism that would make the best of the bomber terrorists blush.

Eduardo Galeano

The best and most beautiful things in the world cannot be seen or even touched. They must be felt with the heart.

Helen Keller

CONTRIBUTORS

MAJDA BECIREVIC is in the Faculty of Health and Social Care at the Open University

BRIAN DOHERTY is in the Department of International Relations at the University of Keele

DAVE HARPER is in the School of Psychology at the University of East London

CHRIS HEWER is in the Department of Psychology at Kingston University

JULIE LLOYD is a clinical psychologist working for Surrey and Borders, and Hampshire Partnership NHS Trusts. She is also a member of MEDACT

NIMISHA PATEL is Head of Clinical Psychology, Medical Foundation for the care of victims of torture, London, and Senior Lecturer in Clinical Psychology, University of East London

STEVE POTTER is Director of the University of Manchester Counselling Service

IAN ROBBINS is in the European Institute of Health and Medical Sciences at the University of Surrey and Head of the Traumatic Stress Service at St George's Hospital, London

RON ROBERTS is in the Department of Psychology at Kingston University

JOHN SLOBODA is in the Department of Psychology at the University of Keele, is co-founder of the Iraq Body Count Project and Executive Director of the Oxford Research Group

WENDY TAYLOR is a UK Government Analyst

HARRIET TENENBAUM is in the Department of Psychology at Kingston University

ACKNOWLEDGEMENTS

First of all I would like to thank all of the contributors for their hard work and commitment to this project. John Sloboda, Nimisha Patel and Dave Harper have been consistently encouraging, for which I am most grateful. I would like to extend particular thanks to Chris Hewer for giving so much of his time, not only to read sections of this book, but also to share thinking and ideas beyond the comfortable boundaries of mainstream psychology. It has been a lot of fun and has contributed considerably, both directly and indirectly, to the contents of the book. I would like to thank Maggie at PCCS Books, who has been a great help in getting this project off the ground and seeing it through, not to mention Sandy for copy-editing and Craig and Guy for helpful suggestions. My friends Merry, Julius, Cockney Dave, Wandia, Subi, Jane, Arike, Delroy, Michael and Pau must also receive a worthy mention. My final thanks go to Majda who has been an inspiration and wonderful source of support.

UN-ACKNOWLEDGEMENTS

I do not wish to thank George Bush, Dick Cheney, Donald Rumsfeld or Tony Blair, nor those members of the US Republican and British Labour Parties who have, in their own ways, done so much to make this book possible.

INTRODUCTION

RON ROBERTS

Afghanistan, Iraq, Lebanon—the numbers of lives lost and people displaced runs into the hundreds of thousands. The 'War on Terror' is, for the people affected directly by this imperial enterprise, a war of terror. As the human cost escalates, the savage brutality unleashed by the United States and its allies is hard to conceal. The invasions of Afghanistan and Iraq and the unbridled support for Israel's wanton destruction of the Lebanon have been re-presented to citizens of the United Kingdom and the United States as necessary responses to the growth of extreme Islamist movements around the world. However the 'War on Terror', rebranded and remarketed as the 'long war' by US officials, has produced a civilian death toll far in excess of anything that al-Qaeda or its allies could boast and the 'benefits' for citizens of the Middle East and Central Asia, where this war is for the most part being fought, appear thin indeed. Certainly, greater democracy and security are not among them. Closer to home, the curtailment of civil liberties, increased surveillance and an elevated risk of terrorist attack hardly provides anything to cheer about. So if we are to understand the origins and consequences of the War on Terror and the Iraq War we must seek an alternative narrative to that provided by official sources.

Considerable evidence exists that both the US and UK have nurtured the growth of extremist movements in areas of strategic interest (Ahmed, 2006), which could provide apparent justification for the huge military presence in these regions. But besides clear identification of the economic and political motives underpinning military action, this 'alternative' narrative involves a profound reframing of the psychology that accompanies acculturation into Western society—in particular how and why people internalise the motives of Western governing elites. To those people on the planet living outside this sphere of cultural conditioning, and here we are talking about most of the world's people, the vindictiveness and aggression of the US–UK alliance (aided and abetted by the US's principal client state, Israel), and its single-minded pursuit of energy, wealth and power has been obvious for some time. To citizens of the US and UK however, it has not. What does this tell us about our own psychology? This book utilises the invasion of Iraq and the 'War on Terror' to deconstruct the psychological and cultural processes which shadow these actions, and which prepare citizens (children and adults alike) to not only accept the state's actions but to assume benevolence in its intentions. A further purpose here is to explore the possibilities that such a deconstruction may open our eyes to. These include a new postmodern variant of totalitarian rule fashioned by the security state to safeguard elite interests at home and abroad, as well as the idea, unspeakable in our own media, that 'we', i.e. the above tripartite alliance of Britain, the US and Israel, do not want peace in the Middle East. Implanted deep in the American and British psyche is the product of a grand deception—the notion that we are continually exploring all means to bring peace, stability, justice, human rights and democracy to the world. The opposite in fact appears more likely to be true: that all available avenues are followed to avoid peace, to wage war, to solicit evidence from torture and to antagonise people around the world toward positions of hatred and violence. All of this in 'the national interest'. This reality somehow survives outside of any critical scrutiny, even in the face of widespread scepticism about the motives of individual politicians. As the window on this hypocrisy opens ever wider, people in the West face the loss of the moral legitimacy of their culture in the wider world. These events, however, also present people with new opportunities to organise, protest and make visible their challenge to the incumbent war 'fever' and suppression of civil liberties. The psychological factors that hinder or promote effective recognition and action are examined throughout the book—particularly in the chapters by John Sloboda and Brian Doherty. A common theme in this analysis is the power of social representations: of warfare, terrorism, and political action to shape our culture (a culture, which has been regularly engaged in military action abroad) and the actions of individuals within it. The theory of social representations makes possible a different kind of critique than that afforded by the experimental social psychology of the 1960s and 70s. It is not that the work of Stanley Milgram and Philip Zimbardo is no longer relevant to any understanding of the events unfolding in Iraq—particularly with respect to the commission of war crimes and torture at Abu Ghraib (see Bruner, 2004)—but in the 2000s there is a need to look beyond these situationist accounts and direct our gaze at the wider culture within which the meaning of these actions are to be found—for actors and interpreters alike. In examining social representations the contributors have adopted a largely UK perspective—though representations of war and terrorism from outside these shores, chiefly from parts of the Muslim world—are an important counterpoint to these.

As well as describing the psychology of the population, one that simultaneously reflects and contributes to the goals of the military industrial complex and the security state, this book is primarily concerned with the relationship between the psychological community and those who wield power. In different ways, many of the contributors to this book consider what exactly our responsibilities as psychologists are and how psychological knowledge can be used constructively in the present climate. Ian Robbins, Nimisha Patel and David Harper in particular—all of them with considerable experience in providing psychological services to people who have undergone torture and inhuman treatment—have made important and powerful statements here concerning our individual and collective responsibility as psychologists. The 'War on Terror' and events in Iraq are perhaps a watershed for the discipline, posing uncomfortable questions for the psychological community regarding the stance adopted towards the powerful and the privileged. The unfolding of this nightmare offers an opportunity to know ourselves a little better and to explore and develop psychological perspectives on peace and conflict, which may not only provide an intellectual defence against the fog of official lies but also permit a platform for action to be constructed that places human rights firmly at the centre of the discipline. This will not be possible without examining the politics of the discipline. In short we need a more socially responsible psychology in the twenty-first century; one unshackled from state interests, that contributes in some small way to a more positive and just world.

Ron Roberts
London, October 2006

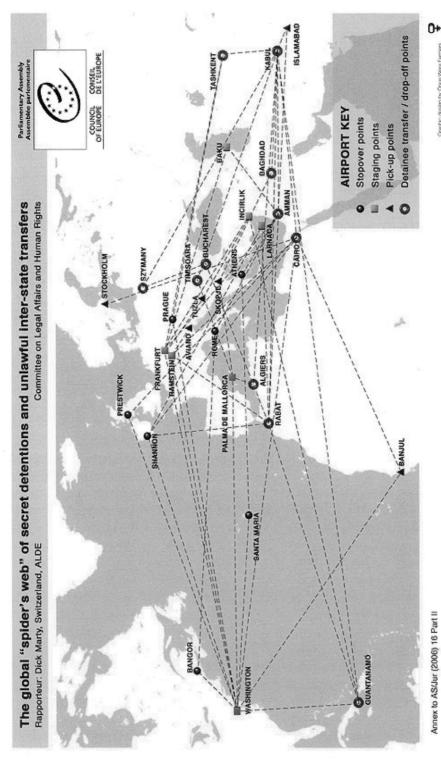

The global "spider's web" of secret detentions and unlawful inter-state transfers

Rapporteur: Dick Marty, Switzerland, ALDE

Committee on Legal Affairs and Human Rights

Parliamentary Assembly
Assemblée parlementaire

COUNCIL
OF EUROPE

CONSEIL
DE L'EUROPE

AIRPORT KEY

Stopover points
Staging points
Pick-up points
Detainee transfer / drop-off points

Annex to AS/Jur (2006) 16 Part II

Graphic design by Once Were Farmers

CHAPTER 1

The Complicity of Psychology in the Security State[1]

DAVID HARPER

A search for the roots of Abu Ghraib in the development and propagation of a distinctive American form of torture will, in some way, implicate almost all of our society—the brilliant scholars who did the psychological research, the distinguished professors who advocated its use, the great universities that hosted them, the august legislators who voted funds, and the good Americans who acquiesced, by their silence, whenever media or congressional critics risked their careers for exposés that found little citizen support, allowing the process to continue. (McCoy, 2006, p. 6)

Introduction[2]

In this chapter I focus on how knowledge gathered by British and American mental health professionals and social scientists (especially psychologists) has been used by the military, intelligence and security communities over the last fifty years. In particular, I will focus on the evolution of psychological torture (i.e. coercive and aversive psychological interrogation techniques) based on this knowledge, but I will also examine the spread of this knowledge into related areas such as surveillance.

As a psychology undergraduate in Liverpool in the mid 1980s, I remember receiving a lecture on the psychology of stress, concerning US soldiers in Vietnam.

1. Parts of this chapter originally appeared in Harper (2004).
2. There is some overlap with Nimisha Patel's chapter in this volume (Chapter 4). However, I have focused more on the psychological research underlying the coercive ways in which psychological knowledge has been applied. Human rights aspects, trauma to detainees, rehabilitation and preventative aspects are covered more fully in Nimisha's chapter.

At the time I didn't really question the ethics of such research or its military application. However, during my third year I undertook a course on the history and philosophy of psychology. The theme behind many of the lectures was the need to view psychology's history in its context and to question many of our taken-for-granted assumptions about the discipline. For this course, I wrote a long essay on the politics of psychology and read up on the use of psychology by the military—especially Ackroyd et al. (1977) and Watson (1978). I was shocked by what I came across. I hadn't realised that the sensory deprivation experiments that had informed our views on perception had, in fact, largely been used to understand 'brainwashing'. Psychologists are often ignorant about this side of the discipline. Indeed, one can sound like a conspiracy theorist just by discussing this research, although it is well established in the public record as a result of UK and US government inquiries, court cases and Freedom of Information requests in the US. For example, at a recent seminar I was discussing secret funding of psychological research by the Human Ecology Fund (a body which covertly channelled CIA funds to researchers) at Cornell University, when another psychologist at the seminar told me that, though she had been at Cornell, she had never heard of this. This is an understandable response, given that this kind of work receives virtually no coverage in psychology textbooks.

There are, therefore, three reasons for focusing on these matters. Firstly, the discipline of psychology positions itself as a science, but there is often scant discussion of the ethics and politics concerning the use of this knowledge. Secondly, psychologists show a remarkable ignorance about the history of their discipline, particularly the application of psychological knowledge by the military and security agencies. Thirdly, because of this ignorance, the discipline runs the risk of repeating previous mistakes. The aim of this chapter is to provide a critical counterbalance to the received view of psychology's history. It is important that we continually revisit this history, and do not forget our complicity in its abuses. My aim, therefore, is to keep this memory alive.

The history of psychological research into torture and interrogation

Alfred McCoy (2006) describes the CIA's research into psychological warfare and interrogation between 1950 and 1962 as 'a veritable Manhattan Project of the mind' (p. 7). In part, interest in this area grew from anxieties regarding reports of American POWs in the Korean war giving information to interrogators as a result of techniques described as 'brainwashing'—from the Chinese *xi nao*: 'wash brain'—(Hinkle & Wolff, 1956; Schein et al., 1961; Lifton, 1967).[3] McCoy points

---

3. Interestingly, Anthony (1990) argues that the notion of brainwashing was promulgated by the CIA as a propaganda strategy to undercut Communist claims that American POWs in Korean War Communist prison camps had voluntarily expressed sympathy for Communism ...

to the significance of a secret meeting in Canada in June 1951 between Henry Tizard (the UK Ministry of Defence's senior scientist) with the chairman of the Canadian Defense Research Board (CDRB), senior CIA researcher Cyril Haskins and other Canadian scientists, including the Canadian psychologist Donald Hebb. McCoy describes how they agreed on a joint behavioural research programme aimed at developing new interrogation techniques.

Sensory deprivation

McCoy (2006) notes that, between 1951 and 1954, Donald Hebb received a small grant from the CDRB to study the effects of sensory deprivation. Twenty-two paid student volunteers at McGill University lay in a cubicle with sensory modalities reduced by soundproofing and low constant noise, wearing thick gloves and goggles to diffuse the light. The results were reported in the *Canadian Journal of Psychology* and the *American Psychologist,* though a fuller account was given at a secret CDRB symposium. The study found that, after continuous isolation and sensory deprivation, the participants began to experience hallucinations and a degraded ability to think clearly. Most students quit the study after 2 or 3 days.

Project MKUltra

In 1953, the CIA gathered together the wide range of psychological research into a programme entitled MKUltra under the control of Dr Sidney Gottlieb of the CIA's Technical Services Division (McCoy, 2006). MKUltra has become widely known as a result of the Rockefeller Commission (Rockefeller et al., 1975) and the Church Committee (US Congress, 1976). Between 1953 and 1963 MKUltra and allied projects dispensed $25 million for human experiments by 185 non-governmental researchers at 80 institutions, including 44 universities and 12 hospitals: 6 per cent of the research funding was provided on a non-contractual basis since many academic researchers feared for their reputations if their work for the CIA became widely known (McCoy, 2006). Lee and Shlain (1992) and Stevens (1987) provide a fascinating account of these bizarre studies and their social, political and cultural context. McCoy provides a pithy summary of their unethical nature:

> Seeking unwitting subjects, the CIA injected not only North Korean prisoners, but also spiked drinks at a New York City party house, paid prostitutes to slip LSD to their customers for agency cameras at a San Francisco safe house, pumped hallucinogens into children at summer camp, attempted behaviour modification on inmates at California's Vacaville Prison. (McCoy, 2006, p. 29)

... and had admitted that they had engaged in war crimes against the Chinese and North Korean forces. Anthony asserts that the brainwashing theory was propagated to the general public through the books of Edward Hunter (e.g. Hunter, 1956) who was a secret CIA 'psychological warfare specialist' with a cover identity as a journalist.

Similar research was going on in the UK. For example, in the 1950s servicemen took part in a study conducted by scientists working for the Secret Intelligence Service (MI6) at Porton Down, the Chemical Warfare establishment. Told that the purpose of the study was to find a cure for the common cold, they were asked to drink a clear liquid, which in fact produced frightening hallucinations. Recently it was discovered that the liquid contained LSD and, in February 2006, three of the servicemen received out-of-court settlements for the distress caused (BBC News Online, 2006a).

More frighteningly, the CIA conducted 'terminal' studies where dubious defectors or double agents in Europe were experimented on (at an Anglo-American facility near Frankfurt) until they died (McCoy, 2006). Despite initial claims of the promises of LSD and hypnosis to enhance interrogation, most of the research came to nought.[4] McCoy (2006) notes that the emphasis then shifted to a Psychological Sciences research programme where $7–$13 million were allocated annually for behavioural studies at major universities 'by channelling funds through private foundations, some legitimate and others fronts—including the Ford and Rockefeller foundations' (p. 31).

Perhaps the most brutal experiments on civilians were conducted by psychiatrists Ewen Cameron and Lloyd Cotter. In 1957, Cameron, at Allan Memorial Institute (McGill University's psychiatric treatment facility), had applied for CIA funds through the Society for the Investigation of Human Ecology. His plan was to use unwitting and non-consenting psychiatric patients to test a three-stage method for what he termed 'depatterning':

> First, drug-induced coma for up to eighty-six days; next, electroshock treatment three times daily for thirty days; and, finally, a football helmet clamped to the head for up to twenty-one days with a looped tape repeating, up to half a million times, messages like 'my mother hates me'. In contrast to Hebb's six-day maximum for voluntary isolation, Cameron confined one patient, known only as Mary C., in his 'box' for an unimaginable thirty-five days of total sensory deprivation. (McCoy, 2006, p. 44)

Cameron was regarded by Hebb as 'criminally stupid' (McCoy, 2006, p. 44) but he had been a member of the Nuremberg medical tribunal (the 'doctors' trial') and went on to become not only the first Chairman of the World Psychiatric Association but also president of both the American and Canadian Psychiatric Associations. The Californian doctor Lloyd H. Cotter further developed Cameron's brutal research. Cotter was sent by the CIA, along with two CIA psychiatrists, to

---

4. Lee and Shlain (1992) note that the US Army's Chemical Corps dispensed with LSD as a battlefield incapacitant after they developed a drug called BZ (Quinuclidinyl Benzilate), capable of knocking out troops for three days. By the 1960s it was the army's standard incapacitating agent and was deployable via grenade and a 750-pound cluster bomb.

Bien Hoa Mental Hospital north of Saigon. The idea, according to McCoy, was to test, under field conditions, whether Cameron's depatterning techniques would work. Cotter's research was published in 1967 in the *American Journal of Psychiatry.*

According to the article, within a short time of arriving at the hospital, Cotter instituted a mass operant conditioning treatment. Patients who wanted to leave were told they had to work for three months 'to prove their capability' (1967, p. 24). This work involved tending crops for American Special Forces troops in Viet Cong territory (ibid., p. 27). Those who refused to work (120 out of 130 patients) received unmodified ECT (i.e. ECT without tranquillisers or muscle relaxants). ECT continued at the rate of three times a week until there was 'evident improvement in the behavior of the patients, the appearance of the ward, and the number of patients volunteering for work' (1967, p. 25). Cotter noted 'ECT served as a negative reinforcement for the response of work for those patients who chose to work rather than to continue receiving ECT' (1967, p. 25). When a similar procedure failed on the second ward—after seven weeks—food was withdrawn until, after three days, all 130 women 'volunteered' for work. In Cotter's words:

> As has been repeatedly demonstrated, when the subject is hungry, food is one of the strongest and most powerful of positive reinforcements. (Ibid., p. 25)

One of the duties for 'recovered' patients was working in US Special Forces 'A camps', which were prone to Viet Cong attack.

The Society for the Investigation of Human Ecology
Both Watson (1978) and Greenfield (1977) have documented military funding of psychological research. In her *APA Monitor* article, Greenfield (1977) describes how the Society for the Investigation of Human Ecology (later called the Human Ecology Fund) was set up and financed by the CIA in the late 1950s. Originally organised to finance research into 'brainwashing' at Cornell Medical School, by 1957, Carl Rogers was on the board of the organisation receiving grants for his work on psychotherapy. He has commented:

> It's impossible ... to realize what it was like in the 1950s. It seemed as though Russia was a very potential enemy and as though the United States was very wise to get whatever information it could about things that the Russians might try to do, such as brainwashing people. (Greenfield, 1977, p. 10)

Others in receipt of Human Ecology Fund grants included the psychologist Edgar Schein, the anthropologist Edward T. Hall (proxemics theorist), psychiatrist Martin Orne (researcher into demand characteristics and hypnosis) and sociologist Jay

Schulman (one of only two of Greenfield's interviewees to have received CIA funds unwittingly). Shallice (1984) also includes Erving Goffman in this list. At the end of this period of CIA co-ordinated research, McCoy (2006) argues that three key behavioural components of psychological torture could now be clarified:

- sensory deprivation (drawing on the work of Donald Hebb);
- self-inflicted pain (drawing on the work of Albert Biderman, Irving L. Janis, Harold Wolff and Lawrence Hinkle);
- obedience to authority (drawing on the work of Stanley Milgram).[5]

These research insights were codified in the CIA's 1963 *KUBARK Counterintelligence Interrogation*[6] handbook. In the UK, they were to form the basis of new interrogation procedures.

Psychological torture in Northern Ireland
In the UK and Europe some commentators have argued that the reported abuses of human rights, as part of the 'War on Terror', are a result of American exceptionalism—i.e. the view that human rights standards only apply to 'foreign' countries (e.g. Ignatieff, 2004). Indeed, even Alfred McCoy refers to psychological torture as a 'distinctive American form of torture' (2006, p. 6). However, this again serves to demonstrate how short our memories are, for most of these psychological torture techniques were carried out by the British army and security agencies in Northern Ireland in the early 1970s. Only after much debate, press comment, two official inquiries and a case at the European Court of Human Rights, were these practices reported to have ended.

       According to Meek (2005), Britain set up an 'intelligence research unit' at Maresfield in Sussex in 1957. By 1962 SAS and paratroop units were being trained to cope with capture. However:

In April 1971, in conditions of great secrecy, a course in sensory deprivation was held at Maresfield for members of the Royal Ulster Constabulary. In the early morning of August 9 that year, the British army began its mass internment programme, arresting and imprisoning, without charges or courts, hundreds of suspected members of the IRA. Hidden within the mass internments was another programme, involving 14 prisoners, to test the new interrogation techniques. (Meek, 2005)

Following the mass arrest of 342 men by Ulster security forces in 1971, this

---

5. Milgram's studies of obedience were funded by the National Science Foundation after some consultation with the Office of Naval Research. Though there is no evidence that Milgram received funding from the CIA or military, McCoy (2006) thinks the timing suspicious.
6. KUBARK was, apparently, a CIA cryptonym for the agency itself.

small group was subjected to several techniques that appeared to serve as pre-interrogation procedures. These included placing a black bag over their heads ('hooding'); being made to stand against a wall with their hands held high above their heads and legs apart for up to 16 hours at a stretch (i.e. in 'stress positions' inducing self-inflicted pain) and being deprived of sleep for the first two or three days. In addition, the men were made to wear boiler suits (perhaps to reduce tactile stimulation) and exposed to continual 'white noise'. It was also alleged that the men's diets were restricted to occasional administrations of dry bread and water (Shallice, 1972, p. 388; British Medical Association (BMA), 1986, pp. 15–16). The British Army termed this 'interrogation in depth' and the methods used (hooding, noise bombardment, food deprivation, sleep deprivation and forced standing positions) were known collectively as the 'five techniques' (Hogg, 2003). At the time, the UK government stated that these procedures were necessary in order to 'provide security for detainees and guards', an 'atmosphere of discipline' and to prevent inter-prisoner communication (BMA, 1986, pp. 15–16). Defence Minister Lord Carrington said the only people subjected to these techniques were 'thugs and murderers' (Hogg, 2003). Commenting on the Northern Irish interrogations, Anthony Storr, however, wrote:

> The hooding and the continuous noise were designed not to isolate the men from each other but as a deliberate method of producing mental disorientation and confusion. (BMA, 1986, p. 16)

The Compton Report (HMSO, 1971) gave justifications for the techniques. Following further outcry, a three-person privy counsellors' inquiry was instituted. Brownlie (1972) notes that the majority report, written by Lord Parker and Mr Boyd-Carpenter, concluded that:

> There is no reason to rule out these techniques on moral grounds and that it is possible to operate them in a manner consistent with the highest standards of our society. (Brownlie, 1972, p. 505)

In a dissenting minority report, Lord Gardiner noted that the 'five techniques' were originally used by the KGB in the 1930s (Hogg, 2003). Brownlie quotes the final paragraph of his report:

> The blame for this sorry story, if blame there be, must lie with those who, many years ago, decided that in emergency conditions in Colonial-type situations, we should abandon our legal, well-tried and highly successful wartime interrogation methods and replace them by procedures which were secret, illegal, not morally justifiable and alien to the traditions of what I believe still to be the greatest democracy in the world. (Brownlie, 1972, p. 507)

Prime Minister Edward Heath accepted Lord Gardiner's minority report damning them (BMA, 1986, p. 18). This may have been related to the fact that the Irish government was in the process of taking the British government to the European Commission of Human Rights (Hogg, 2003). The Commission reported in 1976 and, in 1977, the Attorney General gave an undertaking that the 'five techniques' would not be used as an aid to interrogation again (McCoy, 2006).

The BMA (1986), McCoy (2006), Shallice (1972, 1984) and Watson (1978) all note that these techniques appeared to have been designed in the early 1960s in the midst of burgeoning sensory deprivation research. Both Watson and Shallice make a direct link between this research and the interrogation techniques. Shallice observes, 'not surprisingly, psychologists, by investigating the nature of brainwashing have improved it' (1972, p. 387). Indeed, Shallice (1972) has argued that psychologists have a special responsibility for some British interrogation techniques that appear to have been produced by the 'conscious use of available scientific knowledge' (1972, p. 387).

Current involvement of psychologists, psychiatrists and other health professionals in psychological torture

It would be comforting to report that past abuses of psychological knowledge had now ended, but this would be both inaccurate and complacent. There is evidence of psychiatrists' and psychologists' involvement in interrogations at Abu Ghraib, Guantánamo Bay and other detention centres (Lewis, 2005a, b; Lifton, 2004; Miles, 2004; Bloche & Marks, 2005a, b; Physicians for Human Rights (PHR), 2005) and evidence of enhancements to the psychological torture paradigm, for example, the use of strobe lighting, loud music and repeated playing of bizarre music and sound effects (Ronson, 2004). McCoy (2006) reports that the CIA was allowed to use ten 'enhanced' interrogation methods designed by Agency psychologists for their detainees. One of these is 'waterboarding' where the detainee is tied to a board with the head lower than the feet so that he or she is unable to move. A piece of cloth is held tightly over the face, and water is poured onto the cloth. Breathing is extremely difficult and the detainee will fear imminent death by asphyxiation. Its use is expressly prohibited in the US Army Field Manual 34-52 on interrogation but the CIA is exempt from this. Mayer (2006) notes that soldiers in earlier conflicts have been court-martialled for using this technique.

Behavioral science consultation teams
Following official inquiries into abuse of detainees at Abu Ghraib and elsewhere, the involvement of psychologists, psychiatrists and other health professionals came to light (Lewis, 2005a, b; Bloche & Marks, 2005a, b; Physicians for Human Rights (PHR), 2005). According to McCoy (2006), after Major General Geoffrey D. Miller took over as base commander at Guantánamo, he authorised the creation

of 'Behavioral Science Consultation Teams' (BSCT), which included a psychiatrist and psychologist and which were granted permission to use 16 techniques for 'priority' detainees beyond those in FM 34-52 because of claims that the detainees were resisting interrogation. These enhanced techniques included: stress positions; isolation for up to 30 days; light and sound deprivation; hooding; 20-hour interrogations; and in a possible reference to waterboarding, 'wet towel and dripping water to induce misperception of suffocation' (McCoy, 2006, p. 127). Similar teams were in evidence at Abu Ghraib.

According to one former interrogator 'their purpose was to help us break them' (Lewis, 2005a). Bloche and Marks (2005b) noted that psychiatrists and psychologists conveyed information, including that gained from medical records, regarding areas of psychological vulnerability, for example phobias, to military and other US personnel (e.g. CIA operatives).

> BSCT consultants prepared psychological profiles for use by interrogators; they also sat in on some interrogations, observed others from behind one-way mirrors, and offered feedback to interrogators. (Bloche & Marks, 2005b, p. 7)

Indeed, Major John Leso, whose previous job was assessing aviators' fitness to fly, became the first BSCT psychologist and attended part of the interrogation of Mohammed al-Qahtani, the so-called twentieth hijacker (Bloche & Marks, 2005b). McCoy (2006) concludes that 'Guantánamo's integration of psychologists into routine interrogation perfected the CIA's paradigm, moving beyond a broad-spectrum attack on human senses, sight and sound, to a customized assault on individual phobias or cultural norms, sexual and religious' (p. 187).

Evidence about the involvement of British psychologists and psychiatrists is sketchy. Leigh (2004) reports that psychologists are present during Resistance to Interrogation (R2I) training for British special forces soldiers. Indeed, Leigh argues that the hiring of ex-special forces soldiers as private security contractors may be responsible for the propagation of psychological torture methods in Iraq.

The American Psychological Association's Presidential Taskforce on Psychological Ethics and National Security

In response to public criticism of the role of psychologists in BSCTs, the American Psychological Association launched a Presidential Task Force (American Psychological Association, 2005). Nimisha Patel outlines some of the issues surrounding this report in Chapter 4 so I will avoid unnecessary detail here. However, of note is that the taskforce engaged in 'vigorous discussion and debate and did not reach consensus on several issues' (ibid., p. 9). These issues included whether psychologists should abide by international human rights law. This is significant because previous definitions of torture developed by the Bush administration regarded only practices leading to organ failure or death as torture. That is why US officials could claim that they did not engage in torture, because their definition was much narrower than international human rights standards.

Taskforce members also disagreed about 'the degree to which psychologists may ethically disguise or ethically dissemble the nature and purpose of their work from individuals whom they engage directly' (ibid., p. 9). In other words, some members felt that lying to detainees was ethical. This is not just a technical point— a book by a US Military Intelligence interrogator who served in Afghanistan shows that this tactic was often used (Mackey & Miller, 2004). For example, on one occasion Mackey presented himself to British detainees as a British officer. On another occasion, an interrogator pretended to be from an Arab State that practised torture with the threat that detainees were to be sent to this country. At other times, detainees were warned that if they were spies they could face a death penalty—an opportunity to threaten detainees with death indirectly.

Other professional associations' policies

In contrast to the American Psychological Association, the American Psychiatric Association published a position statement in which it was stated 'no psychiatrist should participate directly in the interrogation of persons held in custody by military or civilian investigative or law enforcement authorities, whether in the United States or elsewhere' (American Psychiatric Association, 2006, p. 10). It is unclear from this statement whether this would cover CIA interrogations. As a result, the US Department of Defense announced 'that from here on they would seek the help of psychologists, but not psychiatrists, when they want advice on how to elicit information from detainees in Guantánamo Bay, Cuba, and other places where prisoner interrogations take place' (Hausman, 2006, p. 4). The American Medical Association also produced a position statement which was broadly similar to the American Psychiatric Association's although it allowed physicians to 'participate in developing effective interrogation strategies for general training purposes' but that these 'must not threaten or cause physical injury or mental suffering and must be humane and respect the rights of individuals' (American Medical Association, 2006). However, the AMA's statement specifically included interrogations conducted as part of national security intelligence gathering as falling within the ambit of the policy.

In July 2006, at the Royal College of Psychiatrists annual meeting in Glasgow, a resolution was passed condemning psychiatric participation in the interrogation of detainees. This resolution welcomed statements in a policy letter from the Defence Medical Service's Surgeon General on medical support to persons detained by UK forces whilst on operations. This stated that health personnel were not to apply their 'knowledge and skills in order to assist in the interrogation of prisoners and detainees in a manner that may adversely affect their physical or mental health' or to 'question detainees about matters unless they are relevant to their medical care' (Royal College of Psychiatrists, 2006).

The American Psychological Association's response to criticism

The taskforce report received considerable criticism. Shinn (2006) provides a summary of the concerns—noting that six out of the ten taskforce members had ties to the Department of Defense. One of the critics was Mike Wessells who had resigned from the taskforce (Shinn, 2006). Following publication of the taskforce report, Leonard Rubenstein (Executive Director of Physicians for Human Rights) wrote to Ronald Levant (President of the APA) and Stephen Benke (APA Director of Ethics). He made three specific criticisms of the report (Rubenstein, 2005):

- that it did not take account of, or issue prohibitions against, participation in highly coercive interrogation;
- that it did not require psychologists to adhere to international human rights law;
- that it did not adequately protect confidentiality with respect to detainee health information.

In the February 2006 issue of *APA Monitor*, Gerald Koocher, APA President, responded to the criticisms defensively:

A number of opportunistic commentators masquerading as scholars have continued to report on alleged abuses by mental health professionals. (Koocher, 2006, p. 5)

However, he argued that no clear evidence had been presented of these abuses. In August 2006 the APA 'adopted as policy long-standing international human rights standards for the prevention of torture and other cruel, inhuman and degrading treatment or punishment' (Foster, 2006). However, it maintained its previous taskforce guidelines. Leonard Rubenstein was critical:

The ultimate question is, should psychologists participate in national security interrogations, and the answer is no … it's a question that other medical groups have addressed and the APA has not. (Foster, 2006)

The evolution of torture policy

There are, no doubt, many contextual influences that create the conditions for torture to take place. Brutalisation of soldiers and dehumanisation of the enemy can create the conditions for abuse (Grossman, 1996). No doubt emotions like fear, anger and frustration and a wish for revenge may also play a role. However, one of the most significant influences in the current development of psychological torture is official government sanction by the Bush administration and ambiguous policies (see also Rose, 2004; McCoy, 2006; Mayer, 2006). Cofer Black, a previous director of the CIA's counter-terrorist unit, stated to Congress in early 2002 that 'after 9/11 the gloves came off' (Barry, Hirsch & Isikoff, 2006). Indeed, soon after the September 11th attacks, Vice President Dick Cheney said 'we also have to work, through, sort of the dark side, if you will. We've got to spend time in the shadows in the intelligence world'. He went on:

> It is a mean, nasty, dangerous, dirty business out there, and we have to operate in that arena. I'm convinced we can do it; we can do it successfully. But we need to make certain that we have not tied the hands, if you will, of our intelligence communities in terms of accomplishing their mission. (Cheney, 2001)

One strategy which has become more frequently used after 9/11 is 'extraordinary rendition', where people are kidnapped and transported to countries where torture is commonplace—a form of subcontracted or outsourced torture (Mayer, 2005). In September 2006, an official Canadian government commission reported on the extraordinary rendition of Maher Arar, a Canadian citizen of Syrian descent. In 2002, returning from a holiday in Tunisia, Maher Arar was arrested at Kennedy airport whilst in transit. He was flown to Jordan in a US government plane where he was transferred to Syria and tortured. The reason for the rendition? He happened to have an acquaintance who was the subject of a terrorism investigation. It was a year before Syrian officials concluded he had no connection with terrorism and returned him to Canada (Austen, 2006). Similarly, Italian prosecutors are seeking the extradition of 22 suspected CIA agents wanted in relation to the kidnapping of Egyptian Muslim cleric Osama Mustafa Hassan in Milan in 2003 (BBC News Online, 2005a).

Despite initial doubts about the existence of this programme, the evidence has been mounting and, in June 2006, rapporteur Dick Marty produced a report for the Council of Europe which documents what he terms a 'spider's web' of secret sites and planes owned by 'shell companies'—front companies for the CIA (Committee on Legal Affairs and Human Rights, 2006), see Figure 1.

McCoy (2006) cites a 2004 *Observer* estimate that 3,000 terror suspects were being held at secret CIA sites and allied prisons in the Middle East. It also estimated that there had been 150 extraordinary renditions of al-Qaeda suspects who were subsequently sent to Egypt, Jordan, Morocco, Saudi Arabia, Syria and Pakistan. As one US official put it 'we don't kick the shit out of them. We send them to other countries so they can kick the shit out of them' (Priest & Gellman, 2002).

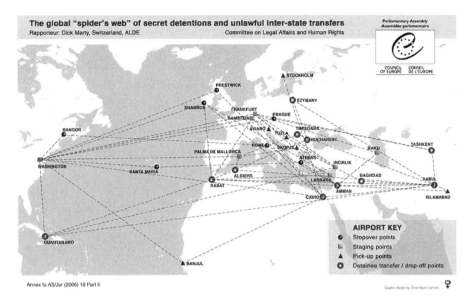

Figure 1. Extraordinary Rendition: The Global Spiders Web[7]

The British government claims it does not use torture and has provided unconvincing arguments that it is not aware of rendition flights though many have transited through Prestwick airport near Glasgow (Corera, 2005). However, a witness told the Special Immigration Appeals Court in 2003 that the Security Service (MI5) 'would use information extracted from tortured prisoners as evidence in court' (Gillan, 2006). However, the Law Lords rejected this argument in December 2005 (BBC News Online, 2005b). Moreover, the recent movement to Guantánamo Bay of 14 'high value detainees' from secret CIA prisons across the world has finally proven the existence of these prison sites (BBC News Online 2006b). Information from interrogations of some of these detainees featured in the 9/11 Commission report (National Commission on Terrorist Acts upon the United States, 2004). The dehumanisation of detainees that such policies inculcate has significant consequences:

> 14,000 Iraqi 'security detainees' subjected to harsh interrogation, often with torture; 1,100 'high value' prisoners interrogated, with systematic torture, at Guantánamo and Bagram; 150 extraordinary, extralegal renditions of terror suspects to nations notorious for brutality; 68 detainees dead under suspicious circumstances; some 36 top al-Qaeda detainees held for years of sustained CIA torture; and 26 detainees murdered under

---

7. Report of the Parliamentary Assembly of the Council of Europe on alleged secret detentions and unlawful inter-state transfers of detainees involving Council of Europe member states. (Resolution 1507 (2006), Recommendation 1754 (2006), Doc 10957 + Addendum, Rapporteur: Mr Dick Marty.) See p. xiv for larger version of Figure 1.

questioning, at least 4 of them by the CIA. (McCoy, 2006, pp. 124–125)

Indeed, at Guantánamo Bay, attempted suicides in 2003 were regarded as 'manipulative self injurious behavior' (Rose, 2004, p. 65). By June 2006, Rear Admiral Harry Harris, camp commander, termed the suicides by three detainees 'an act of asymmetric warfare waged against us' (BBC News Online, 2006c). These attitudes seem to display a total lack of understanding of the stress of indefinite detention. An illustration of this can be seen in the first person account of Moazzem Begg (Begg & Brittain, 2006) and in psychological and psychiatric reports on detainees in the British high security prison HMP Belmarsh (Robbins et al., 2005, see also Chapter 3, this volume) who are now subject to house arrest or 'control orders'. Rose has also reported on the brutal actions of the Extreme Reaction Force (now termed Force Cell Extraction Teams) at Guantánamo where several guards in riot gear assault detainees regarded as breaching camp discipline, bizarrely, whilst a video record is made so senior officers can review whether disproportionate force has been used. According to Rose, the Pentagon told Associated Press in 2004 'that "only" 32 hours of tape showed the ERF using excessive force' (Rose, 2004, p. 74).

This level of official sanction permeated through the reaches of the US military and security apparatus (Rose, 2004; McCoy, 2006). It is not surprising, therefore, that this approach, combined with the argument that the Geneva Convention does not apply to detainees captured in Afghanistan and elsewhere led to consequences at the frontline for military interrogators:

> By the time we left Afghanistan, we had come to embrace methods we would not have countenanced at the beginning of the war. And while those who followed us at Bagram dismissed much of the so-called wisdom we sought to pass on, they took to monstering[8] with alacrity. Indeed, as we left, it was clear they did not regard this as a method of last resort but as a primary option in the interrogation playbook. What was an ending point for us was a starting point for them. (Mackey & Miller, 2004, p. 476)

The assumptions underlying torture

> It is incredible what people say under the compulsion of torture, and how many lies they will tell about themselves and about others; in the end, whatever the torturers want to be true, is true. (Spee, 1631, cited in Rose, 2004, pp. 92–93)

---

8. 'Monstering' referred to an interrogation strategy in which an interrogator did not allow sleep breaks and the interrogation continued 'as long as the interrogator could hold up' (Mackey & Miller, 2004).

So wrote the Jesuit academic Friedrich Spee in *Cautio Criminalis,* his 1631 polemic against the European witch-hunts of the Middle Ages (Rose, 2004). However, it seems his lesson needs to be re-learned in the twenty-first century. The post-9/11 debate about torture has been replete with macho posturing. For example, McCoy (2006) quotes Jane Harman, ranking democrat on the House Intelligence Committee:

> If you're serious about trying to get information in advance of an attack, interrogation has to be one of the main tools. I'm OK with it not being pretty. (p. 179)

A similar line is pursued by the ex-Military Intelligence interrogator Greg Mackey:

> If a prisoner will say anything to stop the pain, my guess is he will start with the truth. Our experience in Afghanistan showed that the harsher the methods we used … the better the information we got and the sooner we got it. (Mackey & Miller, 2004, p. 477)

According to McCoy (2006) an ABC News/Washington Post poll conducted two months after the release of images of abuse at Abu Ghraib, reported that 35 per cent of Americans felt torture was acceptable in some circumstances. This is hardly surprising given the promotion of physical and psychological torture in popular culture, for example in the American TV series *24* where FBI counterterrorism agent *Jack Bauer* regularly tortures suspects (who are always guilty), always producing reliable, timely and useful intelligence (Zizek, 2006).

There has been considerable academic debate about the ethics of torture with the American law professor Alan Dershowitz arguing for the creation of torture warrants. The 'ticking bomb' scenario is regularly used as an argument in such cases. As McCoy (2006) notes, however, real-life examples of this scenario are hard to come by. For example, many cite the interrogation of Abdul Hakim Murad in the Philippines who was linked to Ramzi Yousef, the maker of the 1993 World Trade Centre bomb. However, McCoy (2006) reports that most of the useful intelligence was gathered in the first few minutes of Murad's arrest and Meek (2005) comments that Yousef was arrested as a result of evidence (e.g. the address of his dentist where he was subsequently arrested) found at an apartment in the Philippines. Although the Israeli security services have claimed many examples of torture leading to important information, McCoy (2006) reports that, after considerable investigation, there seemed to be only one case—that of a Hamas organiser.

Rosa Brooks, a law professor at the University of Virginia law school, comments 'the so-called ticking bomb scenario has proved remarkably effective as a rhetorical tactic for defusing opposition to controversial interrogation techniques' (Brooks, 2005). If you acknowledge that you might turn to torture under certain extreme circumstances (e.g. stopping a nuclear bomb) then where does one draw the line? Brooks also identifies a flawed assumption with torture—that the person you are torturing is guilty. This is an assumption shot through Greg Mackey's account, where the default assumption appears to be that detainees are guilty until proven otherwise (Mackey & Miller, 2004). However, what if the person tortured is innocent? How can they establish their innocence? For many, they appear caught up in a Kafkaesque world where they have to confess to things they have not done. For example, Shafiq Rasul, a British detainee in Guantánamo Bay, gave a false confession after months of coercive interrogation and psychological torture. He said that he had met Osama bin Laden and Mohammed Atta (one of the September 11th hijackers) in Afghanistan in 2000 and appeared in a video with them. He was only cleared of this when the Security Service (MI5) produced evidence that he was actually working at a branch of Curry's electrical stores in the West Midlands at the time (BBC News Online, 2004d).

McCoy (2006) identifies other flawed assumptions with the ticking bomb scenario:

- that the person captured has key information;
- that those arresting know when the bomb is going to go off;
- that the person is captured just before;
- that the interrogators know a lot about the plot but are missing a few crucial details;
- that the interrogators know this person has the information;
- that the interrogators will be able to verify the information.

As McCoy argues, such a confluence of factors is unlikely in the extreme. He quotes Georgetown University law professor David Cole: 'You can't know whether a person knows where the bomb is or even if they're telling the truth. Because of this, you end up going down a slippery slope and sanctioning torture in general' (McCoy, 2006, p. 195). Koppl (2005) has identified logical problems with torture—the interrogator needs to know whether information gained is accurate and needs to be able to credibly promise that the torture will stop if the information is accurate otherwise there would be no incentive to give the information—again, he notes that such conditions are extremely unlikely.

Arrigo (2004) identifies other problems with torture, from a utilitarian point of view. She identifies four models of interrogation: (1) the animal instinct model (based on the idea that the subject will tell the truth in order to stop the pain); (2) the cognitive failure model (where the subject tells the truth because the stress of torture interferes with the ability to deceive); (3) the data processing model (where mass arrests are required); and (4) the rogue interrogation services model (where torture is an established part of a brutal intelligence service, like Saddam Hussein's security service). Arrigo finds problems with each of these models: The animal model fails since bodily injury might impair the ability to convey the truth, the subject might die and the torturer cannot control the subject's interpretation of pain. The cognitive failure model fails because interrogators cannot distinguish true from false statements and lengthy interrogation might reduce the value of the information. The data processing model fails because analysts become overwhelmed with data and the mass arrests are likely to motivate more opposition from the population. Finally the rogue interrogation model fails (because the motives of the torturers bias the information) and is likely to empower opposition groups.

Indeed, McCoy (2006) notes that although the French won the Battle of Algiers, they lost the war because their extensive use of torture delegitimised their case for the war. Why then, do interrogators continue to turn to torture? McCoy cites Hinkle and Wolff's Cold War report:

> When feelings of insecurity develop within those holding power, they become increasingly suspicious and put great pressures upon the secret police to obtain arrests and confessions. At such times police officials are inclined to condone anything which produces a speedy 'confession' and brutality may become widespread. (Hinkle & Wolff, 1956, p. 135)

Conflicting models of interrogation

Amidst press reports and official inquiries about psychological involvement in interrogations one clear area of debate concerns the model which drives interrogations (Bloche & Marks, 2005b; McCoy, 2006). Law enforcement agencies like the police and FBI prefer a rapport-based model of interrogation, rather than a coercive one based on inducing fear and anxiety. This is because of widespread evidence of the unreliability of information obtained through coercive interrogation. A major factor in this unreliability is that, under certain conditions, people can be suggestible and confess to things they have not done (Gudjonsson, 2003; Kassin & Gudjonsson, 2004). In the UK, for example, the 1984 Police and Criminal Evidence Act prevented coercive interrogation techniques and introduced a number of safeguards including the audio-taping of interviews, following the experience of wrongful convictions—as a result of forced confessions—like the Birmingham Six and the Guildford Four. Gisli Gudjonsson has been conducting research into suggestibility for twenty years—examining how false confessions, confabulations and false memories may be produced as a consequence of both the circumstances of interrogations (e.g. use of false evidence) and the individual characteristics of suspects (e.g. level of intelligence, suggestibility or anxiety). Yet there is no mention of suggestibility, for example, as an important factor in either Greg Mackey's account, of his work as an interrogator (Mackey & Miller, 2004) or in the APA taskforce report (APA, 2005).

Physicians for Human Rights (PHR, 2005) quote from heavily redacted emails between FBI agents concerning the interrogations at Guantánamo, released following a Freedom of Information Act request:

... in a series of emails about Guantánamo, an FBI agent wrote that 'Our Behavioral Assessment Unit (BAU)[9] disagreed with the use of specific techniques in the case of [redacted] as they opined that the techniques would not be successful and they could produce unreliable results. (PHR, 2005, p. 99)

Similarly, Savage (2005) interviewed Dr Michael Gelles, the head psychologist for the Navy Criminal Investigative Service:

The strategy behind a coercive approach, he said, is to try to 'vacuum up all the information you can and figure out later' what is true and what is not. This method, he argued, clogs the system with false and misleading data. He compared it to 'coercive tactics leading to false confessions' by suspects in police custody.

Gelles noted that 'fellow psychologists, intelligence analysts, linguists, and interrogators' shared his scepticism. In addition, he stated:

We do not believe—not just myself, but others who have to remain unnamed—that coercive methods with this adversary are ... effective ... if the goal is to get information, then using coercive techniques may be effective. But if the goal is to get reliable and accurate information, looking at this adversary, rapport-building is the best approach. (Ibid.)

Savage (2005) also reports on the publication of a memo that described how FBI agents tried to persuade military commanders that coercive techniques were unreliable and recounted:

A 'heated' video teleconference in which the FBI showed the military that certain intelligence produced by coercive techniques 'was nothing more' than what the FBI got with traditional tactics: [The Defense Department] finally admitted the information was the same the Bureau obtained. It still did not prevent them from continuing [their own] methods. (Ibid.)

Johnston (2006) reports how FBI interrogators were withdrawn from interrogating Abu Zubaydah so CIA interrogators could use more aggressive tactics. Of course, gathering information in this manner could mean that courts refuse to accept the evidence and thus the chances of successful prosecutions are much diminished. Johnston notes that, in late 2001 and early 2002 senior CIA officials drew up a list of aggressive interrogation procedures that might be used. As part of this

---

9. The correct title is actually the Behavioral Analysis Unit.

process they 'consulted agency psychiatrists and foreign governments to identify effective techniques beyond standard interview practices'.

Rapport-based interrogation can have significant outcomes. For example, a recent BBC programme by reporter Peter Taylor described how the Malaysian Jihadi Nasir Abbas (who had been head of the military division of Jemaah Islamiya) eventually ended up co-operating with the police, giving evidence in prosecutions against his former comrades. He had been a trainer in Afghanistan in the early 1990s. His view of Jihad was that it was:

> ... acceptable to fight and kill foreign forces occupying Muslim countries like the Soviets in Afghanistan, the Americans in Iraq or the Philippine army occupying ancestral Muslim lands in Mindanao, but killing innocent civilians—men, women and children—is forbidden. (Taylor, 2006)

However, when he discovered that some of his former students in Afghanistan were responsible for the 2002 Bali bombings he was deeply shocked:

> 'I feel sorry, I feel sin,' he said, 'because they used the knowledge to kill civilians, to kill innocent people.' (Taylor, 2006)

Interestingly, rapport-based interrogation disrupted his assumptions about the security forces:

> As he was taken off for interrogation, he feared the worst. 'I believed that the police were very cruel and used torture to get their answers.' he said. But Mr Abbas was in for a surprise. He was treated with civility and Muslim respect. (Taylor, 2006)

This is a good example of how a coercive approach would have been counter-productive, as it would simply have fulfilled Nasir Abbas' expectations and made it unlikely that he would have willingly co-operated in the way that he has— resulting in successful prosecutions. McCoy (2006) gives other examples of how empathy and an understanding of language and culture can be effective in rapport-based interrogation.

Unfortunately, the development of psychological torture techniques is not the only way in which psychologists and other social scientists and health professionals are contributing to worrying forms of knowledge as part of the 'War on Terror'. In the next section I examine the wide array of new technologies of political control.

The 'Manhattan Project of the Mind' rolls on: new technologies of political control

A considerable amount of research funding in the UK and elsewhere comes from military and security agencies. Langley (2005) notes that the UK's defence Research and Development spending is 33 per cent of the total government Research and Development budget, the highest in the EU. He also notes, 'With ESRC funding several research teams are also teasing apart the psychological and societal aspects of terrorism, with a total budget of less than £750,000' (Langley, 2005, p. 65).

Anecdotal evidence suggests that military and security agencies regularly attend academic conferences and approach researchers. I give several examples here from my own experience. I was at a Discourse Analysis workshop where an academic was approached (unsuccessfully) for help by researchers working at the Defence Evaluation and Research Agency. I heard an academic specialising in risk analysis mention, during a presentation at a conference, about giving a talk to Secret Intelligence Service (MI6) operatives. I was emailed out of the blue by the Director of Terrorism Studies at the US Military Academy to contribute to a book, presumably on the basis of an article I had previously written (Harper, 2004). Nimisha Patel (see Chapter 4 in this volume) also reports on how a conference on torture was attended by a military physician from a country where torture was practised.

In the wake of the September 11th attacks the APA sought to offer consultation to a range of intelligence and security agencies. For example, an APA Public Policy Office (PPO) report to the APA's Board of Scientific Affairs outlined a number of initiatives (American Psychological Association, undated) including:

- A meeting in June 2002 between two senior staff members in the National Security Council's Office of Combating Terrorism and APA President Philip Zimbardo, Senior Scientist Susan Brandon and PPO's Heather Kelly.
- In December 2002, APA Senior Scientist Susan Brandon and Science Policy Director Geoff Mumford arranged for Robert Sternberg, PhD, President-Elect of APA, to provide a presentation, hosted by the CIA, on intelligence and cognitive assessment to a group of psychologists from the Intelligence Community who are directly involved in operations.
- Combating Terrorism: Responses From the Behavioral Sciences, 24 one-page summaries of how psychological research could address particular problems (http://www.apa.org/ppo/issues/svignetteterror2.html)
- The production of a report (APA/FBI, 2002) on applying psychology to counterterrorism with a preface written by Dr Anthony Pinizzotto (FBI Behavioral Science Unit), Dr Susan Brandon (Senior Scientist, APA), Dr Geoffrey Mumford (Director of Science Policy, APA). Scenarios discussed included 'a trustworthy local businessman reports suspicious activity by an apparently Middle Eastern neighbour' and 'a woman contacts her

therapist about a friend of her son's "martyrdom mission"'.

Although it is understandable for psychologists to want to put their knowledge at the service of the public, it is vital that the implications of their work are seriously thought through, particularly given the history of psychology's involvement with military and security agencies.

Arming Big Brother

Hayes (2006) has reported on the European Security Research Programme. He notes that its proposed budget of one billion euros per year is almost treble that being made available by the EU for research into the environment, including climate change, and the equivalent of 10 per cent of the entire EU research budget.

Wright (1998, 2002) has reported on a new generation of 'technologies of political control' and 'non-lethal' or 'less than lethal weapons' (see also Ackroyd et al., 1977; Bunker, 1997; Ronson, 2004). This includes: new surveillance technologies (of which more below); innovations in crowd control weapons; new methods of prison control in the private sector; and new interrogation and torture technologies. For example:

> The US Army has identified a range of technologies used to facilitate such options which include anti-traction devices (e.g. liquid ball bearings being researched by South West Research Institute in Texas), acoustic weapons (including Vortex Ring Guns being researched by ICT in Germany), entanglements and nets (produced by Foster-Miller in Mass [Massachussetts]), malodorous munitions (produced the Monell Chemical Senses Center in Philadelphia), obscurant and sticky foams, directed energy systems, isotropic radiators and radio frequency weapons (such as the vehicle mounted $40 million VMAD system which uses high power microwaves to heat up a human target to induce an artificial fever), expected to be in the field by 2009. (Wright, 2002, p. 4)

Wright also discusses worrying research into developing 'bio-weapons for racially selective mass control' (2002, p. 6). His discussion of prison control methods was prescient in that Gordon (2006) has argued that the abuse in Abu Ghraib was, in many ways, the outcome of 'practices, amounting to a condition of permanent imprisonment … pioneered by the US in its super-maximum civilian prisons' (p. 42) especially when many of the abusive Abu Ghraib military police were prison guard reservists. Wright comments:

> With proper accountability and regulation, some of the technologies discussed above do have a legitimate law enforcement function; without

such democratic controls they provide powerful tools of oppression. The unchecked vertical and horizontal proliferation of the technologies of political control described in this report, present a powerful threat to civil liberties in Europe. (1998, p. 59)

Surveillance technologies

Sherrard (1991) investigated why there was so much psychological research on face recognition and concluded that this was because it was applicable to electronic surveillance techniques. In particular, it is directly applicable to Closed Circuit Television surveillance—the UK has the highest density of CCTV cameras in the world. London's Newham Borough Council was one of the first authorities to employ a sophisticated CCTV system called Mandrake where by the 140 CCTV cameras are linked to software that can identify faces and compare it to a database of individuals considered to be 'of interest'. In the probability of an individual project receiving funding, face recognition and 'man-machine interface' (80 per cent) were surpassed by no other research areas according to Sherrard, based on the 1987 edition of Current Research in Britain/Social Sciences. In addition, the US military are extremely interested in visual cognition, having spent 32 per cent of the 1980s 'Star Wars' Strategic Defense Initiative funding on 'Surveillance, Acquisition, Tracking and Kill Assessment' using parallel distributed processing modelling—another area of research which was mainly supported by military funding (Bowers, 1990, p. 136).

Hayes (2006) reports that one of the aims of the EU Security Research Programme is 'situation awareness' which, he argues, is shorthand for surveillance and intelligence gathering. Ten of the first 24 projects funded under this programme concern general surveillance technologies that are in no way limited to counterterrorism. Three of the projects concern EU border controls. Projects here include: surveillance from space platforms (including Europe's new *Galileo* GPS system); biometrics and RFID identification systems (a tiny computer chip which can be 'read' by radio-waves); and border Surveillance by Unmanned Aerial Vehicles. Wright (1998, 2002) details a number of new surveillance technologies including vehicle number plate recognition systems and extensively networked CCTV systems. The reach of computerised information can be seen in the fact that the police are regularly using this information. For example, a recent report indicated that the Metropolitan Police in London had made 243 requests to access people's Oyster card records—these smart cards, used by five million Londoners, record details of each bus, tube or train journey made by the holder over the previous eight weeks. Of these 243 requests, 229 were granted (BBC News Online, 2006d).

Wright (2005) describes the ECHELON surveillance system developed by the USA, UK, Australia and New Zealand (see also European Parliament, 2001).

According to some reports, ECHELON can capture radio and satellite communications, telephone calls, faxes, emails and other data streams nearly anywhere in the world and includes computer automated analysis and sorting of intercepts. According to Halpin and Wright (2002), the organisation Statewatch concluded 'it is the interface of the ECHELON system and its potential development on phone calls, combined with the standardisation of "tappable" communications centres and equipment being sponsored by the EU and the USA, which presents a truly global threat over which there are no legal or democratic controls' (p. 11).

The Office of Surveillance Commissioners (2006) report details the large scale of surveillance conducted. During 2005–2006 there were: 435 intrusive surveillance authorisations; 2,310 property interference authorisations; 23,628 directed surveillance authorisations; and 4,559 Covert Human Intelligence Sources recruited by law enforcement agencies. It needs to be borne in mind that this does not cover surveillance by the security or intelligence services. A report by the American Civil Liberties Union (ACLU) (2004) details other worrying developments in surveillance technology, particularly the increasing crossover of private data into government databases. Of particular concern is the increasing use of data mining.

Data mining
The ACLU report notes that:

> The idea behind data mining is to tap into the ever-growing number of databases containing details on individuals' behavior, aggregate that data to form rich pictures of individuals' activities and then use computer models to scrutinize them en masse for suspicious behavior. (2004, p. 23)

One of the most worrying new technologies is that devised by the Information Awareness Office at the Defence Advanced Research Projects Agency (ARDA) in the US Department of Defense. Originally called Total Information Awareness (TIA) it has gone through a number of politically induced name changes. Next, it was called Terrorism Information Awareness and then the program was supposedly cancelled although ARDA's new Novel Intelligence from Massive Data (NIMD) program seems to be a replacement. Goldenberg (2002) notes that the purpose of TIA is to trawl through huge amounts of data on US citizens in order to 'predict potential terrorists by tracking a lifetime of seemingly innocuous movements through electronic paper trails' for example 'academic transcripts, prescription drugs, telephone calls, driving licences, airline tickets, parking permits, mortgage payments, banking records, emails, website visits and credit card slips'. It was run by Admiral John Poindexter who played a central role in illegally channelling funds from Iranian arms sales to Contra guerrillas in Nicaragua and was convicted of lying to Congress. Poindexter was forced to resign in August 2003 over another information awareness project and Congress has cut the funds allocated to TIA and banned it from focusing on US citizens without congressional oversight (Borger, 2003). Given that previous attempts to block this project have foundered it is likely that it will continue under its new title: NIMD. Of course, the attempted prediction of behaviour through statistical modelling and computation has a long history in psychology and it is, again, likely that this project will be drawing on psychological knowledge. Of course, it is interesting that research in both surveillance and TIA/NIMD technologies is largely conducted by businesses under contract to government agencies since this decreases the amount of direct accountability for their work.

The ACLU report notes that another US programme intended to aggregate and analyse vast amounts of private-sector information on the activities of Americans is the MATRIX (Multi-State Antiterrorism Information Exchange). Like TIA, it is based on bringing together vast amounts of information to detect terrorism and other crimes. It 'combines government databases from participating states with a private database that claims to have 20+ billion records from 100's of sources' (2004, p. 24).

Following Operation Overt in the UK in August 2006 when an alleged plot to blow up transatlantic airliners was disrupted, reports discussing passenger profiling began to appear in the press at the same time as an informal meeting of EU Justice and Home Affairs ministers in London (BBC News Online, 2006e). Criteria mentioned included 'People behaving suspiciously or with an unusual travel pattern could be selected but racial or religious factors may also form part of the criteria' (BBC News Online, 2006e). Mathur (2006) describes the effects of such ethnic profiling, where, after 9/11, there was a 'dragnet' arrest approach where 'thousands of Muslim, South Asian and Middle Eastern men were detained by the FBI, police and immigration officers and held in various prisons in New York and New Jersey' (p. 31).

Goldston (2006) describes the ambitious German profiling operation— Rasterfahndung—carried out from the end of 2001 until early 2003. In this massive exercise, he reports, German police reportedly collected sensitive personal data from public and private databases pertaining to approximately 8.3 million persons. The profile was based on characteristics of members of the 'Hamburg Cell' around Mohammed Atta, one of the 9/11 hijackers. Criteria established at national level included the following:

- 18–40 years old;
- male;
- current or former student;
- resident in the regional state (Land) where the data is collected;
- Muslim;
- legal residency in Germany;
- nationality or country of birth from a list of 26 countries with predominantly

Muslim population / or stateless person / or nationality 'undefined' or 'unknown'.

In the end, apparently not a single terrorist suspect was identified.

What has this to do with psychology? Well, as we shall see in the next section on network theory, rather a lot.

Network theory

Milgram's (1967) 'small world' article reported that two Americans could be linked by six other people (or 'six degrees of separation'). Keefe (2006) describes how this insight has been mobilised to understand affiliations between jihadis. He discusses the work of social network analysis consultant Valdis Krebs who plotted the network of the September 11th hijackers using publicly available information (Krebs 2002–2006). Krebs found that a disproportionate number of links centred on Mohammed Atta. Keefe (2006) reports how:

> Analysts start with a suspect and 'spider-web' outward, looking at everyone he contacts, and everyone those people contact, until the list includes thousands of names. Officials familiar with the program have said that before individuals are actually wiretapped, computers sort through flows of metadata—information about who is contacting whom by phone or e-mail.

However, a practical obstacle is the sheer number of links detected:

> The National Counterterrorism Center's database of suspected terrorists contains 325,000 names; the Congressional Research Service recently found that the N.S.A. is at risk of being drowned in information. (Ibid.)

Sageman (2004a, b) has adopted a different approach to social network analysis by compiling biographies of 400 individuals considered terrorists. He found that they did not experience significant mental health problems. Sageman argues that most of the people he investigated were not very religious when they joined jihad, only becoming religious later—often whilst living in another country from where they grew up. Most were, in some way, totally excluded from the society they lived in. Eighty eight per cent had friendship or family bonds to the jihad. Sixty per cent were associated with twelve mosques and institutions across the world. He notes that there is no profile; just similar trajectories to joining the jihad and that most of these men were upwardly and geographically mobile. They come from moderately religious, caring, middle-class families, are skilled in computer technology and speak a number of languages.

Following the attacks on al-Qaeda bases in Afghanistan, he argues that the network is now self-organised from the bottom up, is very decentralised and grows organically, like the Internet. There are no 'recruiters'. Instead 'spontaneous groups of friends, as in Madrid and Casablanca, who have few links to any central leadership, are generating sometimes very dangerous terrorist operations, notwithstanding their frequent errors and poor training' (Sageman, 2004a).

McFate (2005) describes the long history of the use of anthropology in counter-insurgency. However, perhaps the most bizarre application of ideas has been described by Eyal Weizman, an architect based in Tel Aviv and London, who has conducted research on behalf of the human rights organisation B'Tselem on the planning aspects of the Israeli occupation of the West Bank. Weizman (2006) reports that, via an Operational Theory Research Institute set up in 1996, the Israeli Defence Forces have been heavily influenced by the writings of Gilles Deleuze, Félix Guattari and Guy Debord, as well as more contemporary writings on urbanism, psychology, cybernetics, post-colonial and post-structuralist theory.

Weizman argues that the IDF attack on the city of Nablus in April 2002 was a classic example, described by its commander, Brigadier-General Aviv Kokhavi, as 'inverse geometry', which he explained as 'the reorganization of the urban syntax by means of a series of micro-tactical actions'.

Weizman notes that:

> During the battle soldiers moved within the city across hundreds of metres of 'overground tunnels' carved out through a dense and contiguous urban structure ... Furthermore, they used none of the city's streets, roads, alleys or courtyards, or any of the external doors, internal stairwells and windows, but moved horizontally through walls and vertically through holes blasted in ceilings and floors. This form of movement, described by the military as 'infestation', seeks to redefine inside as outside, and domestic interiors as thoroughfares.

However, he warns that this 'seductive use of theoretical and technological discourse seeks to portray war as remote, quick and intellectual, exciting—and even economically viable'.

Psychology's vulnerability to misuse

Why is it that psychological research has been so implicated in the development of methods of psychological torture and of political control? I would argue that there are four reasons. Firstly, psychologists are often keen to see their work applied but are not always thoughtful about the consequences. Secondly, psychologists are just as vulnerable to the anxieties that citizens experience—for example, much of the research in the 1950s was conducted by researchers who knew full well how their work was to be applied, but these psychologists wanted to help their country in the face of what they saw as a Communist threat from China and Russia. We see the same now as we experience a fear of terrorism. Thirdly, as McCoy (2006) notes, psychologists are not restrained by the invocation to 'first, do no harm'—for example, they do not swear a Hippocratic oath. Finally, as McCoy argues, this makes psychologists 'more flexible in their service to the state, its military, and clandestine agencies' (2006, p. 32).

The social sciences have been involved in military, security and intelligence work for many years. Indeed, as McFate (2005) notes, Darling (1966), writing in the CIA's house journal, *Studies in Intelligence*, reports how Gregory Bateson—a British anthropologist whose research was a major influence on the early development of family therapy—served in the US Office of Strategic Services (the forerunner of the CIA) during World War II. Darling observes that Bateson was one of the first people to call for the creation of a post-war clandestine service. McCoy (2006) goes so far as to suggest that, because hundreds of US psychologists had served in the military or conducted contract research for the Pentagon, psychology was 'the most militarized among the social or biological sciences' and thus it 'already had a professional mind-set that made it a natural CIA ally in the search for new interrogation techniques' (p. 32). The links between psychology and the Intelligence Community continue today—the CIA even advertises for social and clinical psychologist posts on its website.

Of course, it is not inevitable that psychologists become complicit in abusive practice. We have already seen how Dr Michael Gelles spoke out against coercive interrogation tactics, at considerable risk to his career. Indeed, Pumla Gobodo-Madikizela who is a South African clinical psychologist who served on the Truth and Reconciliation Commission has published a brave and insightful analysis of Eugene de Kock, commanding officer of apartheid death squads, based on 46 hours of interviews (Gobodo-Madikizela, 2003).

Psychological warfare: information and perception warriors

There is another use of psychological knowledge by the security state: psychological operations. These are used in both overt and covert ways. Overtly, the British Army maintains a psychological warfare unit: the 15 (UK) Information Support Group—its name changed from 15 (UK) PSYOPS Group in order to distance its work from so-called 'black' and 'grey' propaganda operations which, it is claimed, are 'not practised today' (Jolly, 2001). It has a permanent staff of eight drawn from three services and a reservist group of 28 people drawn from the media, broadcasting and publishing. It is mainly involved in designing leaflets dropped to enemy troops and setting up radio stations. In March 2003 BBC News Online reported that it had set up a radio station in Basra, run by Lt. Col. Mason, deputy chairman of Choice FM in London. The use of psychological operations by the US military is far more substantial than its British counterparts.

However, alongside these overt and openly reported operations it is clear that there are other, more covert, uses of psychological operations: propaganda for the citizens of countries sending forces abroad. In *Weapons of Mass Deception* (Rampton & Stauber, 2003) the authors detail a number of these. Remember the story about Iraqi soldiers removing babies from incubators in Kuwait in October 1990? One of the witnesses to the US Congressional Human Rights caucus, Nayirah, a 15-year-old Kuwaiti girl, gave tearful evidence about this, but what was not reported at the time was that she was the daughter of the Kuwaiti Ambassador to the US and her evidence had been coached by Lauri Fitz-Pegado, the Vice President of Hill and Knowlton, one of the world's largest PR firms. This company had set up a front organisation. This is known in PR circles as 'astro-turfing'—a common PR strategy well known to those observing how pharmaceutical companies set up apparently grass-roots 'patient's groups' to campaign for a particular company's products. In this case the front organisation was Citizens for a Free Kuwait—to which the Kuwaiti government channelled $11.9 million in six months (Rampton & Stauber, 2003). PR consultant John W. Rendon has worked on extensive Iraq-related activities under contract to the Pentagon and the CIA including distributing American flags and the flags of other coalition countries to Kuwaiti residents to welcome coalition troops in Kuwait during the first Gulf War. He has described himself as an 'information warrior' and a 'perception manager'. The Pentagon defines perception management as the combination of 'truth projection, operations security, cover and deception' (Rampton & Stauber, 2003). Bamford (2005) describes Rendon's Pentagon-funded role in laying the ground for the Iraq War and how he not only gathered together disparate groups to form the 'Iraqi National Congress' but even gave them their name.

One key technique in targeting the general public is to get the media to focus on particular stories and to ignore others. John Pilger has noted how, in the run-up to the current Gulf War, the media had been distracted by reports of Iraqi weapons of mass destruction and thus failed to recall statements, like those made by both Colin Powell in February 2001 and Condoleeza Rice in April 2001, that Saddam Hussein had been contained and did not pose an immediate threat (Pilger, 2003b). However, alongside the publication of official reports, it is clear that a more covert PR war has been waged using psychological operations techniques. One example was the February 2003 dossier presented to some journalists in private briefings written by the UK government's Coalition Information Centre headed by Alistair Campbell, then the Head of Communications Strategy at No. 10 Downing Street. This dossier, which used decade-old research from an uncited PhD thesis obtained from the internet, strengthened the language to exaggerate the threat and merged it with information from the Intelligence Community. The aim of this was clearly to present 'new evidence' to make the case for stopping the UN inspections conducted by Hans Blix and to enable preparations for war against Iraq. David Cornwell, writing under his pseudonym of John le Carré, notes how successful this campaign was:

> How Bush and his junta succeeded in deflecting America's anger from bin Laden to Saddam Hussein is one of the great public relations conjuring tricks of history. But they swung it. A recent poll tells us that one in two Americans now believe Saddam was responsible for the attack on the World Trade Centre. (Le Carré, 2003, p. 20)

It is also clear that the security services regularly hold unattributable briefings with selected journalists about the current threat posed by terrorists. These reports are then cited by intelligence sources as proof that the arrests made under current terrorism legislation are necessary (Bright, 2002). Following a Law Lords ruling that indefinite detention of foreigners was illegal under the Human Rights Act, Control Orders—a form of house arrest—were introduced. Control orders 'can impose restrictions including electronic tagging, 18-hour curfews, bans on using mobile phones and the Internet, and limits on who they can meet and allow into their homes' (BBC News Online, 2006f). At the time of writing, there were fourteen control orders in force, five of them on Britons.

It is interesting that many psychological operations at home are conducted by PR agencies. Whilst these may employ psychologists we can see that the use of psychological knowledge is more subtle—it may be drawn on to construct more effective messages in order to have psychological effects (e.g. to support military operations) but be used by anyone. In this context what, as psychologists, can we do? I think we should begin by taking techniques seriously, analysing them within their political and cultural context, understanding their functions and effects and resisting them either by co-opting them or by exposing them.

Resisting psychological operations I: cultural and political analysis of fear of the other

In his analysis of Cold War rhetoric, Kovel (1986) argued that projecting hostile intent onto other nations helped sustain the military–industrial complex and the nuclear state. This effect can be seen more generally: thus, in his history of MI5, Bernard Porter (1992) noted that accounts of IRA bombing campaigns seemed to 'justify the role of MI5 and the Special Branch' (p. 200). Indeed, with the demise of the USSR as a threat to national security, terrorism has become the officially recognised priority of British security services (Norton-Taylor, 1993; Rimmington, 1994). Post-September 11th the Security State has grown massively. For example, the number of UK Special Branch officers (police officers with responsibility for security, intelligence, subversion and terrorism) had gone up from 1,638 in 1978 to 2,220 at the beginning of the 1990s to at least 4,247 by February 2003

(Statewatch, 2003). Kirkup (2005) reports that, in December 2004, the Chancellor of the Exchequer told MPs that overall spending on domestic security would rise from £1.5 billion in 2004–5 to £2.1 billion by 2007–8. He noted that the security budget had more than doubled since September 11th 2001 and that the Security Service (MI5) had seen a massive increase in its budget, which is believed to be rising towards £300 million. Kirkup (2005) noted that the service planned to open eight branch offices around the UK whilst the Security Service website notes 'we plan to increase our staff numbers to around 3,200 people by 2008' (http://www.mi5.gov.uk). A recent BBC TV (2002) series *True Spies* revealed how many of the stories previously seen as paranoid (e.g. surveillance of trade unionists and peace campaigners) have turned out to be more accurate than previously supposed.

Fear-generating processes also have consequences at a more domestic level. López (1991) has described how the cultivation of fear has led to the militarisation of everyday life, with increasing emphasis on personal security and safety leading to political conservatism. Such a context can lead to the dominance of a 'text of fear' which then organises the experience of life with people increasingly retreating to the private space of home, guarded by the technology of the security industry (López, 1991). This has a number of effects, which are both economic (witness the growth in personal and home security alarm systems) and cultural (with society becoming dominated by suspicion and observation—the development of *Neighbourhood Watch* schemes in the UK is symptomatic of this). Noam Chomsky has made a similar point in a comment on the US international War on Drugs policy:

> The more you can increase fear of drugs and crime and welfare mothers and immigrants and aliens and all sorts of things, the more you control people. Make them hate each other, be frightened of each other and think that the other is stealing from them. If you can do that you can control the people. (Noam Chomsky, in López et al., 1996, p. 14)

Some of the most insightful analyses of the current state of affairs have been conducted through documentary films. Adam Curtis'[10] excellent 2002 BBC2 series *The Century of the Self* illustrated the extent of co-operation between big business and the new profession of Public Relations—founded in the US by Sigmund Freud's American nephew Edward Bernays, drawing on many of his uncle's insights. Curtis' thesis was that in an affluent West people no longer consumed out of need—instead corporations decided to sell by capitalising on people's desires. Consequently, we saw clever PR practitioners linking images of smoking with liberation: for example, cigarettes became 'torches of freedom' for women.

---

10. Somewhat bizarrely, Aitkenhead (2006) reports that Curtis serves as one of a small number of associate editors for the emailed celebrity and music gossip newsletter *Popbitch*.

Of course, this can also work by playing on people's fears. In his 2002 film, *Bowling for Columbine*, Michael Moore pushed this further by arguing that there was a link between the promotion of fear and consumer capitalism. In other words, fear sells.

If fear-generating techniques are used in times of relative peace, they become much more overt in times of conflict—we have only to look at the kind of language used. Thus Billig (2001) has noted how the language of war was quickly mobilised in the US immediately after the World Trade Center attacks as a way of attempting to categorise the incomprehensibility of the events. Curtis picked up this theme in his 2004 series *The Power of Nightmares*. In this documentary he argued that, during the twentieth century, politicians had lost the power to inspire the masses, and that the optimistic visions and ideologies they offered were perceived to have failed. Politicians, consequently, had to seek a new role that would restore their power and authority. In his introductory narration, Curtis stated that 'instead of delivering dreams, politicians now promise to protect us: from nightmares'. He made a persuasive case, arguing that, in many ways, the rise of both the American neo-conservatives and radical Islamists were related. For example, each group believed they were responsible for the exit of the Soviets from Afghanistan and, thus, for the ending of the Cold War. He argued that though the threat from Islamic jihadis was real, it was grossly exaggerated (see Chapter 10, this volume).

Resisting psychological operations II: action strategies

Having developed an analysis of the context and effects of psychological operations, what positive action can be taken? In one interview Sheldon Rampton has suggested a number of effective counter-strategies: to understand how propaganda works; to seek information from a wide variety of sources (and not just a narrow diet of mainstream media); and not simply to be passive recipients of the media but actively to engage in the real world and in active means of communication, debate and dialogue (Rampton, 2003). To Rampton's list one might add the need to reveal and question the implicit assumptions underlying political discourse. It is also important to delineate the networks of power and interests at work influencing governmental policy (see for example, the work of the Oxford Research Group) and to organise education and action campaigns against those networks. Within the discipline of psychology we can seek to influence journal editorial policies so that authors are required to state any interests or funding involved in their studies. Most importantly, we need to keep the abusive past of our discipline in mind so we do not make the same mistakes again.

CHAPTER 2

British Psychology's Response to the Invasion and Occupation of Iraq

RON ROBERTS

Intellectuals are in a position to expose the lies of governments, to analyze actions according to their causes and motives and often hidden intentions. (Noam Chomsky, 1967, p. 16)

The regular stance of most intellectuals is a conformist subservience to those in power. (Morgenthau, 1970, cited in Chomsky, 2004, p. 48)

Introduction

In this chapter, the official response of the British psychological community to the war in Iraq will be examined. This response provides a case study of one of the major psychological communities in the Western world. Of course, in this context, the British Psychological Society (BPS), alongside the American Psychological Association (APA), occupies a privileged place in this pantheon of organised academic communities—for the simple and obvious reason that its host country was a leading player in the illegal invasion and ongoing occupation of Iraq. This position confers a particular duty on the BPS to discharge its intellectual and ethical responsibilities independent of government. Thus the principal issue explored here is whether the published output from the BPS during the period of the war conforms to the propaganda model of the media outlined by Noam Chomsky and Edward Herman (Chomsky, 1989; Herman & Chomsky, 1994; Klaehn, 2005).

Briefly stated, this model proposes that the media presents (or withholds) information in such a way as to legitimise the interests of powerful elites against the majority. Whilst psychologists have examined the techniques of persuasion and attitude change, the actual purpose of the mass media, and therefore this model, have received little attention. This issue has major importance for our understanding of the social construction of reality, for it is the media that provides the primary definitions of social reality (Schlesinger, 1991; Taleb, 2004). The question therefore is: to what extent are psychological texts, which purportedly adhere to a strict academic-scientific discourse, subservient to elite interests and serving a propaganda function?

The following analysis of the treatment of the Iraq War in *The Psychologist* magazine therefore serves as a specific empirical test of this thesis. This publication is sent to all graduate and student members of the BPS on a monthly basis and has a readership in excess of 28,000. This analysis will be undertaken using two methods. First of all by examining the range of opinion which is allowed expression, and secondly by paired comparison with alternative press coverage. Before we undertake this analysis, however, it will be helpful to be reacquainted with information about the background to the war and its conduct.

Background

In March 2003, US and UK forces launched an invasion of Iraq. There is compelling evidence that, far from being a humanitarian effort by the US/UK coalition to liberate Iraqi citizens from the tyranny of Saddam Hussein's regime and remove the threat of weapons of mass destruction (WMD), as portrayed by both governments, the war was an orchestrated assault upon the integrity and independence of a sovereign state that posed no threat to the West (Ahmed, 2003). The war and subsequent occupation have been widely recognised as illegal, with critics of the joint action including Kofi Annan, the Secretary General of the United Nations (BBC News Online, 2004a); the deputy legal advisor in the UK Foreign Office, Elizabeth Wilmhurst, whose resignation letter condemned the war as a 'crime of aggression' (Gibbon, 2005); and with the belated exception of the Attorney General, the entire legal team in the Foreign Office, which is understood to have doubted the war's legality (Curtis, 2004). To add to this list there is a 'near-unanimous view amongst international lawyers' (Norton-Taylor, 2003) that the joint US/UK actions were illegal.

The bombing of Iraq, which began with the 'Shock and Awe' attack on Baghdad, (Guardian, 2003) was preceded by a relentless twelve-year campaign that decimated the living standards and morale of ordinary people. In this, the Anglo-American forces not only waged a low-level nuclear war using depleted uranium weaponry, but, through continued sanctions forced through the United Nations by the transatlantic alliance, they deprived people of adequate food and clean water. The UN's Iraq child mortality survey estimated that up to 1.7 million people perished as a result of these actions (Ahmed, 2003, p. 112). This figure is not disputed by any of the major aid agencies or NGOs working in the region.

The British charities *Save the Children Fund* and *CAFOD* have added their voices to the many that have been raised throughout the world against the joint US/UK action. Sadly the British Psychological Society cannot be numbered amongst these.

As well as the slaughter of civilians, and execution of injured Iraqi combatants (incidents described in the UK press as 'alleged shootings' despite extensive witnesses and video evidence; BBC News Online, 2004b), the war has seen journalists targeted, prisoners of war abused and the International Committee of the Red Cross (ICRC) bombed. Pierre Krähenbqühl, Director of Operations of the ICRC, in an unusual statement from the organisation, felt it necessary to remark on the 'utter contempt for the most basic tenet of humanity: the obligation to protect human life and dignity' which has been exhibited during the war and reminded the 'multinational force' that complying with international humanitarian law was 'an obligation and not an option' (Krähenbühl, 2004). Iraqi women's groups have protested at the worsening situation for women (Judd, 2006) and have called on the occupying forces to leave the country. Meanwhile, disturbing evidence of a catalogue of war crimes, including atrocities committed by coalition troops against Iraqi civilians, continues to emerge (Fisk, 2006). In addition to the accusations of war crimes leveled against the UK Government (Wood, 2005) this is producing intense disquiet in the US and UK and fuelling resentment amongst the people of Iraq.

The 2003 war was sold to the British public on the pretext of Iraq possessing WMD, which were deployable within 45 minutes. Thus, only the 'white knights' of the US/UK coalition could save the international community from the threats to world peace and international security posed by a third-world country, whose industrial and military infrastructure had all but collapsed. It is now recognised that Iraq possessed no WMD capability, having been effectively stripped of these during the Anglo-American Gulf War in 1991, and through the concerted efforts of years of inspections by UN officials (Curtis, 2003; Ahmed, 2003).

Though the full consequences of these actions have yet to be understood, the calculus has begun. Curiously, Tony Blair shares the belief, with totalitarian leaders of the past, that the ultimate judgement of his actions lies 'beyond the experience of his contemporaries' (Arendt, 1994a, p. 383). Blair has protested a 'complete inner self-confidence' (Wintour, 2006) in his analysis, and invoked God or 'history' as his ultimate judges, yet the belief that history will judge him kindly does not seem to be well founded—barring an extermination of reason amongst future historians. A study published in the leading UK medical journal *The Lancet* (Roberts et al., 2004) based on a cluster sample survey throughout Iraq (33 clusters of 30 households each being interviewed about household deaths since January 2002; the date, causes and circumstances of violent deaths were all recorded) estimated that over 100,000 people may have died as a direct result of the war.[1]

---

1. In October 2006, Burnham, Lafta, Doocy and Roberts (2006) updated this estimate to 655,000 excess Iraqi deaths as a consequence of the war.

This figure specifically excludes casualties in the city of Fallujah—which, if included, would add substantially to the estimate. Estimates of Iraqi casualties of the war have also come from two other sources. The Iraq Body Count project (IBC: www.iraqbodycount.org) seeks to establish an independent database of media-reported civilian deaths in Iraq resulting from the military action and subsequent occupation. For comparative purposes with *The Lancet* study of 2004, casualties as of January 2005 were estimated to lie between 17,582 (maximum) and 15,365 (minimum). By the end of September 2006, figures are 48,174 maximum and 43,387 minimum. Though the IBC estimates are acknowledged to be conservative, they fall comfortably within the 95% confidence intervals (margin of error) for casualties (8,000 and 194,000) calculated in *The Lancet* study.

A third estimate derives from the UN Development Programme sponsored Iraq Living Condition Survey (UNDP, 2005). This, the largest survey to date, comprised 22,000 households and arrived at an estimate of 24,000 deaths (confidence intervals 18,000–29,000). A direct comparison with *The Lancet* study allowing for the different periods of data collection would yield a scaled-up figure of 28,000 conflict-related deaths in the UN study. For more in-depth discussion and comparison of these figures, readers are directed to the IBC website (see Dardagan, Sloboda & Doherty, 2006). Though all these estimates are shocking, they should come as no surprise. Immediately prior to the outbreak of war, global health organisation *Medact* produced estimates of around 200,000 deaths in the longer term as a result of war, with UN projections suggesting up to 500,000 civilian injuries (Fyans, Stankovich & Paterson, 2003). By November 2003, Medact estimates for fatalities were put at 50,000 (Clark, 2003).

The then British Foreign Secretary, Jack Straw, was moved only to dispute *The Lancet*'s figures (Grice, 2004). He provided no detailed scientific critique of the methodology, merely commenting on the sample size. To help the impartial reader evaluate the merits of the competing claims of the Foreign Secretary and the researchers involved in producing these estimates, it may be useful to recall the words of Mark Higson, former desk officer of the British Foreign Office, who in giving evidence to the Scott Inquiry into arms sales to Iraq, described the Foreign Office as 'a culture of lying' (cited in Pilger, 2003a, p. x).

A further indisputable outcome of the invasion and ongoing occupation of Iraq is that the country has since descended into a state of lawlessness, chaos and civil war (Biddle, 2006), with a home-grown and heavily armed insurgency attracting support throughout the Islamic world (Rogers, 2005)—a fact recognised even by US intelligence agencies (Harris & Beaumont, 2006), in which torture is now more widespread than it was in Saddam's 'Republic of Fear' (Cockburn, 2006).

So where does this lead us? It would appear that the UK Government is prosecuting an illegal war, killing and maiming large numbers of civilians (e.g. through the use of cluster bombs) while attempting to deceive the public by 'spin' and propaganda about its motives, conduct, and consequences. Through the analysis of declassified documents, Curtis (2003) has undertaken a systematic examination of British Foreign Policy in recent times. Charting the activities of British diplomats and armed service personnel in Iran, Iraq, Kosovo, Afghanistan, Guyana, Indonesia, East Timor, Israel, Russia, Turkey and Saudi Arabia (to name but a few), the picture that emerges is of an 'outlaw state' regularly flouting international law, killing innocent people, endorsing systematic brutality and human rights abuses and supporting numerous repressive governments throughout the world. The situation in Iraq led Jordan's Prince Hassan to warn of the prospect of a Third World War brewing in the Middle East as a consequence of the current US and UK actions (BBC News Online, 2004c). So in beginning our analysis of the British Psychological Society's response to these events we must ask, what relevance does all this have to British psychologists?

Psychological issues

There can be no doubt about one thing—the world changed after 9/11—and the change has been psychological as well as political. The world is now awash with new meanings centred on themes that include fear of terrorist action, civil chaos, xenophobia, repressive and totalitarian government and loss of civil liberties. Given that a plausible interpretation of the events of recent years holds that the global emergency we face was in fact engineered by US neoconservatives to permit a more aggressive foreign policy, increased surveillance of the public and a US takeover of Central Asia's oil and gas (Ahmed, 2002), one might characterise state actions in the US and UK as a war *of* terror rather than one against it. Shortly after the inception of the war in March 2003, one of my students expressed fears that Iraqi fighter planes would be heading to London. The meanings generated by the global events need to be understood, challenged and demystified as a matter of urgency.

A further psychological issue raised by the actions of the US/UK invasion of Iraq is how the players in the theatre of war understand their own actions. Iraqi combatants may be certain they are fighting an aggressive invader whose intention is to seize control of their country's natural resources. Western forces, however, were more likely, at least initially, to believe that they were fighting to liberate Iraq—or at least to hope that they were. It is probable that, contrary to the picture painted by UK media, it is the insurgents who have a more thorough grasp of the situation they face, whilst many of the American and British forces have been alienated from the reality that the new military humanism is a pretext for a way to make Iraq safe for foreign investors (Chomsky, 1999a; Ahmed, 2003). Alienated from this reality, troops were accordingly estranged from the political, economic and strategic intentions that drive their own behaviour. So here in the West, the functional explanations required to comprehend the conduct of the war are fundamentally different from those that constitute the 'view from the ground'. At present the general public are not well placed to distinguish between these, although there is undoubtedly widespread scepticism about the motives for the war. The propaganda to which people are subject has as its implied aim, the manipulation of the population—in particular to present the intentions of the Western forces as benign and humanitarian (for this purpose giving air time to the beliefs of service personnel is of particular importance)—and to reduce information about death and suffering. These intentions extend beyond the confines of the UK population in order to influence international opinion about the motives underpinning the UK's actions and increase support for them. Under New Labour this is now called 'information support' at home and 'public diplomacy' abroad (Curtis, 2002, p. 25), yet more evidence—were it needed, of the Orwellian language games at large. That psychologists have been employed in some capacity to design and orchestrate these psychological operations for the government is more than likely (see Chapters 1 and 4). It should not, of course, be forgotten that the conduct of those who perpetrate war crimes or carry out torture, whether under the guise of acting under orders or delivering them, has been addressed by psychological theory before. Milgram's (1974)[2] classical work on obedience to authority appears to have lost none of its relevance and in view of what is known about the events unfolding in Iraq, a reconsideration of our propensity to 'follow orders' could certainly be considered appropriate (Bruner, 2004).

Last, but not least, there is the question of the immense physical and psychological damage being caused to the people of Iraq and to all the combatants involved, where the 'horrors of engaging in the act of killing, witnessing killings and living with the constant threat of being killed' produces mental health consequences which are 'incalculable' (Duckett, 2005, p. 417). Little, if any, media attention has been devoted to this—and it is with respect to the enormous trauma caused that perhaps the silence of the BPS is most damning, for the impact of war on mental health is well known (O'Brien, 1998; Herman, 2001). Let us now examine and compare the responses of the organ of the British Psychological Society to those produced within the UK medical community.

Comparison of responses from the British Psychological and Medical Communities

The analysis to be presented below comprises a survey of *The Psychologist* from March 2003 (the month when the war started) to November 2004 (when the major attack on Fallujah commenced). This will permit us, first of all, to garner a

---

2. In Milgram's experiments participants were asked to deliver what they believed were electric shocks to another person undertaking a learning experiment. Very high rates of obedience were found (around 65% were prepared to deliver shocks to a 'dangerous level') even when the learner, a confederate of the experimenter, complained that they had a heart condition.

reasonable picture of the published response from the BPS to what is almost the first two years of the war and, secondly, to examine its further response subsequent to its being presented with the results of this initial analysis. In effect, this further response—to the results of the analysis—constitutes an additional test of Chomsky and Herman's propaganda model of the media, and provides us with an opportunity to reflect on the conclusions drawn from the initial analysis.

Initial analysis

In the 21 months covered by this period, the President's Column in *The Psychologist* contains no reference to the war. Two of the main articles appearing during this period are of potential relevance. Bull (2003) discusses the nature of public communication with politicians, though again no mention is made of the war, nor British foreign policy, nor the propaganda used to justify it; this despite the title of the piece, '*Slippery politicians*', implying our politicians are economical with truth. By failing to confront the depth and breadth of deception used to pacify the public about the actions of the West, the piece conforms to the same placid, middle-class standard of sanitising reality adopted by much of the British media.

The other article of potential relevance (Silke, 2004) considers the aftermath of the terrorist attacks on New York. Incredibly, no mention is made here of the wars in Iraq and Afghanistan. Silke does acknowledge that the response of the behavioural science community to the events of 11th September 2001 has, in the UK at least, been muted, but his discussion of 'terrorism' is all about *our* responses to *them*—the terrorists or religious extremists *out there* and how *they* affect *us*. There was, of course, no consideration of what some may call the state terrorism practised by the US and UK for decades. Nor any demonstration of awareness that the actions of the US and the UK go a long way toward explaining the existence of these terrorists in the first place—for example the funding and training of the Taliban, Osama bin Laden and the Afghan resistance by the CIA and MI6 (Curtis, 2003). One could also add to the issue of responsibility, the role of the US in preventing any resolution of the Israeli–Palestinian conflict (Chomsky, 1999b) and how this has fuelled the sense of injustice and powerlessness throughout the Arab and Muslim world. Any dispassionate reading of the evidence reveals that it is the Western forces that epitomise terrorist activity and that it is we who taught them how to do it. Curtis makes the point that until the West (read the US and UK) began large-scale arming, training and funding of the Afghan resistance, terrorism, as we understand it, was largely confined to genuine resistance movements and distinct geographic regions of the world, rather than the dispersed global pattern we now have. In a thoughtful letter responding to Silke's article, which perhaps marks the only serious comment in *The Psychologist* over the 21 months, Phil Banyard (2004) remarked:

If there is to be an impact on psychology, then hopefully it will encourage us to describe and understand why groups of people decide to wreak havoc on civilian populations for political ends, and to help develop forums for dissent that are peaceful and constructive. I hope the impact is not, as menacingly suggested by Silke, to focus research on 'attitudes to extremism among ethnic communities' and so risk increasing xenophobia and demonising generally peaceful groups. (p. 624)

When the war has been mentioned in *The Psychologist*, it has been in the context of a handful of minor (less than one page) pieces on the back page 'Media Watch'. The following extract sets the tone:

War is something of a topical issue right now. And our press office has understandably been taking a flood of media requests for psychological comment. But I was surprised to learn that until the first shots had been fired, the psychological angle had not been a priority—a mere trickle of enquiries. I scoured the papers too, and found nothing. There were articles on many aspects of the crisis—even the usefulness of protest songs got a mention! (Bailes, 2003, p. 280)

The writer then proceeds to discuss a study of football referees. So it seems the major interest in the war for the BPS is whether psychologists are appearing in the media. Two months later, again relegated to the back page, we find the potentially more seriously titled 'Blame and responsibility in Abu Ghraib' (McDermott, 2004). After a promising start this short entry again descends into the lugubrious fixation with psychologists in the media.

It is entirely appropriate that psychologists should be finding their voices within the media to comment upon and enhance the analysis of these dehumanising and degrading forms of behaviour. (McDermott, 2004, p. 424)

Finally, in another minor section entitled 'Time to make love not war' which appeared in the month after the war began (Joinson, 2003), the US forces' employment of psychological operations in the war received only a couple of sentences, before moving on to the more serious business of Celine Dion and pop songs.

What then seems to be of a more pressing concern to the BPS? Just consider some of the regular features. Each month readers receive regular news of members, which, on occasion, means being treated to photographs of psychologists on motorcycles, receiving awards at Buckingham Palace and news of their promotion to more prestigious posts. We can also read the prurient details of miscreant psychologists, who are named and shamed for their sins, while regular adverts for the BPS credit card solicit our wealth. There are invitations for members to sign up for media training, and should we forget it, there is the 'Psychology in the Media' section. We also find in the April 2003 edition a full-page advert from the Ministry of Defence seeking Chartered Psychologists to assist in the training of aircrew. Suitable recruits no doubt may contribute to the greater efficiency of illegal actions in Iraq. Ongoing issues addressed include the statutory regulation of psychologists (the Society has been liaising with government on this for some time) and, under the heading of 'Who's the greatest?', members were invited in January 2003 to 'vote for your top psychologists'. The result was announced as the war in Iraq was in full swing. This catalogue of trivial pursuits amounts to a kind of 'Hello' magazine for behavioural scientists—displaying an obsession with frivolity, gossip, celebrity and the quest for power in professional psychology. Meanwhile, huge numbers of people were being slaughtered as a, supposedly necessary, price to pay to maintain our way of life. It is difficult to believe that this absence of critical comment is completely unrelated to the society's political aims, since it is currently lobbying the UK Government for favours. These include the policy to legally restrict the use of the title 'psychologist' to BPS members (such a move would have financial advantages for the BPS and would increase its power base) and the policy to secure a role for Health Psychologists as Public Health professionals.

Further illumination may be gained by drawing comparisons between responses to the war in *The Psychologist* and the two leading medical journals in the UK—*The British Medical Journal* (*BMJ*) and *The Lancet*. Over the same period in which *The Psychologist* was surveyed, the *BMJ* published 22 different news items on aspects of the war. These address a broad range of topics covering political issues, the organisation of health care and the types of health problems which the Iraqi people are experiencing. These specifically include: civilian deaths from land mines and munitions (Dyer, 2003a), the withdrawal of aid agencies from the country (Tayal, 2003), the lack of UN humanitarian aid (Hargreaves, 2003), the funding of health care and mental health services (Dyer, 2003b), increases in perinatal mortality (Dobson, 2003), and infectious diseases (Dyer, 2004), dangerous levels of radiation in the country (Moszynski, 2003), chronic malnourishment in Iraqi children (Moszynski, 2004), and the experiences of medical personnel in the war (Kirkup, 2004). Even if we consider the more frequent publication of the *BMJ,* considerably more attention and column inches have been devoted to the consequences of the Iraq war in the *BMJ* than in *The Psychologist.*

Turning now to *The Lancet.* A search revealed 115 relevant articles and news items between March 2003 and November 2004. In addition to the survey detailing mortality stemming from the war (Roberts et al., 2004), and the accompanying editorial comment (Horton, 2004), numerous articles have examined the political and humanitarian aspects of the war as well as the consequences of pre-war sanctions. I select just a few examples from this literature. Writing three weeks before war broke out, Benjamin et al. (2003) warned of the likelihood of a humanitarian disaster and went on to say:

> A military campaign that does not address the needs of the civilian population of Iraq, and that is likely to result in disproportionate levels of morbidity and mortality of non-combatants, is of dubious legality and questionable morality. (p. 874)

Attempting to draw lessons in the aftermath of war, Burkle Jnr. and Noji (2004) argue that in future the armed forces should be prevented from dominating humanitarian assistance. One of the more frequent themes in the journal is the subject of torture. Rubenstein (2003), for example, discusses its extensive use in warfare—noting that physicians may be involuntarily caught up in this. He makes the telling observation in our troubled times that:

> One of the perverse effects of the war on terrorism has been the revival of the idea that torture can be legitimate in so-called exceptional cases. (p. 1556)

He goes on to make a poignant point to the effect that the medical community must speak out more forcefully against torture. In the period under study, the silence of the British Psychological Society on this matter is striking. Not until March 2005, when the BPS formally adopted a commitment to human rights, has the issue of torture received any kind of official condemnation from it. (See Chapter 1 for further consideration of this.)

Initial analysis: conclusions

What conclusions can be drawn from the picture presented? Given the lack of coverage of the war and its effects on ordinary people in *The Psychologist* it would appear that the war is not a priority for professional psychology. This neglect stands in stark contrast to the treatment of the war in the *British Medical Journal* and *The Lancet*. How can this be explained? Perhaps it is the historical link between medicine and the public health movement, with its associations with advocacy and human rights (Beaglehole & Bonita, 1996) that have enabled the medical community to remain more keenly aware of their ethical and professional responsibilities in wider affairs. Professional psychology, meanwhile, lacks any such roots in projects that have sought to improve the public good and bring radical social change, and from its inception has struggled to justify its own status as an experimentally based scientific discipline (Richards, 2002).

The indifference of professional psychology as a whole stands in contrast to the efforts of some individual psychologists in the UK. For example, John Sloboda at Keele University has been instrumental in setting up the Iraq Body Count project and has also drawn attention to the absence of engagement of British psychology with the substantive issues raised by the Iraq war and the salient psychological issues associated with it. Duckett (2005) makes a similar point, noting critical positions on the war have been confined to radical sections of the international psychological community. Like their British counterparts, neither the American Psychological Association nor the American Psychiatric Association for example has taken a critical stance regarding the war (Soldz, 2005). But leaving aside the indeterminable question of the general level of interest that UK psychologists have toward events in Iraq, it is clear that space in *The Psychologist* reserved for presidential analysis or news commentary (i.e. that which originates with the editors and journalists responsible for copy) contains barely a mention of the war. Instead, the emphasis on trivia, gossip and professional power has been an increasing feature of the publication in recent years, which has been a source of dismay to many colleagues. Neither the *BMJ* nor *The Lancet*, it can be said, displayed any interest whatsoever with the appearance or non-appearance of medical practitioners in the media.

This content is not unconnected with the general direction in which British psychology has been moving. The introduction of market forces and absurd measurements of quality in UK higher education have received no official response from a profession that purports to possess expertise in scientific measurement. It is hard to avoid the conclusion that British psychology, as represented by the contents of *The Psychologist,* has deliberately adapted a stance in which controversial political issues of the day, no matter how relevant to psychologists, are studiously avoided. We therefore ask in whose interests is this agenda being pursued? And what type of Psychology will emerge from it if it continues? At present there is a real danger that in future British institutional psychology will be concerned only with those apolitical issues that satisfy the curiosity of the middle-class citizens of the world who have yet to confront the military reality of Anglo-American capitalism.

Initial analysis: BPS response
The results of the above analysis were initially submitted (electronically) to *The Psychologist* in December 2004. What happened next will be recounted in some detail as it has considerable bearing on the applicability of the propaganda model to *The Psychologist* and the conformity of the BPS to elite interests. Within a single day, the response, in the form of an email from the editorial team was swift:

> Thank you for your article, but I'm not going to send it out for review. As I'm well aware ... this could be seen as me protecting my own behind ... it's the comparison between the medical and psychological communities that I find the weakest. This in particular will seem like a personal defence,

but I think your target is all wrong here. I agree we haven't published much of substance, but the really interesting issue is why we haven't received it. I think you'd be better off just doing a letter of under 500 words saying 'loads of us know this has been an awful and unjust war. Why isn't the Society saying anything about it?' (Jon Sutton, personal communication, 9 December 2004)

Whilst the editorial team of *The Psychologist* saw no merit in a comparative analysis of its content and agreed it had published little of substance on the war, to them it was the fault of people failing to submit anything. Whilst little may have been submitted—itself a reflection on the culture of psychology—the irony of refusing to review material that had been submitted to them appears to have been lost. Further correspondence led to an agreement to publish a short letter, on condition that *The Psychologist* also publish a link to a website, if one could be found, to host the full article.

I'll put a note at the end of your letter saying: 'Editor's note: This letter has been edited down from a submitted article, as I felt this was a better way to present the issue. If you would like to read the original, go to ... (website address given). (Jon Sutton, personal communication, 10 December 2004)

The letter duly appeared—though neither the editor's note nor the link to the website prepared to host the article did. I submitted a formal complaint to the Policy Committee of *The Psychologist*, on the grounds that the editor had failed to honour the agreement made and that a clear conflict of interest could be construed in refusing to review the article whilst accepting an advertisement (and therefore money) from the Ministry of Defence, a body implicitly criticised in the article who are party to what many see as an illegal act in pursuing the war. In reply I was informed that the dispute between the editor and myself '*was resolved*', unbeknown to myself, and that

There is not even agreement by the legal profession or the international community regarding the legality of the war. However, the armed forces are a legitimate employer and employ many psychologists. (Paul Redford, personal communication 12 May 2005)

The relevance of the number of employed psychologists to what is a moral argument is unclear. While the BPS appears unwilling to acknowledge the potential illegality of UK military action in Iraq and its attendant consequences, British Chief of Defence Staff, General Sir Michael Jackson is not so reticent. He is reported to have remarked:

I spent a good deal of time recently in the Balkans making sure Milosevic was put behind bars. I have no intention of ending up in the next cell to him in The Hague. (Norton-Taylor, 2005)

The complaint was now passed to the Chair of the Publications and Communications Board, Pam Maras (later to be President Elect 2006–2007), who declared that the link to the website had already been published, when in fact it had not. Further correspondence failed to produce any response to the issue of conflict of interest. Perhaps this was influenced by the fact that Dr. Maras has been charged by the Society with reporting on its extensive liaisons with UK Government departments (BPS, 2006a). The link was finally published some nine months after it was promised—no note accompanied it.

It is interesting to note that the Editor, Chair of *The Psychologist* Policy Committee, Chair of the Publications and Communications Board and President have all refused to discuss the potential conflict of interest in refusing to review an article which is critical of a body advertising in *The Psychologist* and from whom they have received money—not to mention the relationship of the organisation to central government. Yet it is these issues that lie at the heart of understanding the BPS's role and whether its actions in this affair conform to a propaganda model of the media. Chomsky's (1989) favoured test of this model is to examine the range of opinion allowed expression. I would contend on the basis of the material presented here, with the evident bounds on what the BPS considers permissible, that the propaganda model is supported.

To return again, albeit briefly, to the contents of *The Psychologist*, publication of the letter (Roberts & Esgate, 2005) was accompanied by a response from the President, Ken Brown, both in his monthly column and the letters page. This was notable for the astonishing failure to actually mention the war, beyond a single line in the President's Column alerting readers to the existence of a letter about it in the current issue. Quite some feat given that the letter was headlined under the banner of 'Don't mention the war'. Brown's principal argument is that Charity Commission rules create a legal quagmire for interpreting the kind of political response that is permissible from charitable bodies (Brown, 2005). However, as Roberts and Esgate's original letter makes clear, this is a red herring, as numerous charitable bodies have already spoken out against the events in Iraq. Over the succeeding months several letters appeared in response—two are of particular interest.

The BPS would be ill advised to involve itself in attempting to speak politically for its members. I for one am relieved that the BPS says nothing about the war in Iraq. Yes, there are relevant issues pertaining to the effects of war and violent conflict but the political rights and wrongs are best left to the governments involved … I for one supported the government's decision to go to war on Iraq. (Grose, 2005, p. 199)

> The lack of consensus on this or any other issue does not imply, as the President claims it does, that the Society can take no stance ... If the BPS can take a stance on the ethical treatment of rats, pigeons and monkeys, why is it silent over the ethics of killing innocent Iraqi children, and torturing and humiliating Iraqi prisoners? (Oliver, 2005, p. 198)

Grose's contribution to the debate illustrates the complete abdication of responsibility and subservience to authority that would be welcome news within any dictatorship. In contrast, Oliver draws explicit attention to the moral dimensions of the current inaction. This inaction serves the agenda of those who have prosecuted the illegal invasion and occupation of Iraq. It could be argued, with some justification, that British institutional psychology in fact sees no political role for itself beyond one of self interest—lobbying government in the hope of accruing or protecting power and prestige. Back in the real world, people in other corners of the world can be slaughtered, tortured and exploited for the continuance of the Western way of life.

The following year, 2005, continued with a BPS 'investigation' into 'What psychology has done', discussion of the new Society logo, more interviews with celebrity psychologists, and a plethora of awards for various categories of psychologists. The magazine finally reached its nadir in the April issue with a cover depicting a cartoon workman with his backside hanging out of his trousers. On the Iraq war—other than the handful of letters referred to above—nothing. The only items of note were an article in the March issue on the psychology of suicide bombing (Marsden & Attia, 2005) and following the London bombing, readers were referred to several articles of potential interest, all of which accept a model of terrorism in which 'we' are the victims of terrorist acts perpetrated by individuals whose psychological 'motives' we are charged to understand. The letters from Banyard (2004) and Roberts and Esgate (2005), both of which situate terrorism within a political context, which includes the war in Iraq, received no mention.

Early 2006, saw a news item in the March issue concerning the identification of people traumatised by the London bombings and the psychological treatment which has to date been offered (Jarret, 2006a). Again no discussion of the political context of the bombings was offered. In the April issue John Sloboda and a number of other psychologists replied (Sloboda, 2006):

> While is admirable that British Psychologists are playing a leading role in providing professional assistance to those psychologically wounded by 7/7, it is worrying that questions about the effects of Britain's role in bombing innocent civilians in Serbia, Afghanistan, and Iraq seem of less interest. Data collected by www.iraqbodycount.org shows that on average, 35 innocent civilians in Iraq have met violent deaths every day since March 2003. During the 3-week invasion phase of March–April 2003, the daily

civilian death rate (almost all caused by coalition bombs and bullets) was 315. By now, the Iraq violent death toll exceeds the death toll of 7/7 by over 600:1. This suggests, on a conservative estimate, that there are at least 600,000 Iraqis who are suffering post-traumatic effects, a very large proportion of them directly caused by coalition military aggression, or indirectly by coalition failures to restore and maintain security.

Britain shares with the United States the responsibility for providing the resources for Iraqi people to recover from the psychological traumas caused by our actions. And, on the basis that every human being is equal, the financial and human resources that the UK and US psychological communities should be jointly supplying to Iraq should be 600 times greater than that being given to the British victims of 7/7. Our guess is that the actual ratio is probably reversed (i.e. closer to 1:600).

Standard definitions of terrorism depict it as 'the use or threatened use of violence against civilian populations in order to achieve economic or political aims'. This definition allows one to see the UK and US as perpetrators of terrorism in Iraq, responsible for the deaths of vast numbers of civilians, the numbers of which— as Sloboda's letter makes clear—dwarf those that have resulted from the actions of 'individual' terrorists. We can therefore choose to view the terrorism directed against the UK as one of the consequences of UK and US state terrorism. From a psychological perspective we might learn much more about the phenomenon of terrorism by studying why our political leaders so willingly endorse its use, and how members of the UK population construe our military actions.

The US remains the only country in the world to have been found guilty by the International Court of Justice of perpetrating state terrorism through its support for attacks against the people of Nicaragua. These terrorists are our allies. The views of the majority of the UK population in believing that the London attacks are related to the war in Iraq and that the risk of further attacks has been elevated by the Iraq war (Dodd, 2005) are consistent with this wider notion of terrorism. Sadly the BPS appears to take the narrow view endorsed by the British Government, a view that places our country's terrorist actions firmly outside the zone of responsibility for why others would wish to attack us. Again, the perspective adopted by the BPS is subservient to elite interests. Its designated apolitical stance in fact means 'tacit and silent support in state crimes or direct participation in them' (Chomsky, 2005a).

CHAPTER 3

The War on Terror:
The road from Belmarsh
to Guantánamo Bay

IAN ROBBINS

The use of antidepressant medication for those driven to suicide and the edge of madness by inhumane treatment cannot be seen as anything other than grotesque. (p. 71)

Like everyone else I was horrified when I saw the attacks on the World Trade Centre and the Pentagon. I soon realised that the world had changed following the September 11th attacks. The events had created a climate of fear and a sense of outrage and the responses to these events set in motion a series of changes which have had an impact on the way we view the world and on the way we think about civil liberties. Legislation was passed which altered the normal protections which have existed under both US law and the European Convention on Human Rights. In the US the Patriot Act was passed and Guantánamo Bay was used as a detention centre for those thought to be involved in terrorism precisely because it was deemed, initially at least, to be outside the normal purview of the American domestic legal system. Some of these measures were passed with little protest either because the implications were not fully appreciated or because the sense of violation was deemed to require a harsh response. The 'War on Terror', a creation of the US government, has led not only to invasions of Afghanistan and Iraq but has also been used to justify these increasingly repressive domestic measures. What is of particular concern is the extent to which society's sensibilities become changed to the degree that where new legislation is accepted and ceases to be seen as repressive because of the context in which it is set.

The Patriot Act

Within 43 days of the attacks the Patriot Act was passed by Congress. It had been passed by both houses with virtually no debate and, in some cases, without even an opportunity for members to read the act fully. Neither discussion nor amendments were permitted and members were forced to cast a yes or no vote. The Bush administration implied that anyone who voted against it would be blamed for further attacks. This had a powerful effect at a time when a second attack was expected at any moment and letters containing anthrax were being received in government offices.

The Act made major changes to the powers the government had to carry out surveillance. Most of the changes had been part of a long-standing law enforcement wish list that had been rejected by Congress on previous occasions. It expanded the government's power to search records such as medical records, financial or mental health records. It expanded the ability of government agencies to carry out secret searches without the consent or knowledge of the owner. It also expanded the ability of the government to carry out a physical search or to tap phones without having to prove probable cause (a reasonable belief that a crime has been committed).

The US government no longer has to demonstrate that the subject of a search order is an 'agent of a foreign power': a requirement that previously protected American citizens from abuse of power. The FBI no longer has to demonstrate reasonable cause and does not even have to justify its behaviour by showing that it has a reasonable suspicion that the records it requires are related to criminal actions. It merely has to state that the request is in relation to ongoing terrorism or foreign intelligence investigations. The Act has weakened judicial oversight to the point where it is almost meaningless. The government need only assert to the judge, with no evidence or proof, that a search meets the Act's broad criteria. Having done so, the judge does not have the power to reject the application. Even when an organisation has been forced to hand over records they can be prohibited from disclosing the search to anyone. The American Civil Liberties Union (ACLU) maintains that the provisions of the Act weaken or threaten a number of rights enshrined in the United States Constitution. Furthermore, once these erosions occur they pave the way for even more draconian legislation (www.aclu.org/safefree).

In addition, the Act allows for the indefinite detention of non-citizens. It gives the Attorney General unprecedented powers to decide the fate of immigrants and refugees: they may be detained on the basis of certification by the Attorney General. The certification is issued on the basis that the Attorney General has 'reasonable grounds to believe' that a non-citizen is a threat to national security. Furthermore, if the individual cannot find a country willing to accept them the detention can be indefinite.

The ACLU believes that in excess of 8,000 people have been interrogated simply because of their ethnic background rather than because they have been accused of any criminal activity. It maintains that thousands of men, who are mostly of Arab or South Asian origin, have been held in secret federal custody for weeks or months, and that the government refuses to publish their names or whereabouts even when ordered to do so by the courts. The press and public have been banned from the immigration court hearings of those detained under this legislation.

Given the level of repression possible in the US domestic environment it is no longer hard to understand how the US government was able to set up secret prisons around the world where torture and interrogation could be carried out. Until recently, they had denied the existence of such prisons but, since their admission that they do exist, other activities such as 'special rendition', whereby operating outside the borders of the USA people can be imprisoned and taken to a third country without the knowledge or approval of the country where the individuals are living, are being considered necessary. It is a short step to being able to carry out systematic torture in a prison under direct American control, as happened at Abu Ghraib prison.

Guantánamo Bay

In January 2002, following the invasion of Afghanistan, the American government set up Camp X-ray at Guantánamo Bay, an American enclave on the island of Cuba. Over 600 inmates were transported in very poor conditions. They were usually hooded and shackled during the long flight and were denied access to toilet facilities, soiling themselves in the course of the flight. On arrival they were put in metal cages and were kept under continuous observation. There was a complete lack of privacy and conditions were initially very basic. Prisoners on occasion found scorpions and snakes in their cages. Subsequently the more permanent Camp Delta was built with an improvement in physical conditions if not in treatment.

Military personnel at Guantánamo sought approval for a regime that included sensory deprivation, enforced nudity, forced grooming, isolation and the use of prisoners' existing fears such as a fear of dogs. Approval for this was given by the then Secretary of Defence Donald Rumsfeld on December 6th 2002 (PHR, 2005 p. 25). Prisoners could be held in isolation for prolonged periods. Indeed Human Rights Watch, in 2005, stated that it was compulsory for prisoners to spend their first month in Container Camp, the isolation wing, but they could also be placed there for relatively minor infringements of rules such as having extra items such as cups or salt in their cell. Sometimes, as in the case of Moazzam Begg and Feroz Abbasi, two British prisoners, isolation could be for as long as 18 months. Indeed, in the case of Mr Begg, the guard outside his cell was removed and replaced with a CCTV camera because it was found that the guard had been talking to him (PHR, 2005 p. 28). Rasul, Iqbal and Ahmed, three British prisoners, were also subject to frequent isolation, which ultimately led to them being willing to say anything their interrogators wanted. They found the prospect of isolation to be one of the most frightening aspects of their captivity.

When being transported between different sections of the camp prisoners were shackled and hooded. After each journey they were subject to body cavity searches even though they were unable to reach anything let alone insert it into a body orifice (Rasul, Iqbal & Ahmed, 2004). Clearly the search process was aimed at increasing the humiliation and sense of degradation, seen as essential factors in the process of coercive interrogations (Robbins et al., 2005).

Prisoners were subject to frequent, and often prolonged, interrogations and Rasul, Iqbal and Ahmed (2004) describe the ways in which shackles could be used as part of interrogation and torture. When they were 'long shackled' prisoners could move into more comfortable positions but when 'short shackled' could be pinioned into painful stress positions for many hours. In addition, they could be stripped and subjected to prolonged strobe lighting and music played at very high volume while the air conditioning was turned up to maximum levels. This would be used in connection with sleep deprivation (PHR, 2005 p. 29). Furthermore, they point to the use of sexual humiliation: using female guards and interrogators to achieve this.

Not surprisingly these techniques had a serious impact on prisoners' well-being and mental health, and garbled conversations, disorientation, hallucinations, irritability, delusions and paranoia were frequently observed. Military officials confirmed the impact on prisoners in a BBC interview in 2005. In 2003 there had been 350 acts of self-harm including 120 attempts at hanging including a mass suicide attempt by 23 prisoners. In 2003 a psychiatric ward was opened and, while self-harm reduced, there were still 110 attempts at self-harm in 2004 (PHR, 2005 p. 52). Sadly, rather than accepting these attempts at self-harm and suicide as being an indicator of distress and deteriorating mental health it was referred to as 'manipulative self-harm syndrome'. Depression and anxiety were common and many of the prisoners were prescribed antidepressant medication. Rasul, Iqbal and Ahmed (2004) described psychotropic medication also being administered without their consent. They were also not informed as to the nature of the medication.

On their release I met with a number of the UK citizens who had been detained in Guantánamo Bay. They were hypervigilant and showed exaggerated startle response. They were suffering from insomnia and were extremely anxious about leaving the house they were in. They were plagued by memories of their experience and were suffering from mood swings. The nature of their responses left me in no doubt about the psychological damage that had been done to them as a result of their imprisonment. Without doubt they could be seen as suffering from post-traumatic stress disorder (PTSD), depression and anxiety. Perhaps what was most worrying was the way in which their view of the world had been changed by their experiences. Whether this change is permanent is yet to be seen.

Detention in the United Kingdom

By December 2001, following the attacks, the Anti-terrorism Crime and Security Act 2001 was created as a response to events. The day after the Act received the Royal Assent ten men who were asylum seekers or refugees, were arrested and taken directly to either Belmarsh or Woodhill high security prisons, bypassing police stations. Their families were given no idea as to their whereabouts and the men were not allowed access to lawyers or to make a phone call. By chance, a remand prisoner being represented by Gareth Peirce, a well-known human rights lawyer, became aware of a group of Muslim men who had arrived in the prison and who were being held incommunicado. He contacted his lawyer to let her know what was happening and she set about trying to gain access to the men. As Christmas was approaching it required rapid legal action simply to gain access.

The 2001 Anti-terrorism Crime & Security Act

Article 4 of the Act, which was clearly produced in haste, allowed detention following certification by the Home Secretary on the grounds that the individual, who had to be a foreign national, was a threat to national security. The burden of proof required for certification was only that the Home Secretary had reasonable grounds for suspicion. This is clearly a considerably lower requirement than the 'burden of proof on the balance of probabilities' adopted by the civil courts or 'beyond reasonable doubt' as in the criminal justice system. The requirements for certification were remarkably similar to those of the Patriot Act in the USA. Suspects under the UK legislation were neither charged nor prosecuted for any specific crime and could be detained indefinitely without trial.

The Act required derogation from Article 5 of the European Convention on Human Rights (ECHR): Article 5 provides for the right to liberty and security of the person. Individuals can only be deprived of their liberty as part of a judicial process and are guaranteed the right to a trial. To be able to derogate from Article 5, the Government of the day had to declare a state of national emergency. The United Kingdom was, and remains, the only European country that felt it necessary to derogate from Article 5 of the ECHR in response to perceived terrorist threats.

The Act established that the Special Immigration Appeals Commission (SIAC) was the appropriate jurisdiction to hear appeals against detention. On average, appeals were heard up to 18 months post arrest. The Act had no explicit detention period, which meant that detention would only cease if:

1. The legislation lapsed.
2. An acceptable country could be found to take the suspects and the suspects themselves agreed.

3. SIAC granted the suspects bail if it found no case to support the Home Secretary's beliefs.
4. The Home Secretary revoked the certification.

Appeals against indefinite detention had both open and closed elements. During the open elements the evidence was presented and the suspect and his lawyers were allowed to challenge the evidence. In the closed sections the court was cleared and both the suspect himself and his legal team were unable to be present and hear any evidence. During the closed elements a Special Advocate, who was a senior, security-cleared barrister, was appointed to represent the suspect's interests. The Special Advocate was not, however, allowed to discuss the case with either the suspect or his legal team. This meant that suspects and their legal teams could not know the basis of the case against them or the supporting evidence. Unlike normal criminal cases there was no obligation to disclose any evidence that could help a suspect's case. Because much of an appeal could be held in closed session it was difficult to infer the nature of the case against by the material presented in the open sessions.

The impact of indefinite detention without trial

Sixteen men were initially detained under this legislation. My own involvement came about when, along with a group of psychiatrists, I was involved in producing independent clinical reports on some of the detainees' mental state. I was alarmed by the rapid deterioration that had taken place in a number of the men. When discussing this with the rest of the group we became aware of a number of common issues and decided to produce a joint report addressing these. We aimed to develop a composite report on the impact of indefinite detention on the detainees on the basis of existing specialist clinical reports. In all, 48 reports were used: these reports were prepared by 11 experienced psychiatrists and one psychologist. We also examined the impact of indefinite detention on spouses of the detainees, again using existing specialist reports. A further aim was to review any published material that could help to guide opinion on the impact of detention.

   In total, eight detainees were seen, and all were seen by more than one clinician and on more than one occasion. In some cases they had been seen several times by several clinicians. Six of the detainees came from Algeria, one from Tunisia and one from Gaza. All had had some education, in some cases up to university level. All were literate. Four of the eight detainees had a previous psychiatric history prior to their arrest and three had a clear family history of mental health problems. There were serious physical health problems including bilateral traumatic amputation of arms, the consequences of childhood polio, lower back injuries etc., which interacted with and influenced their mental state. Three of the detainees had experienced previous detention and torture. All had been in situations of political instability and unrest. All had felt themselves to be under serious threat prior to migration. In the case of one, the perceived threat related to his wife. In completing the report, conclusions were only drawn where two or more clinicians had independently made the same observations. While recognising that this was a very conservative approach it allowed for a robust set of conclusions.

There was a high degree of consensus amongst the expert opinion on the detainees. All of the detainees were suffering from significant levels of depression and anxiety. The symptoms were of clinical severity and had shown a clear deterioration over time. In a number of cases where there had been direct exposure to traumatic events there was also a diagnosis of post-traumatic stress disorder (PTSD). This was in relation to pre-migration events, events pertaining to their arrest and imprisonment or both, working in a synergistic fashion.

Deterioration in mood state was clearly linked to a sense of helplessness and hopelessness, which are integral aspects of indefinite detention. It led to a high level of suicidal ideation and attempts at self-harm. The latter ranged from superficial cuttings to attempts at hanging. All of the men and their families were devout Muslims. They originated in countries where mental illness is highly stigmatised. Islam prohibits suicide and the expression of hopelessness as this suggests a lack of faith in God. For them to acknowledge mental health problems, including suicidal ideation, was extremely difficult and was an indicator of their mental states and distress. The married detainees were extremely concerned with regard to the impact of their detention on their wives' and families' mental state and this in turn exacerbated their mental health problems. A number of detainees, as their mood deteriorated, developed significant psychotic symptoms. These symptoms were not present prior to detention.

On a number of occasions, detainees' psychotic symptoms and behaviour was interpreted by prison staff as manipulative, particularly where there had been a failure to co-operate with the healthcare regimes. There was a failure to perceive this behaviour as reflecting a deterioration in mental state and seeing it as being deliberately manipulative impeded appropriate assessment and treatment. Where people had additional complex physical health needs, as for instance in the case of the polio survivor and amputee, these needs were not adequately met within the prison system.

There was a strong consensus that indefinite detention per se was directly linked to deterioration in mental health and that fluctuations in mental state were related to the prison regime itself and to the vagaries of the appeal process. There was also a strong consensus that, while indefinite detention continued, it was highly unlikely that the Prison Health Care team would be able adequately to combat the deterioration in mental health.

There was clearly a high burden of stress imposed on detainees' wives and this was causing significant mental health problems. While having a husband in prison may be seen as stressful for any women, the problems of the detainees' wives were seen as over and above what would normally be expected. Again, the findings of two clinicians who interviewed three wives had a high level of agreement. All three women were showing signs of clinical depression. One was also showing signs of PTSD in relation to her husband's arrest while another had a phobic anxiety state. Their symptoms related directly to the incarceration of their husbands and its indefinite nature. The women were isolated culturally and linguistically. Even within their own communities they were isolated because many of the people they knew were afraid to be involved with them in case they became a target of the security services. Their isolation compounded their own mental health difficulties. The wives' own state fluctuated in relation to the problems that their husbands were experiencing. It was concluded that it was highly unlikely that there would be any improvement while their husbands' situation was maintained.

The report (Robbins et al., 2005) was considered by the Royal College of Psychiatrists in the UK who took the unusual step of issuing a statement in support of the findings and condemning the practice of indefinite detention without trial. To my own embarrassment, being a psychologist, no such statement was forthcoming from the British Psychological Society.

The House of Lords decision

In December 2004 the Appellate Committee of the House of Lords (2004) delivered a judgement that found that indefinite detention without trial was contrary to fundamental legal principles. Lord Hoffman, one of the judges involved, stated:

> This is one of the most important cases which the House has had to decide in recent years. It calls into question the very existence of an ancient liberty of which this country until now has been very proud: freedom from arbitrary arrest and detention. The power which the Home Secretary wishes to uphold is a power to detain people indefinitely without trial or charge. Nothing could be more antithetical to the instincts and traditions of the people of the United Kingdom.

The detainees were released in March 2005, but only after further powers were introduced in the form of control orders under the 2005 Prevention of Terrorism Act. Many of the detainees have been re-arrested but this time under immigration legislation. As the UK cannot deport people to countries where they could be at risk of torture, the UK is attempting to have a memorandum of understanding with a number of countries such as Algeria which would guarantee their safety and allow deportation to occur. This may be a prolonged process and means that the detainees have entered into another round of indefinite detention.

The impact of prolonged immigration detention

Previous published work on detention has been in relation to regimes which also use torture during the process of detention. The closest analogue to the recent situation is the position of asylum seekers in detention awaiting immigration decisions where a number of studies have highlighted the damaging impact which detention may bring about. The Victorian Foundation for Survivors of Torture (1998) in Australia found high rates of mental illness in relation to detention of 17 East Timorese. They found that all suffered from post-traumatic stress disorder (PTSD), 94% suffered from depression and 65% from severe anxiety. Clinically significant suicidal ideation was also reported. In a further group of 46 Cambodian asylum seekers detained for up to two years they found that 62% had PTSD, all were clinically depressed and 94% had clinically anxiety (Steel et al., 2004).

Silove et al. (1998) surveyed 25 detained Tamil asylum seekers held in detention in Victoria. Compared with community-based Tamil asylum seekers, detainees reported a greater level of trauma exposure, were more depressed, suicidal, and suffered more extreme post-traumatic and physical symptoms. Past trauma exposure did not entirely account for symptom differences across the groups suggesting that detention was a cause of mental health problems among detainees.

In the UK, Bracken and Gorst-Unsworth (1991) carried out a file audit of ten detained asylum seekers of whom six had documented physical evidence of torture. All reported depressed mood, appetite loss and somatic symptoms. Suicidal ideation was present in four with two having a history of serious suicide attempts. This was similar to another UK study by Pourgourides et al. (1995) of 15 detained asylum seekers. The majority gave histories of traumatic experience and presented with high levels of depressive and post-traumatic stress symptoms, profound despair and suicidal ideation. There were serious attempts at self-harm.

Sultan (2001), a physician who himself was held in detention, described the situation for 36 detainees held for over 12 months in detention in Australia. Thirty-three were experiencing clear evidence of severe depression, the remaining three experiencing mild depressive symptoms. Six developed clear psychotic symptoms and five had strong aggressive impulses and were persistently self-harming. Most displayed little if any of those symptoms prior to their detention. Sultan and O'Sullivan (2001) described deteriorating psychological well-being in 33 people held for over nine months with the immigration process being implicated in the deterioration—85% were depressed and 32 out of 33 displayed significant symptoms during their detention.

Keller et al. (2003), in a survey of detainees in the USA, found that 77% of participants had clinically significant symptoms of anxiety, 86% depression and 50% PTSD. At follow-up they found that those released had a marked reduction in psychological symptoms while those still detained had deteriorated. There was a strong association between level of symptoms and length of detention.

Review of these finding suggests that asylum seekers and refugees are likely to have had exposure to high levels of trauma in the pre-migration period. Many of them are likely to have experienced systematic torture and, when exposed to detention, their mental health deteriorates. This is true even when detention is in the relatively benign context of awaiting an immigration decision. They describe a sense of hopelessness that ensues as a direct result of the detention process (see Petersen, Maier, & Seligman, 1995 for an extensive discussion of learned helplessness). The studies point to a strong association between length of detention and severity of symptoms and authors are emphatic that detention per se is as strong as the other factors in causing deterioration in mental health. This is over and above any mental health problems that are the result of pre-migration trauma. Release from detention usually brings about an improvement in mental state, although none of the studies have examined the impact of indefinite detention. While these studies can be seen as merely analogous to the position of the current detainees they point to a number of common factors which are highly likely to have an even greater impact when the detention is indefinite.

The implications for health care professionals

There are a number of implications for health care professionals in the events that have occurred post 9/11. People detained under the Patriot Act will be offered the services of health care professionals, especially with regard to their mental health problems. The question is—where do these professionals see their responsibilities as residing? For anyone working in health care within the prison system this remains an issue. For the detainees in Belmarsh the health care team were clearly seen as being allied to the prison regime. In reality I am not sure that this was the case but, to a large extent, the reality is less important than the perception. To be able to use mental health specialists to their full extent there has to be trust and a belief that whatever is discussed remains confidential. There are, of course, issues for professionals themselves who can see the causes of their patient's problems and are only dealing with the effects. They can come to feel that they are part of a regime of control using medication to deal with the impact of incarceration.

When considering the role of health care professionals within the prison system it could be seen that they are passively supporting an unfair system. I posed the question to a group of UK forensic psychiatrists at their annual conference as to what they saw their role as. The consensus was that their duty was to the patient. If they were not offered treatment they would clearly not improve or would deteriorate. They also pointed out that the use of independent assessments by outside professionals acted as a guarantee of the quality of their care. They also saw their role as being able to observe and document the effects of legislation such as the 2001 Act. They did not see refusing to participate at all as an option. More importantly they saw their independent professional status as potentially offering a safeguard to people detained under anti-terrorism legislation.

The issue is somewhat different with regard to those detained in Guantánamo Bay. They do not have the possibility of independent medical care. What care they receive is only obtained via military health practitioners, whose independence gives rise to serious doubt. There is evidence that interrogators had access to prisoners medical files (PHR, 2005, p. 46) and that this was used to facilitate interrogations. Doubts have been cast with regard to the reliability of health professionals in documenting and reporting instances of abuse. There is also evidence that, in addition to sharing privileged information, health professionals participated more directly in interrogations. It is clear that medical opinion was being used to decide whether or not prisoners were able to be interrogated. Furthermore, PHR (2005) point to a memorandum, which stated that dietary manipulation, sleep management and sensory deprivation must be monitored by medics. This goes far beyond the provision of health care.

Rather worrying is the use of psychiatric medication. Comments from those released suggest that medication was administered without consent and may have been used for the purpose of control rather than for a clinical reason. The use of antidepressant medication for those driven to suicide and the edge of madness by inhumane treatment cannot be seen as anything other than grotesque. In these circumstances, without the recourse to independent assessment, there cannot be any justification. The Tokyo Declaration (1975) clearly prohibits the participation of medical practitioners in torture and all forms of cruel, inhumane and degrading treatments. This includes providing the knowledge to facilitate such treatment and also prohibits the doctors' presence when such treatment takes place. The American Psychiatric Association (2006) have made it clear that psychiatrists should not take any part in interrogation and torture. In the UK the Royal College of Psychiatrists have taken a similar stance.

As a psychologist I find the treatment regime disturbing for many reasons, but the realisation that the acts are not random and are clearly informed by psychological principles is especially disturbing. The use of sleep deprivation, isolation and humiliation are not occurring by accident. Returned prisoners have described a regime which is clearly operating on operant conditioning principles and where the approaches are too consistent to have been arbitrarily arrived at. Clearly psychologists have been involved in the design and delivery of these programmes. The American Psychological Association (2006) has reaffirmed its position against torture and abuse. It has however accepted that psychologists may have a role in interrogations, although only non-coercive ones. I would maintain that all of the interrogations carried out in Guantánamo are coercive and that involvement in them has to be an issue for the society to rule on. They can only do this if given unfettered access to the psychologists' working environment.

Lifton (2004) has questioned the role of US doctors, nurses and medics in Guantánamo Bay and the extent to which they may have been complicit in torture or any other illegal procedures. He recognises the problems which being a military physician causes and the responsibilities to both patient and the military organisation. Lifton draws on his previous work looking at the role of Nazi doctors in Germany in WWII (Lifton, 1986). He points to the way in which they are socialised into their profession first, but then also into their military units, before finally, extermination camps. This process of socialisation may lead to people being able to accept increasingly inhumane practices that at the outset would have been completely unacceptable. It is very easy to assume that human rights abuses only occur in other countries. Lifton gives an insight into how this may occur anywhere.

Conclusions

The September 11th attacks set in motion a series of events that have had a profound effect on our world. Afghanistan and Iraq were invaded with disastrous consequences. On the domestic front, in both America and the UK, draconian legislation allowed the indefinite detention without trial of foreign nationals who were deemed to have some involvement in terrorism. The burden of proof was minimal to initiate indefinite detention in the UK and Robbins et al. (2005) showed that it had a very damaging impact on the detainees. In enacting the legislation ancient protections provided against abuse of the legal process were set aside. The legislation was ultimately declared to be unlawful by the Appellate Committee of the House of Lords: the highest court in the UK.

Existing research carried out with those in immigration detention has found a high level of psychiatric morbidity in those detained. The length of detention was clearly related to the severity of symptoms. What is particularly worrying is the fact that the research on detention is readily available and publicised by groups such as Amnesty International and JUSTICE. Governments cannot fail to be aware of this research and its implications yet it does not appear to have altered their approach. Indefinite detention without trial is without doubt psychologically damaging.

The criteria for identifying torture contained in the UN convention against torture are:

- severe pain and suffering whether physical or mental
- intentionally inflicted
- with a purpose
- by a state official or another acting with the acquiescence of the state

When there is a body of evidence which points to the impact of indefinite detention without trial, and the government of the day still proceeds with this as official policy, it meets or comes close to the UN definition. What happened and continues to happen in Guantánamo Bay easily surpasses the threshold criteria for identifying torture. This raises a number of questions about the involvement of psychiatrists, psychologists and other health care professionals in operations in Guantánamo Bay and the responsibility of professional bodies to enforce their professional codes of conduct.

Both the USA and UK have an espoused commitment to equality under the law, yet the evidence suggests that the detainees in Guantánamo, Belmarsh Prison, or those who are detained under the Patriot Act on the American mainland, are not receiving the protection under the law which citizens of the country receive. Singh (2003) suggests that:

> There seems to remain the residual but instinctive feeling that equality is about equality between citizens. Foreign nationals are not regarded as analogous because foreigners are different.

Seeing individuals as different or other is an essential precursor to being able to imprison, torture and ultimately execute them.

As yet there is no clear evidence as to the long-term impact of indefinite detention. There is an assumption that any problems will dissipate following release, but this may not be the case. Eitinger (1961) pointed to a number of long-term features in survivors of concentration camps, notably extreme anger and resentment, self-destructive urges, profound social withdrawal, bitterness, alienation and interpersonal conflict. These features could be triggered by perceptions of threat, frustration, dehumanisation and situations of confinement. Early clinical experience with those released suggests that there may indeed be parallels.

I do not suggest that, in the face of terrorist acts, we should take a passive approach. In fact I am in favour of pursuing anti-terrorist policies vigorously but I only believe in doing so within a normal legal framework. Individuals against whom there is evidence should be arrested and charged and have the evidence against them tested in a court of law. The burden of proof rests with the prosecution and should be of the same standard as for any criminal act. To do anything else means that we have allowed terrorists to move our society to a less liberal and caring position. This should not happen by default. The issue of a trade-off between human rights and public protection is not a new one but is again being tested in Blair's Britain. Another Mr Blair, Eric Blair, otherwise known as George Orwell, has commented on this previously. We need to consider whether this is what we want to be done in our name.

> … the choice for mankind lay between freedom and happiness, and … for the great bulk of mankind, happiness was better … the party was the eternal guardian of the weak, a dedicated sect doing evil that good might come, sacrificing its own happiness to that of others. Orwell (1970, p. 210)

CHAPTER 4

Torture, Psychology and the 'War on Terror': A human rights framework[1]

NIMISHA PATEL

Any involvement by psychologists in interrogations involving torture or other cruel, inhuman or degrading treatment or punishment for 'national security' or other purposes, not only perverts the ethos of all psychological practice, but inevitably and justifiably, erodes and undermines the public's trust in us, in our profession and in our activities.

Introduction

For practising psychologists, the 'War on Terror' has highlighted the complexities and ethical concerns arising from 'dual loyalty': a clinical role conflict between professional duties to a client and for some, obligations to the state. I argue here that psychologists have a professional obligation to uphold and defend the right to health and welfare of not just their clients, but all those affected by armed conflict and detention, torture and ill-treatment perpetrated by the US/UK military and intelligence personnel in all theatres of the 'war'.

I begin by providing a human rights framework to the 'War on Terror', defining torture and its prohibition in international law, before considering how torture has featured in Iraq, during Saddam Hussein's regime, and subsequently in the 'War on Terror', with reflections from refugee torture survivors, in the UK. The methods of torture used in the 'War on Terror' are examined, highlighting how psychologists have historically shaped these methods, and how, in

---

1. An earlier version of this chapter was presented at the Inaugural Meeting on Human Rights and Psychology, British Psychological Society Quintennial Conference, March 2005, Manchester, Britain.

participating in, and advising on, the application of interrogation methods involving torture, psychologists' direct and indirect role and complicity in torture has breached professional ethics and international law. The response of professional bodies is critiqued, with a specific emphasis on psychologists.

In highlighting psychological arguments beyond philosophical and legal positions against torture, I address whether torture 'works', examining the health and psychological impact of torture, emphasising that as psychologists we can never justify torture, or any involvement in torture. I conclude, with examples drawn from my own work, that psychologists have an important role, not in justifying and facilitating torture, but in preventing it and promoting international law.

A human rights framework: the 'War on Terror', torture and international law

Based on the premise that all human beings are born free and equal in rights and dignity, the United Nations Universal Declaration of Human Rights, 1948, specifies rights that seek to regulate nation states in their conduct to ensure the freedoms and protection of all human beings. Values enshrined in human rights law are mirrored in the professional codes and endeavours of health professionals, thus a human rights analysis, drawing on international human rights and humanitarian law provides a resource and an overarching framework to inform and guide the ethical practice of all health professionals and academics, particularly relevant to the 'War on Terror'.

The current 'War on Terror' has crystallised legal and moral problems associated with the notion of 'striking a balance' between human rights and security, in the face of terrorism. It has involved many state acts ranging from military conflict to the use of torture. Whether such acts are seen as self-defence, retaliation or a demonstration of the force of powerful nations, determines whether they can be considered a 'war', or a form of state terrorism itself, and balanced against the terrorist acts to which they are responding, whether they can be considered proportional and justifiable. No agreed definition of terrorism exists in international law; though many definitions have been proposed, with most agreeing that terrorism includes the targeting of civilians for death and destruction (Hoffman, 2004). Sterba (2003) suggests that, given that state-sanctioned terrorism is acknowledged by the US (2000), an inclusive definition would be that:

> Terrorism is the use or threat of violence against innocent people to elicit terror in them, or in some other group of people, in order to further a political objective. (p. 206)

Such a definition might allow attacks like 9/11, the invasion and war in Iraq, as well as previous US sponsored sanctions in Iraq which killed several thousand children in Iraq each month (Indemyer, 2001), to be defined as terrorism.

In the US's use of language in describing 9/11 as an 'act of war', there is an attempt to create an image of a war, rather than terrorism, positing al-Qaeda members as too fanatical to be defeated by traditional law enforcement methods, thereby creating an argument to undertake a 'War on Terror'. Whilst resorting to the use of force in self-defence is permissible under Article 51 of the United Nations Charter, the 'War on Terror' is still open to criticism in terms of proportionality and its duration—in essence it is an open-ended 'war', despite difficulties in demonstrating that the risk is enduring and the danger is constant.

Despite existing human rights law providing flexibility to states to protect national security within strictly defined limits, post 9/11 the balancing rhetoric, and use of 'special circumstances' in the 'war' (thereby evading strict definitions of war and emergency) has been used by states to violate human rights. Even when terrorism constitutes an emergency threatening the life of a nation, some rights must never be suspended, specifically the prohibition on torture and on the arbitrary deprivation of life (Fitzpatrick, 1994). Torture is frequently practised by emergency regimes (Amnesty International, 1984) and has been associated with other human rights abuses characteristic of emergencies, such as incommunicado detention, disappearances, administrative detention and secret trials (Fitzpatrick, 1994). The casualties of human rights in the current 'war' are evidenced in a number of ways. For example, the 500 plus Guantánamo detainees, transported to a supposed human-rights-free zone, held in incommunicado detention beyond the reach of any body of law, some in secret detentions, refused the designation as prisoners of war, denied hearings before competent tribunals, held indefinitely without charge and subjected to torture, cruel, degrading or inhuman treatment, provide testimony to the abuses of executive power unchecked. In the UK, anti-terrorism legislation targets non-citizens, so that British citizens receive the full panoply of protections if suspected of terrorism, while non-citizens, subject to immigration control, were until recently being detained indefinitely without trial or charge (See Chapters 1 and 10, this volume). The discrimination is fuelled by, and supports, a political environment where minorities, particularly, though not exclusively, Arab, Muslim and migrant people, are targeted for racial abuse and violence, including death threats and killings (see International Council on Human Rights Policy (ICHRP), 2000).

The illegal extradition procedures (expulsion and return) and the violations of the rights of asylum seekers are also areas of concern. Extraordinary renditions without rights for people suspected of terrorism, to countries in which there is reason to believe they will be subjected to torture (breaching Article 3 of the UN Convention against Torture), (United Nations High Commission for Human Rights (OHCHR) 1984), provides another systematic example of the cost to human rights of the 'war'. The use of phone and wiretapping, surveillance, control of the Internet and other measures in the 'war' also breach the right to privacy, but have enjoyed increasing protection under new legislation in various countries.

According to ICHRP (2002) serious errors have also been made in the 'War on Terror' where civilian casualties have occurred (e.g. being bombed because ordinance was misdirected, civilians being identified erroneously as combatants or civilian buildings being thought to be military targets). The number of civilian deaths remains unknown, although figures on military casualties are meticulously kept. Thousands of civilians have also been killed in Iraq since the invasion with the rise of insurgent bombings (arguably Iraqis exercising their right, enshrined in international law, to resist an illegal invasion) and sectarian execution-style killings in the civil conflict.

Central to anti-terrorism efforts is the recognition that all human beings have a right to security and to life, and all governments have a responsibility to respect, ensure and fulfil these rights and to take measures to prevent or punish terrorism. It is in the recognition that the right to security is not absolute—that no country can ever be protected completely from terrorism—that the arguments for balancing security and liberty emerge. Essentially, the right to security must be fulfilled within the framework of protecting human rights, not at their expense. Poignantly, Hoffman (2004) asks why the 'War on Terror' has received so many resources and so much attention at a time when more people in the world continue to experience suffering, harm and hardship as a result of the failure of states to uphold human rights standards, than exist victims of terrorism. More pressing issues of human security, argues Hoffman, include extreme poverty and substandard shelter and medical care which affect the well-being of millions. According to the World Bank, the Millennium Development Goals will not be achieved, in part because the 'War on Terror' is shifting attention and resources away from long-term development issues (Bulstein, 2004).

For psychologists, there are many questions. How relevant is our knowledge and experience to debates on the impact of the 'War on Terror' on people's security, health and well-being? Is there a role for psychologists in any aspect of the 'War on Terror', such as in interrogations? Unfortunately, the use of torture and the controversial role of psychologists, physicians and psychiatrists in interrogations involving torture and other ill-treatment has been a hallmark of the current 'War on Terror'. Whilst subordinating loyalty to the client/patient (even if a detainee) to the interests of the state can sometimes be argued to be permissible to serve a higher social purpose, violations of human rights cannot constitute permissible social purpose (Physicians for Human Rights (PHR), 2002). Torture is prohibited by international human rights law, the laws of armed conflict and customary international law. This prohibition is a non-derogable right under global and regional treaties, even in times of war. Torture was first defined in the UN Convention Against Torture and Other Forms of Cruel, Inhuman or Degrading Treatment or Punishment,1984 (UNCAT), and more recently in Article 7.2 (e) of the Rome Statute of the International Criminal Court (ICC) (1998) as:

the intentional infliction of severe pain and suffering, whether physical or mental, upon persons in the custody or under the control of the accused; except that torture shall not include pain or suffering arising only from, inherent in or incidental to, lawful sanctions.

Currently, over 104 countries in the world practise torture (Amnesty International, 2006a). It can be perpetrated by states or by individuals, though here I focus on state torture, where torture is used as a deliberate government policy, often to suppress political opposition. Torture is as much about the silencing and terrorising of societies, by using brutal techniques to heighten fear, as it is about 'getting people to talk', to obtain information (Reyes, 1995). State torture is also used to forcibly engage people in collaborating with government to incriminate others, as part of ethnic cleansing (e.g. in the Balkans) and in oppressing religious and ethnic minorities.

The involvement of health professionals using their knowledge and skills to participate in, guide or contribute to torture is a grave human rights violation, violating the right to be free from torture, the right to security and potentially violating the right to life (UNCAT and UN International Covenant on Civil and Political Rights) (OHCHR, 1966). Whilst history is replete with examples of such violations by health professionals, the context of the 'War on Terror' creates a unique landscape, one that has led the Bush administration to narrowly redefine torture in US domestic law, and to pass new legislation in 2006 which not only denies the right of habeas corpus to detainees—preventing an independent judge from ruling on the legality of the detention, and thus reducing the right to a fair trial before an independent court—but which may also allow the authorisation and sanctioning of methods amounting to torture and cruel, inhuman and degrading treatment, with immunity granted against prosecution for such violations in the last five years, even retroactively. However unique the landscape, there can be no justification, legal, ethical or otherwise, for the practice of, or complicity in, torture as defined in international law.

Torture in Iraq

They [Iraqi people] deserve better ... we want the people to be free to live fulfilling lives without the oppression and terror of Saddam. (Tony Blair, TUC Conference, 10th September 2002)

The question of what exactly the Iraqi people 'deserve' and who is to decide what is best or 'better' for them is a political question, requiring consideration, amongst other things, of the cost to human beings in suffering, injury and death. In initiating a war and occupation, supposedly in defence of human rights, the coalition has supplanted one form of suffering and fear with another. Torture, far from being part of Iraq's past history, after Saddam, became one of the defining features of the US/UK-led illegal invasion and occupation of Iraq and of the 'War on Terror'.

Torture and human rights violations in the Saddam years
During Saddam Hussein's dictatorship (1979–2003) human rights violations included high levels of torture, summary executions including public beheadings of women, targeted assassinations, chemical weapons and the widespread persecution of Kurds, Shi'ites and others. The latter included the disappearances of thousands of Kurdish males and children, some known to have been tortured and killed; the chemical bombing of the Kurdish town Halabja in 1988 with a combination of nerve agents, mustard gas and cyanide, killing in a single day 5,000 and injuring a further 10,000; and the Anfal campaign which included the forced displacement of hundreds of thousands of villagers, arbitrary imprisonments, executions by beheadings and chemical attacks against Kurdish civilians and destruction of Kurdish villages, in total killing between 50,000 and 100,000 people. Further massacres followed the uprisings by Kurds and Shi'ites after the first Gulf war, killing over 100,000 people. Compounded by restricted political participation at the national level to the 8 per cent Arab Ba'ath Party only, the banning of legal assembly except to express support of the government and very tight control of the membership of the government, change and opposition to the government was stunted and heavily punished. As head of state, head of government, leader of Iraq's only political party, head of the armed forces and head of security services, Saddam Hussein's control was extensive, with oppression sustained by widespread discrimination and terror, supported by torture, a systematic tool against political detainees and their families.

Torture in Iraq was carried out with impunity in many purpose-built torture centres and prisons. Torture methods (see Foreign and Commonwealth Office, 2002) included; suspension from the ceiling, beatings with fists, boots and implements, whippings with cables, whips and metal rods, piercing of hands with electric drills, electric shocks applied to genitalia, ears, tongue and fingers, sexual ill-treatment including rape of men and women, sexual threats and forced nakedness, falaka (beatings on the soles of feet with cables/implements), extraction of nails, acid baths, mock executions, being forced to witness others, including family members, being tortured, forced confinement in small metal boxes, solitary isolation for months in sound-proof and dark rooms with no ventilation or light, deprivation of food and fluid, cigarette burns and appalling prison conditions including deprivation of sanitary facilities, deprivation of light or sufficient space to lie down and infestation of lice and rats. Iraqi survivors of torture in the UK report also having experienced suffocation, submersion or immersion, enforced standing, hosing by cold water, torture using medical methods, administration of unknown substances, sleep deprivation, use of loud noise, threats of death to self and detention/imprisonment and violent death of family members, with almost all having experienced rape or other sexual ill-treatment in detention (Patel et al., 2006).

In Abu Ghraib, a notorious torture centre built by Saddam Hussein, nearly seven thousand political prisoners were executed as part of a prison 'cleansing' campaign. Many had previously been held there in solitary confinement (Foreign and Commonwealth Office, 2002). The reputation of Abu Ghraib, and the torture and killings within, were well known by all Iraqis prior to the US/UK invasion. The role of health professionals in such torture was also known by Iraqis, with psychiatrists forced to work within the Iraqi Military Psychiatric Services during the 1980s and 1990s, forced to torture, aiding interrogations using electric shocks to the body, administering depot neuroleptics to produce distressing side effects, striking the person, maintaining people in poor detention conditions and depriving them of contact with families whilst in hospital (Al-Ganimee, 2005).

The suffering of Iraqi people was arguably further compounded by the US and UK bombing raids on Iraq since 1991, many resulting in civilian casualties (Rangwala, 2002). Economic sanctions, imposed in 1990 by the United Nations and strongly supported by the US and UK, have led to a dramatic deterioration in humanitarian conditions; infant mortality rates becoming the highest in the world, children under five dying at more than twice the rate they were ten years previously, chronic malnutrition affecting every fourth child under five, only 41 per cent of the population with access to clean water, the health system in a dire condition with rising epidemics in communicable diseases such as malaria and water-borne diseases and a 157 per cent rise in the numbers of people with mental health problems attending health facilities (Rangwala, 2002).

Torture and abuse by the US/UK occupying forces
According to Amnesty International (2006b) more than 60 countries have violated or tolerated human rights abuses on the basis of new security laws introduced since September 11th 2001, with torture featuring prominently. In breaching human rights, the 'War on Terror' has created more victims in its recourse to torture and other ill-treatment, extraordinary renditions, outsourcing torture, and armed conflict.

In Iraq, occupation by coalition forces has led to an intensification of violence, with torture and abuses by the US and UK coalition resulting in more civilian deaths, injuries and suffering. Torture since the occupation has increased, perpetrated by security forces, militia groups and insurgents, as well as abuse and torture under extremely harsh detention conditions by US personnel, including food and liquid deprivation, forced nakedness, sexual humiliation, being drenched in cold water and then interrogated in air-conditioned rooms or in cold weather, solitary confinement, sleep deprivation, electric shocks, severe beatings and being sodomised with bottles (Schmitt, 2006). There are also reports of US troops killing civilians (Broder, 2006), raping a teenage girl and then murdering her and her family (Cloud & Semple, 2006) and newspaper reports of British troops abusing civilians and causing deaths, with several facing trial for war crimes under the International Criminal Court Act 2001. The effect on families and the local community of the loss of civilian lives and the abuses by coalition forces, their ongoing fear, suffering and rage, and the likely long-term political consequences of this, both in Iraq and closer to home in Britain, cannot be underestimated, dismissed, sanitised and obscured in the language of war—'collateral damage' (civilian deaths), 'entitlements under rules of engagement to use lethal force' (under the Geneva Conventions), 'clearing by fire' and 'prepping the room' ('you stick the weapon around and spray the room')(Broder, 2006).

Torture survivors living in UK
For many survivors of torture living in the UK, including Iraqis, clinical experience at the Medical Foundation for the Care of Victims of Torture, a human rights organisation, has shown that the media reports of the war, torture, abuse by occupying military personnel and continued civil violence in Iraq has a powerful effect. Experiences of clients affected by the war and its media coverage include one Algerian man expressing shock not just at the photos of Abu Ghraib but at the naïvety of those who believed 'democratic and civilised countries like the USA and the UK could not do' such things, stating that:

> I could send a message to everyone who has been shocked seeing the photos … do you still remember the photos? Do you think about those people who have been tortured? Every single day? No, of course not. I am not blaming or judging you, I am trying to tell you that when the general public finish their chat with friends and colleagues about torture and things related to it, they go home and we return to hell. (Medical Foundation, 2004, p. 4)

Others, current clients, expressed shock and profound despair, with many experiencing recurrent painful memories and nightmares of their own torture experiences. Many, with families still in Iraq, sat 24 hours a day by any television set they could find, desperately searching for news of the fate of people in their home towns, watching helplessly as the war progressed and the daily violence and news of abuse by troops unfolded. One client, an Iraqi Kurd, expressed ambivalence about the invasion, but was unequivocally against the continued occupation: 'with Saddam it was terrible, our lives were terrible, the torture was brutal, but we knew what to expect, with the US and the British, they came to 'rescue' us from Saddam—is this what they call rescuing?' For her, the sense of betrayal and injustice by the US and UK governments magnified the suffering related to her own torture, and to her experience of losing many family members during the chemical bombing of Halabja, when the international community, including Britain, was silent. Many other clients commented that the world is only interested in torture and Iraq for a moment, and fails to see similar violations in other countries, where torture continues with impunity. Many commented on the hypocrisy in the media coverage of torture by coalition troops, whilst simultaneously fuelling negative media images of asylum seekers, many of them fleeing torture. As one African client stated, 'This is British justice, I don't understand it, really, torture is torture, why can they not see all our suffering?' One wonders why there is now more general interest in torture, particularly since the Abu Ghraib photos, given how widespread it has always been. Perhaps because it is Western states who are the perpetrators, and after all, torture has been portrayed as a medieval, barbaric and importantly, a 'foreign' practice, not one practised by Western democracies.

On the ongoing occupation, abuses by coalition forces and the daily killings of civilians, one client remarked:

> We are like insects that can be crushed with no regard, it is as if the life of an Iraqi or a Lebanese person is not equal to the life of a British person, we are just dropping like flies, people in the West do not see that we are also human beings with children, mothers, fathers, with feelings and hopes, that we also feel fear, no, we are just insects, who cares how many of us die and suffer?

In Iraq, new centres for the treatment of survivors of torture have been established in Baghdad since 2004 and in Basra since 2005, for those who had survived torture during and after the Saddam regime. In contrast, the conflict in Iraq, the impact on the health and lives of civilian populations and the torture perpetrated by coalition forces, with the help of psychologists and medics, has attracted little consideration, let alone debate amongst British psychologists.

Psychological torture and the role of psychologists: past and present

The release of the infamous pictures from Abu Ghraib in 2004, followed by revelations about the use of torture in Guantánamo, Iraq and Afghanistan, exposed the participation and complicity of health professionals, including psychologists. These raise particular questions: What role have psychologists historically played in torture, either in researching and developing interrogation methods involving torture, in facilitating training of military/intelligence personnel in such methods, in implementing or monitoring torture and in advising military and intelligence agencies on the use of torture to further security measures? What are the related ethical concerns for psychologists and how have professional bodies responded?

Torture in the 'War on Terror'
In Abu Ghraib torture by US military forces was at first portrayed as random acts of abuse, violence and misbehaviour, though Danner (2004a) questions how isolated these abuses could have been when one of the most notorious images, that of several naked detainees stacked in a 'pyramid', served as a screen saver on one of the computers in the military intelligence office (Fay, 2004). The

techniques used in Iraq, Guantánamo and Afghanistan were later revealed to be part of a much more systematic policy, designed, refined, assisted and monitored by psychologists and other health professionals.

A report by Physicians for Human Rights provided the first comprehensive review of the use of psychological torture by US forces in the 'War on Terror'. This had gone unreported by official Pentagon investigations, including the report by Church (2005). Despite being based on incomplete evidence, there is sufficient indication that psychological torture was central to the interrogation process in US custody centres in Guantánamo, Iraq and Afghanistan since 2002: practices which followed directly from decisions by civilian leadership and military officers (PHR, 2005). According to PHR (2005) the psychological torture methods used were applied in combination, involving:

Prolonged isolation was used in various US custody centres. In Iraq isolation was used, and according to ICRC (2004) in one place detainees 'were held for nearly 23 hours a day in strict solitary confinement in small concrete cells devoid of daylight' and in Abu Ghraib the use of total isolation was routine and repetitive (Fay, 2004), with detainees in the 'isolation section' in 2003 being 'deprived of their liberty, completely naked, in totally empty concrete cells and in total darkness, allegedly for several consecutive days' in a system in which detainees were 'drip fed', given new items and privileges ('rewards') in the form of clothing, bedding, and light in exchange for cooperating (ICRC, 2004). In some cases detainees were segregated from other detainees, in total isolation (known as ghost detainees), in preparation for interrogation by the CIA, and denied visits by the ICRC. Even after the Abu Ghraib scandal, around 500 detainees continued to be held in isolation in Guantánamo (PHR, 2005), some for over 30 days in maximum security units composed of sealed boxes made of steel, concrete and aluminium, modelled on the US supermax prisons. British men released from Guantánamo have reported experiencing up to 19 months in solitary confinement (Meek, 2005; Begg & Brittain, 2006).

Sleep deprivation was commonly used in Afghanistan, Guantánamo and Iraq, and in Iraq was facilitated by 'playing of loud music or constant light in cells devoid of windows' (ICRC, 2004) and by varying the detainees' feeding schedule to disturb the biorhythm, making them walk, stand or putting them in different positions, waking and taking detainees from their cells, stripping and showering them with cold water and then subjecting them to interrogation, sometimes after up to three to four days of sleep deprivation (Fay, 2004). When asked about the infamous picture of the detainee placed on a box with electric wires attached to his fingers, toes and penis, the female soldier replied that it was her 'job to keep detainees awake' and that military intelligence wanted them 'to do things for MI [military intelligence] and OGA [other governmental agencies, a euphemism for the CIA] to get these people to talk' (Danner, 2004a). British prisoners released from Guantánamo have testified that British soldiers and intelligence officers interrogated them following sleep deprivation, as well as using hooding, beatings and short-shackling (Meek, 2005).

Severe humiliation/sexual torture using forced nudity, shaving and cavity searches, being photographed in shaming positions, inappropriate touching, and sexually provocative behaviour by female interrogators, forced to wear female underwear, forced to watch pornography, to simulate homosexual acts with other detainees, to masturbate, to drink urine and being denied food and water were also reported as being used in the 'War on Terror' to deliberately humiliate and break down detainees (see Fay, 2004; PHR, 2005) by violating cultural, religious and other taboos. According to ICRC (2004), detainees in some detention facilities in Iraq were paraded naked outside cells in front of other detainees, sometimes hooded or with women's underwear over the head whilst guards laughed at them. Reports of sexual torture in Iraq included threatening male detainees with rape, sodomizing a detainee with a chemical light and broom stick (Danner, 2004a) and the sexual torture of women, with one example of an elderly woman being subjected to being ridden like a horse, with a rope in her mouth and across her eyes, being beaten and having a stick inserted in her anus, whilst being insulted and sexually threatened as others looked on and laughed (PHR, 2005, p. 38). A British prisoner released from Guantánamo described being painted with his own urine while being racially abused (Meek, 2005).

Use of threats of beatings or electrocutions, the use of military working dogs to induce fear of death or injury and use of mock executions was used by interrogators in Afghanistan, Iraq and Guantánamo (PHR, 2005). In Iraq the use of dogs to instil fear amongst detainees was confirmed by dog handlers (White & Higham, 2004). One incident (Fay, 2004) involved dog handlers using snarling unmuzzled dogs with two juveniles to instil fear, in a game to see which handler could scare the teenagers first to a point where they would defecate. The use of staged mock executions was also common (PHR, 2005). Frequent insults and physical and verbal threats, threats of death and indefinite detention, and threats to wives and daughters of detainees have been alleged by detainees (ICRC, 2004).

Hooding was used in Iraq, from several hours to several days, to disorientate people, to prevent them from seeing, and to allow interrogator anonymity. It was used in conjunction with beatings to create anxiety about subsequent blows (ICRC, 2004).

Restraints and stress positions were reported in Iraq by ICRC (2004) including handcuffing with flexi-cuffs, which can cause skin lesions and long-term nerve damage. In addition, being attached repeatedly over several days with handcuffs to the bars of their cell door in humiliating and/or uncomfortable positions causing physical pain, and being forced to remain for prolonged periods in stress positions such as squatting or standing with or without the arms lifted were also reported.

Exposure, while hooded, to loud music or noise and prolonged exposure to the sun over several hours, while hooded, when temperatures could reach 122°F or higher were also reported in Iraq (ICRC, 2004).

The ICRC (2004) described methods in Iraq as 'physical and psychological coercion ... used by the military intelligence in a systematic way to gain confessions and extract information'. Other methods reported by released prisoners from Guantánamo include being forced to take suspect medication, being forcibly injected with unknown substances, being urinated on, being deprived of food and being made to run in shackles until injured (Allard, 2004). Some of the techniques described are similar to those used in the 'Resistance to Interrogation' (R2I) training for British soldiers to inoculate them against psychological coercion, abuse and torture if captured (Leigh, 2004) and to the corresponding Survival, Evasion, Resistance and Escape training programme used by the US army (Mayer, 2005).

As the ICRC stated in their leaked report (Lewis, 2004) 'the construction of such a system, whose stated purpose is the production of intelligence, cannot be considered other than an intentional system of cruel, unusual and degrading treatment and a form of torture'. Taken in concert, the combined use of these methods in a system deliberately devised to break people can amount to torture and have a devastating impact with long-term consequences for the individual and their families. The argument that this is 'torture-lite', and that individual acts do not constitute torture, ignores this reality.

Human rights violations are often justified as being 'part of the job', though such normalisation of abusive practice is also commonly reported by survivors and perpetrators of torture in other contexts—in dehumanising and criminalising the 'other', with detainees portrayed as the enemy, subhuman, barbaric and a danger to the welfare of 'Western democracies' or as Bush stated, to 'those of *us* [italics added] who love freedom'. Torture in the 'War on Terror' has been a part of a systematic abusive practice in an environment that normalised the abuse of human rights, even where criminal homicides of detainees took place. For example, in 2004, five men were found to have died as a 'result of abuse by US personnel during interrogations' (Schlesinger et al., 2004, p.13), or more accurately, were 'tortured to death' (Danner, 2004b) with 23 detainee deaths under investigation at the time (Schlesinger et al., 2004).

The involvement of UK military and intelligence personnel in such abuses is highly pertinent. The House of Lords and House of Commons Joint Committee on Human Rights' Report (2006) assessing the UK's compliance with the UN Convention Against Torture and Other Cruel, Inhuman and Degrading Treatment or punishment (UNCAT) states that 'questions remain' regarding the extent to which UK troops have engaged in practices amounting to torture, yet acknowledges that some British personnel have committed grave violations of human rights of persons held in detention facilities in Iraq. Prisoners released from Guantánamo have also testified that British officers interrogated them at the US base and in Afghanistan whilst being subjected to many of the torture methods previously described. Yet, the Intelligence and Security Committee's (ISC) (2005) report into the handling of detainees by UK intelligence personnel states that of the thousands of interviews conducted or witnessed in Afghanistan (2,200), Guantánamo Bay (100) and Iraq (2,000) there were fewer than 15 incidents, at the time, identified as actual or potential breaches of either UK policy or the international conventions. The ISC report states that in Abu Ghraib, there was evidence that UK personnel were 'embedded' with the US and they may have observed US interrogations, though with no records of concerns being raised. The report concludes that in Iraq the SIS (Secret Intelligence Service), security services and civilian Defence Intelligence Staff (DIS) were insufficiently trained in the Geneva Conventions prior to their deployment to Iraq and they were not aware of the interrogation techniques that the UK had previously banned. Shiner (2005), from Public Interest Lawyers, comments: 'Are we to assume that the officers and soldiers who tortured to death Baha Mousa [killed whilst under arrest by British forces] and Kifah Taha A-Mutari to the brink of death were ... unaware? And that soldiers were unaware that repeatedly kickboxing hooded detainees in the head, or beating [them] for not remembering footballers' names was also prohibited?'

The ISC report menacingly notes that only trained interrogators were actually used to conduct interviews but the 'DIS civilian technical experts supporting these interviews, who were either in the interview room or outside it, had no training on the principles of interrogation' (Intelligence and Security Committee, 2005, para. 82, p. 21) nor had received any training concerning the Geneva Conventions. Later the report quotes the Chief of Defence Intelligence as saying 'for our civilian experts ... on this occasion they were closer to the front line, they were more intimately involved with the interrogation process than was our experience in the past ... it was still supporting professional interrogators, but more intimately: they were present at more interviews, rather than just prompting questions' (ibid., para. 89, p. 23). Who were these 'civilian technical experts', 'present' in interrogations, helping to 'just prompt questions'? Were they psychologists or others with health backgrounds?

The history of psychologists developing and refining methods of torture
    Psychology as a discipline appears to have played no verifiable role in the
    development of torture techniques ... there does not seem to be much that
    psychologists could add, or have added, to the tools already at hand.
    (Suedfeld, 1990, p. 105)

In contesting the view that the reports of abuse and torture by military personnel in Iraq, presented by the Bush administration as a 'few bad apples', were isolated examples of bad behaviour by a few junior staff, McCoy (2006) meticulously documents the development of such techniques by the CIA over the last 50 years, pointing to a systematic policy, supported by CIA interrogation manuals, to use psychological torture methods dating back to the Cold War. Torture reported in the 'War on Terror', and authorised by the army commander for Iraq, involved many techniques derived from the CIA's methods, coded in interrogation manuals in seemingly innocuous ways:

Dietary manipulation: Changing the diet of a detainee.

Environmental Manipulation: Altering the environment to create moderate discomfort (e.g. adjusting temperatures or introducing an unpleasant smell).

Sleep adjustment: Adjusting the sleeping times of the detainee … (e.g. reversing sleeping cycles from night to day).

False flag: Convincing the detainee that individuals from a country other than the United States are interrogating him.

Isolation: Isolating the detainee from other detainees … use of this technique for more than 30 days … must be briefed … prior to implementation.

Presence of military working dogs: Exploiting Arab fear of dogs while maintaining security during interrogations.

Sleep management: Detainee provided minimum four hours of sleep per 24-hour period, not to exceed 72 continuous hours.

Yelling, loud music, and light control: Used to create fear, disorientate detainee and prolong capture shock. Volume controlled to prevent injury.

Deception: Use of falsified representations, including documents and reports.

Stress positions: Use of physical posturing (sitting, standing, kneeling, prone etc.) for no more than 1 hour per use. Use of technique(s) will not exceed four hours and adequate rest between use of each position will be provided. (See McCoy, 2006, pp. 134–5.)

The use of scientific research to develop such methods dates back to 1951, when Canada and Britain joined forces with the CIA to research into 'confessions', 'menticide' and 'intervention in the individual mind' as part of their 'mind control' programme (cited in Victorian, 1996). From this grew operation ARTICHOKE and research grants were given to psychologists to conduct research into 'attitude changes' in individuals (e.g. exploring the use of sensory deprivation and isolation). The CIA provided the majority of funding (reputedly one billion dollars a year) for around six leading psychology departments, and to some 185 non-governmental researchers (McCoy, 2006). Research on torture and interrogation included using electric shocks and giving LSD, dubbed the 'truth serum' to unsuspecting subjects

(Bennett, 2005). Other research, allegedly funded and used by the CIA includes the work of psychologists Stanley Milgram, John Lilly, Harold Wolff, Lawrence Hinkle and others (McCoy, 2006; Bennett, 2005; Harper, 2004; see also Chapter 3 in this book). Mayer (2005) reports that interrogators at Guantánamo were particularly interested in research into learned helplessness by Martin Seligman, a former President of the APA, which Seligman reportedly presented to military interrogation specialists. Though approached for interview, Seligman has refused to comment on the matter (Bennett, 2005).

One psychologist researching sensory deprivation openly stated that, 'while our goal is pure knowledge for its own sake, we have no objection to someone's use of that knowledge' (Vernon, 1966, p. 16). Similarly, Suedfeld (1990), commenting on psychological involvement in methods drawn from psychological theory and research, such as the use of drugs, conditioning, behaviour modification, psychoanalysis, sensory deprivation, encounter techniques, aversive conditioning, psychosurgery, sensory over-stimulation, cognitive effects of fatigue and electroshock, states: 'if torturers use dental drills on healthy teeth, this does not imply that researchers and practitioners who develop, improve, and use such drills in the course of ethical dental practice should feel guilty' (p. 106). The ethical responsibility of psychologists to ensure that their knowledge is not misused and the legal obligation to not engage in, support or be complicit in any acts of torture is thereby obscured.

Cameron (1957), a Canadian psychiatrist in the 1950s, attempted to produce an effect akin to brainwashing, arguing that 'depatterning' learned psychotic and neurotic thoughts could pave the way for 'implanting' adaptive ideas by using 'psychic driving' involving weeks of induced sleep, frequent and severe electroconvulsive shocks, the use of psychotropic drugs, prolonged monotonous stimulation, thousands of repetitions of particular words or phrases (research subsequently funded by the CIA—see McCoy, 2006). In describing this work, Suedfeld, (1990, p. 108) asserts: 'there is no evidence that any governmental agency anywhere has ever used a torture technique remotely similar'. Evidence of torture and abuses in the 'War on Terror' suggests otherwise.

The results of these early CIA torture experiments were codified in 1963 in a secret manual known as 'KUBARK Counterintelligence Interrogation' (McCoy, 2006) at a time when the CIA operated many interrogation centres and supported army mobile training teams working worldwide. The authors of the CIA's 1963 interrogation manual KUBARK (cited in Hodge & Cooper, 2004), write that psychological rather than physical debility will break a suspect sooner: 'the threat of coercion usually weakens or destroys resistance more effectively than coercion itself. The threat to inflict pain can trigger fears more damaging than the immediate sensation of pain … intense pain is quite likely to produce false confessions, concocted as a means of escaping from distress'. The manual, which cites numerous psychological studies, says all detainees should be given a psychological assessment and contains descriptions of different personality types and the specific techniques to use to interrogate them. All of the basic techniques used in Iraq are found in the manual's pages: sexual humiliation, sensory deprivation, sleep deprivation and disruption, solitary confinement and the use of stress positions. The manual also suggests threatening a detainee suspected of feigning mental illness by telling them that they might need 'a series of electric shock treatments or a frontal lobotomy'.

The British, Meek (2005) argues, refined some of these early methods, which were used in interrogations in Northern Ireland by the Ulster security forces. They were produced by the 'conscious use of available scientific knowledge' (Shallice, 1972, p. 387) developed by psychologists and in 1972 were banned by the British following a ruling by the European Court of Human Rights.

The KUBARK manual in 1983 provided the model for the CIA's Human Resource Exploitation Training Manual, an interrogation manual, listing coercive techniques such as those used in Abu Ghraib, Guantánamo and Afghanistan (McCoy, 2006). In 2005, following evidence of abuse of detainees held by the US in Iraq, the US Army announced that it would be issuing a new manual for army interrogators ('Human Intelligence Collector Operations'), with specific guidance on interrogation procedures and scenarios which prohibited stripping of prisoners, forced stressful positions, dietary restrictions, the use of police dogs and sleep deprivation, though not stating what else is specifically banned (Schmitt, 2005), or which psychologically abusive techniques can be used. Adding to speculation about what else happened in Iraq, Thomas Gandy, director of human intelligence and counterintelligence for the US Army said in an interview (see Schmitt, 2005) that the manual barred interrogators and other intelligence officials from posing as medics, journalists or chaplains to gain information from detainees, though falsely promising prisoners release in exchange for information is allowed. Whilst it bans the CIA from using army prisons for holding 'ghost detainees', the manual (and its guidance and prohibitions on interrogation procedures) only applies to the army, not to interrogations by the CIA or other agencies.

Psychologists' participation and assistance in torture in the 'War on Terror'
Recent evidence of the involvement of psychologists, psychiatrists and other doctors in torture and interrogation in the 'War on Terror' has highlighted the continuation of psychologists' participation and complicity in torture. Evidence that medical personnel were aware of abuse but failed to report it (Fay, 2004) and evidence that confidentiality was breached, in that medical files were accessible to interrogators (Lewis, 2004), was followed by evidence of the existence of the Behavioural Science and Consultation Teams (BSCTs) at Guantánamo and Abu Ghraib. These comprised health professionals, including psychologists and psychiatrists, tasked with helping US intelligence and military in conducting interrogations of detainees.

In Britain, psychological expertise is integral to the delivery of Resistance to Interrogation (R2I) training provided to British soldiers where psychologists or psychiatrists are always present to check on the (non) induction of psychological damage (Leigh, 2004). In the corresponding US military training programme, the psychologists involved in developing their programme were the very same US psychologists also reportedly working in the BSCTs aiding CIA and military interrogations in the 'War on Terror' (Mayer, 2005). The role of BSCTs in facilitating interrogation was addressed by Vice Admiral Albert Church III, Director of Navy Staff for the US Department of Defense, in a report (Church, 2005):

> These personnel observe interrogations, assess detainee behaviour and motivations, review interrogation techniques, and offer advice to interrogators. This advice can be effective in helping interrogators collect intelligence from detainees; however it must be done with proper limits. We found that the behavioural science personnel were not involved in detainee medical care (thus avoiding any inherent conflict between caring for detainees and crafting interrogation strategies) nor were they permitted access to detainee medical records.

Bloche and Marks (2005a) report evidence questioning this reported separation of roles between care giving and assisting in interrogation. Strikingly, Church (2005) positions international humanitarian law, and 'US military doctrine', as being responsible for the nature of assistance given by behavioural science personnel to interrogators 'evolv[ing] in an ad hoc manner' because 'neither the Geneva Convention(s) nor US military medical doctrine specifically addresses [this] issue', failing to acknowledge that, nevertheless, international law is unambiguous about the illegality of torture; and that all BSCT personnel, as those with health/'behavioural science' backgrounds would be bound by medical (or psychological) ethics.

According to Bloche and Marks (2005b) one principle BSCT function was to engineer the camp experiences of 'priority' detainees to make interrogation more productive. Health information (e.g. detainees' phobias) has been routinely available to BSCT consultants responsible for crafting, advising on or carrying out interrogation strategies, including those using extreme stress, combined with behaviour-shaping rewards, which, since 2002, psychologists and psychiatrists have taken part in, with the limit being that they may not act as interrogators, though they were required to give clinical information to military and CIA interrogation teams on request, as well as to volunteer information believed to be of value. They reveal that a psychiatrist and a psychologist had each headed BSCTs to assist interrogations in Guantánamo, and did have access to medical records, preparing psychological profiles for use by interrogators, sitting in on interrogations and observing others behind one-way mirrors and offering feedback to interrogators. Further, health personnel conveyed information about detainees' mental health and vulnerabilities (e.g. phobias, relationships with a parent or significant other) directly to the interrogators (ICRC, 2004). Interestingly, Gray and Zielinski (2006) remark on the US government website for government psychologists, which has an extensive bibliography on torture treatment literature, implying a systematic use of such knowledge.

Ethical considerations and the response of professional health bodies

Exposure of the role of psychologists and other health professionals in the 'War on Terror', specifically in interrogations, has thrown into turbulent waters the various professional bodies, including the American Psychological Association, the American Psychiatric Association, the American Medical Association, the British Medical Association and the World Medical Association: all of whom have issued policy statements responding to revelations about health professionals' involvement in interrogation processes in Iraq, Guantánamo and Afghanistan. Notable in its silence is the British Psychological Society (BPS).

The UN Principles of Medical Ethics provide explicit guidance for health personnel charged with the care of prisoners and detainees (United Nations, 1982): principles which echoed the World Medical Association's Tokyo Declaration 1975 on torture, recently revised in light of events at Guantánamo (WMA, 2006). In short, any participation and complicity in torture or other ill-treatment is a breach of medical ethics. However, these declarations are only guidelines and are not legally binding for health professionals or their bodies. The American Medical Association (see Ray, 2006) also joined the WMA in approving a policy, supported by military physicians (Moran, 2006), which rejected the Pentagon's stance on the use of military physicians to support individual interrogations, though it has areas of ambiguity. Unlike the American Medical Association, the American Psychiatric Association has been explicit and unambiguous in stating that it believes interrogation to be inherently coercive and deceptive, thus strongly stating that no psychiatrist should participate in, or otherwise assist or facilitate, the commission of torture of any person and that no psychiatrist should participate directly in interrogation of persons held in custody by the military or civilian investigative or law enforcement authorities, whether in the United States or elsewhere. The policy also states that psychiatrists should not, in any way, assist in so-called 'coercive interrogations', which are also commonly described as 'torture-lite', which the Association goes on to define clearly.

The controversy on ethics was sparked by the American Psychological Society when it established the Presidential Task Force on Psychological Ethics and National Security (PENS), with the aim to explore the ethical aspects of psychologists' involvement and the use of psychology in national security-related investigations. In so doing it provided guidance to its members, (APA, 2005) by stating that 'it is consistent with the [American Psychological Association] Ethics Code for psychologists to serve in consultative roles to interrogation and information-gathering processes for national security-related purposes, as psychologists have a longstanding tradition of doing in other law enforcement contexts'… whilst such action does 'not threaten or cause physical injury or mental suffering', though it is not clear how mental suffering is defined, how an assessment of whether there was any mental suffering or physical injury is to be made, and by whom, and when.

The PENS report listed 12 statements regarding psychologists' ethical obligations in national security work, including statements contradicting their overall position that psychologists do have a role in interrogation: 'psychologists do not engage in, direct, support, facilitate, or offer training in torture or other cruel, inhuman, or degrading treatment' and 'psychologists are alert to acts of torture and other cruel, inhuman and degrading treatment and have an obligation to report these acts to the appropriate authorities' (without stating which authorities) and 'psychologists who serve in the role of supporting an interrogation do not use health care information from an individual's medical records [implying, though not specifying, psychological records] to the detriment of the individual's safety and well-being'. The report brought into fierce debate the issue of whether psychologists had any role in matters of national security, and highlighted the question of whether psychologists' ethical obligations to the State override their obligations to the recipients of torture, and whether such obligations superseded those under international human rights law. In Britain, the report was criticised by the BMA, though not the BPS, as part of a trend of 'governments and professional bodies rewriting existing ethical guidance in the service of abuse' (Wilks, 2005), or to be more precise, in the service of State abuse.

What is clear is that the APA does envisage a role for psychologists, even suggesting that they be engaged in conducting research into 'benign' interrogation methods. As Bloche and Marks (2005a) point out 'proximity of health professionals to interrogation settings … carries risk', which in interrogation-related research can be the risk of involvement or complicity in torture or other ill-treatment. As such, psychologists, in making judgements about what constitutes 'benign' interrogation, are already implicated in addressing questions on which particular methods, applied in which way, under which particular circumstances, in which context, could cross the threshold between 'benign' and 'harmful' for a particular person. This carries such significant risk of harm that it would be hard to justify under any prevailing research ethics.

The APA's argument that psychologists have historically been involved in interrogations for criminal/law enforcement purposes is also problematic. Psychologists have engaged in research on interrogation (though not involving torture) and its effectiveness in obtaining confessions (e.g. Gudjonnson, 1999), but the issue here is of torture, cruel, inhuman or degrading treatment or punishment. The principle remains the same: psychologists should have no role in coercion, or in the use of psychology to facilitate interrogations involving deliberate suffering amounting to torture or cruel, inhuman or degrading treatment for anyone, whether civilian, soldier, criminal or 'terrorist'. In addition, invoking 'greater cause' as a common justification for psychologists' involvement in interrogation further circumvents both ethical obligations to the detainee, as well as obligations under international law, which does not permit the violation of human rights, for any 'greater cause'.

Introducing further ambiguity is the report's statement that 'psychologists do not engage in activities that violate the laws of the United States, although psychologists may refuse, for ethical reasons, to follow laws or orders that are unjust or that violate basic principles of human rights'. Reference to the laws of the United States is insufficient and denies the overriding obligations under international law. Interestingly, in suggesting that psychologists may refuse to follow laws or orders for ethical reasons implies that the responsibility is not on the State, nor the professional body, but on the individual to make a judgement on what is 'unjust' and violates international law. In this relegation of judgement on the legality of their actions, the report cites UNCAT and the Geneva Convention, and 'encourage[s] psychologists working in this area to review essential human rights documents', implying that individual psychologists are responsible for acquainting themselves with, and interpreting, international law vis-à-vis their activities, something probably beyond their competencies. It is also unlikely that psychologists would be fully and adequately informed of the nature and extent of the use of their knowledge and skills, which would be essential in enabling them to judge the ethics of their actions. In the absence of specific guidance, and under duress in particular situations governed by military policy, this risks individual (potentially inconsistent) and lay (potentially incorrect) interpretations of international law.

The PENS report's statement that 'psychologists are sensitive to the problems inherent in mixing potentially inconsistent roles, such as health care provider and consultant to an interrogation, and refrain from engaging in such multiple relationships', legitimates psychologists' consultative role in interrogations: as long as there is no overlapping or contradiction in providing healthcare and in then being involved in offering advice which can be potentially harmful to the recipient. This statement leaves open the loophole of teams of psychologists who could simultaneously be involved in psychological assessment, and/or treatment and interrogation, but not all three activities for their own clients—there is no prohibition on aiding interrogation of each other's 'clients'.

Refraining from the use of professional titles such as 'psychologist' and using titles such as 'behavioural science consultant', as suggested by the statements from the Pentagon, could sidestep the ethical obligations in professional codes which apply whatever name or title is used, whilst privileging obligations to the state over professional obligations to individuals subject to state abuse. The PENS report itself affirms the application of the APA Code of Ethics to all psychologists, in any position they are recruited to, by virtue of their training, experience and expertise as psychologists. Given that the specific knowledge, understanding and skills of psychologists are precisely why they are asked to assume such roles, to use alternative titles is nothing but deception.

Most alarmingly, the APA report states that 'psychologists may serve in various national security roles, such as consultant to an interrogation, in a manner that is consistent with the Ethics Code and, when doing so, psychologists are mindful of factors unique to these roles and contexts that require special ethical considerations'. 'Mindfulness' does not prevent torture or complicity in torture. The 'special ethical considerations' are simple: to do no harm, to not deliberately cause or facilitate the infliction of suffering and pain. In the absence of clear, specific and unequivocal guidance, ambiguity about techniques or methods used in interrogation (that is, doubt about how they may be classified in law, or uncertainty about the negative long-term health consequence) can be exploited to continue interrogation methods that amount to torture or ill-treatment. Further, any such involvement, under the current guidance, may lead to no disciplinary action from the APA, though this does not preclude action by complainants against named psychologists (where names are known) before civilian professional ethics boards in their home states in the US.

Not surprisingly, given the American Psychiatric Association's subsequent position statement explicitly prohibiting participation of psychiatrists in detainee interrogations, the Department of Defense announced that the American Psychological Association's stance is closer to the military's than the American Psychiatric Association's, contributing to their decision to use psychologists, not psychiatrists as advisors during interrogations of detainees (Lewis, 2006; Hausman, 2006). Of note is the fact that the Task Force responsible for the PENS report included six (out of ten) psychologists with ties to the Department of Defense, four with involvement in Guantánamo, Abu Ghraib or Afghanistan (Benjamin, 2006), thus introducing the possibility of vested interest, or situational pressures to conform to, even defend military rules and procedures. One of the other members, Mike Wessells, resigned, stating that to 'continue to work with the task force tacitly legitimates the wider silence and inaction of the APA ... [which] has not made a strong, concerted, comprehensive, public and internal response ... affirming our commitment to human well-being and sounding a ringing condemnation of psychologists' participation not just in torture but in all forms of cruel, inhuman and degrading treatment of detainees' (cited in Shinn, 2006, p. 2).

Amidst continued criticism, the APA maintains its existing policy, allowing psychologists to assist in national security interrogations, though it has recently adopted a policy against torture, stating that it 'condemns torture or other cruel, inhuman or degrading treatment or punishment' and that this policy 'applies to all psychologists in all settings' (American Psychological Association, 2006). Nevertheless, the APA position fails to acknowledge how any complicity in torture, however indirect, breaches international law and contributes to a climate of disregard and abuse of 'other' human beings deemed to be a threat to 'us', thus justifying torture in certain circumstances. In a twisted irony, psychologists' identity, as endeavouring to apply psychological knowledge to facilitate the well-being of all people, rings hollow. We become arbiters of moral judgements about who should be tortured, and who not, under which circumstances and even how.

In Britain, the BPS's first ever declaration concerning torture and other cruel, inhuman or degrading treatment or punishment (BPS, 2005) was laudable: though it fell short of providing an unequivocal policy against torture and did not specify that any complicity or participation in any interrogations breaching international law would be investigated, punished, and the person barred from membership of the BPS and from practising as a psychologist. The BPS has until now refrained from any formal and specific policy or ethical guidance. In a press statement, Jarrett (2006b) quotes Richard Kwiatkowski, current chair of the BPS's ethics committee, as saying that it is unusual for the Society (BPS) to set out ethical guidance on specific issues: 'The BPS code says: here are the basic principles, here are the values ... we say in the code, thinking is not optional (p. 9), you have to think about your action and if you think you can justify it, go ahead, but if it is questionable, then go through the appropriate stages'. The quality of thinking, or ethical questioning, depends on being adequately informed of existing international standards. In the current state, the BPS's Code of Ethics and Conduct (BPS, 2006b) and the declaration against torture, have little chance of preventing any British psychologists' participation or complicity in torture without clearer guidance reiterating our obligations under international law.

On the subject of appropriate punishment Gray and Zielinski (2006) ask: 'Is there to be no penalty for US clinicians who participate in torture, whose names, rank and branch of service are published, or whose job résumés or memberships reveal their history in torture? Will they be accepted at international symposia, will their papers be published, and will they be given university posts, fellowships, or other jobs?' (p. 132). However, expulsion from professional bodies and isolation from academic and clinical communities may not suffice. Justo (2006) calls for an international medical tribunal to denounce those who have committed documented violations of human rights, and to exert influence on national medical associations to revoke such doctors' licence to practise. Without legislation compelling disclosure to relevant health professional regulatory bodies; and without consensus amongst the academic and professional health communities on the prohibition on torture and other ill-treatment; and without clear and specific procedures for the investigation and punishment of personnel involved in torture by health professional bodies, there is little hope of progress. Essential ways forward would be first, for all health professional bodies to incorporate explicit reference to obligations under international law, within the rules and codes for ethics and conduct. Second, there should be clear mechanisms to support those who may face difficulties (e.g. with their employers) as a result of compliance with such ethical codes, also providing support to those who wish to report breaches by others. Third, there should be explicit mechanisms to investigate breaches, and to enforce ethical codes and rules, ensuring effective punishment for those found to have breached such codes. Fourth, mechanisms are essential to make publicly available the decisions made by relevant professional committees related to such breaches.

Additionally, in existing legal mechanisms for upholding international law, torture is a crime and in much the same way as torturers can be held to account and punished for human rights violations, so can individuals (including practising and non-practising psychologists) who were active or complicit in torture, and potentially even professional bodies. However, the added risk of professional censure could serve as a useful deterrent.

Under international humanitarian law, both the US and UK, as occupying powers in Iraq, have legal obligations to protect the Iraqi population, which includes the duty to respect the prohibition of torture and of deportation and transfer of the inhabitants of occupied territories. Under international human rights law, the catalogue of torture and ill-treatment by occupying forces against the Iraqi people and others in the 'War on Terror', with the complicity of health professionals, is a breach of an absolute prohibition. As psychologists, if we are unwilling to take a clear and committed stance on actions causing deliberate suffering and pain, what credibility do our ethical claims have? Regardless of how we may debate the definitions, morality and scientific merits of interrogation; no one is above international law.

Does torture 'work'?

Apart from professional and legal obligations, moral arguments abound for and against the use of torture in counter-terrorism measures. For example, utilitarian arguments for using torture hold that the harm prevented by gathering information by torture can outweigh the moral harms inflicted by the practice of torture. But such arguments rely on the reliability and validity of information extracted in torture, a highly dubious premise given research based on the civilian criminal justice system which suggests techniques less coercive than torture have produced false confessions (e.g. Gudjonsson, 1999; Kassin & Gudjonsson, 2004). This is supported by historical accounts of travesties of justice where convictions were based on information extracted in torture. A statement by former US Army Interrogators and interrogation technicians further refutes the assertion that 'coercive interrogation techniques' (or as the CIA describes them, 'enhanced interrogation techniques') and torture are necessary, adding that prisoner/detainee abuse and torture is counterproductive to the intelligence-gathering mission and must be avoided at all costs (Bauer, 2006). Apart from psychological and stress factors which impact on the quality of the information extracted, physical pain and suffering can account for information being given, which later reveals itself to be inaccurate and only offered as a means for ending the pain of torture. All this amounts to a rejection of utilitarian arguments for the use of torture: simply put—because torture is unlikely to yield helpful information, despite being an effective method for instilling fear and intimidating, coercing and politically controlling people. From the viewpoint of the 'War on Terror' if torture was shown to reduce terrorist activity by using fear and intimidation, then it might be argued that torture was morally justified, its benefits outweighing moral harm. However, the harm to society, not just individuals, in using torture, and its striking similarity to 'acts of terrorism', denounced in the 'War on Terror' highlight its paradoxical and precarious status as a possibly morally justifiable, and useful 'weapon' in the 'war'.

The ticking bomb scenario is also often enacted as a justification for torture—that is a scenario where the person being tortured holds vital information that could help prevent the killings of many other people. As McCoy (2006) points out, in four years of torture in the 'War on Terror' the CIA could only say that they had 'documented [unnamed] success' but nothing akin to stopping a ticking bomb. In exploring three models (animal instinct, cognitive failure and the data processing models—see also Chapter 1, this volume) Arrigo (2004) provides a convincing utilitarian argument against torture of 'terrorists', concluding that torture fails overall as a counter-terrorist tactic to create national security. Torture is also never limited to the 'guilty'. Many innocent civilians can be subjected to torture, cruel, degrading or inhuman treatment, resulting in injury and even death. Not only potentially catalytic in the institutional degradation of the government, police, judiciary and military, Arrigo argues that state-sanctioned torture programmes inevitably result in damaging social consequences with breakdowns of institutions and community, with errors in torturing innocents remedied by scapegoating, cover-up, discrediting of victims and token reparations.

Justifying torture is a slippery slope, whereby arguments that certain torture methods do not yield information potentially lead to still harsher methods. As Waldron (2003) highlights, this tendency for torture to be metastatic (Shue, 1978), illustrates the dangers of powers that may be increasingly assigned to governments, and perhaps to psychologists. If psychological coercion does not work, can specific physical torture be effective and justified? For example, if beatings and suspension don't work should waterboarding by forcing fluids into the throat to simulate the effects of drowning be considered, and if this does not work should sexual torture be considered? What works best, for whom? Can this ever be a legitimate quest for psychologists or other health professionals?

The impact of torture and the 'War on Terror' on health and well-being

The dominant security-oriented discourse in the 'War on Terror', perpetuating breaches of human rights, has subjugated discourse on the health effects and harm to innocents by the use of torture and ill-treatment. Likewise, in dominant discourses within psychology and medicine, war and its aftermath are constructed as life enhancement, as struggles for freedom, democracy and defence of human rights rather than as mass killing and an assault on health and human rights (Boyle, 1997). Psychologists have tended to focus more on the health problems of war veterans and victims of 'war' or 'terrorist attacks' in the UK, than on the costs of conflict and human rights violations perpetrated by Western states to civilians in terms of death, destitution, poverty, bereaved families, unemployment and related physical and emotional health consequences (Patel, 2003). Even within the context of the 'War on Terror', the dominant psychological discourse conflates torture with trauma, reducing it to sanitised, depoliticised and pathologising constructs such as PTSD, locating the problem within the psyche of individuals, thereby averting gaze from the causes, and the wider impact on the welfare and fabric of communities affected by war and torture.

The short- and long-term health effects of psychological torture and other cruel, inhuman and degrading treatment can be devastating. My own clinical experience suggests that the nature and number of detentions and torture experiences alone cannot reliably predict the likely psychological experiences and effects, their severity, duration or trajectories. Responses to torture can vary with age at time of torture, life trajectory and life context at time of torture, family support, experience of other abuses or violence in one's life prior to torture, political, religious, cultural or other beliefs, context of torture, execution and/or torture of other family members, friends or comrades. Reviews of research studies suggest that the severity of torture, post-torture psychosocial stressors and social support, family history of mental health problems and 'psychological preparedness for trauma' can predict long-term psychological effects (Basoglu et al., 2001). Psychological preparedness (including cognitive processes e.g. strong political or religious beliefs, the ability to rationalise and give meaning to the torture experience and behavioural processes e.g. prior exposure to torture) is reported by the authors as being the strongest predictor of post-torture psychological health.

Pain is one of the commonest reported health difficulties following torture, being chronic and experienced in multiple locations (Amris, 2000; Thomsen et al., 2000; Williams et al., 2003). Many psychological problems and diagnoses of PTSD and depression have been reported in various studies, though as Quiroga and Jaranson (2005) comment, numerous methodological problems exist in studies with torture survivors, including insufficient description of the interview and assessment procedures, instruments and diagnostic criteria; failure to report the length of time between torture and assessment, and failure to consider how gender, age, education, culture etc. relate to the post-torture difficulties. The diagnosis of PTSD has also been criticised for medicalising the socio-political problem of torture, for its eurocentricity and its individualised and depoliticized approach (e.g. Bracken et al. 1995; Summerfield, 1995; Patel, 2003). Whilst there is no evidence of a torture syndrome (Basoglu et al., 1994; Westermeyer & Williams, 1998) beyond narrow diagnostic descriptions such as 'PTSD', there appears to be some consensus amongst clinicians that torture, as a deliberate political act, impacts on emotional, physical, social, existential, spiritual and political dimensions of human experience, compounded by the experiences of loss, uncertainty, fear and hostility for those in exile.

Torture is not just violence—it is a crime, a political tool in oppression and terror—and it is this context, specific to the particular experience of a person and the way they make meaning of these events, that can shape its effects. In a consideration of the context and the totality of experiences of detention, torture and persecution, where the meaning of these experiences is explored, it is apparent how penetrating, profound and chronic the effects can be, not just on the individual, but on their families too. Further, the distinction between physical and psychological torture (implying that in moral and health terms the former is more serious), is artificial with regards to the longer-term health effects of torture. Psychological and physical health problems are reported by many survivors of torture, some physical health problems being specific to the nature of the torture (Rasmussen et al., 2005, 2006). For example HIV infection, STDs, pregnancy and complications resulting from rape, pelvic pain, infertility, fractures, dislocations, visual and hearing loss, head injuries, post-traumatic epilepsy, physical disabilities and organ damage—and many of the psychological difficulties being related to all forms of torture (Patel & Granville-Chapman, 2006).

Psychological problems most commonly experienced by torture survivors include sleep problems with nightmares related to torture experiences, insomnia (often related to intrusive thoughts about torture experiences, ruminations about the safety of those left behind, fear of sleeping because of nightmares) and frequent wakening, poor concentration, memory difficulties, outbursts of anger, irritability, hypervigilance, hypersensitivity (e.g. to sounds/visual cues similar to those experienced when blindfolded/hooded during torture), intrusive thoughts and images related to torture, helplessness, hopelessness, despair, loss of interest in life, withdrawal, feeling numb or having a restricted range of emotions, extreme fatigue, hearing voices (e.g. of 'comrades reminding me not to forget those languishing in prisons', or 'my family, my mother screaming in pain and begging for the torture to stop, asking me to help', or 'my angel telling me I will be alright', 'my ancestors speaking to me in my suffering'), avoidance of thoughts, people, situations or places which remind them of torture previously experienced (e.g. avoiding friends or people who were also imprisoned at the same time in the same country, avoiding cell-like small rooms, confined spaces, clinical spaces with medical instruments), sexual and relationship difficulties, or difficulty forming new relationships, suicidal thoughts, substance misuse (e.g. using alcohol or drugs to help sleep, to cope with nightmares, distress and intrusive memories) and an inability to function in daily activities (see Patel & Granville-Chapman, ibid.). In addition, extreme mistrust, often mistaken as paranoia, profound guilt, shame and existential despair are common. Many have experienced multiple losses of people, their health, mobility, status, work etc. and can also experience extreme grief and despair, feeling that their lives have no meaning.

Torture is often deliberate in targeting a person's identity: religious, political, ethnic, gendered and sexual, deeply affecting a person's sense of self, destroying the fabric of one's internal and external worlds, an attack on one's values and beliefs, often experienced as annihilating. As one woman stated, having been tortured for her religious and political beliefs, 'they broke the threads inside, and I feel nothing, what is and where was God, I don't want to see or talk to anyone from my [place of worship], I don't want to talk or do anything political, that life is over, I am empty, silent inside … who am I … I don't know anymore?' Torture, and the conditions and the regime of detention, are also deliberate in their intention to render people powerless and to induce loss of control (including bodily control), which not only increases the sense of vulnerability and dependency on the captor, but can give rise to learned helplessness, sometimes mistaken as indifference or apathy. A man who had endured months of solitary confinement with almost daily torture of beatings, suspension, rape, submersion in foul water, had sometimes been incontinent of urine and faeces during torture, and faced further degrading ridicule and abuse by his torturers. He commented:

I can't even breathe properly, walk properly, I can't go out because I am afraid I will be incontinent, I can't even make love to my wife, she takes care of me, like a baby, I feel so ashamed, I can't concentrate or learn [English], I can't control my temper, my tears, nothing—am I a human being? I don't care if I live or I die.

The systematic attack on the psyche (torture was once described as the 'rape of the mind', Meerloo, 1956) parallels attacks on the body, with many describing feeling disintegrated (at the bodily, emotional and existential levels), and feeling that they have lost all sense of coherence and of who they are.

On release from Guantánamo, the Tipton Three reported that many detainees showed signs of extreme distress with 'at least 50 … their behaviour is so disturbed as to show that they are no longer capable of rational thought or behaviour … something that only a small child or an animal might behave like' (Tipton Three, 2004: para. 267). Amnesty International (2006b) have also described the experiences and situations of those incarcerated in Guantánamo, documenting the hunger strikes of up to 131 detainees protesting at their detention conditions, the many suicide attempts and the impact on families as they wait to hear news of their family member detained indefinitely for over four years. Following three suicides in Guantánamo, the five Special Rapporteurs of the UN renewed their calls for closure of Guantánamo, stressing that 'the treatment of detainees since their arrests, and the conditions of their confinement, have had profound effects on the mental health of many of them' (UN, 2006, para. 17) and that 'the totality of the conditions of their confinement at Guantánamo Bay constitute a right to health violation because they derive from a breach of duty and have resulted in profound deterioration of the mental health of many detainees' (ibid., para. 92).

The ICRC (2004) found that detainees in Iraq presented with concentration difficulties, memory problems, incoherent speech, acute anxiety reactions and 'suicidal tendencies', thought to be caused by the methods and duration of interrogation. Other health difficulties reported by PHR (2005) include disorientation, hallucination, irritability, anger, delusions, paranoia, depression, nightmares, ongoing memory loss and difficulties with relationships and maintaining employment subsequent to release.

In acknowledging that psychologically abusive interrogation techniques were usually applied in combination, and that separating unique effects specific to particular techniques is almost impossible, the PHR review of relevant studies, most conducted in the 1950s and 1960s (active years for the 'mind control' research programme), summarises the health effects of techniques used in the 'War on Terror' (PHR, 2005). For example, the report suggests that sensory deprivation can lead to profound and prolonged visual perception disturbances; short-term isolation can cause an inability to think or concentrate, difficulties in memory, anxiety, somatic complaints, temporal and spatial disorientation, hallucinations and loss of motor coordination; and long-term solitary confinement can lead to depression, anxiety, difficulty with concentration and memory, hypersensitivity to external stimuli, hallucinations and perceptual distortions, paranoia and problems with impulse control. Also, sleep deprivation can lead to cognitive impairment, including impairments in memory, attention, learning, logical reasoning, arithmetic skills, speech, complex verbal processing and decision-making, as well as decreasing pain tolerance.

Sexual torture and sexual humiliation also have devastating consequences, and as with all torture, the context in which these methods are used is central to their impact on the individual and their families and communities (see Patel & Mahtani, 2004). For example, the effects of rape, electricity on the genitalia, forced nudity with the constant threat of sexual aggression, sexual taunting, forced shaving, forced masturbation, the use of female interrogators behaving in sexually provocative ways, smearing red ink on detainees (believed by the detainee to be menstrual blood) and not allowing the detainee to wash before prayers, all have a specific meaning within the cultural and religious backgrounds of Muslim male detainees—and it is precisely these meanings which shape the beliefs about the torture and the emotional responses to it: in violating the most sacred beliefs and, hence, the core of one's gendered, cultural and religious identity, one's intimacy and sense of self, and violating cultural rules and taboos. The methods are intended to render the detainee powerless, humiliated, passive and submissive: responses which often induce further shame, self-disgust and guilt, long after the torture has ended, with their isolation intensified by a self-imposed silence and withdrawal, for fear of being further humiliated and ostracised by family and community.

Threats to induce fear of death or injury can have both short and long-term consequences. Clients have reported feelings of terror and powerful desires for the execution to take place rapidly—the anticipation and threats being experienced as prolonging intense fear, sometimes to the point where the captive may lose bodily control or beg for reprieve. One client, tortured several years ago, who had experienced and witnessed staged executions described it thus:

> You see no light from the dark cells, no day or night, you just wait for death. You are made to hear everything, the torture and the threats of death to others, the voice of the guard reading out the names of all those who would be executed at dawn, you wait for your name, you tremble with fear, you wish your turn comes swiftly and the agony would end, then at dawn, every day, you hear the screams as people are pulled out of their cells, you hear the guns being loaded and pulled, you hear the shots and you wait for your turn—they tell you it will come soon. Then when it is your turn, the shot is pulled, nothing happens, you fall to the ground, crying, not sure whether you are dead or alive, I may as well have been dead with fear … how I waited for death … keeping me alive, threatening me with death was the real torture.

Years later, he is troubled by nightmares of mock executions and other torture he endured, preoccupied with suicidal thoughts, ambivalent about being alive: 'I am dead inside, that's what they wanted, they killed me anyway', unable to trust even his own family, living in self-imposed isolation, unable to have relationships or friendships with others ('what for, I am dead, I am nothing inside, nothing outside, just a shell').

Torture impacts not just on individuals, but their families too. Detention can lead to loss of income for families depending on the person who is detained, life trajectories are interrupted and, in some cases, suspended—plans or progress in education, work, political activities, relationships or marriage can all be affected, not just for the person who was tortured, but their family members too, some of whom may have been persecuted, tortured and even executed. Torture affects the capacity of families to support one another, secrets intended to protect can come to destroy family relationships, sometimes leading to permanent breakdown in communication and trust. According to Danieli (1998) torture can have intergenerational effects with parent's experiences of trauma affecting children, even into second and third generations, though others report differently (e.g. Bilanakis et al., 1998). Torture resulting in physical disability, cognitive impairment, fertility difficulties, sexually transmitted infections etc. can all further compound the suffering of family members, who may have to cope with economic and physical hardship, emotional difficulties, social isolation and even ostracism.

Torture as a tool of oppression can affect whole communities, in instilling terror, controlling them with the perpetual threat of arbitrary detention, execution, disappearances, and other ill-treatment. Fear and suspicion of one another, even family members and neighbours, can permeate whole societies. As one client put it:

> You cannot trust even your wife, your children, you believe nobody, trust nobody, how can you, anyone can betray you to the authorities, they [the regime] get everywhere, nothing, no home, no relationship is sacred … soon you feel nothing but fear and dread in your heart.

Torture with impunity can further contribute to the normalisation and acceptance of torture in society, fostered by a culture of fear, whereby even torture comes to be seen as a viable 'solution' to an assumed perpetual threat from the dangerous 'other'.

What can psychologists contribute to prevention?

Ironically, the 'War on Terror', with revelations about the extent, nature and history of methods of torture developed and practised by the US/UK, has served as a clarion call to psychologists and other health professionals, demanding of the academic and professional community an active engagement with the justifications for, and the consequences of, torture and war. What is required of us is not a distant, intellectual muse, or a short-lived burst of shock and moral outrage. What we need is both the sustained courage to critique psychology and the practices of psychologists, and the firm commitment to envision and create a different, more socially responsible psychology in the twenty-first century. What is required is for psychologists to see and realise their potential as activists, promoting and contributing to peace and security, and protecting the right of all human beings to be free from torture. The role of psychologists in preventing torture and in promoting related standards in international law can be varied, with some examples given below, with the preface that such work is still in its infancy.

Tertiary prevention

Tertiary prevention is concerned with activities that aim to prevent ill health or the further deterioration of health, and to promote the well-being of those who have survived torture. Psychologists can provide therapeutic care, support and intervention, where appropriate, and ensure that those survivors of torture who come to the UK, often as asylum seekers, are afforded the same dignity, opportunity and access to healthcare as a fundamental human right. This can necessitate campaigning, and developing appropriate services, for survivors of torture within the NHS (for further discussion see Patel, 2007) with the aim to avoid the replication and reinforcement of the injustices and inequalities experienced by survivors of torture; and to promote the rights of survivors of torture to reparation (treatment or rehabilitative services) enshrined in international law and reinforced in the relevant European directive (European Union, 2003). Therapeutic work often entails not rigid applications of traditional approaches to therapy, but an integrated approach within an explicit human rights framework, incorporating a rights-based analysis and focusing on the totality of the person's/family's experience and addressing the multi-contextual dimensions of emotional, physical, relational, welfare, political, spiritual and legal experiences.

Our role can be not just in providing direct support, but in providing indirect support, in the form of training, consultation and joint working with others engaged in similar work in statutory and voluntary sectors. In addition, psychologists can play a vital role in critiquing and deconstructing traditional psychological theories and approaches for their eurocentricity and tendencies to pathologise, rather than to politicise distress resulting from deliberately inflicted harm and suffering. Theoretical contributions to understanding the nature and impact of human rights violations, such as torture, and psychological perspectives on social action as a means to health are also useful avenues to support primary prevention. A critical review of psychological models also requires that we explore, and expose, the potential for ideological abuse in every theory, and in research, examining any for their potential to condone, facilitate and to reinforce torture. For example, critiquing psychological theories which imply that, in particular social contexts and circumstances, anyone has the potential to become aggressive and to use torture, which can be defended by arguing that one was 'obeying orders from superiors', or that one was 'under duress', despite their being thousands of survivors of torture worldwide who, when being forced to torture others, refuse to do so, risking further torture and even death.

Secondary prevention
Secondary prevention is aimed at ensuring the legal protection of survivors of torture, primarily to prevent *refoulement* (being returned to a country where they are likely to face torture again—prohibited in UNCAT, Article 3) and to ensure that they are also able to access appropriate healthcare, where necessary and appropriate. Prevention activities include the assessment and documentation of health (in formal psychological reports) in support of allegations of torture and other ill-treatment made as part of an asylum (or other) claim, processed within the asylum and immigration courts, or actions for reparation and/or redress in respect of torture or other forms of abuse. Using such documentation to ensure that the person is able to access relevant and necessary follow-up health care, where appropriate, is also an important advocacy and prevention activity, and Articles 19–21 of the UN Basic Principles and Guidelines on the Right to Reparation identify access to healthcare, including the provision of funding where appropriate, as part of the compensation and reparations process.

In detention, particularly where detainees are at risk of torture, cruel, inhuman or degrading treatment, an important role for psychologists could be the assessment and documentation of the detainee's health, providing evidence on behalf of the detainee. This could also include immediate assessments at the time of detention/ imprisonment, prior to and post interrogations and at regular intervals during a detention period, to monitor the psychological health effects of detention and possible ill-treatment, as is currently the UN guidance for physicians in detention centres (United Nations, 1982).

Conducting research and developing methods to ensure that vulnerable survivors of torture are identified as early as possible provide further opportunities for psychologists. One example is of an ongoing initiative to implement good practice clinical guidelines for assessment (Patel & Granville-Chapman, 2006), with related specific training for health staff working in the induction process for asylum seekers, specifically to facilitate the early identification and health assessment of vulnerable survivors of torture. Early identification of torture survivors facilitates the proper preparation of the asylum case prior to the initial decision, which in turn enhances the quality of decision-making, preventing unnecessary suffering and enabling an efficient use of resources. The New Asylum Model (NAM) (Home Office, 2006) is premised upon a desire for faster recognition and integration of refugees, more sustainable negative decisions and fewer successful appeals. Currently the induction process, as part of the UK asylum policy, involves all new asylum seekers being immediately dispersed to geographical areas in the UK, with limited or no services for survivors of torture, held in 'accommodation centres', and given a medical and psychological health 'screening' (in approximately 40 minutes total). With the estimated proportion of torture survivors being between 30–60 per cent, such an asylum policy risks vulnerable torture survivors not being identified, being unfairly refused asylum and removed without legal protection or rightful healthcare. Another example is of a current research project with advocacy potential that involves evaluating medico-legal reports (including psychological reports), written by physicians, psychiatrists, psychologists and counsellors in support of allegations of torture, for their impact on decision-making by the judiciary in UK asylum and immigration courts.

Primary prevention
Primary prevention is aimed at the macro level, promoting international law, in activities aimed at education, regulation, redress, reparation and litigation. For psychologists there are many potential roles in contributing to prevention activities aimed at combating torture. Psychologists can contribute to the promotion of international law and human rights principles within many settings, for example, in teaching in schools, universities and for professional psychology postgraduate training programmes. Psychologists can contribute to the training of other health professionals and the judiciary on the assessment and documentation of the psychological impact of torture to ensure effective monitoring of health, effective gathering of evidence—which detainees or prisoners may subsequently use in prosecutions—and appropriate evaluation of such evidence by the judiciary. Psychologists can also contribute to independent investigations in cases of breaches of international law, for example by other health professionals and breaches by other figures, including current and former heads of states.

Developing research which integrates clinical knowledge and acumen within a human rights framework can be useful in documenting and publicising the nature and impact of different types of torture and related human rights violations, within particular historical, political, social and geographical contexts. For example, research exploring the forms of torture commonly experienced by women in a particular country, within a particular historical time frame, and identifying patterns of abuse (e.g. psychological torture and rape) and their impact. Such research can be used in partnership with relevant human rights organisations to lobby treaty bodies for change, and action. Research exploring survival or coping in torture survivors, whilst potentially powerful as a prevention tool in the therapeutic arena, in the wrong hands can be exploited as a tool in refining further torture methods. An anecdote from colleagues relates to this specific point: that at one professional conference on therapeutic work with survivors of rape and sexual torture, one of the delegates was found to be a military physician from a country renowned for such torture. Nevertheless, psychologists can conduct research facilitating and evaluating the promotion of human rights (e.g. in education systems, from schools to postgraduate health professional courses at universities). Research evaluating the short and longer-term impact and effectiveness of training on medical and psychological health assessment and documentation of torture, for the judiciary, police, military and civilian health professionals (an important prevention activity in itself, particularly in countries where there are high proportions of torture survivors) is a promising avenue for refining such prevention activities.

Psychological research can also be conducted with, and for, refugee community organisations, for example, one such project was initiated by a minority ethnic refugee community, seeking to document the effects of torture endured in order to submit a report to the UNCAT committee monitoring the use of torture in their country. Psychological research can be combined with legal research to lobby UN member states at the UN Commission on Human Rights and to ensure effective use of the UN's or the Council of Europe's monitoring mechanisms, for example by exploring how best the documented torture and its impact on health can contribute to the reporting and monitoring process, and help condemn and combat torture in different countries.

Psychologists can also contribute to advocacy efforts aimed at the UK Parliament, as well as the UK authorities involved in asylum procedures, to enable appropriate interviewing of asylum seeking torture survivors, and appropriate evaluation of evidence provided by torture survivors and by health professionals documenting their health problems. This can involve research, specific training for interviewers and decision-makers and the submission of formal expert reports (e.g. on rape as torture and its psychological impact in different cultural, religious and political contexts). Advocacy efforts can be targeted to influence legislation that may adversely affect survivors of torture (e.g. counter-terrorism legislation).

Psychologists can also actively lobby public authorities, such as the NHS, to ensure conformity to the standards specified in international law on torture and in the European Directive, laying down minimum standards for the reception of asylum seekers, particularly as it applies to survivors of torture and promoting knowledge and understanding of such standards amongst health professionals within the UK.

If the opportunity arises, psychologists can help clients access redress in relation to their experience of torture. This may involve collecting their testimonies, documenting the impact of torture on their health, enabling clients to seek compensation, accessing information about the necessary criminal procedures involved in bringing torturers to justice and supporting them in seeking retributive justice.

What can the BPS do to help prevent torture?

Psychologists have a public health duty which requires not just a critical analysis of the relationship between social conditions, inequities, human rights abuses and health, but a concerted strategy from the BPS for action involving advocacy on the harmful effects of policies and practices and awareness-raising and education of psychologists and the general public. The BPS needs to consider how teaching of human rights principles, including the prohibition on torture, can be made mandatory in all undergraduate and postgraduate psychology courses.[2]

The BPS also has a public health obligation to develop appropriate policies and mechanisms to prevent torture. As stated earlier, a declaration against torture is insufficient and has no legally or professionally binding authority—in short, it is a declaration without teeth. Prevention requires an organisational commitment to upholding and promoting standards in international law. The BPS needs to go beyond providing a declaration condemning torture and to reflect this commitment and its obligations under international law. This, I suggest, can only progress with firstly, specific reference to awareness-raising, amongst the psychological community, of these ethical principles and legal obligations; and secondly, with a specific policy, reinforced by revised codes for ethics and conduct integrating these legal obligations, which unequivocally prohibits the role of psychologists in the development, assistance, facilitation of, and participation in, torture or other ill-treatment, directly or indirectly, in all circumstances. In addition, the BPS must establish mechanisms to ensure that human rights principles—specifically the absolute prohibition on torture and other ill-treatment—are upheld and breaches investigated and punished, and criminal prosecutions assisted where relevant.

---

2. This is the case on the doctoral degree course in clinical psychology at the University of East London.

Conclusions

It is difficult to see how the challenges posed by 'international terrorism' can be addressed by 'striking a balance' between security and human rights, or by justifying the violation of the right to be free from torture. From legal and moral perspectives, torture can never be justified. From the perspective of psychological ethics and health, torture, the deliberate abuse of another human being, with potentially severe and devastating health consequences, is absolutely unacceptable. As psychologists, representing a discipline upholding humanitarian values, we have no choice but to actively engage with the current questions that the 'War on Terror' poses for us. To do this, we have to ensure that our activities are framed and informed by a human rights perspective, one which reminds us of the potential for psychology to support, and to promote, the health and well-being of all human beings equally—surely the measure of our commitment to humanity?

Acknowledgements
For critique and invaluable comments, I would like to thank Amanda Williams and Ellie Smith. For help with obtaining information, thanks to Cristian Peña and Boris Savic.

CHAPTER 5

The Psychology of Anti-War Activism: 1. The British anti-war movement 1956–2006

JOHN SLOBODA AND BRIAN DOHERTY

Most of the leading peace move ment organisations had been in existence for some time before the 1979 INF [Intermediate-Range Nuclear Forces] decision, carrying on their activities without publicity or popularity. They developed critical views of nuclear deterrence and the partition of Europe between spheres of superpower influence, but their ideas received little attention beyond the circle of those already committed. Had they not seized the opportunity for mass mobilization presented by INF, peace movement organizations would have been doomed to continuing marginality. The stratcgy of mass mobilization limited the ability of the movement to preserve its critique of the political system and to maintain its focus on cultural revolution. The dilemma for a new social movement is that the alternative, to remain a counter-cultural sect, presents even dimmer prospects of achieving significant change. (Rochon, 1990, p. 120)

The British context: the normalisation of expeditionary war

Resistance to military violence has taken many forms throughout history. This chapter focuses on forms that are prevalent in contemporary Britain. These are not necessarily the same forms, or driven by the same motivations, as may be found in other parts of the world and in other historic periods. Britain is part of a distinct group of modern wealthy democracies, most of whose citizens have not endured invasion or occupation in living memory, but whose armies have regularly engaged in military expeditions abroad. This group of nations includes the USA, Canada and Australia. Anti-war activism in these countries has thus been predominantly concerned with efforts to reduce the capacity and will of one's own government to prepare for, or engage in, wars on foreign soil, and personal refusal to participate in, or support, such wars.

Even within this small set of nations, Britain is unique. It has been a major colonial power over several centuries right up until the 1960s, and was the world's largest, and most effective, military power for a considerable part of that time. It retains one of the world's largest military budgets (surpassed only by the USA and Japan) (Skons et al., 2005) and has fought in more international wars in the last 50 years than any other nation. Britain has engaged in 21 wars since 1946 (as compared to 16 for the USA, seven for Australia and five for Canada). Adding together the duration of each conflict involving British troops yields a total of 77 'conflict years' since 1946, making Britain the sixth most conflict-prone country in the world (exceeded only by, in order, Burma (232), India (156), Ethiopia (88), the Phillipines (86), and Israel (79)) (Mack & Nilezen, 2005). Furthermore, for a period of nearly 50 years, Britain has retained and actively enhanced its capacity and readiness to kill millions of civilians through thermonuclear devastation. There can be few national psyches on which the famous words of George Washington, from his 1790 State of the Union Address, will have a stronger resonance:

To be prepared for war is one of the most effectual means of preserving peace.

The military are held in very high esteem, and local regiments are, in some parts of the country, viewed with the kind of proprietorial pride that is accorded to top football or cricket teams, as evidenced by the recent popular outcry when high-profile local regiments were proposed for disbanding or merger (see 'Boost for the Black Watch', *The Scotsman*, 10 November 2004).[1] This means that an anti-war posture has been, within a UK context, profoundly 'counter-culture', and its deepest challenges may not be related to responding to acute political crises as much as they have to do with working year-in-year-out in the face of deeply embedded cultural and institutional inertia which reinforces centuries-old beliefs about the moral and practical value of British militarism.

In 2003, some six months after the start of the Iraq War, one of the authors—a committed anti-war activist—spent three months in Quebec. It was an unexpectedly deep and restorative experience to live in a society where popular instincts appeared non-violent and cooperative. Violent crime is almost unknown in Quebec. The military is almost culturally invisible. Anti-war views and attitudes appeared within the cultural mainstream as a viable, if not universally accepted, norm. At the end of the stay, going back to England genuinely felt like going back to a battle zone, a place where every day was a struggle to maintain integrity, vision and energy in the face of, what seemed in comparison, a suffocating

---

1. http://news.scotsman.com/opinion.cfm?id=1297492004 Accessed 16 September 2006.

militaristic ideological landscape, capable of draining all those energies that had so recently produced the largest peacetime demonstrations in British history (numbers far in excess of anything achieved in Canada). This chapter will examine the principal forms of anti-war activism in Britain in recent decades, contrasting the consistent but small anti-militarist core of the movement with the periods when there have been mass movements based on a broader coalition, united by more limited and specific policy objectives.

An account of UK anti-war activism

Conscientious objection and pacifism

Contemporary anti-war activism has its roots in a long tradition of pacifism and non-violence, whose greatest twentieth century proponent was Gandhi, and whose primary political expression in countries such as Britain has been the refusal to bear arms or be conscripted into military service. Conscientious objectors have often paid a high personal price for their beliefs, facing imprisonment, and, in some societies, the death penalty. However, there has been no military conscription (draft) in the UK since 1956, and therefore tax resistance (withholding that proportion of taxes that a government allocates to military spending) has been the only clearly articulated alternative form of conscientious objection, which so far remains universally criminalised even by the most 'advanced' democracies.[2] However, the number of people willing or able to withhold taxes in an economy where the vast majority of workers have tax deducted by their employers at source, makes this a minority form of activism, even within a minority movement. Conscientious objection in all its major forms has been particularly strongly associated with religious groups, notably, but not exclusively, the Quakers. Socialism as a political force also gave early and consistent support to pacifists.

Very recently, in the light of deeply held views about the illegality of the Iraq war, a small number of serving soldiers have resigned their commissions on grounds of principle,[3] but these actions are based firmly within an acceptance of the necessity of war, and relate to judgements of the illegality of this one. This is not blanket conscientious objection of the traditional type, although it may well have, in current contexts, considerably more political impact.

The Campaign for Nuclear Disarmament (CND)

A very significant form of anti-war activism, which has at times achieved the status of a mass political movement, is the campaign against nuclear weapons,

2. http://www.conscienceonline.org.uk/Pages/_subSections/homePages/whatIsPeaceTax.html Accessed 15. September 2006.
3. http://www.telegraph.co.uk/news/main.jhtml?xml=/news/2006/03/12/nsas112.xml&sSheet=/news/2006/03/12/ixhome.html Accessed 16 September 2006.

first developed and deployed by Britain in the 1950s. British civil society was among the first in the world to develop a coordinated mass national campaign, and the London to Aldermaston marches, inaugurated by CND in 1959, became an iconic symbol of lawful civil protest. The basic motivation for protest was, and always has been, the memory of Hiroshima and Nagasaki, and the wish to play no part in the indiscriminate damage that any use of nuclear weapons would do to people and planet. The core activity for CND was, from the start, the public meeting and the mass peaceful demonstration, often a march, ending in a rally. This was a form of activism familiar to, and substantially supported by, the British Labour movement, but capable of attracting wider constituencies, including scientists, academics, artists and musicians, and religious groups. The strong support of Labour Party rank and file as well as considerable numbers of MPs, and Labour-controlled local authorities in the 1980s, meant that anti-nuclear activism entered the political mainstream, and was pursued with the full range of party political activities, although it has been a consistent feature of British politics that senior Labour MPs tend to abandon their anti-nuclear convictions on entry into government.

Although the great majority of activists in the anti-nuclear movement remained committed to actions within the law, a significant minority engaged in law breaking through forms of civil disobedience and non-violent direct action (NVDA), such as sit-ins and blockades. These grew as a proportion of peace movement activity in the early 1980s (Rochon, 1990). The most significant manifestations of NVDA have been actions at military establishments where nuclear weapons are developed or housed, or where key control systems are operated. These include 'breaking and entering' and symbolic acts of damage to nuclear delivery systems. NVDA has also extended to factories where military components are manufactured (e.g. Rolls Royce), and also to nuclear power plants, in recognition that such plants are essential for the manufacture of fissile material for use in nuclear weapons. NVDA has consistently involved establishment figures whose abhorrence of war has prompted them to undertake actions that have led to their arrest. Britain's most eminent twentieth-century philosopher, Bertrand Russell, was arrested in 1961. Since then 2,000 members of both the Scottish and European parliaments have been arrested for participation in blockades of the Faslane naval base, home of the British Trident nuclear submarines. Prison sentences have, by and large, been short and symbolic, but it is still of note that significant numbers of activists have had multiple arrests and sentences for very similar actions, often spread over many years. For instance, Lindis Percy, co-founder of the Campaign for Accountability of American Bases, has been arrested more than 150 times, mainly in connection with acts of protest at or near Menwith Hill, Yorkshire, the US-controlled NSA (National Security Agency) monitoring centre, which is the world's biggest spying centre outside the USA.[4]

---

4. Peace protester appeals as judge makes tagging order.
http://www.thisisbradford.co.uk/bradford_district/otley/news/OTLE_NEWS3.html Accessed 19 May 2005.

The most notable manifestation of the NVDA wing of the UK anti-war movement of the 1980s was the formation and long-term maintenance of several peace camps, mostly notably the women's camps surrounding the Greenham Common Air Base, where American nuclear-powered cruise missiles were sited from 1983 to 1991, but also the mixed camp at the Faslane nuclear submarine base in Scotland, which is still in existence. In many cases, activists lived in the camps continuously—in conditions of considerable privation—for months on end, leaving jobs and family behind. The feminism of the Greenham camps has been a particularly powerful framework in which anti-war activities have been developed, with non-violence at their core (Roseneil, 1995).

The cruise missile crisis sparked a massive increase in CND membership at a time when a former Catholic priest and serving soldier, Bruce Kent, was its general secretary. Kent became an iconic figure of international stature, possibly the first 'superstar' of the movement, with his charismatic rhetoric and skill in handling the media. Kent is not a pacifist, and has gone on record as supporting war under certain circumstances (such as the war against Hitler). CND's high point was October 1983 when it held its largest ever London rally (400,000). In 1985, national membership passed 100,000 (Hudson, 2005), while the overlapping membership of local groups was around 250,000 (Byrne, 1997). CND became of such concern to the government of Margaret Thatcher that she set up well-funded units to monitor and undermine CND by a variety of means, both fair and foul, including the irresponsible but widely believed allegation that the movement was funded by the KGB (Kent, 1992). The British establishment promoted the false popular belief that anti-war activists were dominated by communists and appeasers, who, if not malicious traitors, were at best 'misguided'.

Academic and NGO activity
Although individual academics, scientists and intellectuals have been active in the anti-war movement, it was not until the 1970s that organisations began to bring intellectuals together to study and promote non-violent conflict resolution. A key milestone was the foundation of the first Peace Studies programme within a British university, at Bradford in 1973 (O'Connell & Whitby, 2001). Although not engaging in direct activism, its programmes have now informed and empowered students from all over the world, many of whom have gone on to become change agents in various walks of life. In the wake of this, an increasing number of peace-oriented think tanks and NGOs have been formed, and these have often been articulate critics of government military policy while refraining from direct oppositional campaigning. A small number of people have been able to gain paid employment in these organisations (funded by trusts and foundations, by membership subscriptions, and latterly even by government), creating a new species of 'paid peaceworker'. In general, however, employment in the sector is both poorly paid and insecure (Perks, 2005). The development of an NGO sector also brings with it the internal tensions experienced by the 'aid and development'

sector (cf. recent debates about Live 8 and Jubilee 2000), where influence with governments is often bought at the price of critical independence. This means that a significant sector of the peace movement remains ideologically opposed to the professionalisation of peace activism.

The development of an NGO peace and security sector has also led to the phenomenon of peace activists and researchers visiting countries where wars were being fought, such as Operation Omega when peace activists went to what later became Bangladesh, the International Solidarity movement in the Palestinian occupied territories, groups such as Peace Brigades International and the Human Shield volunteers who went to Iraq before the invasion in 2003, (on whom more below). All these groups exploited the greater attention paid to Westerners prepared to place themselves at risk in solidarity with people in the South who were vulnerable to military violence. In cases where British activists went to countries where Britain has intervened, in a variety of roles, issues about how to relate to UK military and political representatives (on whom one often has to depend, at least in part, for security and access) have raised new dilemmas. These were strikingly illustrated through the kidnapping of peace activist Norman Kember in late 2005 by Iraqis who he was aiming to support and his ultimate release by the British military forces whose actions he went to Iraq to oppose. Kember's actions, culminating in his alleged refusal to express sufficient gratitude to his rescuers, have led to censure, even from elements of the peace movement.

The Falklands War
Because the Wilson government declined to accede to US requests to send combat troops to Vietnam, the 1960s and 1970s were decades where the British anti-war movement concentrated on hypothetical nuclear war more than actual conventional war. The Falklands/Malvinas conflict of 1982 offered a chance for anti-war activists to respond to a real war fought by British troops. Despite strong editorial opposition to the war from the *Daily Mirror,* and a few high-profile dissident MPs (notably the maverick Scottish Labour MP, Tam Dalyell), several factors hindered a strong anti-war campaign:

1. The Argentine invasion came, with almost no notice, on 2nd April. Ten weeks later, on 14th June, the war ended with the official surrender of the Argentinian forces. There was little time to mount or build new forms of protest before the war ended.
2. The intense and organised focus of the UK peace movement at that time was on the Cruise missile protests, which were numerous and well organised.
3. Some anti-nuclear campaigners supported the Falklands War, or were, at best, neutral—believing that the movement should remain concentrated on nuclear issues, and not get diverted by 'side issues' (as evidenced by the correspondence columns of *Sanity*, the house magazine of CND—see

letter by Norman Liverwich and others).[5]
4. Despite more than a thousand military casualties there were, amazingly, no civilian casualties. Setting aside reservations about whether war had been necessary to achieve desired political ends, the war itself was conducted entirely within the letter and spirit of international law.

The Falklands War did, however, sow one very profound seed. During the 1983 election campaign, Margaret Thatcher was confronted on the BBC television programme *Nationwide,* by Diana Gould of Cheltenham, over her role in the sinking of the Argentinian battle ship *General Belgrano*, allegedly set on a course away from, rather than towards, the conflict zone. This confrontation, one of the most remembered and replayed of the entire political debate over the Falkands, has become an iconic symbol of citizens using the media to 'speak truth to power' without deference or equivocation.

The decline of the 1980s peace movement
In the early 1980s the peace movement had a major impact on British politics. Its actions, leaders, and the issues it raised, received extensive media coverage and it was arguably the major issue in the 1983 General Election, which the Labour Party fought on a platform of support for British nuclear disarmament. Yet, Labour performed very badly in that election and this also revealed some of the limits of the movement's achievements. Polls consistently showed that only between twenty and thirty per cent of the public supported CND's main aim, which was unilateral British nuclear disarmament.

The peace movement of the 1980s was part of a wider Western European reaction against the increase in tension between the USA and the USSR in what was known as the Second Cold War. The first wave of peace activism, in several European countries and the USA in the late 1950s and early 1960s, died out because the two superpowers seemed to have developed negotiated means of balancing the deterrent effects of nuclear weapons. The era of détente ended effectively in 1979 when NATO decided to station intermediate range US Cruise and Pershing missiles in Western Europe, ostensibly to counter the threat posed by similar range Soviet missiles. Political leaders in Western Europe favoured deployment because it seemed to guarantee that the USA would use its missiles to deter an attack on Western Europe. Others, however, were concerned that this signalled a new NATO strategy based on fighting a nuclear war in Western Europe. It was this specific development that led to the unprecedented levels of peace activism across Western Europe in the early 1980s. The peace movement was unable to prevent the deployment of Cruise and Pershing missiles in 1983 but it put the issue at the centre of the political stage and was able to sustain its activity enough to keep it there. The crucial change came with the accession of Mikhail

---

5. *Sanity,* June–July 1982, no. 3, p. 4.

Gorbachev to power in the USSR in 1986. Gorbachev accepted a 1983 NATO proposal that effectively withdrew all SS20 and Cruise and Pershing missiles from Europe.

Although both NATO leaders and the peace movement claimed credit for this disarmament, neither was wholly responsible. Gorbachev had decided in effect to withdraw from the arms race, in part to reduce the pressure on the Soviet economy. NATO argued that it had kept the pressure on the USSR and so forced it to breaking point. The peace movement saw, in Gorbachev's espousal of a doctrine of nuclear sufficiency, an adoption of some of the ideas of its own strategic research (Carter, 1992). There is some evidence to support the latter view, but it was essentially Gorbachev's own strategic vision and courage that achieved the breakthrough on disarmament. His opening up of the Soviet political system and economy and refusal to suppress political change in Eastern Europe led in the end to the collapse of the system that Gorbachev had intended to reform.

Just as the NATO alliance floundered for lack of a clear role after the collapse of the Soviet Union, so did an anti-war movement premised on opposition to those same NATO Cold War policies. With the removal of Cruise missiles from Europe after the INF (Intermediate-Range Nuclear Forces) agreement in 1987, the main focus of the movement disappeared, most of the peace camps, including in 2000 those at Greenham, disbanded, and the UK anti-war movement lost its high profile. Many put their faith in the promised 'peace dividend' that was predicted to flow from the end of the Cold War.

Peace activism certainly went into sharp decline in the late 1980s, but most of the core activists failed to recognise this (Maguire, 1992). Many sought to link peace activism to new goals, for example by making the links between the arms trade and instability in the global South under the slogan of 'Food not Bombs'. This process of frame alignment made sense to peace activists, committed as they were to an internationalist agenda of social justice, but failed to mobilise the same level of support from other political groups. Membership of CND remained reasonably high (see Table 1), probably because the nuclear threat had not disappeared, but the wider peace movement infrastructure of local CND groups, peace camps and other peace organisations withered. The CND groups that remained active locally were dominated by long-standing activists of retirement age.

The 1980s peace movement did not decline as much as the movement had in the 1960s and 1970s. After the mid-1960s, very little was left of the British peace movement. It was essentially the pacifist Quakers and the anti-NATO Communist Party of Great Britain that kept CND alive as an organisation in those decades (Byrne, 1997). The 1980s movement involved more people and a wider range of groups in society and this had a legacy. Organisationally, groups such as CND held on to substantial numbers of members, albeit largely passive 'chequebook activists', and other organisations such as the Campaign Against the Arms Trade, were also able to continue. Many local authorities remained 'Nuclear Free Zones'

Table 1 National CND Membership

1970s	Members	1980s	Members	1990s	Members	2000s	Members
1970	2120	1980	9000	1990	62000	2006	32000
1971	2047	1981	20000	1991	60000		
1972	2389	1982	50000	1992	57000		
1973	2367	1983	75000	1993	52000		
1974	2350	1984	100000	1994	47000		
1975	2536	1985	92000	1995	47700		
1976	3220	1986	84000				
1977	4287	1987	75000				
1978	3220	1988	72000				
1979	4287	1989	62000				

Sources: Byrne, 1997, p. 91; 2006 figures cited in *The Guardian* 28 July 2006.

and some trade unions continued to support the campaign. The NVDA wing of the movement also had a significant legacy. Groups such as the Ploughshares activists[6] continued to take action against nuclear bases and arms manufacturers.

As well as these, a new young generation of activists emerged in the early 1990s whose main focus was direct action on environmental issues, particularly protests against new roads. But, although this meant the focus was no longer on peace issues, this was not a movement in competition with the peace movement. The new generation of activists benefited from advice from 1980s peace campaigners on direct action and establishing protest camps, and new and older activists took joint action against arms manufacturers (notably at the Defence Systems and Equipment International (DSEI) exhibitions in London in 2001 and subsequent years) and in protest against British foreign policy. Both groups shared a worldview that Roseneil summarises with reference to the precursors of Greenham Common as:

> a legacy of anti-establishment attitudes, a strong strand of anarchist hostility to hierarchies, a critique of the materialism of industrial societies and of representative forms of democracy and the state, and a belief in the legitimacy and necessity of non-parliamentary forms of action. (Roseneil, 2000, p. 95)

This counter-cultural current remains small, but due to the willingness to take direct action, an important part of the British anti-war movement.

---

6. www.tridentploughshares.org

The Kosovo/Serbia War

It was arguably the series of joint UK/US military interventions, beginning with the 1999 NATO bombing of Kosovo/Serbia, that re-ignited and refocused the movement. The 1999 war differed in almost every respect from the Falklands War, in ways that enabled a refocusing of the movement. Key enabling factors were that:

1. The war was illegal. All parties, even proponents of the war, accepted that it was not legitimate under international law, and could not have obtained UN Security Council approval.[7]
2. The war was a violation of NATO's purely defensive posture. No NATO member was being attacked, or was in imminent prospect of being attacked.
3. It was the first post-Soviet-era war involving UK military where there were significant civilian casualties on the ground (as well as damage to infrastructure, unexploded ordnance and long-term radiation damage from depleted uranium), but almost no coalition military casualties. New moral and humanitarian issues were raised about a war where the military forces of the aggressor risked little (by exclusive reliance on air strikes) and the civilian population of aggressor nations risked nothing (because of geographical distance and the incapacity of the Serbian military to threaten them).
4. The war brought no quick end to violent conflict involving military and paramilitary forces, and left many intractable political problems unresolved. Violent conflict, resulting in death and displacement of civilians, persisted for many years after the 'war' was declared over. There was much for activists to engage with on a long-term basis.
5. The war was very much a personal mission of Tony Blair soon after a landslide electoral victory, and was tied to an explicit philosophy of 'humanitarian intervention' in which it was assumed that Britain would act alongside the USA (Sloboda & Abbott, 2004). As well as gaining majority support from the UK electorate and the Conservative Party, he also gained the overwhelming support of the Parliamentary Labour Party and significant support from the Liberal Democrats. Given all that, it was almost inevitable that he would look to take Britain into future wars on a similar prospectus. The UK anti-war movement knew it had a long-term mission again, one which also meant, for many seasoned Labour Party supporters, a fight for the soul of the Labour party and the survival of a viable British left.
6. There was a significant population of British Serbs, who vocally mobilised within British society against the war. This set a precedent for seasoned

7. The UK Foreign Affairs Select Committee Report on Kosovo (2000) http://www.parliament.the-stationery office.co.uk/pa/cm199900/cmselect/cmfaff/ 28/2802.htm

anti-war activists taking common cause with diasporas of the countries under threat of attack, mainly people that had no prior history of engagement with anti-war issues, a precedent which was to be of vital importance after 9/11.

One key consequence of the Kosovo/Serbia War was the strengthening of two other strands of activism, which came neither from CND roots, nor from pacifist/ NVDA roots (of the sort epitomised by the longstanding publication *Peace News*). The first was an alliance of the disenfranchised political left (fronted by dissenting Labour MPs such as Tony Benn, Alice Mahon and Jeremy Corbyn) together with Serbian émigrés, regional activists, lawyers and humanitarian workers. The second, most curiously of all, was drawn from elements of the libertarian right, particularly strong in the USA, driven in part by opposition to anything that Clinton and his political twin across the Atlantic, Blair, stood for, and a more principled distaste for interventionist foreign policy (for instance, the right-wing Washington think-tank, the Cato Institute, published some of the most trenchant critiques of the Kosovo Intervention—see Carpenter, 2000). Although this alliance was sometimes uneasy, it was less straightforward for government or populist media to typecast this movement, and it arguably opened up a new arena for anti-war activism, which was not rooted in traditional anti-nuclear networks[8] and forms of engagement.

A core focus of the movement was the 'Committee for Peace in the Balkans', led by Alice Mahon, MP, which was able to focus in particular on post-war tracking of the complex mix of political and humanitarian dilemmas that the war failed to resolve. Campaigning materials between 1999 and 2001 show significant focus on civilian casualties (including memorial activities), depleted uranium used by NATO forces, refugees, effects of sanctions, and other threats to ordinary people in the region.[9]

The War on Terror

Then came 9/11. One of the most extraordinary consequences of this was the speed and multifaceted nature of a civil society response, based on profound fears of what the USA might do in reaction to the 9/11 attacks. Within days, a whole range of anti-war letters, petitions, and caucuses had formed, enabled by the new societal familiarity with the Internet. Soon, millions of people were networking worldwide in a plethora of dialogues about how to prevent the gathering rush to war.

In the UK a range of individuals and organisations (representing mainly the political left) rapidly came together to form a new organisation, the 'Stop the War

8. Benn and Corbyn had been long-standing supporters of CND, but this was not their principal political identity and, as leading left-wing Labour MPs, they had strong ties with many other groups on the British Left.

9. See for instance: http://www.balkanpeace.org/events/index.shtml

Coalition' (STWC). It was formed at a notoriously fraught meeting on 21st September attended by 2,000 people, ten days after 9/11, but which succeeded in electing a steering committee and agreeing a basic, shared, three-point platform which proved effective in holding the coalition together (Stop the War; Defend Civil Liberties; End the Racist Backlash). By as early as November 2001, the Stop the War website was listing 92 separate anti-war events taking place across the country on the first weekend of November alone. The organisational capacity and leadership of the Trotskyist Socialist Workers Party (SWP) played a central role in this development, which created some tensions between STWC and the traditional peace movement, represented by CND. These tensions were contained, if not resolved, and a key turning point for the British anti-war movement was the entrance of British Muslims into the STWC. Although the first activists were politically radical and not representative of the Muslim mainstream, this changed quite quickly. In Spring 2002, the Muslim Association of Britain became a leading partner in the coalition, and by the time of the build-up to the Iraq War, all anti-war events, marches, and demonstrations were characterised by a new representation from all sectors of British Muslim life, including Muslim women and youth in unprecedented numbers (Murray & German, 2005).

The charting and understanding of the specific psychological factors at play within the contemporary Muslim anti-war movement is not yet well developed. However, the conflicts of dual identity are bound to be central. On the one hand, British Muslims are British citizens, thus at some level are identified with the acts of the British Government. On the other hand British Muslims have shared identity (based on race, nationality and religion) with those against whom Britain is acting in Pakistan, Afghanistan and Iraq. The latter identification (first a Muslim, second British) may dominate in motivations for protest. The almost complete absence of British Serbs from active participation in anti-war activism post 9/11 suggests a similar motivational orientation for their engagement (Serbian nationalism is infected with strong anti-Muslim sentiments). And of course, those who oppose the Western alliance's actions in Muslim countries include the radical minority that engages in, or supports, political violence—something which is anathema to the traditional peace movement, built as it is on a foundation of non-violence.

The Iraq War
Whilst bringing together new constituencies in new alliances, the organisational strategy of STWC was traditional and recognisable to activists, and based itself—like CND—on marches, rallies, vigils and other symbolic protests, within the law, including both large national events in capitals, and smaller regional and local events all over the country. Indeed, many of the key events were jointly sponsored by STWC and CND. This led to the largest UK rally in peacetime history, in London on 15 February 2003, weeks before the start of the Iraq War, in which up to two million people participated. There were simultaneous co-ordinated

events in many countries round the world, and the event received considerable attention from social scientists, including a group that surveyed participants in seven different countries.[10]

But traditional mass protest was not by any means 'the only game in town'. One of the most remarkable, if controversial, manifestations of the anti-war impetus of early 2003 was the mobilisation of a group of volunteers prepared to go to Iraq and act as human shields. The term 'human shield' has more commonly been used to describe the tactics of military powers, who force civilians to remain close to potential enemy targets in order to deter the enemy from attacking them. International Law deems the use of involuntary human shields as a war crime.[11] However, the human shields of 2003 were civilian volunteers (mainly citizens of the countries of the coalition being mustered to invade Iraq, including several British people) who freely chose to go to Iraq in order to place themselves under coalition bombs. The principal aim was to deter a military attack on Iraq. In this they were not successful, mainly because there were too few of them, but those 70 or so who remained in Iraq during the invasion were situated at key infrastructure installations (e.g. power plants, water purification plants) chosen because many of these installations had been illegally bombed by the USA and Britain during the 1991 Gulf War. None of these installations were bombed by the coalition while the human shields remained there (Simonowitz, 2003).

The heroism of the human shields cannot be doubted. Deliberately putting one's life at risk to protect the lives of innocent others is an act of immense moral courage and intrinsic virtue. Whether or not such action achieves its ultimate goal, its impact on global consciousness is immense. However, much mainstream coverage of the Iraq human shields was astonishingly negative, and focused on highlighting personal shortcomings of the leadership of the movement, gloating in the difficulties experienced by the volunteers, and casting slurs on their motivations.[12]

Also noteworthy were the unprecedented multiple acts of symbolic protest that occurred on the day that war broke out (20 March 2003). Thousands of school students boycotted their classes and joined spontaneous and planned protests around the country, which included roadblocks in city centres. Many employees also left the workplace for a variety of acts of protest. In our workplace, a university campus, protesters left their desks, went to their cars, and sounded their horns continuously for five minutes, at midday. Nothing like this had occurred in living memory.

---

10. http://nicomedia.math.upatras.gr/conf/CAWM2003/Papers/Verhulst.pdf   Accessed 16 September 2006.

11. Geneva Convention Relative to the Protection of Civilian Persons in Time of War. 12 August 1949, 6 UST 3516, 75 UNTS. 287, art. 28.

12. See for instance: Saddam's Idiots. Jonah Goldberg. Townhall.com. 10 January 2003. http://www.townhall.com/columnists/JonahGoldberg/2003/01/10/saddams_idiots Accessed on 16 September 2006.

Post-invasion activism

Although UK civil society has seen no further mass demonstrations on the scale of 15 February 2003, the UK has witnessed a range of post-invasion civil society initiatives and projects motivated by opposition to (and growing revulsion with) the ongoing UK military presence in Iraq, where violence continues to claim at least 40 lives per day at the time of writing (August 2006) (Chamberlain, 2006). These initiatives include, for instance, various legal challenges to actions of British military personnel in Iraq, a campaign mounted primarily by widows and mothers of British soldiers killed in Iraq (Military Families Against the War),[13] campaigns documenting and publicising ongoing civilian deaths in Iraq (e.g. the Iraq Body Count Project),[14] campaigns against torture, illegal detainment, and rendition of prisoners (specifically focused in the UK on the alleged involvement, or complicity, of the UK government in these actions—e.g. Below the Radar: Secret flights to torture and disappearance).[15] These, and many other 'niche' projects, are supported by key mainstream press and media (notably *The Independent* newspaper), as well as by opposition political parties. However, the number of activists involved in any one activity tends to be small (sometimes pitifully small) and there is no uniting philosophy or charismatic leader.

A large minority of the Labour Party (both within and outside parliament) has remained opposed to the government's Iraq policies ever since March 2003, and the most iconic symbol of such dissent (and of the government response) came during the 2005 Annual Conference of the Labour Party when an 82-year-old lifelong party member (and anti-war activist) was assaulted by conference stewards and expelled from the conference hall under anti-terrorism legislation for shouting 'nonsense' during a speech by Foreign Secretary Jack Straw. This was one of many signals of an increasingly anti-democratic political party doing all in its power to stifle legitimate dissent within its own ranks. No strong or confident party would ever treat its own senior members so shabbily. But, despite the manifest weakness of Blair's Iraq policy, no credible opposition has been mounted from the other two major political parties in parliament, or from Labour rebels in parliament. In many ways, parliament and parliamentarians have ceased to function as a watchdog on government in this respect, and the damage done to 'public confidence' in the parliamentary system is enormous and possibly irreversible (Beetham, 2003; The Power Enquiry, 2006).

Three years after the invasion of 2003, Iraq is more unstable than it has ever been, and the USA and the UK have together created the one thing they most feared—a weak and failing state which is a recruiter and exporter of international terrorism—when none was based there before. As a result, the UK has now to

---

13. http://www.mfaw.org.uk/
14. www.iraqbodycount.org
15. Amnesty International. 5 April 2006. http://web.amnesty.org/library/Index/
ENGAMR510512006?open&of=ENG-USA

deal with an entirely new form of domestic terrorism, manifested in the actions of the four UK citizens who took their own lives and that of 53 others on 7 July 2005. Abortive copycat attempts followed, and more can be expected.

Despite 7/7, or perhaps partly because of it, opposition to the UK presence in Iraq has increased steadily among the UK population as a whole. A *Yougov* poll reported on 3 April 2006 showed that 57 per cent of respondents believed that Britain was mistaken to invade Iraq, and that 55 per cent of respondents wanted Britain to withdraw its troops now, or within the next 12 months, without conditions. These are larger percentages against the government than at any time since the invasion. Similar levels of opposition to government policy are found in the USA.[16] And yet, at the time of writing, there are few indications of a significant change of heart in government thinking. Robust assertions of the need to 'stay the course' remain the prevailing mantra. In a speech delivered to the Australian Parliament on 27 March 2006, Tony Blair said, 'This is not a time to walk away, this is a time for the courage to see it through.'[17]

Conclusions

Anti-war activity since 1945 has gone through three major phases, each characterised by a high level of protest and impact on public consciousness and debate, followed by a rapid decline. After 1964, the peace movement almost disappeared after failing to maintain the support of the Labour Party for unilateral British nuclear disarmament. In the 1980s, CND and a wider peace movement re-emerged from obscurity to become a major political force but were unable to achieve significant changes in policy and declined after the 1987 INF agreement. The 'New World Order' of US-led interventions sparked the largest protest in British history in 2003 but this still failed to prevent the UK from joining the US-led coalition in the invasion of Iraq. Since then peace and anti-war activity has continued but at a much reduced level.

We examine the psychological dimensions of different phases of UK anti-war movement activity in the next chapter, but before doing so, it is important to summarise some of the consistent aspects of anti-war activity in the UK.

As we noted at the outset, anti-war activity in Britain has to struggle against a cultural and historical attachment to the military as a significant source of national pride. This is not unique to Britain, but it is exacerbated by Britain's imperial past and the fact that its wars have been fought overseas. The peace movement itself has been accused at times of sharing in some of these imperial perspectives.

---

16. Time to pull out of Iraq, voters tell Blair. Anton La Guardia. *Telegraph*. 3 April 2006. http://www.telegraph.co.uk/news/main.jhtml?xml=/news/2006/04/03/wirq03.xml&sSheet=/news/2006/04/03/ixnewstop.html
17. http://politics.guardian.co.uk/foreignaffairs/story/0,,1740545,00.html

James Hinton (1988) argues that at times the commitment of CND to the importance of Britain taking a moral lead and setting an example to the rest of the world through unilateral disarmament was a case in point. In practice the anti-war element of these three successive mobilisations has been only a minority part of the larger movement. A majority of the UK population opposed the deployment of Cruise and Pershing, but only at most 30 per cent favoured British nuclear disarmament and even fewer, withdrawal from NATO (Rochon, 1990; Carter, 1992). CND and other European peace movements became less far-reaching in their aims as they drew in more established political allies and so the anti-war and peace culture aims of the movement receded. In the 1980s Byrne (1997) estimates that only just under half of CND's membership was pacifist in orientation. CND combines its opposition to weapons of mass destruction with a commitment to general disarmament but that has always been seen as a long-term goal. In each era when the movement has grown larger, it has been because a particular policy or issue provided the opportunity for a broader alliance, going beyond the anti-militarist core. It is misleading therefore to see in the mass mobilisations support for the most radical goals of the movement.

The movement has also differed on tactics. In the 1980s there were tensions between the proponents of NVDA (in which over half the actions were by women's peace groups, inspired by Greenham) and the wider movement over the effectiveness of disruptive and symbolic NVDA as opposed to more conventional tactics such as peace petitions, mass demonstrations and winning the support of political parties, trade unions and professional groups. The NVDA wings of the movement have seen the emphasis on large-scale demonstrations as likely to produce diminishing returns. The media has shown itself less and less likely to report subsequent demonstrations in a campaign, even when these have been sizeable. On the other hand, while NVDA groups have often gained media coverage out of all proportion to their size, this has frequently been hostile. In 1980 for instance, 41 per cent of people polled did not know that there were nuclear weapons in Britain but in 1983 only 4 per cent of those polled were unaware of the Greenham Common peace camp (Rochon, 1990). Yet, while they knew about Greenham, it is hard to know what they thought of it. Media coverage of Greenham focused increasingly negatively on the details of the feminist community's lifestyle and said less and less about their ideas. A similar process occurred in coverage of direct action in the 1990s. Thus, it is difficult to communicate a vision of an alternative society through the media lens, which is how most people see direct action protests.

CND generally avoided making strategic choices that would alienate one or other wing of the movement. Thus, it remained committed to unilateral nuclear disarmament, withdrawal from NATO and support for NVDA, even though these were all rejected by a public that did support the short-term goal of opposing the deployment of Cruise and Pershing. CND was controlled by its members and dependent upon a wider and largely autonomous movement of local groups over which it had no practical control. It was therefore not in a position to narrow its strategy without splitting the movement. A similar Broad-Church alliance, perhaps even broader, characterised the anti-war movement in the 2000s.

There is, then, a tension between the social movement politics of those who live activist lives directed toward deep and long-term social changes and the broader mobilisation on specific crises and policies. As Rochon says:

> To the extent that a movement attempts to achieve specific policy goals, its broader aspect of cultural criticism and transformation is necessarily subordinated. (1990, p. 118)

This does not mean that, either the long-term project of building a peace culture, or the short-term policy goals of broad alliances, are both doomed, but it does mean that they cannot always be pursued effectively, simultaneously, in the same groups.

CHAPTER 6

The Psychology of Anti-War Activism: 2. Building an enduring anti-war movement

JOHN SLOBODA AND BRIAN DOHERTY

Peace issues touch on the very heart of how nations and communities perceive the source of their power in relation to others, so they are often politically 'locked down' and democratic distance is created between a relatively elite group of decision-makers and the people; as a result, there is often a feeling of powerlessness. There is also a fierce national pride attached to the dignity of the armed forces, and thus of militarism. Peace work is usually political and is harder to fund. There are relatively few sources of funding. The human interest angle that is such an effective spur to action is much more difficult to identify with peace and security issues than it is with development issues. We do not have the same general consensus of public opinion to draw on as Make Poverty History—few would believe that poverty can ever be justified, but many believe that war is sometimes justified ... In the face of these obstacles, in many ways we do quite well. (Director of UK-based Peace and Security NGO— unpublished discussion document 'Winning for Peace: Making Peace and Security NGOs more effective' circulated among directors of the UK NGO Peace and Security Liaison Group. Oxford Research Group, April 2006)

It is hard to point to unequivocal and universally recognised long-term successes of the UK anti-war movement. The above quote represents about as optimistic a view of the movement as one is likely to find expressed in thoughtful reflection. It encapsulates three key components of understanding the psychology of the movement. First, there is the national context of history, politics, and a deep-seated culture of militarism, as examined in the preceding chapter. Second, there is the organisational and societal context in which UK anti-war activists operate, and the specific government actions against which they are able to mobilise, more or less effectively. Third, there is the question of what motivates and sustains activists, and from where they derive their sense of purpose and fulfilment.

Although the third of the above components is the primary topic of this chapter, and one which can be illuminated by reference to general concepts and theories in psychology and allied disciplines, the analysis remains politically and practically ungrounded if it has not been informed by the specific historical and social context provided by the former two components. As scholar-activists we are committed to an analysis that reveals and draws on our political convictions and our experience as activists rather than one that attempts to conceal or stand outside them. We therefore approach our topic through our shared understanding of the historical actualities of the last 30 years during which we have witnessed and participated in the UK debate on war and peace.

Assessing and explaining the health of the movement

The dilemma for British anti-war activism may, in its starkest form, be expressed thus. At the height of the Cold War in the early 1980s, when the majority UK public opinion was firmly in favour of the retention of Britain's nuclear weapons, and there was little realistic chance of shifting the balance of British public opinion, the peace movement was strong, united, and remarkably sustained in its effort. In 2006, in the midst of a disastrous intervention which has widely been acknowledged as the worst foreign policy blunder since Suez, which is killing thousands of women and children year on year, and when majority public opinion is against the war, the anti-war movement is weak, diffuse, and dispirited. What psychological processes and constructs might help us to understand, and remedy this profound paradox?

Table 1 provides a summary of some key differences between UK anti-nuclear activism of the 1980s and post 9/11 anti-war activism. These differences will be used as a framework for applying psychological considerations as a basis for understanding the UK anti-war movement as it has moved through different phases of its life in the last quarter century.

Quality of human relations within the Anti-War Movement: Socio-emotional inter-individual bonds

Activism requires coordinated and well-organised action, sustained over time and space. It is, therefore, based on the ability of groups to function well together. One feature of nearly every activist group is that it exists to get things done. A large focus is on planning, executing, and evaluating agreed projects or tasks. This requires co-operation, and an appropriate division of labour. In these respects an activist group may be considered as similar to a team, of the sort that has been extensively studied, either in occupational settings (e.g. military, industrial, managerial) or in leisure pursuits (e.g. sports, hobbies).

Table 1. Contrasting features of two phases of the UK anti-war movement		
1980s anti-nuclear activism	Post 9/11 anti-war activism	Psychological theme
ASPECTS OF UK SOCIETY		
Grounded constituencies rooted in long-term local communities	Ungrounded and virtual constituencies depending on the internet and electronic communication	Quality of human relationships within the movement
Strong cultural identities, 'peacenik, feminist' and socially homogenous activists: white, with higher education and working in public sector professions	Weaker collective identity, and shifting multicultural and multiracial coalitions	Cultural unity/identity of anti-war movement
Consensus of the political left against Thatcher's conservatism	No consensus within ruling Labour Party or Labour supporters. The left is split	The fragmentation of the British left
ASPECTS OF CAMPAIGNING ISSUES		
Focus on averting 'ultimate' nuclear war	Focus on stopping normal conventional war	Global significance of threat
High perceived level of personal danger (nuclear annihilation of millions in the UK)	Low perceived level of personal danger (terrorist suicide bomb killing tens or hundreds)	Level of fear in the general population
One simple campaigning message 'ban the bomb'	Multiple and shifting campaigning messages	Simplicity of campaigning message
Focus of movement broadly stable across time	Focus of movement rapidly shifting (in response to events)	Stability of movement
ASPECTS OF CAMPAIGNING CONTEXT		
Obvious long-term symbolic geographic sites of resistance (e.g. nuclear bases)	No obvious geographic symbolic sites of resistance	Geographic focus of activism
Activism grounded in traditional well-practiced activity (providing expertise and 'well-oiled' organisational structures)	Activism includes much new and unpractised activity (within experimental organisational structures)	Skills base among activists

Making the best use of the individual contributions of team members depends upon those members learning about, and effectively deploying, individual strengths, and addressing individual weaknesses. That learning only takes place when there are frequent and extensive opportunities to interact. It follows that teams which are able to meet together regularly, at the same place and time, are likely to develop a higher level of functioning. Teams which function at a distance, or who coalesce around time-limited projects, operating by correspondence and other remote communication methods, rarely meeting one another, are at a signal disadvantage when needing to plan new activities, and particularly when crises of one sort or another occur. When a team is geographically together, a whole range of personal, social, emotional, and cultural support mechanisms can be easily deployed.

There is considerable suggestive evidence that what keeps many activists engaged in the difficult work of anti-war activism, which rarely yields major visible shifts in government policy, is the possibility of obtaining personal psychological rewards directly from the strong contact and experiences shared with other group members, which become part of a bond (of shared support, shared adversity, and, hopefully, shared moments of transcendence and beauty).

Jasper (1997) has shown that many activist groups have developed what he calls 'collective rites', such as vigils, use of art forms, song, etc. to 'remind participants of their basic moral commitments, stir up strong emotions, and reinforce a sense of solidarity with the group—a "we-ness". He goes on to propose 'rituals are vital mechanisms keeping protest movements alive and well' (ibid. p. 184). It is implicit in his analyses of such rituals that they are a strong part of cementing lasting interpersonal bonds of friendship and mutual personal commitment, which can, in many cases, persist over many decades. This emotional dimension of social movements has become increasingly acknowledged as significant by researchers (see Aminzade & McAdam, 2001).

Public acts of witness are particularly powerful rituals of group solidarity. During a period of personal despair and deep anger, in late 2002 and 2003, when war with Iraq loomed and then began, one of us was deeply nourished by his participation in a small group of peace activists in his local town, who stood in a circle together for two hours every Saturday morning in the centre of the crowded market square in silent witness against the war. It mattered immensely that it was the same people week after week. Our shared commitment to this ritual was a profound support to each other, and a reminder to each of us that there were others for whom this mattered as much as it did to us. It was vital that everyone there was a citizen of this town, thus emphasising BOTH identities—member of the local community, but also member of the countrywide (even worldwide) anti-war movement; cutting across all other things that might divide us (such as age, gender, ethnicity, level of income and education etc).

In terms of Social Identity Theory (SIT—Tajfel and Turner, 1986; Brown, 2000) we were engaged in making more salient the identities that joined us together, and de-emphasising those that separated us. This is well documented as a means of increasing group cohesion and positive interactions between people. It is at least a conjecture worth considering, that key aspects of modern communication (particularly the Internet) are not strong vehicles for the socio-emotional-cultural binding that creates strong and lasting networks of personal commitment and co-operation (Nie, 2001). For the most extreme contrast to the 'virtual community' of the Internet, we can do no better, in Britain's case, than to turn to the extraordinarily rich and long lasting communities formed at the Peace Camps of the 1980s, particularly the women's peace camps of Greenham Common (Roseneil, 2000).

The Greenham camps were not simply premised on sharing a common identity and lifestyle. For many women, to fully participate in the life of the camps meant explicitly and deliberately leaving other identities and commitments behind. One Greenham woman summed this up very clearly:

> My husband didn't understand and didn't like me getting involved outside the home. When I wanted to go to Greenham it was the last straw. He said, 'you either stay at home and be a proper wife and mother, or you go to Greenham, but not both' … Since going to Greenham, my own family have rejected me and feel I've disgraced them …. (Source: *You Can't Kill the Spirit: Yorkshire women go to Greenham.* Bretton Women's book fund, Wakefield, p. 26. Reprinted in Hudson, 2005, p. 138)

Psychological studies have made it clear that the greater the personal cost involved in making a decision, the more committed one is to that decision over the long term, having taken it (Festinger, 1957). Therefore, explicit (and possibly irreversible) rejection of something that has had prior value can be the strongest motivator for long-term activism. For many women, the total community offered by Greenham, which could involve, if so desired, permanent residence over years, was the catalyst for profound personal change, and the development of lifelong relationships based on shared experiences and shared values.

Other research on 1960s activists shows that those who were most involved in high-cost activism, such as the 1964 Freedom Summer campaign of the US civil rights movement, remained committed decades later to the ideals that motivated them in their youth (McAdam, 1988) Those who had been most heavily involved in activism still lived political lives, sustaining the radical identities that they had cemented in early adulthood. This also fits the growing weight of biographical research on the later careers and values of young activists (McAdam, 1988; Whittier, 1997; Braungart & Braungart, 1991).

In this respect, it may be that making a particular act of protest *too* easy, and *too* mainstream, diminishes its motivational value in encouraging long-term activism. One of the possible shortcomings of the 15 February 2003 'March of two million' is that its very acceptability to a broad social spectrum lowered its long-term motivating value. It didn't cost very much (personally, or culturally) to join the march. And for many, no new or powerful relationships formed after the event to encourage and sustain further activism.

This has implications for some of the most important ideas about protest and social movements. Granovetter has argued that movement networks based upon weak ties between groups not normally connected to each other will spread to mobilise more people than will action based in a network of strong ties between people who are very similar socially. A weak ties network, then, will be most conducive to mobilising more people for a mass demonstration. He also acknowledges, however, that a 'strong ties' network may sustain more demanding action for longer because of the interdependence of those involved (Granovetter, 1973). Thus, a strong ties network will be most likely to develop an enduring and sustained movement based on a high level of activism. This can be connected to a second point: Tarrow (2000) has argued that the nature of protest mobilisation is changing. The large and intense organisations such as CND in the 1980s with a culture of local groups, based on weekly or monthly meetings, and sub-groups are being replaced by a new kind of organisation of the kind that the Stop the War Coalition seems, in part, to represent. This is much smaller, and able to mobilise large numbers of participants for demonstrations without the scale of bureaucracy and organisational time previously required. This is partly a consequence of the Internet and the ease it allows in distribution of information, but it is also a result of the accumulation of activist experience across the generations, which allows activists to rejoin protests regularly. The now extensive biographical research on the subsequent careers of 60s and 70s activists suggests that those involved in intense social movement activity do not so much retire as move into less publicly visible action, but without giving up on their core ideals. As a result they;

> … remain available for mobilisation in times of stress or opportunity and keep the flame of activism alive for another day. This continuity also helps to explain why small and apparently weak organizations can produce surprisingly large explosions of protest activity. After the high points of contention pass, these activists remain part of critical communities connected to centres of innovation and potential insurgency. (Tarrow, 2000, p. 278)

On the one hand this suggests a long-term and latent population of post-60s activists. On the other hand, if past activists return only for major events, such as the February 2003 anti-war demonstrations, are the new large protests a weaker form of mobilisation than the smaller but more intense culture of the 1980s peace movement? The challenge for contemporary anti-war activists is to develop a form of participation capable of re-involving those who are already sympathetic to their cause in a more sustained way.

Cultural unity/identity of the anti-war movement

The coalescing of people from different backgrounds under a common cause is never an easy process. Cultural and social differences cannot be ignored—they can obtrude into activities, and become a source of intra-group conflict in, and of, themselves. They have to be dealt with. And therefore, it seems fairly reasonable to suppose that the more shared identities that exist in a group of activists, the easier it will be to handle intra-group conflicts, and sustain the pursuit of common activities in the long term.

The British anti-nuclear movement of the 1980s and that of the 1960s was, while culturally inclusive in some ways (for instance in age and gender), quite culturally narrow in others. Other than the dominance of the middle-class public sector professions, the most obvious feature of the movement, if compared to the 'rainbow' of 15 February 2003, was its ethnic uniformity (Byrne 1997, p. 65). The vast majority of visible activists were white and UK-born. In addition, there were very specific sub-identities, which provided interrelated 'niches' for different activist groups. These included groups developing feminist practices (including radical feminism and the challenging of gender stereotypes in personal lifestyle decisions), groups oriented around religion and spirituality (particularly of a non-traditional and non-hierarchical kind), groups engaging in lifestyles that prioritised conservation and harmony with nature (ecologists, vegetarians etc.) and groups developing alternatives to prevailing economic practices with respect to family, property, and income (e.g. the co-operative movement). Moving between these different types of activism was relatively easy, as they all shared a certain overarching 'world-view'. This meant that different types of activism interacted and fed each other. An activist could sense that going and working on an organic farm was in some deep way the same thing as participating in a blockade of a nuclear facility, or becoming a radical feminist. We were all 'peaceniks'.

Anti-war activities of recent years have, in contrast, involved a complex and shifting kaleidoscope of groups, alliances, and impulses. The most radical change has been the participation of diaspora and ethnic minorities, often bringing with them strong cultural and religious affinities representing mainstream or even conservative (rather than fringe or progressive) values of the countries and regions with which they identify. For instance, the Serbian community that played such an important role in the anti-war activities of 1999 were predominantly politically conservative, many being devout Orthodox Christians, and quite hostile to Muslims. Similarly, many of the Muslims who played a major role in the anti-war activism that developed after 9/11 were religiously and politically conservative, and would find little or no common ground with the set of values that characterise the more seasoned peace activist. Many compromises over quite fundamentally different world-views were needed to hold the Stop the War Coalition together at the height of its influence. There was a sense that the different communities did not interact easily, and those of us who attended the many marches, rallies, and meetings in the 2001–2003 period could not fail to notice how little real interaction there was between the Muslim and white groups represented. The construction of coalitions of anti-war activists varied in response to each successive military campaign. People who were central to the movement in one conflict simply disappeared in the next one. Those of us committed for the long haul have had to remake our constituencies several times in the last decade. This has drained time and energy.

National political landscape: fracturing of the traditional left
In the UK peace movement of the 1980s, Thatcher and Reagan were the hate-figures that united the movement, and the Labour Party in opposition provided plausible 'glue' for a left-leaning activist community. For 18 wilderness years (1979–1997 representing the adult lifespan of many people) progressive hopes had focused on the eventual return of Labour to power. Successive electoral Labour defeats may have dejected the progressive left, but the fact that Labour remained the principal opposition party, with massive electoral support, particularly in the cities and in Scotland and Wales, gave the left hope that, with appropriate leadership, and with the eventual disillusionment of the electorate with conservatism, Labour's time would come, and progressive policies would once again enter the mainstream. Long-standing hopes were raised to new heights on the euphoric day in May 1997, when Tony Blair's Labour party swept to power on a landslide victory. But it did not take long for most of these hopes to be dashed.

It would be hard to overestimate the depth of the disillusionment and disorientation experienced by many supporters of the political left as Blair's New Labour quickly revealed itself to be far from progressive on a whole range of issues. The rightward move of the Labour leadership increasingly disenfranchised the left of the party, and many left-leaning citizens felt equally disenfranchised. The third major party, the Liberal Democrats, showed few signs of resolutely filling the political gap vacated by Labour, and fringe parties, such as the Greens, did not have the electoral appeal in a 'first past the post' electoral system to fill the vacuum left by Labour.

Given the record of previous Labour administrations on matters of war and peace it was perhaps naïve of the anti-war left to pin their hopes on Blair, but it is pretty clear that the anger felt by those on the left towards one-time member of CND, Blair, was far more motivationally debilitating than the anger felt towards Thatcher which, for many, was energising. Fighting a common perceived enemy is far easier than dealing with, what one perceives to be, a betrayal by someone who was supposed to be on the same side. Blair's repositioning of Labour meant that the anti-war movement had no real home in mainstream British party politics.

Since 1999, pro-war and anti-war camps have increasingly formed independently of party-political allegiance. Some of the most hawkish proponents of war have been found on the Labour back benches, and some prominent Conservatives (such as ex-Governor of Hong Kong and EU Commissioner Chris Patten) have found themselves considerably to the left of Blair. An extraordinary example of 'crossing the floor' came in June 2006, when Michael Portillo, a former minister in the Conservative government, joined the ranks of the anti-war left in calling for unilateral British nuclear disarmament (Portillo, 2006).

Activist movements are at their most healthy and vibrant when they can command the resources of major societal organisations that adopt and organise around their agendas (be they political parties, churches, or charitable organisations). Denied a home in New Labour, the UK anti-war movement currently has not succeeded in recruiting organisational sponsorship of the sort that would underpin its long-term health. This is in contrast to the movement in the 1980s, which had the support of Labour, trade unions, and many local authorities. It is also in contrast to the environmental movement, the anti-poverty/ development movement, and human rights movement, all of which have managed to win organisational support on a large scale from political parties (across the spectrum), faith groups, conservation groups (countryside and heritage), as well as the business community.

There is no inherent reason why wealthy and societally powerful organisations, such as major churches, should not actively support and nurture anti-war activism. Many high-profile religious leaders have expressed profound unease at the direction in which Blairite foreign policy is taking Britain, yet anti-war issues are hardly raised in most churches. This is in contrast with the 1980s when Church groups were to the fore in peace movements in many European countries (Klandermans, 1990). Opportunities are there for the grasping, but to exploit them possibly requires a deep understanding of and engagement with the organisations involved, an engagement for which people exercising leadership within the current movement may be ill-equipped.

One sign of hope is the recent decision by the Roman Catholic Bishops of Scotland to oppose the replacement of the British nuclear deterrent. In April 2006, they issued a joint statement urging:

> The Government of the United Kingdom not to invest in a replacement for the Trident system and to begin the process of decommissioning these weapons with the intention of diverting the sums spent on nuclear weaponry to programs of aid and development. (Scottish Bishops, 2006)

To what extent this position was arrived at through efforts of anti-war activists is as yet unclear.

Global significance of threat and levels of fear

One reason for the lesser involvement of the Churches in the contemporary anti-war movement, compared to the 1980s, is likely to be the greater moral ambiguity of the contemporary wars. The war on terror requires political judgements that are more in the tradition of the 'just war' theory: is more harm than good likely to result from an invasion of a country that will remove a brutal and repressive regime (Afghanistan and Iraq), for instance? The reasons that we would argue 'yes' in these cases are political and contextual, including the question of who carries this out. Such reasons do not entail that all efforts to remove tyrants are wrong.

In contrast, the threat that motivated anti-nuclear activists of the Cold War was ultimate and apocalyptic. They argued that it was clearly morally wrong to plan a defence system based upon the 'hair-trigger' readiness of both the USSR and the USA to instigate 'mutual assured destruction'. This also had a strong cultural impact. It burrowed its way deep into cultural consciousness, as manifested by a spate of novels, films and docudramas (such as *When the Wind Blows*, Briggs, 1992) providing graphic depictions of the fate of ordinary people in the West, which etched themselves in the memory and the imagination. These threats were given added reality by (a) regularly repeated footage of Hiroshima and Nagasaki, and (b) a series of actual nuclear crises and stand-offs (e.g. Bay of Pigs) which made it seem only too plausible that nightmare scenarios could be enacted. These crises were given a heightened 'fear factor' by the virulent and all-encompassing anti-Soviet propaganda that spewed out of all major Western capitals, depicting Soviet leaders as fundamentally malign and intent on conquest of the West at all costs, justifying the refusal of the USA and its allies to accept a 'no first use' policy, and to intensify the arms race. This propaganda had the effect of making many people believe that nuclear war was likely. In 1983 the doomsday clock of the *Bulletin of the Atomic Scientists* was set at three minutes to midnight (it was only closer than this in 1953 when both the USSR and the USA exploded thermonuclear devices in separate tests). For most of the 1990s the clock receded further than 10 minutes from midnight (Bulletin of the Atomic Scientists, 2006).

In a major nuclear exchange there could be no 'unaffected survivors'. A prolonged nuclear winter could destroy civilisation and result in the death of billions, regardless of the location of explosions. Anti-nuclear activists were explicitly fighting for human and planetary survival. This was nowhere more powerfully expressed than in the Russell–Einstein manifesto, issued in 1955 by a group of concerned scientists, led by Bertrand Russell and Albert Einstein (Born et al., 1955).

> It is feared that if many H-bombs are used there will be universal death, sudden only for a minority, but for the majority a slow torture of disease and disintegration ... Here, then, is the problem which we present to you, stark and dreadful and inescapable: Shall we put an end to the human race; or shall mankind renounce war?

The only contemporary campaigns that have the same level of appeal to public consciousness and human survival are environmental campaigns (such as those against global warming or destruction of the rain forests) and some public health campaigns (e.g. against HIV-AIDS). They share with anti-nuclear campaigning that same irrelevance of geography. Wherever the damage is started, the whole world will eventually suffer for it. It is perhaps no surprise that these campaigns have more widespread public support than current anti-war campaigns.

In contrast, the wars against which UK activists currently campaign kill mainly foreigners in far-off places, and any potential 'blow back' to the UK is slow and indirect. It is hard to persuade the average person that life in the UK would be greatly better than it is now had we not bombed Belgrade, or retaken the Falklands. There is a growing public consciousness of the ways in which the Iraq fiasco could rebound to broader international disadvantage (e.g. more terrorist attacks, rising oil prices), but none of the potential scenarios share the simple global inevitability of the consequences of a nuclear war or of global warming. That being the case, the motivations for becoming a contemporary anti-war activist and sustaining that activism must, of necessity, be more diverse, and more complex. Campaigning messages must also be similarly diverse and conceptually rich. That makes for difficulties in focus and compellingness.

Simplicity and stability of campaigning message

The anti-nuclear movement of the Cold War had the best campaigning slogan imaginable—'Ban the Bomb'. A highly paid advertising copywriter could not have done better. Instantly recognisable, rhythmically and phonetically symmetrical, and of utter simplicity, this slogan served as a rallying call for several generations of activists. It is as relevant for anti-nuclear activists today as it was when first invented in the 1950s, even if it has a somewhat culturally dated feel ('the bomb' no longer has a clearly understood referent among younger people).

In contrast, the slogans spawned by the anti-war movement of the Blair era have come and gone. 'Don't attack Iraq' was probably the phrase that rallied the greatest number of people in 2003. But the moment the first bomb dropped on Baghdad the slogan became useless. It is not fanciful to attribute some of the failings of the movement to the transient and time-limited nature of its slogans. Slogans are psychological anchors. They bind people together, literally (they are good for coordinated chanting and marching) and metaphorically—by providing a clear 'brand' identity. They are also easy to remember and call upon at times of stress and challenge. They have, in this respect, some of the 'grounding' properties of mantras and other meditative devices.

But slogans only go skin deep. Committed activists must be able to call on a clearly articulated repertoire of arguments to justify their position. The more stable a particular issue is (and the longer time over which it remains an issue) the better the opportunity for learning, rehearsing, and enriching one's understanding, and the flexibility and convincingness of one's campaigning message. Someone who campaigns against nuclear weapons will be able to call on knowledge that was often acquired decades ago, but is still relevant today. The same states possess the vast majority of the world's nuclear weapons as did 30 years ago, and the destructive capacities of these weapons remains much the same.

In contrast, someone campaigning against a potential US military strike on Iran will need to have acquired much new (and constantly updated) knowledge. As something of a hoarder, one the authors occasionally looks back over old campaigning material. Although much anti-nuclear literature from the 1980s can still be read with profit today, boxes full of Balkans-related literature have almost no relevance to current conflicts, except in a rather academic, historical sense. Being an effective anti-war activist today means constantly following the twists and turns of international events. Arguments deployed against an air-attack on Iran's nuclear facilities will not be the same as arguments deployed against the ground invasion of Iraq, and cannot easily or plausibly be recycled.

So, today's anti-war activists may be increasingly 'tied up' in the sheer business of 'keeping on top of events'. This takes energy from all the other necessary components of activism (e.g. planning, organising, inspiring, building relationships, evaluating). How can the movement overcome the ephemerality of specific events? One way is to locate a conceptual framework that sits above specific conflicts, and may be re-applied to successive crises without starting from scratch. Different wars may therefore be interpreted and understood as context-specific manifestations of the same thing.

A strong motivation for many of those who have remained active throughout the Kosovo-Afghanistan-Iraq sequence of wars is a perception of an underlying (and basically unchanging) US strategic vision, which has a number of elements, but in which military and political control of areas of geo-strategic importance (particularly oil-producing regions) is paramount. Opposition to this succession of wars can then be based on a set of unchanging principles—e.g. that wars promoted as being for the benefit of the peoples of the countries attacked are actually pursued for reasons of imagined self-interest, and that any benefit to the people of those countries is incidental.

It should follow that individuals who are able to articulate overarching concepts to explain their anti-war stance will be more likely to remain active in future conflicts than individuals whose opposition to a particular war is motivated primarily by specific aspects of the conflict in question. For instance, a substantial number of opponents of the Iraq War based their opposition on the absence of a Security Council Resolution. The presence of such a resolution in the case of Afghanistan would therefore be sufficient reason to explain why such people did not oppose the Afghan invasion (or might not oppose a future attack on Iran or some other country, should Security Council approval be given).

To build long-term commitment to anti-war activism will require (among other things) the intellectual leadership of the movement to provide a compelling narrative that is both comprehensive enough to be a reliable framework for several decades to come, and flexible enough to take account of the very different conflicts, in different parts of the world, which any future UK government might be tempted to take part in. One example of such a framework is that being developed by the Oxford Research Group (Abbott, Rogers & Sloboda, 2006).

The campaigning context

It has been hugely grounding to the anti-nuclear movement that nuclear installations have clear and long-term physical manifestations on UK soil. Aldermaston, Greenham and Faslane have been just three of several high-profile sites. These are both physical and psychological foci for activists. These sites have properties that enable certain kinds of engagement. They have high security, large numbers of military and related personnel going in and out, are often located in relatively remote areas of some natural beauty (thus 'engaging' for those who have concerns for the natural environment), and are in a real sense 'shrines' to the lethal and costly weapons and plant within their boundaries. For the committed activist this is 'distilled evil', which stays put and cannot easily run away. There are simple logistic and planning advantages. People can become familiar with the geographical specificities. Local residents and local politicians can be engaged over the long term.

But there are also more subtle motivational advantages. It is no accident that so many of the actions around nuclear bases have a 'spiritual' component, in the broadest sense of the word. Activists engage in rituals of various sorts (from explicit prayer, within mainstream traditions, through to improvised symbolic acts—e.g. tying of flowers and pictures to the perimeter fence) which aim to summon up and project 'good energy' to counteract the 'evil energy' emanating from within the perimeter fence. Spiritual rituals need physical focus. That is why people need churches and shrines. In the case of the nuclear base there is even a suggestion of 'exorcism': the uttering of sacred words and the enactment of sacred rituals as a deep transformative act. It matters to the activist that they are in the physical presence of the evil they seek to transform.

An activist against the Iraq occupation has no such clear geographical focus. Military personnel and plant come from all over the country, and, as troops rotate, the geographical mix of the deployment changes. No one local military base is any more or less an appropriate target for activists than any other. Political targets are equally amorphous. There is no symbolic substitute for Parliament and Downing Street, but these are the foci of any type of political activism relating to any action of the current government on any topic whatsoever. There is nothing specific to war. Also, few activists, even the most ardent, would want to identify the entire parliamentary and government machine as 'evil' in the way that anti-nuclear activists can identify a nuclear base as such.

The only potential long-term 'shrine' for the UK anti-war movement is Parliament Square, where, at the time of writing, despite the government's best efforts, a chaotic collection of handmade anti-war banners and posters has been maintained by a small group of activists ever since shortly after 9/11. However, this presence has never caught widespread support, and, on the many occasions when one of the authors has walked past this (on the way to meetings with parliamentarians or civil servants) the installation has a neglected air, with few people near it. It is a fragmentary patchwork of differently pitched messages. It does not attract or inspire with a clear and focused message.

Finally, it can be argued that new-wave anti-war activism has 'deskilled' traditional campaigners. Where so much is new, experimental and transitory, involving shifting constituencies, skills acquired over decades may become, at best, in need of re-shaping, at worst, irrelevant. There is much creativity, and, out of that creativity, success may emerge. But the flip side of trial and error is many failed experiments, and increased levels of disagreement about strategy and tactics. Where activism involves new skills (e.g. Internet), new issues (e.g. terrorism, civilian casualties), new constituencies (e.g. British Muslims), and new organisations (e.g. STWC) then there is bound to be a strong learning curve, at the beginning of which, the general level of effectiveness is low.

It may be optimistic to hope that international affairs will ever regain the 'frozen' stability of the cold war decades. The conditions for the steady development of a skill base may never again be as good as they were through the three decades of the 1960s–1980s. But this means that activists must think even harder about how new activists are recruited, trained, developed and retained. What are the conditions that will ensure that the person you invite to join you in an upcoming action or project is still going to be in the movement, using and developing their skills in ten year's time?

Psychological studies of skill (e.g. Ericsson, 1996) provide some potential answers:

1. Frequent opportunities to exercise skills (ideally daily).
2. Early opportunities for success, leading to a sense of personal efficacy.
3. Appropriate feedback, both positive and negative.
4. Opportunities to increase skill levels through engagement in more challenging activities as skill levels rise.

Most committed activists will probably realise that these things happened for them, but in an unplanned and random way. Can anti-war organisations become strategic enough to ensure that these things are guaranteed to large numbers of people? This may be the key challenge facing the UK anti-war movement.

CHAPTER 7

Relational Psychology in the War Speeches of Bush and Blair: Beyond 'Us' and 'Them'

JULIE LLOYD AND STEVE POTTER

If he uses weapons of mass destruction, that will just prove our case, and we will deal with it. We've got one objective in mind: that's victory. And we'll achieve victory. (Tony Blair, Camp David Speech, 27 March 2003)

Introduction

This chapter explores the relational psychology embedded in the speeches of George Bush, President of the USA, and Tony Blair, Prime Minister of the UK, relating to the war in Iraq. It borrows a method of analysis from psychotherapy (Cognitive Analytic Therapy) to examine how these two leaders, with very different political agendas, came to speak with one voice, sharing a confrontational, righteous and heroic position against the more sober and traditional grain of international diplomacy. As such, it is not a review of the various social, psychological and linguistic tools that are currently in use that could be used to examine political speeches. Dialogical Sequence Analysis intends simply to describe what appears to be said—to reveal the voices that are present, hidden and silenced. We believe quite strongly that accurate description is challenging to prejudiced and condensed thinking on all sides.

In the build-up to the Iraq war, the President and Prime Minister presented their decision to go to war with Saddam Hussein as essential to the defeat of the global threat of terrorism. It was going to be 'us or them'. They gave idealistic and triumphant accounts of the freedom, security and progress that would flow from victory. An analysis of their speeches before, during and 'after' the war reveals a 'head-to-head' mindset that sets an 'us' against a 'them' and approaches international conflict as personalised and epic. Despite the apparent locality and personalisation of issues, the 'enemy' in Iraq is also presented as abstract and generalised. This chapter explores how a one-dimensional psychology of war is used to address a more complex psychology of conflict that is always multiple-positioned and global.

Cognitive Analytic Therapy (CAT) is a collaborative, relational psychotherapy developed by Anthony Ryle in the UK National Health Service. Using a philosophy of dialogism, it combines elements of psychoanalytic and cognitive behavioural understanding in a unique and versatile way. Cognitive Analytic Therapy has developed a method of mapping some of the limiting, dislocating and harmful ways in which we interact when we aren't functioning well. The relational processes that describe someone in a traumatised, paranoid, cut-off, or angry state of mind can be usefully applied to the collective states of mind among proponents of war. This is true even if the war (as in Iraq) is being fought for primarily economic or political reasons, as elite decision makers may be alienated from the forces driving their own thinking.

A key feature of CAT is its methodological versatility. It weaves a general, plain-language, description which connects the detail of momentary experiences of emotion, behaviour, body and thought to the 'big picture' relations between assumptions, roles, identities and self-understanding. In this respect, as a psychotherapy, it is able to weave a double-dialogue between the inner, relationally intimate psychological processes and the more social and interpersonal, sociological processes without giving priority to either. As humans, in any moment, we are actors caught simultaneously within a high-level orchestration of several positions and processes in our minds, bodies and interactions with others. As described by Donald (2001) these operate in complex layers of neuro-cultural mental history combining episodic, mimetic, mythic, and theoretic processes. Our social and personal intelligence is rooted in relations between ourselves and others. Our challenge is to develop the flexible relational thinking among ourselves that can measure up to this complexity. To do this CAT proposes we look at ourselves, with a skilled helper at hand, to see how we move between repeating restrictive positions and patterns of interaction.

An example might be someone viewing his heavy drinking as Dutch courage to gain confidence in socially anxious situations. In so doing he is taking a position on his drinking and giving it a justification. In CAT terms this might be formulated as in Figure 1. The man feels anxious about going out socially. This is fed by his anticipation that others will find him boring and will avoid him. He predicts being in a position of anxious exposure and coping by taking one of two positions. He is either hurt and in retreat and becomes isolated, or he is angry, defiant and full of resentment and unpopular. Both positions confirm his basic assumption about how others will treat him. As a way of coping with this dilemma he may adopt a procedure of drinking alcohol to give himself courage against the wish to retreat and to reduce the feared anxiety about exposure. His drinking may make him even more nervous, or conversely, *too* free of inhibition and actually be off-putting to people. He may avoid the impact of these responses by benignly calling his drinking 'Dutch Courage' and 'my little helper'. His drinking becomes increasingly his only way of coping and prevents an accurate dialogue with his emotional experience or social situation. This results in him not being able to remember how his social interactions went, or how he felt, leaving him more anxious about going out socially. The drinking increasingly masks his dialogue with any other solutions. Drinking too much alcohol is more than a behaviour, or a resultant feeling, or solution. It is a complex relational position that can only be tackled if understood in the round, and considered in relation to the more distressing positions against which it is a partial solution.

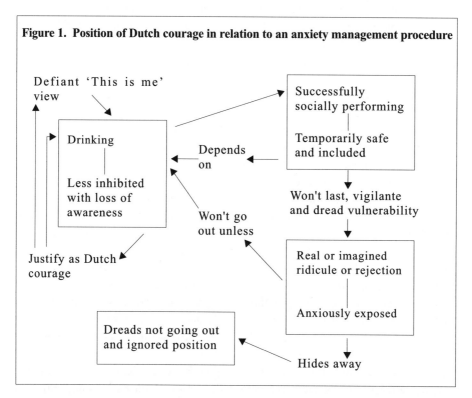

Figure 1. Position of Dutch courage in relation to an anxiety management procedure

Patterns and positions like this play a part in the establishment and maintenance of emotional distress, physical symptoms, restrictive self-management or conflict with self or others.

CAT captures the importance of the interactive nature of patterns and positions in terms of roles and our capacity to internalise knowledge of the reciprocal positions involved in playing the role. For example, if I feel *loved* and cherished by a caring parent, I know what it is to be in the reciprocal *loving* position. If we learn one role, such as pleasing and placating a demanding parent, we also learn, and take in as part of our identity, the reciprocal position to this role. So if I am obliging to a demanding 'other' I know what it is to be demanding (even if I don't express it, I know the role and how to play to it and, under certain circumstances, may shift into it). We may have a strong familiarity with the position of obliging and placating the high expectations of a demanding parent and only a slight or dreaded awareness of the possibility of shifting to another position such as rebelling against these demanding expectations. We may dissociate from, or repress, knowledge of a traumatic position.

According to CAT thinking, someone functioning well would have a wider range of patterns and positions and seek reciprocation with less rigidity. They would be more able to switch between conscious and collaborative choices of how to live their lives, in any particular situation, and demonstrate sensitivity to self and others in the moment. Someone functioning badly would rely on a narrow set of positions and procedures (actions), which are fixed and are experienced as hard to control or negotiate. The therapeutic goal might be appropriately evoked as developing a sense of dialogue and emotional democracy in the negotiation and orchestration of movement between patterns and positions. The same could be said of a national political culture or an international political process as typified by the speeches of political leaders.

It is central to CAT's relational thinking that any particular problem or distress is likely to be maintained by many factors. The client's distress can only have a hope of changing if the interaction of many factors is accurately described in a safe, collaborative and constructive way. CAT works with these many factors by integrating different levels of relational analysis. So at one level, it is a strong feature of our early bio-cultural evolution and cultural development that, for example, we are easily pushed to coping with distress and problems by going head to head in an emergency mode charged with myths of survival and combat. At another level, the CAT approach focuses on the intentional reciprocal nature of our human interaction. Like chess players or lovers, pedestrians or investment bankers we have evolved (in our minds, bodies and personalities) to intentionally calculate our moves in relation to the moves we see, or anticipate, from people and things around us.

The focus is not on how the client should be, or moral judgements about good health and bad health, but on accurate description of the overlapping internal and external relational world that shapes his or her distress and their ways of coping. The healthy aim is the internal emotional democracy of an individual self that is adaptive and relationally responsive in a complex world. This mapping of healthy and damaging patterns can be extended to a nation or its leaders. Looked at from a relational point of view, the structural similarity in relations between individuals and societies is striking.

CAT has developed many psychological tools to assist its therapeutic work. One of these is the mapping of reciprocal patterns of interaction that make up a position or identity. This aspect of CAT is richly informed by the work of Mikael Leiman (1997) who has added dialogic sequence analysis to this process of mapping out relational positions and identifications. The art of mapping out these reciprocal role patterns can be represented as simplified diagrams of personal identity in action with others.

In CAT, the narrative process of telling is kept open and made useful by an analytic process of mapping out the relational patterns and positions embedded in someone's story of distress. As the client speaks, the therapist is listening out for the patterns that may be recurring, general and pivotal. The therapist holds this thinking in mind in a tentative way, and looks to join with the client's own inherent tendency to map out their own story, for them to develop a judgement or evaluation of themselves. Typically, this brings a quality of recognition such as 'There I go again' which is coloured by a self-evaluation: 'aren't I pathetic', or 'I can't help it'. Change in CAT therapy involves the double task of linking recognition of general and recurring patterns to the general self-evaluative position taken by the person.

One cluster of people treated by the CAT approach, (those with a narcissistic structure to their relational thinking), tend to find it initially very hard to notice their own processes. They hold to a superior position and tend to associate any troublesome insight very strongly with humiliation. This group live a life of narcissistic solutions as a defence against difficult feelings about themselves. Grandiosity for them is a defence against more complex relational understanding. This can be usefully kept in mind in the subsequent analysis of the speeches below.

The method of applying CAT to speeches works by viewing them as a series of positions in which the moral, emotional, value and relational content has been condensed. These positions are uttered (enacted) through the words, references and images of the speeches, in ways that justify, deny, distance or address the expected reactions of others. The speeches of President Bush and Prime Minister Blair use various declarations of intent, assumptions, and avowals of feelings to move between a series of linked positions in relation to a perceived threat to Western interests. They are analysed for their implicit positions as a step to drawing out the relational consequences of these.

Analysis

A CAT analysis is applied to four instances of speech making; Blair in the UK, 18 March 2003; Bush and Blair at Camp David, 27 March 2003; Bush and Blair looking back 26 June 2006; and Bush and Blair in Russia, 18 July 2006.

The first speech analysed is by Prime Minister Tony Blair to the UK House of Commons on the eve of the Iraq War.[1] Elements of the analysis presented here

---

1. <http://www.pm.gov.uk/output/page3295.asp>. Van Dijk (2006) presents a critical discourse analysis of parts of this speech, emphasising the manipulation of general, socially shared representations.

have been taken as extracts from a paper by the authors (Potter & Lloyd, 2005). In this speech the middle two reciprocal roles (patiently reasoning—cooperate or treacherous games [C] v threaten use of force—fearfully submit or stand up [D] see Figure 2 below) are at the heart of the argument, and rely first on the assertion of 'us' as good, patient and democratic and 'them' (rogue nations—personified by Saddam Hussein's Iraq—and terrorists groups) as beyond reason and dialogue. The argument relies upon the self-evident evil of Saddam Hussein to stand as the generalisable evil of *all* regimes and groups who are judged to threaten us. Blair's case for taking a different position (D) is that Saddam or Iraq (Saddam and Iraq are interchangeable terms in the speech) have failed to reciprocate as they 'should' by being co-operative in response to our reasonableness. Their response of 'treacherous game playing' needs a new reciprocation promoting a very different state of mind, which Blair suggests is against our nature ('the natural urges of our democracy towards peace') [author's emphasis]. Where? One effect of setting our reasonableness against Saddam's failure to co-operate is that it hides any treachery in our dealings in the past (the history of supporting Saddam Hussein by the West is denied), in the present (the West's economic interest in oil goes unmentioned), or in the future (our lack of preparation for a just and humane peace). The speech creates a shared position of the reluctant, patient warrior.

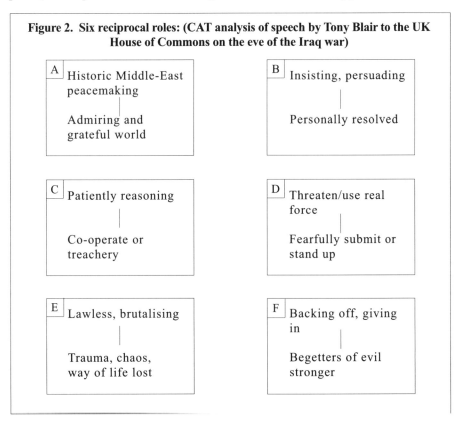

Figure 2. Six reciprocal roles: (CAT analysis of speech by Tony Blair to the UK House of Commons on the eve of the Iraq war)

A | Historic Middle-East peacemaking

Admiring and grateful world

B | Insisting, persuading

Personally resolved

C | Patiently reasoning

Co-operate or treachery

D | Threaten/use real force

Fearfully submit or stand up

E | Lawless, brutalising

Trauma, chaos, way of life lost

F | Backing off, giving in

Begetters of evil stronger

Similarly, the reciprocal role (E) of 'lawless and brutalising' implies the trauma and brutalised experience of loss of life and chaos. To know the meaning, value and purpose of force (which the speech advocates) we must know of its impact in terms of the experience of suffering and terror. The nature of suffering and the meaning of trauma are hidden in the speech. The actual terror that the people of Iraq will experience goes unmentioned in the speech, as does the wider consideration of options in the face of trauma, damage and loss in the world. In contrast, the fear that we should feel and act upon in the face of an imminent threat to *our* way of life is emphasised. Fear, danger and threat to 'our way of life' provide a reason to make us firm, whereas for Iraqis—it is described as the only means to make them submit. The top two reciprocal roles A and B in Figure 2 are idealised positions: the promise of peace in the Middle East, and the Churchillian and historical grandeur of being led by someone who is convinced of the wisdom and necessity of his position and knows the danger of being feeble. Perhaps one of the restrictions of the psychology evidenced in the speech is that it names only a victor's peace, a golden time when all will be in order. Oliver Richmond, (2005) in his rich conceptualisation of peace, points to the difficulty of moving from a 'victor's' peace, to a more constitutionally maintained peace.

In Figure 3 the six reciprocal positions sketched out in Figure 2 are linked to show how a CAT analysis of the speech highlights particular patterns in more detail. Some of the key sequences of the speech have been placed into the basic diagram. The speech dwells at length on two themes, the West's placation and patience (which affirms our goodness and reasonableness but also casts doubt on it as being of no avail). The speech recasts our twelve-year-long trap of being reasonable and patient democrats (*'our inspections drew no co-operation or results'*) as a polarised choice of action between threatening and using real force: '*The only persuasive power to which he responds is 250,000 allied troops on his doorstep*' (Procedure 3 in Figure 3*)*. Something hard and forceful is being said here but is embedded in a blurred psychological equation of '*holding firm or turning back*'. It is described as a tough choice with no middle way between retreating (with all its connotations of weakness) or holding firm (with many connotations of strength and wisdom and none of violence, unpredictability or destructiveness). In implying that it is a course *we* have set, it suggests the path is already chosen and it would be a further weakness to change our minds at this point.

> This is a tough choice. But it is also a stark one: to stand British troops down and turn back; or to hold firm to the course we have set. I believe we must hold firm.

In threatening force it is assumed that 'Saddam' (and all other forces of evil) will only occupy one of two narrow and polarised positions and will either comply through fear or not comply through treachery. If they resist, then war will follow.

Figure 3. Six reciprocal roles: (Further CAT analysis of speech by Tony Blair to the UK House of Commons on the eve of the Iraq war)

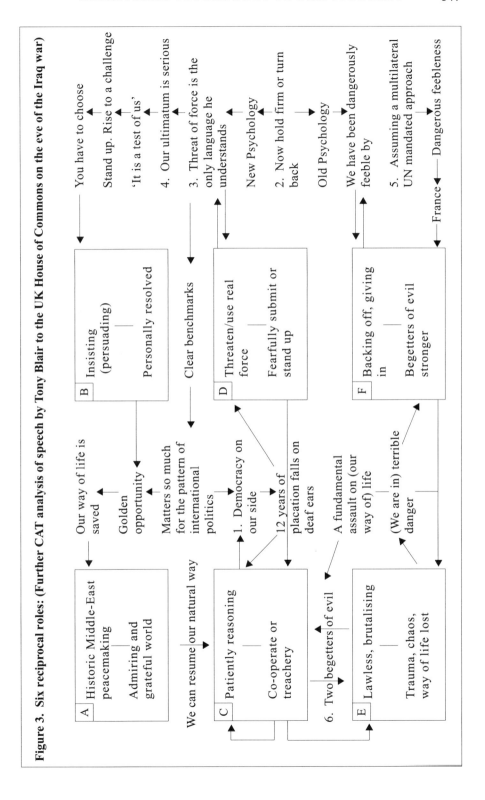

Though the Prime Minister's speech is coy and vague about the realities of war—hindsight shows that if war does follow, it means an overwhelming use of force, with heavy bombing characterised in melodramatic psychological terms as a 'shock and awe' approach. The threat of force is embedded in the notion of the righteousness of 'our' position because *we* are reasonable and democratic and therefore can be trusted to use violence wisely and only when necessary.

Whilst the speech emphasises the way in which Saddam Hussein's regime and the terrorists will join hands to be brutalising forces, there is dissociation from the way in which the threat and use of force can lead to the Western powers being the lawless brutalising party. The military emphasis on the technology of smart weapons and damage limitation hides the dissociation from any psychology of destructiveness and terror on 'our' part. Only their weapons of mass destruction (WMDs) are described as threatening to play a part in the brutalising loss of life. The unspoken or dissociated part is that the UK has many WMDs, but since *we* are reasonable we are entitled to have them and they do not need to be mentioned. This might best be understood as the dominant positional sequence of the West—to avoid being seen as weak and appeasing. We have to use force as a necessary evil, but the harm and damage of this must be disguised by taking an idealised position of it being for a greater good and based upon our greater integrity and wisdom. This seems to draw very much on the Project for the New American Century, which has considerable influence on the Bush administration. On its website (www.newamericancentury.org) PNAC describes itself as:

A non-profit educational organization dedicated to a few fundamental propositions: that American leadership is good both for America and for the world; and that such leadership requires military strength, diplomatic energy and commitment to moral principle.

The Prime Minister's speech refers to a dialogue between the West and the 'two begetters of evil' most clearly identified as the Iraqi regime and global terrorist organisations. Behind them, as observers, are other tyrannical regimes. Tony Blair is telling Parliament how our weakness will be perceived by these begetters of evil, and by other regimes that observe us. In so doing he is positioning those who will not now stand firm with him as being in the position of giving strength to a dangerous enemy. All dialogue is drawn into this 'head-to-head mindset', and there is no scope to analyse the danger and calculate the least harmful or most productive strategy.

In returning to the theme of the old psychology, Mr Blair justifies his 'hold firm' position, with its inevitable progression to war, by contrasting it in dismissive ways with the feebleness of backing-off and colluding with these new forces of darkness. France, in general, rather than any particular French politician, serves to represent the risks of collusion and the placatory foolishness of trying for a multilateral solution. On the other hand, leaving the misunderstood US to act alone would just encourage unilateralism.

Finally, to underscore the importance of holding firm (in a sequence linking the top two reciprocal roles in Figure 3), the aim is to involve the British population directly. Morally charged and personal, motivational language is used. '*Stand up, rise to a challenge, you have to choose.*' This top right-hand reciprocal role is a familiar one from the Prime Minister. He uses *his* commitment as a measure of the truth that calls for *our* personal consent. This (the top right-hand reciprocal role procedure) suggests that, if we are personally resolved, it will be a great opportunity and many things that are now stuck will be freed. The disavowed option that is not considered is that 'personally resolved' could be associated with anything other than military intervention.

The next speeches were made at the Bush and Blair Camp David meeting of 27 March 2003.[2] As with Blair's parliamentary speech in 2003, these speeches deny the legitimacy of a difference of view. They deny the complexity of the situation and contain a grandiose polarisation of positions in the form of 'all will be well if you follow us but disastrous if you don't'. The aim is to keep it simple, reduce ambiguity; we must all appear the same, the Heads of State are the same as each other, just as the enemies of our States are all the same as each other. This is described in Figure 4.

1. Nobly sacrificing—disdainfully sacrificed
The speech started with mutual admiration:

> We've learned that he's [Tony Blair] a man of his word. We've learned that he's a man of courage, that he's a man of vision. And we're proud to have him as a friend.

The Prime Minister's speech began in a supplicatory role: '*Thank you for your strength and for your leadership at this time*'. Historical differences are now irrelevant, as the Prime Minister affirms: '*The alliance between the United States and Great Britain has never been in better or stronger shape*', but also this alliance is presented as having been ever the case, as the President ends his speech by declaring:

> For nearly a century, the United States and Great Britain have been allies in the defence of liberty. We've opposed all the great threats to peace and security in the world. We shared in the costly and heroic struggle against Nazism. We shared the resolve and moral purpose of the Cold War. In every challenge, we've applied the combined power of our nations to the cause of justice, and we're doing the same today. Our alliance is strong, our resolve is firm and our mission will be achieved.

---

2. The White House (2003). Operation Iraqi Freedom.
http://www.whitehouse.gov/news/releases/2003/03/20030327-3.html March 2003.

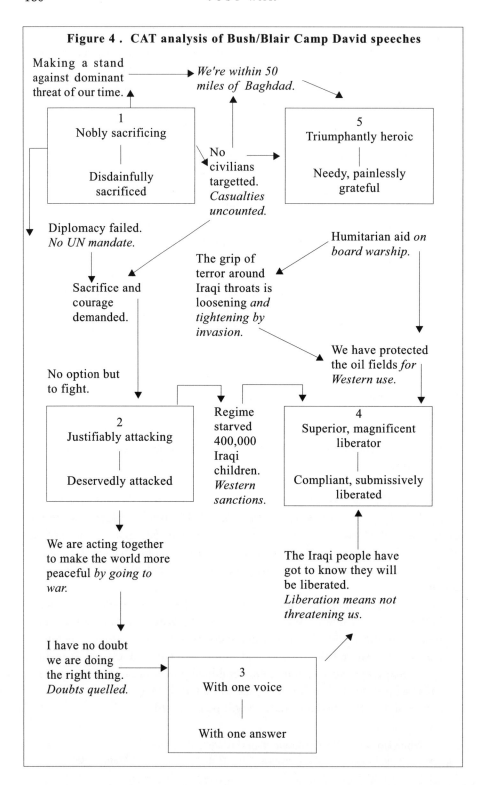

Figure 4. CAT analysis of Bush/Blair Camp David speeches

Now that their credentials are established, both leaders describe our sacrifice demanded by the situation:

We're sharing the sacrifices of this war ... the campaign ahead will demand further courage and require further sacrifice ... we're sharing the sacrifices of this war ... together we have lost people, and the American people offer their prayers to the loved ones of the British fallen, just as we offer our prayers to the loved ones of our own troops who have fallen.

The Prime Minister echoes laments for the American and British dead. Praying for the unmentioned, fallen enemy is however overlooked. He states that our actions bring liberation and security and wards off doubts through pointing out that those who fight against us do so because they have no choice, rather than any nationalistic wish to repel invaders.

Iraq will be disarmed ... our coalition will stand with the citizens of Iraq in the challenges ahead ... history requires more of our coalition than a defeat of terrible danger ... there will be people fiercely loyal to that regime with no option but to fight all the way ... the justice of our cause lies in the liberation of the Iraqi people ... our world more secure.

No mention is made of the civilian casualties, but rather we are positioned as bringing aid:

Sir Galahad [the ship] is loaded with tons of supplies; the oil for food programme will re-start ... we will affirm Iraq's territorial integrity ... so we must prosecute military victory with utmost vigour ... the campaign has targeted, very specifically, military command and control, not the civilian population.

The damage to civilians is omitted, as if they are an inevitable sacrifice. The ship's name constructs an image of the knightly, courtly conduct of Arthurian legend and ordinary Iraqis as fair damsels in distress yearning for rescue from the dragon. That idealised, rescuing mindset is expanded as the president describes:

Together to make the world more peaceful ... to make our respective nations and all the free nations of the world more secure ... to free the Iraqi people ... British, American, Australian, Polish and other coalition troops are sharing the duties of this war.

2. Justifiably attacking—deservedly attacked
This position follows logically from our quest to bring peace and freedom, and leads to:

> The coalition's professionalism and integrity stands in sharp contrast to the brutality of Saddam's regime ... this is a regime that has brutalised its people for well over two decades ... I am not surprised he is committing crimes against our soldiers ... I am not surprised that regular army forces are trying to desert but get blown away by fellow Iraqi citizens ... if he uses WMD that will just prove our case and we will deal with it.

There is no direct mention of how it would be dealt with, but, presumably, it would be by bigger WMD. This chilling statement is isolated from any consideration of the thousands who would die on both sides—his usage would merely prove we are right, and our usage merely provide victory; all else becomes irrelevant. The effects of Western sanctions go unacknowledged, as we are needed

> ... to bring a better future to the Iraqi people. 400,000 Iraqi children under five have died of malnutrition and disease because of the nature of the regime.

There are no other options than military action because diplomacy could not work:

> If we wanted to make a stand against the dominant security threat of our time, the combination of WMD in the hands of unstable, repressive states and terrorist groups we had to act. We tried to make the diplomatic process work, but we weren't able to do so.

However, this action will lead to a more peaceful world. The Prime Minister comments on the professionalism of our soldiers:

> ... their skill and bravery, stands in sharp contrast to the brutality of Saddam's regime. Day by day we have seen the reality of Saddam's regime—his thugs prepared to kill their own people; the parading of prisoners of war; and now, the release of those pictures of executed British soldiers. If anyone needed any further evidence of the depravity of Saddam's regime, this atrocity proves it. It is yet one more flagrant breach of all the proper conventions of war.

We have learnt to be proud, and responsible for good, and it is *they* who have been taught to hate us, they who are guilty, they who are violating obligations, and they who are responsible for evil. Sadly, later reportage was to show that both sides exercised depravity. This was a blow to our image of ourselves as innocent, put upon, but obliged.

3. With one voice—with one reply

The unspoken implication is that if we are divided, we may fall. Therefore differences have to be absolutely disavowed. In habitually employing the rhetorical device of repeating the initial phrase, '*we're working together*' the President is saying that '*working together*' is what matters to the exclusion of anything else. If united we stand, we will prevail. The vital point is that liberty is all we have ever desired.

> We are acting together to make the world more peaceful ... for nearly a century we have been allies in the defence of liberty and opposed all the great threats to peace and security in the world ... our resolve is firm ... however long it takes, the Iraqi people have got to know they will be liberated ... the UN will endorse the post-conflict administration.

Here 'Our History' is used to place this current action within a single time frame; it has always been so and thus it will always be.

President Bush does not respond directly to a question from a journalist asking why he had not received the support of past firm allies. Instead, he emphasises the grandiosity of the coalition and the dominance of the threat posed by WMD.

> We have a vast coalition ... People hesitate before committing to conflict and war ... the diplomatic process is unable to work against the dominant threat of our time: WMD in the hands of unstable, repressive states and terrorist groups ... if we want to make a stand we have to act.

Any self-doubt is also silenced:

> I have no doubt that we are doing the right thing, I have no doubt that our cause is just and I have no doubt that, were we to walk away from this conflict at this time, we would be doing a huge disservice to future generations.

Tony Blair is willing to admit a more complex picture:

> Yes, there are countries that disagree with what we are doing. I mean there's no point in hiding it ... I hear people constantly say to me, Europe is against what you're doing. That is not true. There is a part of Europe that is against what we are doing. There are many existing members of the European Union, and virtually all the new members of the European Union, that strongly support what we are doing. So there is a division, but we have many allies.

4. Superior, magnificently protecting liberator—Compliantly, gratefully, submissively liberated
There is no in-depth exploration of what 'liberation' means and this speech appears to define it in terms of an absence of threat to us, and encouraging compliance across the world.

> The grip of terror around the throats of the Iraqi people is being loosened. If the world walks away from the security threat facing us, and if we back down and take no action against Saddam, think of the signal that would have [sic] sent right across the world to every brutal dictator, to every terrorist group.

'Freedom' is similarly idealised, remaining a vague term that also requires no definition beyond removal of the previous regime.

5. Triumphant heroic leaders of men—deprived, needy, painlessly grateful at no cost

> In just under a week into this conflict, let me restate our compete and total resolve ... in less than a week we have secured the southern oil fields and facilities and so protected that resource and wealth for the Iraqi people and avoided ecological disaster ... our forces are now within 50 miles of Baghdad ... they've paved the way for humanitarian aid to flow into the country ... the vast majority of ordinary Iraqi people are desperate for a better and different future, for Iraq to be free ... the day of your freedom draws near.

The expectation is that the Iraqi people will now be gratefully free to enjoy our aid to them and to develop civilisation. The Prime Minister explains that he understands why people hesitate before committing to conflict and to war. For the only time in the Camp David speech, everyone is included in the concept that war is a brutal and bloody business, but this was the price that had to be paid as the only way to take a stand against the dominant security threat of our time. Allied weapons of mass destruction do not need mentioning, as we are obviously stable, open and democratic.

The President assures that world that:

> Iraq's greatest long-term need is a representative government that protects the rights of all Iraqis. The form of this government will be chosen by the Iraqi people, not imposed by outsiders. And the Prime Minister and I are confident that a free Iraq will be a successful nation.

At the prospect of a peace that appears spontaneous and inevitabe, hopeful ripples are felt throughout '*the entire Middle East*'. For the Prime Minister, a little more is required for this to happen. He reverts to the British government's previous, but unsuccessful, (having failed to secure a second UN resolution prior to declaring war) aim of involving the United Nations, describing working with the UN to affirm Iraq's territorial integrity and endorse an appropriate post-conflict administration for Iraq. A number of speculative interpretations are possible regarding this intention. Does this reflect a desire for the arms of globalisation to extend into Iraq, or merely a recognition that constructing peace is something more than an absence of threat, and is simply not a task for the Heads of State who are leading the cavalry charge to war?

The Prime Minister points out that George Bush is the first President to publicly commit to a two-state solution between Israel and Palestine, and Bush, according with a view of the responsibilities of the West to the Middle East, commits both countries to implementing that solution. Blair continues:

We will carry on until the job is done … we will achieve our objectives.

The President echoes this:

I urge those Iraqi generals who have any doubt of our word to be careful, because we'll keep our word. We're going to keep our word to the Iraqi people and we'll keep our word to those war criminals in Iraq.

So, whereas *we* are resolved, the regime is hardened and desperate. The only path left leads to Iraqi defeat. The horror of what they are doing is not only minimised, it is presented as humanitarian. Peace is presented as a prospect that will appear automatically. 'Peace' does not require defining and can be left vague because what is actually meant by the word 'peace' in this context is an absence of threat to 'us' through 'them' being passively compliant. Sadly, and perhaps inevitably, in Iraq, the conflict has become protracted—a war of dominance—as the criminality, aggression and anarchy has not been crushed by military might and coercion. Attack through 'shock and awe' did not construct the peace, and by minimising the options available to adversaries, has exacerbated small-scale, fragmented terrorism. Using our power to humiliate and denigrate merely produced seething resentment, leading to further violations of human respect, in a mutual spiral of fear and hatred.

With one voice

Excerpts from the anniversary speeches of March[3] and May[4] 2006 show that their

---

3. 'Blair takes on war critics' http://news.bbc.co.uk/1/hi/uk_politics/4827680.stm Accessed 21 March 2006. See also http://www.number-10.gov.uk/output/Page9245.asp. 'Blair to tough …

mindset has changed little. In a speech to the Australian Parliament, the Prime Minister stated:

> If we want to secure our way of life, there's no alternative but to fight for it … We must reject the thought that somehow we are the authors of our own distress, that if only we altered this decision or that, this extremism would fade away.

'Somehow', here implies that any alternatives were inconceivable, and our stance singular, exclusive, unquestionably inevitable and righteous. We must reject the notion that we are in any way culpable for outraged responses by insurgents and terrorists to our actions or that what we did cost us dearly. This is a position of 'dread' in which the Prime Minister has to silence his own doubts by seeing his actions as a moral imperative that called out to an admiring and grateful world.

> These are not Western ethics but universal ones which should be the right of the 'global citizen' … this is not a clash between civilisations. This is a clash about civilisation … the struggle in our world today, therefore, is not just about security. It is a struggle about values and about modernity, whether to be at ease with it, or enraged.

Yet again, this moral high ground distinguishes us from the enemy.

> The only way to win is to recognise this phenomenon as a global ideology, to see all the areas where it operates and to defeat it by values and ideas set in opposition to those of the terrorists.

Those who fail to see the honour in our actions do not make sense; The Prime Minister is bewildered by the '*madness of anti-American feelings in Europe*'. We must soldier on and stick doggedly to our course, neutralising any urges to reconsider:

> If the going gets tough, we tough it out …This is not a time to walk away but to have the courage to see it through.

Pausing to re-consider who is the real enemy:

> We are active … [contrasted with] … the benign inactivity of those who say that intervention is wrong.

… it out on Iraq'. http://news.bbc.co.uk/1/hi/world/asia-pacific/4848278.stm   Accessed 27 March 2006.

4. 'Bush and Blair admit Iraq errors' http://news.bbc.co.uk/1/hi/world/americas/5016548.stm Accessed 27 March 2006. See also http://www.number-10.gov.uk/output/Page9549.asp

How wars attract this narcissism, which compels their proponents to ward off any wider range of thinking, is further revealed by the contrast in actions and responses the two world leaders consider in relation to two different situations. The press and public responded seriously to the material we will now examine— taken from a transcript of an unguarded conversation between Mr Bush and Mr Blair at the G8 Conference in Russia (July 2006).[5] This material was regarded as honest and, therefore more revealing, because it was not staged for the public as neither leader realised they were being overheard. In the absence of rhetoric, were different positions revealed? The transcript shows an informal, jovial and friendly relationship.

In the first topic, the President came over as more open minded as he made a realistic appraisal of a situation, attempted to gather allies, stated his opposition and then moved on. The reciprocal role might be described as *protesting but letting go* in relation to *expecting to hear with own agency acknowledged.* Mr Bush, when discussing an issue to do with trade, accepted Mr Blair's point that they may not be able to move things forward and acknowledged that he can nevertheless respond by expressing his opposition. He then let the topic go.

With the second topic—Israel's bombing of Lebanon—there was a return to positions adopted for the Iraq War. The solution, from the President's point of view, was obvious and simple; for Israel '*To stop Hezbollah doing this shit*'. The Prime Minister tried to offer a wider approach through volunteering to prepare the way for a US diplomatic move, whilst recognising the weakness of the position of the Secretary General of the United Nations. As with Iraq, for the President the answer was the same; use of superior force in the belief that people can be bombed into neutralised compliance and an agreement with his world-view. Although initially the Prime Minister preferred a wider diplomatic response, when facing the option of righteous attack, he abandoned a more troublesome and patient path.

There is a joint view in all the speeches that, as the US/UK knows best, it is our duty to promote our interests and exercise global leadership. We must shape circumstances before the crises emerge, meet threats before they become dire. This view is encouraged by the aforementioned Project for the New American Century. Its idealism feeds a sense of urgency that reduces the opportunities for rational doubt that would allow consideration of a more flexible range of possibilities.

Both Heads of State appear to believe their own rhetoric. Their sense of destiny fosters grandiosity and narcissism. They appear shameless. In a state of cognitive dissonance, their determination works against the spirit of democracy. Baumeister and Zhang (2006) describe how people who depend on being seen to be successful can become ever more entrapped in a losing position and procedure. They increasingly expend resources in the belief that their effort will eventfully

5. Bush and Blair's unguarded chat http://news.bbc.co.uk/1/hi/world/americas/5188258.stm Accessed 18 July 2006.

force a win instead of considering that they might have made mistakes and therefore search for alternative approaches. 'The motivation [is] to maintain and enhance favourable views of self.' Admitting an unwise decision threatens such views.

The context to the Iraq war and the Anglo-American alliance was the trauma and shock to the Western psyche of the terrorist attacks on the United States in September 2001. A trauma-based politics took hold in which further diplomacy was described as, at best, impotent and, at worst, colluding with terrorists and rogue national states in possession of weapons of mass destruction. Decisive war action was portrayed as transformative with gains in freedom and justice that would bring benefits in the Middle East and beyond.

Conclusions

This analysis has offered the opportunity to draw out the defining and hidden voices and positions in the speeches. The speeches quoted and analysed merge many local and specific threats and challenges to peace into one global and general challenge. The threat is generalised and branded as global terrorism. In being non-specific it is more easily opposed in simple psychological terms which bypass the possibility of, or need for, a more detailed, versatile and subtle analysis. In particular, the notion of an 'axis of evil' reduces a plurality of conflicts and threats to one abstracted enemy. This denial of differences within the enemy is matched by a collusive denial of difference between Bush and Blair themselves. In the process, any possibilities of an emerging democracy of international politics is reduced.

Without too much simplification, the Bush–Blair approach might be described as the 'old psychology of war and peace'. This 'old psychology' is closely mirrored by many of the nations or groups declared as the 'global enemy'. It is a psychology of 'us or them' centred upon a linear path to victory or defeat. Analysis highlights the polarised either-or and if-then quality of the thinking in the speeches. The relational thinking seems to be: if victory, then freedom and prosperity; either complete victory and justice, or total defeat and evil.

A newer, more relational, psychological approach to war and peace may yet emerge, evident in some collaborative NGO thinking and in international organisations and efforts at global governance. It is implied in the Charter of the United Nations and is one thread in the tradition of diplomacy. A more relationally complex approach to war and peace making may well have as many military exponents as peace activists. Generals and soldiers may be less driven by shameless narcissism and grandiosity than their political companions or paymasters. In their speeches, Bush and Blair derided such thinking as soft, weak and giving comfort to the enemy.

The Bush–Blair speeches, despite their speakers' different levels of sophistication and rhetorical styles, share a powerful tendency to rely on the win–lose psychology of war. They offer a narrow psychology of victory or defeat. This victor's psychology (Richmond, 2005), which ignores the human, environmental and economic costs of war and the complexities of securing a post-war peace, has been tragically exposed and extensively covered by commentators in international relations and diplomacy. The victor's dilemma of win or lose bears close similarity to elements in the classification of narcissistic personality disorder[6] (if we are single-minded, indestructible and powerful we will be triumphant and admired; if we show weakness and suffering we will be humiliated and destroyed and be distracted). As a set, the speeches of Bush and Blair address the world with a personalised view of international relations and a strategy justified by inner conviction in search of admiration in an ideal world— driven by what Socrates would describe as 'thymos' or spiritedness.

To some readers this chapter may seem to have been describing the obvious. Teasing out the old psychology of war from the Bush–Blair speeches does a number of things. It changes the focus away from the personalities of Bush and Blair, their unequal power relationship, the merits of the truth about claims of weapons of mass destruction, and it turns attention to the psychology of a 'victor's' war. By thinking with a more relational and psychological subtlety there is a challenge to look at our collective participation in a certain mindset of war victory and the deep levels of cultural spin on which a simple psychology of war relies. It is hoped that links to more relationally effective and less harmful psychological responses can be constructed within both the mass politics and the elite politics of global leadership. It may make it easier for ordinary people and elected politicians to *not* join the win–lose mentality of their leaders and the inevitable victor's dilemma. This chapter stops at an important, but fuzzy, point. How a more complex psychology would appear is likely to be varied, subtle, and responsive to the relational context—and more than likely, explicitly concerned with conflict resolution.

There is an interesting psychological parallel between this challenge to show resolve and take up the fight, to face the threat head on, with the everyday threats and challenges we experience as individuals. We use general terms of resolve such as 'pull your self together', or 'blame so and so'. As experience has so eloquently shown us that exhortation, retaliation, or grandiose dreams don't seem to work to solve individual psychological problems, it would be surprising to see them work at the massively more complex level of international relations.

---

6. 'Narcissism' as a term existed before it was appropriated by the *Diagnostic and Statistical Manual* (DSM). CAT has been critical of the DSM–IV (APA, 2000) as reductive, non-dialogic and of poor value as a clinical tool.

CHAPTER 8

Power, Illusion and Control:
Families, states and conflict

RON ROBERTS

The statesmen of the world who boast and threaten that they have doomsday weapons are far more dangerous and far more estranged from reality than many of the people on whom the label psychotic is affixed. (Laing, 1965a, p.12)

The standard view of how the system works is at serious odds with reality. (Herman & Chomsky, 1994, xi)

Introduction

The postmodern society of rich Western countries envelops us in a paradoxical linguistic new world where the struggle for meaning is waged against a system of represented social relationships stripped bare of the struggle for power between oppressed and oppressor. Of course, the old inequalities of power remain—arguably in the most brutal form for more than half a century. We debate post-feminism in a world in which women vie to sell their bodies in the global multimedia sex and pornography market; we speak of a post-industrial world where inequalities in wealth and death are manufactured with celebrity endorsement, precision marketed and cheap (and dangerous) industrial production has been resized and relocated to those corners of the earth where the majority of the planet's inhabitants actually reside—the developing, or is that the underdeveloped, world?

Thus it is that we live in a world of illusions—a manufactured non-sanity of runaway consumption, financed by international capital and predicated on the control of energy resources, through military force, by the world's remaining superpower—the United States: aided and willingly abetted by the United Kingdom and a cavalcade of client states. Together, they constitute a coalition of the willing, the fearful and the forced, acting as one to ensure a healthy climate for transnational corporations to conduct their business (Chomsky, 1999a). This view, familiar perhaps to intellectual dissidents and those at the sharp end of Western practice, has not been widely disseminated in the Western media and, consequently, is largely absent from popular discourse and understanding. The failure to represent this perspective in the mainstream can be attributed to the operation of one simple factor—power.

This chapter seeks to cast light on the operations through which power functions to manufacture the confused psychological realities, which are both the by-product of the modern age and the prerequisite for its continuation. This task recognises that international relations shape our experience of the world and influence our individual psychology. The task will involve examining the ideas of both Laing and Chomsky and the relations these have to each other. Considered together their work provides a clinical dissection of how power operates in various domains so as to construct our social, economic, political and psychological realities.

In Laing's case, the analysis of power was directed to understanding the interpersonal and intrapersonal (intrapsychic) operations on our experience—particularly as they occurred in the micro-social context of the family, though understood as applicable to other social institutions (e.g. the army, the nation), and carrying historic repercussions (see Laing, 1967, 1968, 1971). In contrast, Chomsky's work examines the macro-social context of international relations, politics and the media to unravel the workings of power, chiefly US power, on the global stage. Here in its most naked form (summoned at the behest of the elites who control international capital), military force, or the threat of it, is used to terrorise, punish and enslave those who perceive as subservience, economic dependency and imperialism, the benefits of what our politicians and media commentators call democracy. In a calculus of misery, death and suffering, Chomsky's writings have catalogued the many 'benefits' which this exported democracy has brought to the citizens of Latin America (e.g. Chomsky, 1992; Herman & Chomsky, 1994), the Middle East (e.g. Chomsky, 1999b), the Balkans (Chomsky, 1999a) and Southeast Asia (e.g. Herman & Chomsky, 1994; Chomsky, 1967). Closer to home, in its host environment, a more subtle manifestation of power prevails, working through a loyal media to channel thought within acceptable boundaries and thereby manufacture political obedience and consent (Chomsky, 1989, 2003a; Herman & Chomsky, 1994).

It is argued here that Laing's unravelling of family dynamics, alongside Chomsky's functional analysis of international power relations, reveals to us the origins of the irrationality underlying the 'total world system' (Laing, 1968), that threats, violence and deceit underlie the fabric of consensual reality, and that the operations of power in the construction of our 'internal' mental life mirror those operations used to fashion the external world. The major illusions underpinning the reality and experience of Westerners, the operations by which they are maintained, the functional role which these serve in society and the nature of the institutional purveyors of these illusions will be examined in what follows.

Illusions

In a recent work, Chomsky (2004) describes the guiding principle behind imperial action in the world (and permissible discourse dealing with this), as one so obviously true that it is 'often considered unnecessary to formulate' (p. 42). This principle holds that the imperial power (the US and/or UK) is the vanguard of history, motivated solely by noble intent, righteously intervening in the world to bring justice, stability, liberty and democracy to the darker uncivilised corners of the earth. Whilst postmodern challenges to the idea of an inherent direction to history may have sufficed to curtail vulgar Marxist assertions of the inevitability of revolution, they have fuelled Western reactionary opinion with an overwhelming sense of urgency. Faced with climatic change, dwindling oil supplies, and the consequent reduced possibilities for centralised power, the imperial quest must now assume greater importance lest any reduction in Western power leaves the floodgates open to the tides of chaos which threaten to overwhelm our civilisation. So simply put—we are the benevolent agents of good, forever on guard against malevolent others who threaten our way of life. It is *we* who are good, and *they* who are evil. And what is so bad about them, the opponents of Western intervention and influence? If a thorough examination of the historical record is anything to go by, it would seem to be *their* desire for independence and national self-determination that arouses our displeasure. One important but little mentioned factor behind the invasion of Iraq was the Iraqi regime's move from the dollar to the euro as the currency for oil transactions. Such a move could, in principle, have started an international stampede amongst OPEC countries that would have seriously weakened Washington. The war saw the new US-favoured Government in Iraq revert back to the dollar (Clark, 2004). The ongoing threats against Iran must also be understood, at least in part, against its intentions to open an energy market in euros in the near future.

Laing wrote extensively on the means by which we arrive at notions of 'them' and 'us'—whether as family member, political ideologue, soldier or national citizen. These are complex abstractions whereby group identity emerges as the product of a set of reciprocal internalisations of each by each other. Thus we all belong in the same family/group/nation because we believe that we all share the same set of values and beliefs, which includes our beliefs about our own identity. Of particular interest in the present context, Laing argues that the precondition for the stability of this *nexus* of relationships is the generation of terror and violence within the group. Only then, as a consequence of such destructive action on our experience, are we ripe for the destruction of others. This usually becomes apparent only when the set of reciprocal internalisations producing stability and consensus breaks down and 'you' become no longer one of 'us' and therefore subject to whatever sanctions 'we' must apply to uphold our identity. Thus;

> If our experience is destroyed, our behaviour will be destructive … Normal men have killed perhaps 100,000,000 of their fellow normal men in the last fifty years (Laing, 1967, p. 24).[1]

The numbers of such killings by 'normal men' which have arisen directly or indirectly from the complicity of US 'peacemakers' in Washington make for disturbing reading. Consider just a few of the locations where US action has been felt. In Guatemala around 200,000 people were killed by the US-backed counter-insurgency campaign and its death squads (Chomsky, 2003a, p. 6), in Nicaragua 40,000 were killed by the US-backed contras. Death squads in El Salvador and in Honduras saw another 75,000 and 10,000 respectively shuffled from their mortal coils (Chomsky, 2003a, footnote 13). In Vietnam, Laos, and Cambodia (the so-called Indo-China wars) upwards of 4 million people were killed (Chomsky, 2003a, p. 90), a figure which includes approximately 750,000 deaths attributed to the Khmer Rouge (Herman & Chomsky, 1994, pp. 383–384) whose emergence and campaign of slaughter, subsequent to the illegal bombing initiated by Kissinger and Nixon, did not preclude it from later enjoying the backing of the US and UK Governments at the United Nations. Following the US-backed military coup in 1965 and installation of Suharto as President, the Indonesian army killed 700,000 people followed, in the late 1990s, by another 200,000 people in East Timor, all with the diplomatic and military support of the US and UK (Chomsky, 2004, p. 53). To these figures we can now add the recent estimates of 1.8 million deaths as a result of the sanctions and ongoing war in Iraq (Roberts et al., 2004), not to mention the enormous numbers of tortured and displaced people resulting from US attempts to ensure democracy—for example in South Vietnam 8 million people were forcibly displaced (Chomsky, 2003a, footnote 52), in Columbia 2.7 million (Chomsky, 2004, p. 52), and in Kosovo 350,000 (Chomsky, 1999a, p. 16). And in passing, lest one should think that the UK has a more honourable record in the international arena, analysis of declassified UK government records by Mark Curtis (2003, 2004) should suffice to set the record straight. Curtis estimates that the UK has had direct responsibility for between 4 and 6 million deaths in conflicts since the end of the Second World War. As we remember the Holocaust 60 years on, it seems that the principal lesson which the current imperial powers have taken on board is to make sure they hold on to power.

---

1. Estimates for the total number of deaths in the twentieth century due to organised violence range from 167–188 million (Ferguson, 2006).

The maintenance of illusion

It is evident that for this catalogue of horror to have somehow eluded one's attention, and for our belief in Western 'goodness' to have survived relatively intact, significant forces must be operating to maintain the denial of reality. Chomsky (2004) moves into psychological territory in identifying several core mental mechanisms responsible for sending information 'down the memory hole', as he puts it. To Orwell's 'double think' he adds 'loyalty to power', 'denial syndrome' and 'intentional ignorance'. While Sartre and Laing may have used the concept of 'bad faith' to explain all of these phenomenon, bar loyalty to power, Chomsky's terms are additionally useful inasmuch as they make explicit reference to the operation of these processes in subservience to violent political power. They are the building blocks of, what Marx described as, 'mystification', a concept invaluable to Laing (1965b) in his elucidation of family systems.

> This entails the substitution of false for true constructions of what is being experienced, being done (praxis), or going on (process), and the substitution of false issues for the actual issues … If we detect mystification, we are alerted to the presence of a conflict of some kind that is being evaded. The mystified person, in so far as he has been mystified, is unable to see the authentic conflict … He may experience false peace, false calm, or inauthentic conflict and confusion over false issues. (p. 344–345)

For Laing, as for Marx, the function of this trickery was clear—to enable

> … a plausible misrepresentation of what is going on (process) or what is being done (praxis) in the service of the interests of one socioeconomic class (the exploiters) over or against another class (the exploited). (Laing, 1965b, p. 343)

Intentional ignorance is of specific interest, a term which ably captures both the intentions of the relevant authorities to instil ignorance in the population, and the resulting intentions of people to maintain their own psychological comfort in ignorance. Furthermore, by never actually talking about these matters, the processes of intentional ignorance in effect hide all traces of the intent to forget, thus wiping their existence from conscious thought in a meta-level of forgotten thoughts. So we come not to know what it is that we have forgotten we ever knew. In this state of enlightenment we are permitted to pronounce on our free will, but such are the means by which our own thoughts directly mirror the will and intentions of outside agents. Laing (1971) considered these matters in *The Politics of the Family*. For example:

It is mandatory to project bad onto the Enemy, whoever they may be; and it is *mandatory* to deny that this is a projection. (Laing, 1971, p .92)

And again:

We at this moment may not know we have rules against knowing about certain rules. (Laing, 1971, p. 100)

No wonder that Laing questioned whether much of what we customarily feel is a result of having been hypnotised to feel it. Experience, he argued, is normalised through the operation of a whole host of, what are usually described psychoanalytically as, defence mechanisms—these comprise such actions as denial, splitting, projection, introjection, repression, rationalisation etc. plus rules against acknowledging that we are in fact doing these things. In discussion with Richard Evans, Laing argued that these systems and structures of communication, underpinning as he put it 'a multitiered system of lies' (Evans, 1976, p. 66), fitted perfectly well the day-to-day functioning of political elites—as exemplified in the Watergate affair, for example. Thus, like Chomsky, he was clear that such defences are not merely defences for us but defences for powerful elites to continue with business as usual. In domestic and international politics, reality is what is believed, not what is known. One is forever confronted with the façade of plausible deniability behind which truth lies who knows where? Behind the mirror of illusion is the concealment of power. These distortions of our psychological reality mean that we seldom get to ask the most obvious questions about what is going on around us. As an example, there has been much speculation, in Government, the media, and academia about how best to combat the threat of terrorism. However, a very obvious, significant step never gets considered in these deliberations:

Everyone's worried about stopping terrorism. Well there's a really easy way: Stop participating in it. (Chomsky, 2003b, p. 141)

Chomsky reminds us that it is not simply a matter of psychological processes, operating independently of the social and economic realities in our midst, that are responsible for this onslaught on truth;

Throughout the modern period, measures to control 'the public mind' have been employed to enhance the natural pressures of the 'free market', the domestic counterpart to intervention in the global system. (Chomsky, 1989, p. 31)

Repression always has functional significance—whether on the personal or political stage—and the mainstream press are one of the principal means by which the public mind is controlled. In both *Manufacturing Consent* (Herman &

Chomsky, 1994) and *Necessary Illusions* (Chomsky, 1989) the workings of a 'propaganda model' are explored, explaining how 'totalitarian thought control' is maintained by self-confessed 'free agents' of the press and an elite intellectual culture following an agenda loyal to corporate business interests. Like intentional ignorance, 'loyalty to power' may operate on different levels. It describes the functional workings of the press as a corporate institution selling readers of different social groupings to the markets controlled by other corporations. Equally, it applies to the motivations of individuals who are selected, or self-selected, to perform their 'duties' as reporters of events deemed permissible to discuss within the system. At the level of the individual these motivations may, or may not, be conscious. The rewards for such loyalty can be great, one reason why Chomsky believes that, if you find yourself being accepted in elite company, it probably means you're doing something wrong! Chomsky usually reserves discussion of double-think to the willed intentions of the elite, though he is not unaware that the consequences of these intentions are played out in our own obedient psychology. Compare the following:

> Throughout history, aggressive and provocative measures have been justified in terms of defence against merciless foes; in Kennedy's case, defence against what he termed 'the monolithic and ruthless conspiracy' dedicated to world conquest. (Chomsky, 2004, p. 225)

In such forms have US ruling elites always portrayed the 'enemy', communist or not. Compare this with a presidential address at West Point military academy:

> The plan is for the United States to rule the world ... it calls for the US to maintain its overwhelming superiority and prevent new rivals from rising up and challenging it on the world stage ... It says, not that the US must be more powerful, but that it must be absolutely powerful. (Quoted in Ahmed, 2003, p. 17)

Evidently the idea of world conquest lies close to the heart of some people. Rather than come clean on this to the public—not considered a good idea—better to impugn these motives to others (projection) and use these projected motives to justify one's own aggression against the enemy in order to protect and defend our interests. In this way the invasion of South Vietnam by US forces, for example, becomes an act of defence, the invasion of Iraq an act of liberation—in fact all such acts of naked aggression by US and UK forces are rendered invisible—as being conducted by the benign and merciful Anglo-American alliance. Employing a psychoanalytic perspective, perhaps the nation states of the US/UK have been internalised by their populations as parental figures who must undertake stern action in the best interests of the wider family of nations. They may even have to destroy in order to save and protect the greater good. They may have to defy the

United Nations and invade Iraq in order to uphold the 'principles of the United Nations': *ipso facto*, we cannot be malign, because *we* would never do bad things. Only *they* would. *We* are trustworthy, *they* are not. *Our* sources are reliable *theirs* are not. In Bush's words 'We are good, they are evil'.

In fact the more outlandish the US/UK alliance's actions are, the more psychologically paralysed the population becomes, unable to build bridges between their own identity and the actions of the nation state carried out in their name. Anyone who seriously questions the basic 'goodness' of the British character for instance may well find themselves out on a limb, psychologically speaking. The splitting between the good *us* and the bad *them* can be seen then to set in motion an elaborate public fantasy system to justify continued aggression. In *Sanity, Madness and the Family* (Laing & Esterson, 1964) and in Schatzman's *Soul Murder* (1973) (principally Laing's work: see Mullan, 1995) such public fantasy systems operate to curtail and restrict the independence of particular family members who threaten to blow open the machinations of family life. As we embark once more on the 'War against Terror' (recall the prior instalment, courtesy of President Reagan in Latin America, now obliterated from memory), the war without end, 'the ongoing war' of the Bush/Blair *folie á deux,* it is important to realise that, like the tangled wars within the family, this one too is fought against those who seek (national) independence and self-determination.

Chomsky describes the efforts to maintain the current fictions shielding us from reality as 'thought control'. Making assertions of thought control in the real world can be dangerous, since it may attract psychiatric attributions of delusional ideation, particularly if one speaks of thoughts being broadcast into one's head, by radio waves for instance. But, of course, it is not a question of whether others really are trying to control and direct our thoughts—they are—it is rather a question of how distressed we are when we make public our realisation of this. A person who appears in a state of great distress over the lack of control they have over their own thoughts may, in one sense, be considerably more in touch with reality than another, not so distressed person, who appears oblivious to the fact that this kind of thing is going on all the time. Accordingly, the notion of thought control can be viewed either as a symptom of mental illness or as a strategy of power. Which of these we choose to endorse perhaps says something about the level to which we have internalised society's rules on permissible thinking, and how we have managed to deal with the prevailing realities so far.

That such a matter of choice is possible at all is surely no coincidence. To unravel this further, an authentic behavioural science would need to unearth the history of ideas of thought control and its incorporation into a system of policing thinking—a history of the origins of the 'thought police' no less. Throughout the world the mental health system has always been used to patrol internal dissidence. We do not stand apart from the Soviet Union in this respect—it is not that *they* are repressive whilst *we* are humane and benign. The mental health system is subservient to the 'great game'—the power play of politics—Soviet dissidents knew this well—but we too have our own dissidents. Just as citizens of the USSR and Maoist China were subject to suitable 'education' about the need to 'reform' the malcontents in their societies, we have our own 'public relations' system embodied in institutional psychiatry. And 'public relations' is after all just another term for propaganda (Curtis, 2002). The threat of mental illness is the sword of Damocles hanging over all our heads. The politics of mental health have always been inseparable from the power-play politics of the domestic and international arena.

Reclaiming reality

Each of us is living in a society that has a vested interest in our alienation from reality and the indoctrination of new recruits into the collective fantasy of Western benevolence. The struggle to regain our own thoughts is a political struggle in the fullest sense. We need to wake up from this dream world urgently, and win the struggle within ourselves. In Orwell's *1984*, Winston Smith finally loved Big Brother. We must avoid that fate. Discerning what is actually going on from what we are told is going on will not be easy; such is our present state of alienation. The possibility of an authentic mode of being was a central issue for Laing— similarly for Chomsky, the concern is how to remain free from the imposition of a mentality imposed by propaganda emanating from a dysfunctional social system:

> Citizens of the democratic societies should undertake a course of intellectual self-defense to protect themselves from manipulation and control. (Chomsky, 1989, p. viii)

The struggle for people in the West today, to reclaim some credible version of the truth behind the operation of our modern societies, is vital. It is time for the behavioural sciences to play their part in this and to aid what Chomsky calls the second great superpower—public opinion. To do this, exposing the lies and hidden intentions of government (Chomsky, 1967) must assume a higher priority. In the modern age the survival of the human species is under threat from induced climate change and human folly in the pursuit of greed. We should not underestimate the risk, nor presuppose that our political leaders will come to their senses. In the US and UK our peaceful and benevolent governments are the world leaders in disregarding international law, promoting mass murder and accruing and developing armouries of devastating biological, chemical and nuclear weapons. They have made it clear that the risks these pose are, to them, inconsequential. Their fundamental operating principle as Chomsky tells us, is that

> Hegemony is more important than survival. (Chomsky, 2004, p. 231)

The other human inhabitants of the planet—those on the receiving end of Western 'hospitality and justice' have long known this. For them it is '*not wise to live with illusions*' (Chomsky, 2004, p. 168). We must free ourselves from the imposition of an acquiescent psychology that stems directly from the global dominance of pharmaceutical, petrochemical and other corporations allied to military power and realise, before it is too late, it is not that wise for us either. The twin aims of the power that threatens life on this planet—as Orwell knew,

> ... are to conquer the whole surface of the earth and to extinguish once and for all the possibility of independent thought. (Orwell, 1970, p. 156)

CHAPTER 9

Children and War:
Making sense of Iraq

RON ROBERTS, MAJDA BECIREVIC
AND HARRIET TENENBAUM

There are many kinds of tigers. Some roam the jungle of human desires.
You must learn to conquer the ones within (Author unknown, quoted in
Padel, 2005, p. 123)

The most innocent—those who had nothing to do with whatever distortions,
whatever dislocations led to war—are children, and yet they pay the highest
price. Children are least able to defend themselves against aggression, and
they suffer the most both physically and psychologically. (Olara Otunnu,
UN Under-Secretary-General, 2002)

Introduction

In this chapter we present the results of an empirical study into children's and
early adolescents' reasoning about the Iraq War and their emotional reactions to
it. We examine children in two countries, the UK and Bosnia. The UK has not
experienced war on its soil during the lifetime of the children interviewed. The
situation for Bosnian children is different, following three years of warfare in the
1990s (1992–1995). This crucial difference, we believe, enables us to develop a
deeper understanding, not only of how children's reasoning is related to the socio-
cultural context in which they live, but to the processes by which social
representations of war are taken up and circulated in a society. For a more detailed
discussion of the theory of social representations, see Moscovici & Duveen (2000).

We believe that it is also important to gather the views of children because,
all too frequently, it is they who shoulder the burden of modern warfare, since

civilians are the principal victims rather than military personnel. Despite the targeting of civilians being designated a war crime, the proportion of civilians killed in conflicts has risen steadily throughout the past century (Ferguson, 2006), so that now, some 80–90 per cent of casualties are non-combatants, most of them children and women (Williams, 2006). In the decade between 1993 and 2003 approximately two million children were killed and a further six million injured or permanently disabled in war zones (Williams, 2006). Iraq—a country with a young population, where almost two-fifths are below 15 years of age (United Nations Development Programme (UNDP), 2005)—has also seen large numbers of its young people lose their lives as a direct result of the war. According to the Iraq Living Conditions Survey (UNDP, 2005), children below 18 years of age comprise 12 per cent of the war-related deaths in the country. The same survey reports that about 5 per cent of under-fives in the country are currently living in homes damaged by military activity or looting whilst up to 62 per cent can hear shots being fired within the vicinity of their homes several times a week.

Several studies have given us a picture of the psychological effects on children of living in combat zones. These have largely focused on children caught up in the Balkan wars and Middle East conflicts (the Lebanon, Israel, Palestine, Iraq and Afghanistan). In a study of displaced Bosnian children during wartime, the majority had faced multiple traumas: separation from family (91.3 per cent), bereavement (64.2 per cent), direct exposure to war and combat (58.9 per cent) and extreme poverty or deprivation (59.4 per cent). Over 90 per cent of the children experienced significant sadness and over 95 per cent reported high levels of anxiety, with 94 per cent of the sample meeting criteria for post-traumatic stress disorder (PTSD) (Goldstein, Wampler & Wise, 2005). More than three years after the end of the war, the prevalence of PTSD among Bosnian refugee adolescents was still high (62 per cent), with those who had been internally displaced showing higher levels of both PTSD and acculturation problems (Hasanovic, Sinanovic & Pavlovic, 2005). Similarly, in studies of children exposed to war stress in Croatia, higher levels of sadness, fear (Zivcic, 1993), intrusion and avoidance (Kuterovac, Dyregrov & Stuvland, 1994) were found in refugees compared to other children who lived locally.

In the Middle East, studies of pre-school children in the Gaza Strip exposed to day raids and tank shelling by Israeli military revealed elevated emotional and behavioural problems (Thabet, 2006). However, older Palestinian children (aged 12–15 years) exposed to violence have demonstrated fewer behavioral problems than younger children (aged 6–9 years), suggesting that age may serve as a protective factor (Garabino & Kostelney, 1996). A UNICEF study (2003) of children in Iraq who had lived through the first Anglo-American Gulf War in 1991 found extremely high levels of unhappiness and anxiety comparable to that documented in children in Bosnia. Four out of five expressed fear of losing family members through death or separation and three-quarters felt sad or unhappy. The numbers of young children (aged 0–6 years) attending outpatient mental health facilities rose from 200,000 in 1990 to almost half a million by 1998. The report also found that war and sanctions had left the home environments of many children depleted of toys, books and other essentials which provide opportunities for self-directed learning and achievement. The 1991 Gulf War also saw Israeli civilians targeted by Iraqi missiles. Laor, Wolmer and Cohen (2001) found a persistence of post-traumatic symptoms in children five years after the attacks. Again, greater disturbance was found in those who had been displaced as well as those living in less cohesive families. Investigations of children in the Lebanon prior to the recent Israeli attacks, once again, showed that multiple war traumas predicted the development of PTSD (Maksoud & Aber, 1996). Data from Afghanistan, where warfare has been a continuous fact of life for over 20 years, adds to the depressing picture for children in conflict zones. Bhutta (2002) describes some of the consequences. Almost half had lost a parent because of conflict, more than half had witnessed torture or violent death and over 90 per cent expressed a fear of dying in the conflict. The majority of children interviewed (80 per cent) felt they could not cope and that life was not worth living.

Consideration of the effects of war on children, however, is not restricted to mere descriptions of the frequency and nature of the psychopathological categories to which they can be assigned. Young children—chiefly boys—may be drafted into combat themselves. In Rwanda 1,800 children have been held on charges of genocide (Palmer, 2002) and an undisclosed number of children have been detained at Guantánamo Bay (Human Rights Watch, 2004). While boys may be forced into perpetrating violence, the experience of Bosnia and Rwanda shows that girls are vulnerable to sexual assault. For example, according to Human Rights Watch (2003) 80 per cent of the girls who fled Kigali during the genocide in Rwanda had been raped. Children who are at a distance from war may also feel its effects. Indeed, research indicates that the extent to which a child is exposed to the media (print and television) is related to negative emotional reactions as well as post-traumatic stress symptoms (Pfefferbaum et al., 2003). This was true of children living 100 miles from a terrorist event.

Although available data paints a picture of children that have been psychologically traumatised through exposure to war (Jensen & Shaw, 1993), a number of authors also point out that the experience of living through war may not necessarily result in functional impairment (e.g. Sack, Him & Dickason, 1999). In a study of Israeli children, Punamaki (1996) provided evidence that ideological commitment—perhaps by providing a sense of meaning to events—could offer some protection against increased anxiety and insecurity. In a study that explored the role of psychosocial support given to children, Kos and Derviskadic-Jovanovic (1998) argue that the psychological consequences of warfare on children have been overstated and that children's perception and social construction of the world can be accommodated within the normal range of human feelings and memories. They comment:

Positive influences of war on personality, values, relations and behaviour are rarely quoted. The war experience can, however, enrich one's personality as any difficulty in life can. It can encourage empathy and positive social behaviour, enhance coping capacities and social maturity. Many well-adjusted Bosnian adolescents reported that the war experiences, related losses and the adversities of asylum life mobilised their strength and enhanced their personal and moral development. (Ibid., p. 4)

They further note that although much emphasis has been placed on identifying psychopathology, mental health professionals have paid little attention to understanding how children exposed to war actually function—or to how and what they think. Hoffman and Bizman (1996) make a similar point—children are rarely asked for their views. In a noteworthy exception Hakvoort, Hägglund and Oppenheimer (1998) conducted a series of semi-structured interviews with a group of Dutch and Swedish children aged between 7 and 17, eliciting their views on war and peace and strategies to attain peace. Many of the children equated peace with the absence of war and described the process of attaining peace as the responsibility of people in powerful positions who could 'talk with their soldiers' and negotiate with other leaders. What is interesting here is that the children singularly omitted to consider force as a strategy for producing peace—rather they saw peace as arising from social interaction and communication with others. Furthermore, the older children (aged 13–17 years) employed more sophisticated value systems in their conception of peacemaking. In Hakvoort and Hägglund's (2001) terms the older children had shifted from a purely negative conception of peace (i.e. the absence of war) to embrace a wider more positive conception, using ideas such as democracy, equality, tolerance and ending discrimination. Differences between the Swedish and Dutch children were also manifest, Swedish children tended to adopt a more international orientation to peace making (e.g., positive international relations, global meetings, conferences, and trade exchanges), whilst the Dutch children employed more abstract ideals (e.g democracy and equality). Hakvoort and colleagues relate these differences to the distinct historical experiences of war in the two societies.

Hakvoort and Hägglund (2001) contend that children's conceptions of war and reactions to it, like much of children's development, are located within the cultural and historical context in which their life is unfolding. Indeed, a study asking early adolescents (mean age 11.8 years) to list their fears, found that Swedish children were more likely to cite war (26 per cent) as a primary source of fear than were Albanian children (3 per cent) (Tarifa & Kloep, 1996). When asked whether they thought that war might occur in their country, Swedish children were six times more likely to say that they were very afraid that war might happen. In contrast, Albanian children were three and a half times more likely to say that they were not at all afraid of war in their country. Tarifa and Kloep (1996) argue that these findings are especially noteworthy given that Albania is much more likely to experience war than Sweden, given its location and the volatility of political events in the region. Our present study focused on children from Bosnia, which has recently experienced war, and children from the UK, in order to examine the ways in which recent direct experiences of war affect children's reasoning.

Exposure to conflict affects individuals' relationship to war in complex ways. For example, adults in Northern Ireland who were reared during the 'Troubles', and who had direct experience of the violence, rated politics higher in importance than those who did not have direct experience (Whyte & Schermbrucker, 2004). However, in a younger cohort (aged 17 years) those with Troubles-related experience were described as more cynical and less willing to become involved in politics. Direct experience of violence may thus deter some people from direct involvement in the political process.

To bring matters up to date it therefore seems important to ascertain the views of children on the war in Iraq, to explore their views on how to change the world and to establish how they construct the nature, causes and consequences of the war. We seek to locate these views in the context of the children's main sources of information about the war and the national and cultural context from which they view the conflict. What follows is a study that has undertaken to gather the perspectives of children in two countries: the United Kingdom and Bosnia. It is therefore a study of children's common sense about the Iraq war, situated within Moscovici's theory of social representations (Moscovici & Duveen, 2000). We present the preliminary findings from this study below.

The study

Sixty-one children from two age groups were interviewed; 31 from the UK, whose troops are directly involved in the Iraq War, and 30 from a post-conflict society—Bosnia (BiH). Interviews took place in Surrey in the UK during February and March 2006. Interviews in Bosnia were conducted in Sarajevo during December 2005. Responses from the Bosnian interviews given here have been translated from Bosnian into English by one of the authors (MB). The mean age of all children in the younger age groups was 9.88 years (UK=9.93, BiH=9.83) and for the older groups 14.95 years (UK=15.82, BiH=13.97).

The children were asked questions in six areas: (1) what they knew about the war/why they thought the war took place; (2) who was involved; (3) their sources of information about the war; (4) the effects of the war on themselves; (5) how they thought the war would affect the world; and finally, (6) what they would like to see changed in the world. We made developmental comparisons between the children within each country and cross-cultural comparisons across each age group. Here, we principally describe the cross-cultural comparisons that were statistically significant and judged to be thematically important.

Findings

Cross-National comparisons
1. Knowledge about the War/Reasons for War.
Of the younger children from the UK, six (42.9%) described the war in terms of the US/UK coalition acting benevolently (e.g. bringing democracy to Iraq, preventing Saddam Hussein from attacking Iraqis). One girl, aged twelve, remarked:

> Well that Saddam Hussein had weapons of mass destruction and he was killing all his people—he was like a dictator and the Americans went in and the British went in with them and tried to stop it.

None of the children from Bosnia described the war in these terms. The Bosnian children were, however, significantly more likely to describe the war in terms of people being killed or injured (N=8: 53.3%), terms not used by any of the UK children. Amongst the older children a noticeable difference was that none of the UK sample described the US/UK coalition as responsible for the war whereas eight (53.3%) of the Bosnian children did. In the words of one fourteen-year-old Bosnian boy:

> Oil, money. America wants to be powerful. Oil is the basis of that war. America wants it, and Iraq doesn't want to give them it because it is their national treasure.

2. Who is involved in the war?
Amongst the younger groups the UK children were more likely (N=8, 57.1% v N=2, 13.3%) to cite British/UK/English involvement in the war. This was also true for the older children (N=15, 88.2% v N=3, 20%). The older Bosnian children were more likely than their British counterparts to mention American (N=15, 100% v N=12, 70.6%) and Iraqi (N=12, 80% v N=6, 35.3%) involvement. Of particular interest, several older children in the UK named specific individuals (for Bush N=6, 35.3%), for Blair N=4, 23.5%) as being involved in the war. None of the Bosnian children in either age group did this.

3a. Have any of your parents/grandparents/teachers/friends said anything about the war? (If Yes) What have they said?
No significant numerical differences were observed amongst the younger children, although a higher proportion of the Bosnian than British children (N=9, 60% v N=5, 35.7%) indicated that their parents/grandparents had spoken about the war. Differences between the UK and Bosnian children in the content of parental conversations noted were evident. Quite a few of the older Bosnian children noted discussions at home about the war.

It is not a war against terrorism, that terrorism scare is blown out of proportion. It is because of the money (14-year-old girl, Bosnia)

Well we say that this war is not needed, because we know what a horrible war we had here before. When there is an action to send aid, we always do that. But, that war is stupid, it shouldn't have happened. They should have resolved that peacefully. With the war nothing can be solved, there are only victims. (14-year-old boy, Bosnia)

With the UK children, the topics of the conversations were somewhat different:

I think we once had a conversation about it over dinner, about the whole thing. My mum says we are losing troops and we should let them sort themselves out. We stayed in there too long, we're dragging it out and we are losing our troops. (17-year-old boy, UK)

It's been mentioned a few times but not talked about too much. (17-year-old girl, UK)

Amongst older children, British children were more likely than Bosnian children to have heard their teacher(s) say something about the war (N=13, 76.5% v N=6, 40%).

3b. Have you heard about the war on the television?
(If Yes) What have you heard?
On this question younger British children were more likely (N=9, 64.3% v N=3, 20%) than younger Bosnian children to have heard about the war on the TV.

Yeah, on the news about the car bombings—loads of cars blowing up and 103—it's 103 isn't it?—soldiers have died, our soldiers. (12-year-old girl, UK)

Some of this reflected a distorted view of the relationship between the events of 9/11 and the Iraq War.

Yes a lot, I saw there was a picture of the man in the plane destroying the building and apparently he's up in the mountains in Iraq. (9-year-old boy, UK)

This view, probably referring to Osama bin Laden, and purported links between al-Qaeda and the Iraqi regime in the 9/11 attacks, is similar to those widely held by people in the US just prior to the war's instigation (Chomsky, 2005b—see also Chapter 10, this volume)—itself a testament to the role of the media in influencing what people say about the Iraqi regime.

4. Has the war had an effect on you in any way?

Stark differences were observed in answer to this question, which were very revealing of the cultural settings within which the children reside and within which war is interpreted. A majority of the Bosnian children both younger (N=10, 66.6%) and older (N=9, 60%) commented on feeling sad about the war.

> Yes it did. I am sorry for people who get killed and those who die, and many are in danger; then people don't have anything to eat and they are very poor. (10-year-old boy, Bosnia)

> I am sad because of that, because many Muslims there get killed and die. I don't want any wars. (10-year-old girl, Bosnia)

In contrast, only four (28.6%) of the younger UK children felt sad about the war—and all of these had familial connections with the UK military. Amongst older UK children only one reported feeling sad (6.7%). For several of the older Bosnian children (N=6, 40%) the war in Iraq evoked feelings about the Bosnian war. Many of the children in this age group were alive during the war and had been evacuated.

> Yes, it did. When I see what pictures they send us, they show on the news, I cannot but remember our war. Even though I wasn't here, I was in Germany for five years, but I know how it was here, from news, and these war criminals stories. Even though I wasn't here, I can feel like I was going through it all. (15-year-old boy, Bosnia)

> Well, of course I was sad, because I immediately remember what they were doing to us ten years ago. Nobody deserves that. (14-year-old girl, Bosnia)

5. Will fighting affect the world?

The most frequent response was that the war would make things worse. This was a more frequent response amongst Bosnians, both young (N=14, 93.3% v N=7, 50%) and old (N=14, 93.3% v N=9, 52.9%).

> It will be probably worse in the world. Because America will probably win, and then other world powers will think they can attack anyone if they want. (14-year-old girl, Bosnia)

> It does affect me. If it continues like this it will be a nuclear war. I am sure someone will drop atomic bomb and pollute the whole world. It will be the worst! (14-year-old boy, Bosnia)

Yes, I think people have seen how it was a pointless war, it was not really needed, and they have just fought for no reason, so I think people will see what's happened and see that wars are useless. (14-year-old girl, UK)

Many children, in particular the older ones, (N=8, 57.1% UK v N=9, 60% Bosnia) also spoke about the war involving other countries. Amongst younger children only those from the UK made this suggestion (N=5, 35.7% v N=0).

6. If you could change one or two things about the world, what would they be? Children from both the UK and Bosnia offered a range of ideas for changing the world. One British girl remarked:

Probably ban guns and I'd probably get rid of the nuclear weapons, because there is no reason to have them, it's stupid, we're only going to kill ourselves. (16-year-old girl, UK)

By far the most popular response was to 'stop fighting' and 'stop war'. Bosnian children were more likely to make these proposals, particularly amongst the older children (N=12, 80% v N=6, 35.3%). They were also more likely to refer explicitly to having, or creating, peace.

To influence people in a way to stop the war, so that people never go to war again, and to not think about the war. To make peace in the whole world. (14-year-old girl, Bosnia)

I wish there was no war, and that everybody joins some peace community, something like the European Union. So that everybody is one country. We should all look after each other, not fight against each other. (14-year-old boy, Bosnia)

Bosnia and Herzegovina should send a letter or something to America, to stop that, because we want peace. (15-year-old boy, Bosnia)

These latter remarks are a clear reflection of the political and historical context in Bosnia, where many have aspirations for their country to be integrated within the European Union—perhaps for economic development, or perhaps as a protection against any future outbreak of war.

Discussion

Although this is a relatively small-scale study, the systematic nature of the differences observed is striking, and we believe is informative of important differences in the views of children from the two countries. As such the interviews tell us something about the social construction of the Iraq war in British and Bosnian society and echo the views of Hakvoort and Hägglund (2001, p. 329) that listening to children enables us to '*gain insights into the norms, values and attitudes a particular society holds*'. It would appear that the Bosnian children were more affected by the Iraq war and were more aware of who is involved in it. They also had different views about its causes; they viewed the consequences of the war with more gravity and expressed a greater desire to end war and have peace. How are we to understand these findings? What are likely to be the principal causal factors for these differences? Two main factors seem possible—recent Bosnian history and the nature and role of UK media.

Though still young, the children in Bosnia belong to a society that has very recently been traumatised by war. Most children there have had some member of their immediate or extended family killed in the Bosnian war. The children interviewed here were all Bosnian Muslims—a people who were the principal target of a war prosecuted by Serbian forces. As such, through their own experiences (in the case of the older children), their home life and their media, they are keenly aware of the real destructive and horrific nature of warfare. They referred to 'innocent people being killed', 'homes destroyed', and the 'violation' of people's 'human rights'. These accounts remind us that every war may evoke painful memories for those who have, and are still, experiencing the consequences of previous wars. Although 11 years have passed since the ending of war in Bosnia, the children who were born during that period, as well as those who were born shortly after, still suffer the consequences. There are vivid and constant reminders of war in the lives of children; large numbers still live in refugee camps and children are still killed by landmines.[1] The homes of many remain damaged by war, a part of the disfigured urban landscape of Bosnia's towns and cities where the scars of bullets and shells abound. In addition, the media provide a constant flood of images reminding people of the war. A sample of television news in Bosnia during August and September 2006 for example included: newly discovered mass graves, identification of bodies, stories about war criminals and protests by families of victims or war veterans. Inevitably, these images provoke discussion within families and raise questions among children.

Bosnia then has a cultural repository—a repertoire of images—social representations of warfare that are invariably negative. Bosnian children are able to draw upon these dramatic and traumatic first-hand representations of warfare. They may also feel solidarity with Iraqis because of their own negative perception

1. There are an estimated one million mines and around 30,000 minefields still in the country (Save the Children Norway, 2005).

of the West and because Iraqis too are Muslims. Within the UK, children have no such experience and consequently lack access to such representations. For some UK children the war had a positive focus. Nine cited the benevolence of the coalition forces in explaining the reasons for war. The UK children were more likely to draw on media (television) representations for their knowledge about the war (although scholars have found these to be subject to considerable distortion—see Miller, 2004). Weapons of mass destruction (N=8), Iraqi aggression (N=1), and Osama bin Laden (N=4) were all cited as reasons for going to war. Bosnian children cited none of these. Many older Bosnian children were also informed by the media about the Iraq war, but their strong identification with the victims of war suggests that their media representations were interpreted in relation to their own store of knowledge about war—both their own experiences as refugees or as a result of discussions within the family, among people who had lived through war and had lost loved ones.

That younger British children were less likely to engage in conversations about the war with their parents than were younger Bosnian children is a factor that may contribute to British children's misconceptions. Within the family, parents may provide a framework for young children's incipient views of international politics. Kos and Derviskadic-Jovanovic (1998), for example, emphasise the critical role of natural social interactions in both recovery and making sense of war. As a result of Western inaction in the Bosnian war, many Bosnians felt abandoned and now feel disenchanted with Western ideals. Perhaps it is inevitable that this is communicated to their children, several of whom in this study were able to question the US's professed motives for the Iraq war. The UK children, even those who have family in the armed forces, are unable to draw on these same interpretive repertoires. Perhaps making sense of the war, for them, is more difficult—faced as they are with a familial loyalty to the military or to their country but with possible unease about the UK forces' role as aggressors in Iraq.

Nevertheless, it should not be forgotten that many children in the UK have made vocal protests against the Iraq war (Rai, 2002; Curtis, 2003), although interestingly, coverage of this in the British press has focused primarily on the susceptibility of young people to adult manipulation and their competence to exercise political judgments (Such, Walker & Walker, 2005)—concerns which are absent when it comes to evaluating the effect of UK government propaganda in favour of the war. Behind this concern may be a fear that the growth of children's political awareness could herald a loss of adult control and authority. Neither should it be thought that Bosnian children's moral reasoning has escaped unscathed from the war in that country (Garrod et al., 2003). The findings in this study draw attention to national differences in the socialisation of children, and the way in which representations of war are culturally embedded. They provide us with further knowledge about social influence and how knowledge is disseminated in a society (Moscovici & Duveen, 2000) and, perhaps most importantly, they show us that alternative constructions of warfare are always available.

CHAPTER 10

Sleepwalking into Totalitarianism: Democracy, centre politics and terror

RON ROBERTS

Something happened on 11 September 2001 that caused the West to lose its moral bearings in a way that led government machines, and those who worked in them, to move a significant way down the path of contempt for individuals. The Nazis went much further down that path, but it is undeniably the same one.
 (Murray, 2006, p. 12)

Tell me how you'll know when this war is over.
Because this war will never be over.
It will just keep moving from place to place.
(Laurie Anderson, 2005)

Since the invasion of Iraq and the advent of the 'War on Terror', a number of domestic political initiatives have been launched which challenge fundamental rights and freedoms. These initiatives, with the nature of UK foreign policy that they assume, raise questions about the kind of society we wish to live in. The curtailment of civil liberties, in tandem with attempts by the government to involve the police in driving through new anti-terror legislation (BBC News Online, 2005d), has led a number of commentators to question whether these herald the transformation of the UK from a democracy to a totalitarian or police state. This possibility merits serious consideration. The postmodern age carries particular risks. Where concepts of truth have been abandoned, the distinction between fact and fiction obscured, and the reality of experience no longer held sacrosanct, the foundations for totalitarian systems of thought to flourish have already been laid. In short, intellectual tyranny may be a sign of physical tyranny to come (Roberts, 2001). Whether these moves foreshadow the demise of a democratic system in the United Kingdom should be a matter for debate. Should this ever come to pass it would not be the first time that war has been used to further authoritarian or totalitarian rule. First however, it will be necessary to discuss the psychological barriers that make this prospect seem so unimaginable and which therefore could be said to stand in the way of producing any effective resistance to it.

The belief that the horrors wrought by totalitarian government no longer pose a real and present threat to the citizens of the West is not easy to dispel. Our 'common sense' understanding places the assaults on humanity from Nazi, Stalinist and Maoist terror in the bygone days of the twentieth century. From the vantage point of our contemporary halcyon days, whatever evils bestride the modern world, the totalitarian project appears not to be one of them.

In this chapter historical and contemporary social representations (Moscovici & Duveen, 2000) of totalitarianism will be explored in order to understand how belief in our immunity from it is sustained. As it is Moscovici's contention that the character of social representations is more clearly revealed during times of crisis and upheaval, the 'War on Terror' and the current period of international instability would seem to provide an opportune moment for examining these. This approach differs from the one usually adopted by psychologists when faced with the challenge of addressing political violence or inter-state conflict. Dispositional constructs, such as unconscious hostility or authoritarian personality structures, were at one time frequently invoked, though attention is now more commonly directed to group processes—those deriving from a shared sense of identity or the strategic interactions between groups that give rise to conflict escalation or reduction (Christie, Wagner & Winter, 2001; Pruit & Kim, 2004). With the notable exception perhaps of Reich (1975), totalitarianism itself has rarely been contemplated by professional psychologists.

A 'social representations' approach to understanding the genesis of totalitarianism has the advantage, that of necessity; it is rooted in the specific shared meanings and values that are transmitted within and across generations. Van Dijk (1996) considered such shared representations, when they govern the operation of more specific group beliefs, as defining an ideological system. Consequently if we desire to understand the allure, the power, indeed the vulnerability of a population to seduction by totalitarian ideology or practice, perforce we must contend with the nature of the shared meanings that underpin it. Our approach must be cultural and historical. The historic movements toward a totalitarian form of life can be viewed organically, as specifically rooted in people's changing relationships—with each other, with their construction of the past and with the systems of knowledge and power coursing through the veins of a given culture and society.

Beliefs

Widespread belief in the benevolence of our ruling elite (discussed in Chapter 8) must inevitably play a part in explaining our self-perceived protection from tyrannical rule. Of course it remains possible that beliefs in the inviolability of the British political system are essentially correct and are rooted in a clear understanding of the potential directions in which society could move, though it should always be remembered that the absence of a written constitution leaves open myriad possibilities. Two sources of evidence have potential relevance here. The first concerns people who have experienced totalitarian rule in other societies. Were they, prior to its emergence, able to foresee it? And if they did, how did they respond to it? Second, is the question of how deeply rooted in our society is an awareness and understanding of events which have already occurred or are currently unfolding and which may shape our broader political future? The answers to these may tell us much about how well founded the public's belief is in the benign evolution of the state power that governs it and their assumed protection from totalitarianism. Should it transpire that members of previous totalitarian societies failed to discern the future toward which they were heading or indeed welcomed it where they did, or that people's knowledge and understanding of events which shape the political landscape is poor, then the public's beliefs would appear to be resting on shaky foundations.

Europe provides several case studies where we have been afforded a wealth of information on the civic atmosphere and beliefs of people prior to the onset of totalitarian rule. From a comparative point of view these are of most relevance to the task here of considering the possible emergence of a new strand of totalitarianism. The period between the two World Wars saw the rise of Mussolini's Fascist party in Italy, the National Socialists in Germany under Hitler and, following civil war in Spain, Franco's assumed leadership of the Nationalist forces and seizure of power, aided by troops from the Fascist Italian and Nazi states. In recent years, following the break up of former Yugoslavia, ethnic cleansing and genocide of the Bosnian Muslims was allowed to proceed unhindered by either the European powers or the United States.

Both the National Socialist Party (NSPD) of Germany and Mussolini's Fascists came to power through a well-organised mass movement via the ballot box (Fest, 1974; Farrell, 2004), whilst in Bosnia a newly sovereign country was attacked and its population terrorised by the agents of nationalist parties (the Serbian Democratic Party, SDS; and the Croatian Democratic Union, HDZ), who again had gained ascendancy through the ballot box (see Vulliamy, 1994; Woodward, 1995). In the case of Spain, Franco's nationalists fought their way to power following a narrow election loss, though again enjoying considerable popular backing. All these examples should be considered to provide little comfort for those who believe a democratic electoral system provides a guarantee of protection for democratic and civilian rule. How could it, when totalitarian rule itself appears to rest on mass support (Arendt, 1994a)?

The citizens of pre-war Italy, Germany and Spain were, without doubt, hindered by the absence of any recent historical precedent for totalitarian rule—but it is nevertheless legitimate to ask whether their citizens were in a position to anticipate the likely direction their societies would take. There is abundant evidence that in Germany many people were all too aware of the direction in which their government was heading and enthusiastically contributed to the destruction of civil liberties and the persecution of Jews and other minorities (Goldhagen, 1997; Rees, 1997). From the available evidence Arendt (1994a, p. xxiii) concluded, '... mass support for totalitarianism comes neither from ignorance nor from brainwashing'. Only when the course of the war turned, and people began to see their ordered society crumble before them, were many shaken from the National Socialist reverie that had slowly overtaken them (Kershaw, 1987). Mussolini likewise incurred the wrath of those around him only when military defeat loomed large. Franco's guile enabled him to stay in power beyond the war, having switched alliance midway through it, and subsequently, despite the suppression of trade unions and political opponents, to garnish support from the United States through his anti-communist stance (Preston, 1995). The transition to democracy following Franco's death has been a success story, but it was neither guaranteed nor predictable.

The dilemma for us in examining the German, Italian and Spanish experiences is to appreciate that totalitarian rule was not simply imposed from above—that a sizeable number of citizens helped bring it about and saw no danger for themselves in doing so. Only in retrospective accounts do we find evidence of the twilight moral world for example, in which Germans were both simultaneously aware of atrocities—be they the killing of disabled and psychologically disturbed individuals (Sereny, 1974, Goldhagen, 1997), or the operation of the death camps—and yet professed ignorance of their existence. Sereny's (1995) interviews with Hitler's chief architect, and later heir apparent, Albert Speer, are a masterly exposition of the double-think which seems to have pervaded the German psyche of the period, and must be considered a warning against any reliance on the normative moral standards of a society being an effective guard against a drift into the politics of cruelty and inhumanity.

Bosnia provides a different but no less compelling lesson. Even after war had broken out between Serbia and Croatia, many Bosnians did not predict that carnage would be heading in their direction (Hunt, 2004). A multiethnic state where Serbs, Croats and Muslims had lived together peacefully for years, the Serbian-led assault on the integrity of Bosnia and Herzogovina, began a three-year war against the country's civilian population, culminating in between 100,000 and 150,000 dead (Nilson, 2004), 2 million refugees and a state of two semi-autonomous regions following the Dayton agreement, seen by many as rewarding the perpetrators of war (Power, 2003). Simply because Bosnia was considered to lack strategic significance after the demise of the Soviet Union, the European powers, together with the United States, saw no political capital in risking the lives of its own troops to prevent the worst atrocities in Europe since World War II. In the words of Peter Galbraith, a member of the US Senate Foreign Relations Committee, 'We did not want to know what was going on, did not want to confront it, and did not want to act' (quoted in Cohen, 1998, p. 220–221); and so, the Nationalist forces in Serbia and Croatia, hell-bent on an ethnically motivated land grab (which saw concentration camps, mass rape and ethnic cleansing as acceptable political tools) were effectively condoned and implicitly encouraged by our democratically elected governments. Their stated policy aims are widely acknowledged to have been a disaster (Perry, 1995; Power, 2003) and their diplomatic efforts to end the war described as 'reducing the moral temperature to nil' (Hitchens, 1995).

The psychological lesson of Bosnia for the Western public is that their governing elites were not prepared to take sides in a conflict initiated by Fascists, even though intervention was favoured by their citizens (Power, 2003). Rather, they stood idly by and watched a return to the standards of civility set by the worst totalitarian governments on record. The operating principles on offer were to place political wheeler-dealing and self-interest ahead of any moral commitment to protect the principal targets of the war—civilians.

We turn now to the question of public understanding of events that have shaped our past. Systematic enquiry into the Western public's understanding of the causes (and consequences) of the wars in the Balkans is sadly lacking, as indeed is similar information regarding a number of other major conflicts. Research by the Glasgow Media News Group (Philo & Berry, 2004) into public under-standing of events in the Second World War, the Vietnam War and Israeli–Palestinian conflict however has been carried out and reveals considerable confusion and inaccuracy in the public's interpretation of events. This misunderstanding closely follows patterns of media coverage. Philo and Berry conclude, as many others before them have done, that popular conceptions of history are shaped by the perspectives and interests of those producing it. A particularly startling illustration of this comes from the US. In December 2001 less than 5 per cent of the American population believed in a link between the Iraqi regime and the events of 9/11. By December 2002, after an extensive media propaganda assault in preparation for the Iraq war, this figure had risen to over 50 per cent (Chomsky, 2005b).[1] Simply put, history is written by the victors, and those who side with them. Accordingly it is marked by conformity to elite interests (see Chapter 2). Under the current free market system of information production and distribution, public misapprehension is typical and unlikely to change in the immediate future.

---

1. In September 2006, the US Senate finally agreed that prior to the outbreak of war in 2003 there were no formal links between al-Qaeda and the Saddam Hussein regime (US Senate Select Committee on Intelligence, 2006).

The confusion wrought by a loyal media tends to both produce and reinforce particular kinds of attributional bias; especially what is called the 'fundamental attribution error' (Ross, 1977). In this the reported actions of others are 'explained' or attributed to internal or dispositional factors—such as national character. The social representations that circulate as purported 'explanations' for why particular countries wage war, or are susceptible to totalitarianism, frequently invoke this attribution in the form of deficiencies in national character (see Hall, 1994 for an example in relation to the wars in former Yugoslavia). Policy makers are also as likely to invoke these representations as lay people (see Hunt, 2004). The converse of this is that the actions of one's own side are attributed to external or situational factors—the search for weapons of mass destruction, the necessity to oust an evil dictator (read Saddam Hussein in Iraq, General Noriega in Panama), to bring democracy to a troubled region, or protect international order, rather than explanations closer to home—our being an aggressive expansionist power, greedy for oil/money and resources for example.

Media treatment of the Balkan wars depicted the conflicts as civil (rather than inter-state) wars between the different ethnic groups in the region, whose volatile national characters had enslaved them in the grip of a historical warring psychosis, the result of which was that all sides in the conflict were hell-bent on slaughtering each other. Little attempt has been made to understand the instability of the socio-economic and political environment, which precipitated the mayhem, and yet it is precisely such environmental instability that is recognised by political scientists (e.g. Woodward, 1995) and psychologists (Haslam & Reicher, 2005) alike as a major contributor to the onset of political tyranny. In a related manner, for all the European cases considered here, media presentations typically highlight and mythologize 'charismatic' leaders (see Kershaw, 1987)—Mussolini, Hitler, Franco, Milosevic, in explaining why the totalitarian systems took root, rather than examining in depth the link between economic and political breakdown and the rise of political extremism, precipitated often by the actions of major corporations and domestic and international powers with an antipathy to communism.

Reporting of the Iraq war (Miller, 2004; Scatamburlo-D'Annibale, 2005) has also been subject to intense distortion, hindering the prospects for a clear public understanding of the events. Coverage has often sought to legitimise the interests of the Anglo/American invaders within a framework set by the instigators of the war (whose own public pronouncements on the reasons for war have displayed little consistency). This is in part because editors and journalists tend to share the same ideological assumptions as government. Rarely do readers actually get the opportunity to see the legitimacy of warfare challenged (Freedman, 2004). The ongoing situation in Iraq now presents entirely new difficulties, though once again the public remains shielded from the unpalatable reality created by the occupation. Engelhardt (2005) quotes journalist Maggie O'Kane:

The hacks are corralled in a single hotel where huge egos bang off the wall and each other. After a week or two, the atmosphere becomes suffocating … Since Al-Zarqawi's people started cutting off heads it is too dangerous for foreigners to go out. So, instead, his poor Iraqi fixer is off to some hell hole to count the bodies and get the pictures … And that is the great tragedy for war reporting now. We no longer know what is going on but we are pretending we do. Any decent reporter knows that reporting from Baghdad now does a disservice to the truth.

All of the countries considered here, Italy, Germany, Spain and Bosnia/former Yugoslavia, were advanced technological societies, driven forward on a modernist project. The paradox of the totalitarian system is its appeal to a rationalist, systematic, scientific order to bring an end to chaos and uncertainty, yet it is built on the fundamentals of unreason, irrationality and nationalism. The examples from the past enable us to see how the populations of entire countries, sometimes willingly, sometimes not, sleepwalked, or were carried disbelievingly, into a future political and psychological nightmare—a reality whose final consequences they could not fully anticipate. That we may one day wake up and find ourselves living in such a scenario runs counter to our belief in a just world, a belief aided and abetted perhaps by the socially constructed history of our 'benevolent' state's intentions. Our desires for stability, order and justice then, formidable as they may seem, do not provide an insurmountable psychological barrier for the realisation of a totalitarian reality.

There are, meanwhile, additional psychological factors that may lower the threshold for its appearance in future. The historical precedents set by totalitarian movements of the left and right have led us to expect that totalitarianism must always be associated with extreme political movements. Such social representations have been recycled ad nauseum, perhaps to bolster perception of the superiority of our own society. It is as easy to conceptualise the extreme right as the extreme left, but what of the idea of the extreme centre? How do we conceive of this? Are we now blinded by expectation to the possibility of a totalitarian government of the centre? Our myopia with respect to this possibility carries interesting historical parallels with the measurement of political attitudes in psychology, where first right-wing authoritarianism and later left-wing authoritarianism were recognised as measurable entities in order to come to terms with the twentieth century realities of fascism and communism (Richards, 2002). Perhaps the problem lies with an implicit conceptualisation that political authoritarianism is opposed to a democratic posture. Clearly this precludes any notion of democratic authoritarianism, a construct not too distant from the idea of a species of totalitarianism bound to the political centre.

Furthermore, from a British or American perspective, totalitarianism may be represented as a purely foreign phenomenon. As such it can more easily be removed from our sphere of moral relevance. By so removing it, we may be more likely to reduce in significance any role, major or minor, which our own country may have played in supporting or contributing to the international circumstances that nurtured the birth of any of the major totalitarian systems. The comment of former British Prime Minister, Ted Heath, provides a typical illustration. Heath remarked that if people wished to murder one another, as long as they did not do so in his country, it was not his concern and nor should it be the concern of the British Government (Becirevic, 2003). The implicit assumption is that people murdering one another outside of the UK is unrelated to the activities of the UK Government, a stance somewhat at variance with British history. Reich's (1975, p. 18) position on the matter is more instructive and more credible:

> The fascist madman cannot be made innocuous if he is sought ... only in the German, or the Italian and not in the American and the Chinese man as well; if he is not tracked down in oneself; if we are not conversant with the social institutions that hatch him daily.

A 'mass psychology' of totalitarianism, in the manner conceived by Reich, is not the aim in these pages i.e. the intention is not to source fascism, or any form of totalitarianism, in the internalised repression of one's impulses toward love and life, or the character structure of the masses. However, what is being argued is that widely shared internalised beliefs about the nature of the governing state and its people, and the attendant psychological processes that support these, are key pillars in disarming any potential opposition to anti-democratic developments. We must therefore examine our own beliefs carefully if we are not to remain complacent about the dark historical possibilities on offer. Hannah Arendt's (1994b) observations on the 'banality of evil' are also particularly relevant, not just in terms of the failures in thinking and judgement of any individual regarding the moral nature of acts—but of the thinking and judgement pertaining to our own susceptibility to reprogramming and restructuring of the moral order. Like Milgram (1974) she recognises that totalitarian societies are not comprised of monsters, but fallible, ordinary individuals, susceptible to the moral maelstrom unleashed by malevolent authority.

The historical representations of totalitarianism—situated in foreign lands, a phenomenon of political extremes of the left or right, gullible masses seduced by alluring leaders, alongside belief in both the benevolence of the state and a stable order immune to totalitarianism, creates a psychological climate in which citizens are not well positioned to detect and recognise its emergence. In the section that follows, the importance of these psychological vulnerabilities will be further explored through an examination of the UK political climate since the invasion of Iraq and the country's continued allegiance to the 'War on Terror'.

Contemporary realities

In recent years the political climate within the UK has been shaped to a considerable degree by international events. To assess the possible ramifications of these, it will be useful to have some indication of the pre-existing psychological and civil climate into which these events project their influence, elaborating in the process the notion of psychological resilience to totalitarian ideology.

In Western cultures, the ethos of free market capitalism has now made substantial inroads into the personal domain achieved through multiple media channels, pornography and the 'talk show' (Roberts, 2001). The distinction between public and private life is dissolving before one's eyes, as citizens and celebrities routinely bare their bodies and their souls for mass entertainment. In the eyes of Seabrooke (1988) these may be considered further instances whereby human beings have become the 'raw material' for consumption and industrial processing, the reality of which resonates symbolically in the plethora of media features in which cannibals, vampires and zombies munch their way through scores of people in the course of an evening's viewing. The philosophy of consume and be consumed finds other outlets; addiction to celebrity, seduction into virtual realities (Baudrillaud, 1994) and invitations by the psychiatric-cum-pharmaceutical establishment to ease one's discomfort with the social malaise by tranquilising one's *self* out of existence.

Belief in political stability and state benevolence, auto-consumption and the social alienation of modern life—to this litany must be added a widespread denial of the horrors of contemporary life, and of our roles, personal and social, in creating and responding to them. The field of denial has been elegantly explored by Cohen (2001), delineating its various forms (literal, interpretive, implicatory) with an understanding of its ubiquitous nature in both the private and public realms. He raises uncomfortable questions concerning what we choose to excise from thought in the course of engaging with suffering in the world, and how organised collective contemporary and historical denial manufactures for us a picture of the world that perhaps bears little resemblance to the actual events that unfold. This brings us full circle to a feature of totalitarian life—which Todorov (2003), like Orwell before him, recognised was critical to its pursuit—the control of information about the past. Primo Levi referred to this as the 'war on memory'. A survivor of the Bosnian war puts it succinctly:

> In order to kill people, you must kill memory, you must destroy everything that belongs to that people (quoted in Vulliamy, 1994, p. xx)

How much more efficient the process would be if the destruction of memory was carried out from within! Referring to the liquidation of the Polish intelligentsia by the Nazis, Himmler famously remarked:

You should hear this but also forget it immediately. (quoted in Arendt, 1994a, p. 372)

To my knowledge, no British journalist has ever questioned the Prime Minister about Britain's role in arming the Iraqi regime, nor about improving the credit ratings to the regime following its use of chemical weapons—on no fewer than 195 occasions (Power, 2003) including its gassing of the Kurds (see Gittings, 1991)—these occurring of course before it was decided to 'take Saddam out'. This recent history in Anglo–Iraqi relations has been expunged from mainstream news reporting and likely, public memory with it. And what of Blair's repeated exhortations to 'draw a line' under the Iraq war and 'move on'? What resilience do we have to this kind of thing? What happens to public memory when events pass out of personal autobiographical memory? Who are the guardians of public memory, if it is not those charged with reporting it? Is it the World Wide Web that may ultimately preserve some faithful rendition of the past free from the intimidations of power? But if so how will we recognise it?

To appreciate fully the risks of sleepwalking into totalitarianism, the foundations from which it might emerge must be clearly understood. Its wellsprings can in fact be identified in many areas of life today: increased surveillance, imprisonment without trial, anti-terror laws, electoral rigging, an obedient press, control of information, reconstruction of the past, the realisation of eugenics via the use of genetic and reproductive technology, calls for euthanasia, nationalism, xenophobia and institutionalised racism. One might also ponder whether the UK's proposed move to meet its future energy needs, through the expansion of its nuclear power programme, might accelerate existent trends toward a police state, requiring as it would, enhanced security for the transport, processing and storage of nuclear material, all of which could act as a magnet for a terrorist attack. All the activities on this list posit the necessity for standardising and controlling different facets of life, the unpredictability of which are deemed to induce fear and dread into our political masters. The paradox here is that totalitarianism thrives on the maintenance of fear, sustaining it through the very means which, it is argued, are necessary to defeat it. Many of these measures— surveillance, imprisonment without trial, anti-terror laws, pressures on press freedom, xenophobia and nationalism—have been stepped up in the aftermath of the invasion of Iraq and warrant closer attention.

Surveillance
Modern British society lies enthralled with technologies which afford multiple possibilities for monitoring people's daily activities: credit card and mobile phone tracking, ID cards, CCTV (with software to facilitate face recognition and road vehicle number plate identification) are but a few examples. Little or none of this has been subject to electoral accountability or control. State intrusion into people's private lives is now considered necessary to maintain the security of the state,

just as intrusion into the private sphere is now considered necessary to maintain the survival of the capitalist enterprise. By preventing terrorism, aiding the fight against organised crime, and tackling illegal immigration and fraud more effectively we are told, mass surveillance will bring noticeable improvements to our quality of life. The contrary arguments however are that the UK suffered terrorist attacks from the IRA for many years without any need to introduce measures such as ID cards, and that the anti-civil libertarian measures introduced then did nothing whatsoever to combat terror or improve quality of life—just the opposite in fact. Furthermore, Spain, a country that has had identity cards for years, found them to be of little help in preventing the Madrid bombings of 2004. Indeed the perpetrators of both the Spanish attacks and the attacks on the Twin Towers all possessed valid identification. Former MI5 Chief Stella Rimmington has gone on record as saying that the cards could turn out to be 'absolutely useless', and that many within the security services have shown no enthusiasm for their use. Others have branded the cards 'bogus' and 'an unnecessary incursion on people's privacy' (Woodcock & Ross, 2005). Why the pressure for their introduction continues despite the absence of any reasoned argument must remain open to question. In the present climate it is not surprising that suspicions exist about the government's true motives.

Detention without trial/anti-terror legislation
The citizens of Iraq know all too well what the coalition really mean by liberty and freedom as, at any one time it is estimated that around 10,000 of them are being detained without trial by the US and UK forces (Rogers, 2005), with over 4000 of these having being detained for more than a year (Amnesty International, 2006d). UK citizens are also now being detained without trial under the guise of protecting the public from psychiatric inmates or terror suspects. In December 2004, the Law Lords adjudged the indefinite detention without trial of 'potential' terrorist suspects in Belmarsh Prison, in accordance with UK law, breached European Human Rights legislation (see Chapter 3). Pulling no punches about the threats to liberty that this posed, one of the Lords (Hoffman) observed, 'The real threat to the life of this nation ... comes not from terrorism, but from laws such as these' (House of Lords, 2004, p. 53). Another, Lord Nicholls, took the view that 'indefinite imprisonment without charge or trial is anathema in any country which observes the rule of law' (House of Lords, 2004, p. 47). The clear implication of the judgement was that the age-old democratic traditions of the country were now under a real threat from the Government.

The perceived erosion of human rights in the UK signalled by these events is exacerbated by the UK's moves in concluding a *Memorandum of Understanding* with both Jordan and Libya, and actively pursuing one with Algeria and other countries in North Africa and the Middle East, which would allow it to sidestep moral and legal responsibilities to refrain from deporting individuals to countries where there is a high probability that they would suffer torture and other human rights abuses. These developments alone prompted Amnesty International to instigate a high-level investigation of the UK's current record on human rights (Allen, 2005). The ensuing report concluded that the UK's policies were 'effectively sending a 'green light' to other governments to abuse human rights' (Amnesty International, 2006e, p. 5). Amnesty warns that new laws to combat terrorism contravene existing human rights law, have led to serious abuses of human rights, and threaten the independence of the judiciary.

The UK's respect for human rights has been further called into question by logistic and political support given to the CIA in snatching terrorist suspects and flying them outside the US, thus avoiding US legal restraints, to countries where they may be tortured (Cobain, Grey & Norton-Taylor, 2005). One of the many disturbing outcomes of the war in Iraq and the 'War on Terror' has been the growing acceptance of the use of torture, which now appears to be approaching the status of normative action (Gray, 2005). Former British Ambassador to Uzbekistan, Craig Murray for example has provided extensive documentary evidence that the UK Government, under the mantle of gathering intelligence has frequently condoned its use (Murray, 2005, 2006). The erosion of moral sensibilities, which this signals, bodes ill for any triumph of liberal Western values over fundamentalist demagogy. A review of recent UK Government policy and its stated objectives—which includes reduction of the right to trial by jury, attacks on the independence of the judiciary, limitations on suspects' right to silence, abolition of the double jeopardy principle, cuts to legal aid, and neighbourhood curfews on young people—bear all the hallmarks of a concerted war on freedom (Ali, 2005). The apotheosis of this assault on freedom can be found in the original proposals for the Legislative and Regulatory Reform Bill (House of Commons 2005/6) that sought to grant ministers the right to amend, repeal or replace existing legislation without parliamentary scrutiny. Had these proposals remained unaltered they would have effectively created a legal framework for totalitarian government in the UK.

Press freedom
The obedience of the press has been referred to throughout this book; a particularly sinister manifestation concerns the sacking, just prior to the onset of the Iraq War, of Palestinian and Iraqi journalists working for the BBC World Service. They were dismissed by its Head, Mark Byford, a personal friend of Geoff Hoon then UK Defence Secretary. The latter end of 2005 also saw the Attorney General threaten UK national newspapers with the Official Secrets Act. This followed revelations by the *Daily Mirror* newspaper of conversations between George Bush and Tony Blair in which Bush had proposed taking military action against the Arabic TV station Al-Jazeera following their coverage of the bloody US assault on Fallujah in November 2004 (Norton-Taylor & White, 2005). This example not only illustrates the fact that journalists operating in war zones have now become acceptable targets—but that the US, having already launched air strikes against

Al-Jazeera's offices in Baghdad and made death threats against its workers (Bodi, 2004) without fear of condemnation from the British Government, considers the UK to be a willing aide to the military curtailment of a free press. Can we assume assassinating and threatening journalists is an activity that meets with wholehearted approval in the echelons of Whitehall so long as strategic objectives are met (Bodi, 2004)?

Coverage of the invasion and occupation of Iraq has been further distorted by the procedure of embedding journalists within the military—a process that has serious shortcomings for the impartial reporting of events (Freedman, 2004). The most public manifestation of the Government's attempt to control the agenda of the media concerns the aftermath of the Radio 4 interview in which BBC journalist, Andrew Gilligan, suggested that the government had 'sexed up' the contents of the intelligence services' report on Iraq and weapons of mass destruction—the so-called 'dodgy dossier'. Whatever the conclusions of the Hutton Report (Hutton, 2004), the wealth of detail in its contents make it absolutely clear to anyone who has bothered to read it that the Government did indeed exaggerate the strength of the case for Iraq possessing weapons of mass destruction, and that the US–UK case for war was 'an audacious fraud' (Edwards & Cromwell, 2004, p. 212). Still this did not prevent a major crisis at the BBC and the forced removal of its Director General, Greg Dyke and its Chairman, Gavyn Davies.

Xenophobia and nationalism

One of the corollaries of the attacks in New York and London has been an increase in attacks on Muslims in the US and the UK. In the study by Sheridan and Gillett (2005), Muslims were the only religious group to report significant increases in prejudice following 9/11. Almost 14 per cent reported a specific personal experience of racism or discrimination related to the events in New York. Following the London bombings in July 2005, figures from Scotland Yard revealed a 600 per cent increase in religious hate crimes in the capital (Brown & Morris, 2005). Similar findings have been reported from the International Crime Survey (Manchin, Kury, Van Dijk & Schaber, 2006).

It would be tempting to view these incidents as simply an uncoordinated expression of people's fear of further threats and attacks. Alas the picture is somewhat more complicated. Hostile government policies and media coverage in recent years have contributed to the aggression directed toward minority groups, one result of which has been the transformation in the meaning of the term 'asylum seekers'. It no longer simply denotes people seeking refuge from human rights abuses abroad, but has come to signify, for many, those looking to come to the UK 'because it is a soft touch'. An Oxfam report (Mollard, 2001) argues that the incessant negative press coverage and posture emanating from central government (which includes the removal of judicial review in asylum cases) has helped to create a climate in which:

It is acceptable to detain asylum seekers, give them support payments worth only 70 per cent of Income Support levels, to make that payment in vouchers, to provide sub-standard accommodation, and to disperse people across the country without recourse to individual need. (Mollard, 2001, p. 4)

The scapegoating of this group of vulnerable individuals has contributed to a brutish environment in which the expressed willingness of Britain to meet its obligations under the 1951 United Nations Refugee Convention is looking increasingly hollow, as political parties and media compete to adopt the harshest stance against foreigners, to pander to their own racist constituencies. According to Williams (quoted in Mollard, 2001) the tone in which the political and media debate is being conducted is giving succour to racists, respectability to racism and encouragement to those who perpetrate racist attacks against refugees and asylum seekers. One can hardly escape the comparison between the upsurge of racist attacks in the UK and the fact that the armed forces of the country are currently occupying a foreign land and killing and abusing the citizens there, in order it seems, to expropriate their resources.

A disquieting element to emerge from the debris of the London bombings has been the repeated calls from some quarters for Britain to turn its back on multiculturalism (BBC News Online, 2005d; Pfaff, 2005), that the bombings reflect a failure of multiculturalism (Hardy, 2005). Malik (2005) has argued that the multicultural experiment has led to a politicization of identity in terms of ethnicity and religion, and that a core feature of these identities is victimhood, while the Head of the Commission for Racial Equality, Trevor Phillips (2005) has argued that we are drifting toward a climate of segregation that will further exacerbate the risks of extremism in the Muslim communities. The tide of alienation can only be reversed, these analyses suggest, by establishing 'Britishness' as the nucleus of a new post-July 7th identity, as if such a magical rewiring of our sense of who we are would eliminate the problems throughout the world caused by the invasions of Iraq and Afghanistan, and the policies of the US and UK in the Middle East.

A lone voice, given less prominence than the clarion calls for 'New Britons' comes from Madood (2005) who notes the arrival of this strand of thinking predates the London bombings and owes much to the tenure of reactionary Home Secretary David Blunkett. It is more, not less multiculturalism that is needed says Madood. The cry to extend the multicultural project to a politics of equal respect that includes British Muslims is unlikely to have been aided by those who effectively blame the multiculturalism of the last 30 years for the weaknesses inherent in modern British identity. Neither will they be helped by the aspirations of that other noted supporter of the Iraq invasion, Gordon Brown, to resurrect the British Empire as a noble enterprise (Brogan, 2005). With UK military forces tied up in the Middle East, the resurrection of empire from the heart of government should perhaps not come as too much of a surprise, though perhaps it may serve as a warning of the dangers yet to come from the current administration and the type of heroic, nationalist identity the government hopes to foist on the populace.

Fascism, fundamentalism and the War on Terror

Thus far, the argument advanced here has been that people in the UK (by dint of the social and historical representations of totalitarian and domestic political systems) are imbued with beliefs that render them complacent with regard to the prospect of totalitarian government in the UK: complacency which could reduce the effectiveness of any public resistance should this be necessary. These beliefs are currently held in a context in which a series of political developments in the UK, justified on the grounds of national security and maintaining morale in the ongoing 'War on Terror' and occupation of Iraq, are pushing the UK state in a direction where fundamental freedoms and democratic rights are being sacrificed with depressing regularity. All this is accompanied by a torrent of propaganda to exaggerate the terror threat (Chu, 2005; Jenkins, 2005). The curtailment of liberties, paradoxically, is being done ostensibly in the name of protecting them from the onslaught of radical Islamists and followers of al-Qaeda. The pattern is reminiscent of that brand of military logic whereby 'what we are fighting for must be destroyed in order to save it'. Here freedom is sacrificed to protect us from its loss.

As the suicide bombings in London on July 7th clearly demonstrated, a serious terrorist threat does now exist: one which in the eyes of a majority of the public, is linked to the invasion of Iraq (Glover, 2005). It must be asked why the presence of terrorists operating in the UK has only now led the British Government to place draconian restrictions on civil liberties. Certainly, the speech of MI5 Head, Manningham-Buller (2005) in which she calls for civil liberties to be eroded to protect 'Britons from terrorism' contains no satisfactory explanation. During the heyday of the IRA's campaign in London no calls were made to introduce internment on the UK mainland (a policy instituted in Northern Ireland between 1969 and 1971, now widely recognized as a failure (Cash, 1996) or to detain people for up to 90 days without charge. Furthermore the UK's intelligence services have been aware since the mid-1990s that people involved in promoting, funding and planning terrorism—in the Middle East for example—have used London as a base (Gregory & Wilkinson, 2005). Such was the extent of this that in some circles the capital city was referred to as Londonistan (O'Neil, 2002). Ahmed (2005, 2006) provides details of several well-known individuals and organisations that have routinely broken UK anti-terrorism legislation and have faced no charge, even after 9/11. He writes:

> Under the Prevention of Terrorism Act the government has detained more than 7000 people. The vast majority, were released without charge. Only a small fraction has ever been charged with offences relating to terrorism.

Indeed, rather than targeting genuine terrorists, 'Current anti-terror laws are being used to quell peaceful protest, to detain foreign nationals without trial, and are fostering discrimination against the Muslim community in Britain'. Meanwhile, unscrupulous operatives connected to Al-Qaeda, who do fall under anti-terrorism legislation, are permitted to continue their activities unsanctioned. (Ahmed, 2005, p. 108)

Ahmed also notes that the culture of 'tolerance' toward the al-Qaeda network and its affiliates existed in both the UK and the US for a number of years. Regarding the 9/11 attacks the evidence, he argues, points toward not incompetence or failure on the part of the various intelligence agencies, but political obstruction and negligence from the highest echelons of the US Government. The background to the London bombings appears to follow a similar pattern (Ahmed, 2006). We need to ask therefore, why the threat perceived to emanate from the radical Islamist groups and the perceived means to deal with it warrant such drastic measures now. Curtis (Curtis, A., 2004) sees something sinister: the 'War on Terror' as a mask for restoring the declining power and authority of the political elite.

Instead of delivering dreams, politicians now promise to protect us from nightmares. They say that they will rescue us from dreadful dangers that we cannot see and do not understand. And the greatest danger of all is international terrorism. A threat that needs to be fought by a war on terror. But much of this threat is a fantasy, which has been exaggerated and distorted by politicians. It's a dark illusion that has spread unquestioned through governments around the world, the security services, and the international media.

Ahmed (2005, 2006) likewise sees a hidden agenda behind the 'non-existent' war against terror—a Faustian pact comprising multiple regional Western/al-Qaeda relationships to bolster elite interests (control of raw materials and strategic resources) by creating global instability and enhancing the security state. Congruent with the thesis espoused here, he contemplates an engineered drift into a new variant of totalitarianism.

National security has quite deliberately been sacrificed by Western governments, especially the United States and the United Kingdom, to secure the interests of the corporate-military-industrial complex ... to consolidate the power of both the state and the corporate-military-industrial complex, and the latter's interests, under the guise of fighting the 'War on Terror'. The consequence is an ever deepening vicious circle of escalating insecurity and intensifying police state powers on a national and international scale: a guaranteed recipe for the emergence of a new form of postmodern fascism. (Ahmed, 2005, p. 270)

Ahmed's position takes us into territory previously explored by Arendt (1994a, p. 381), though her remarks were intended to express the logic underpinning the evolution of the Nazi and Soviet systems:

> Totalitarian regimes, based on a fiction of global conspiracy and aiming at global rule, eventually concentrate all power in the hands of the police.

Allowing Islamic terrorist networks to flourish, would, as a matter of course, lead sooner or later to the emergence of a credible threat; one that could instill fear into the population.[2] At a stroke, it now appears this 'threat' is being used to justify the sacrifice of traditional freedoms, enhancement of the security state, and validation of an aggressive foreign policy (of which the invasion of Iraq is but one aspect) whilst simultaneously promoting nationalism, feeding the military industrial complex and making a scapegoat of Muslims. Inevitably this will alienate Islamic communities still further and likely produce more recruits for attacking Western targets.

Tariq Ali (2002) sees the current 'War on Terror' as a clash of fundamentalisms—not between the Zionist Christian crusaders and Islam as seen through the eyes of radical Islamists—but the fundamentalisms of the market and the Jihadists. In their professed certainties, intolerance, social destructiveness, disregard for human rights and democracy they provide mirror images of one another, locked into a mutual spiral of antipathy and fear. At issue is whether the West, in its promotion of radical capitalism, is courting the growth of the Islamists in order to engineer the social conditions for the population to embrace a totalitarian 'solution', a postmodern managerial fascism, and thereby further the interests of those whose power remains tied to the global energy market. Yergin (2006) for example argues that global developments in security must be developed to maintain stability in an oil industry which is now increasingly subject to disruption. In accord with those who question the compatibility of democracy with capitalism (e.g. Bernholz, 2000) and warn of the inherent instability of the free market (Gray, 2002), the new totalitarianism could be presented as a necessary price to pay in order to retain hegemony. Such a strategy could only enhance global insecurity and have untold psychological consequences.

Terror promoted by the state to justify the waging of aggressive war and domination of the body politic, together with a penchant for propaganda unrivalled in British political history, now tower over the political scene. These two features, terror and propaganda, in the view of Hannah Arendt (1994a), comprise the most critical elements of totalitarianism. That so many more of those elements also cast their shadow over domestic and international life might prompt us to re-evaluate beliefs apropos our vulnerability to a new 'postmodern totalitarianism',

---

2. See Mueller (2005) for a discussion of how the 'terrorism industry' massively inflates the perceived threat that would be involved in any attack or series of attacks.

courtesy ironically of 'New Labour'. Perhaps spin doctors will yet give us *'neue arbeit macht frei'*.[3]

Earlier in this chapter the social representations of European totalitarianism were seen to provide little basis for any psychological anticipation of the phenomenon in the UK. One clear factor however, does distinguish the present situation from previous historical examples in Europe. In all prior instances totalitarianism rode into town on the back of economic and political crisis. This has yet to occur in the UK—though the signs of political crisis are most certainly there—an ominous atomising of social and political life and an utter contempt for civil liberties. At best one could argue that current trends are the result of a misguided desire to impose what politicians believe is good for us. But as Todorov cautions:

Why is the plan to impose good so dangerous? Assuming that we knew what good was, in order to achieve it we would need to declare war on all who disagreed. (Todorov, 2003, p. xix)

From a less charitable, but no less dangerous, perspective, politics in Great Britain is now marked by an insatiable hunger for power,[4] which the electorate shows little appetite for. The last Blair Government was elected by only 21.8 per cent of eligible voters—as a percentage, the lowest won by any governing party in recent European history (Ali, 2005). Two of the literary classics about totalitarian life originate from English writers—Huxley and Orwell. We must hope that our contemporary reality is not about to furnish us with a third.

---

3. 'New Labour sets you free.'
4. 'I have taken from my party everything they thought they believed in. I have stripped them of their core beliefs. What keeps it together is success and power.' (Tony Blair, quoted in Sampson, 2004, p. 78.)

CHAPTER 11

Deconstructing Terrorism:
Politics, language and social representation

CHRIS HEWER and WENDY TAYLOR

> Just because we condemn does not mean that we should not strive to comprehend. (Burke, 2004, p. 250)

In recent years, the conflict of culture between the Middle East and the West has culminated in extreme acts of violence. The moral, religious, social and political differences are not, however, just differences of opinion; they are founded on competing realities generated by two different civilisations. This chapter considers these two positions and reviews our psychological understanding of politically motivated violence, arguing in favour of an approach that combines elements of social constructionism (Gergen, 1999; Burr, 2003) and social representations theory (Moscovici, 1961/1976). The principal contaminating factor within contemporary social and forensic psychological analysis is, in our view, the recourse to individualism, which obscures an alternative and more persuasive theoretical narrative that accounts for suicide attacks and the factors likely to mobilise individuals to carry them out. Producing explanations at the level of the individual also limits our understanding because it moves the analysis away from an examination of the significance of language, which within both a social constructionist critique and social representations theory, is critically important. The central idea is that the selective use of language and discourse, the arbitrary identification of historical precedent and the formation of culturally derived constructs actively structure and generate cultural meaning. This form of knowledge, which may be laden with political and/or religious import, is systematically endorsed by the culture to provide a basis for collective explanation and understanding. The result is a subjective view of the world that ultimately accounts for a broad repertoire of social behaviour including politically motivated violence. Notwithstanding these processes, the tendency to explain politically motivated violence in terms of cognitive states and motivations of the individual persists due to a combination of common sense on the one hand and the influence of scientific orthodoxy on the other.

In the world of science, solutions to practical problems ranging from the identification of a virus to the mundane malfunction of a washing machine are deduced from the systematic analysis of component parts. The cause is identified, isolated and rectified; the problem is solved and our understanding enhanced. Consequently, when scientific reductionism is applied to the social world, the environment, group culture or populace is reduced to its primary component— the individual—whose behaviour thus becomes the object of analysis. The consequence of this is that the source of what appears to be aberrant, bizarre or alien behaviour is always seen to emanate from within the dark, unexplored psyche of the individual. This is the domain of the psychologist; real and fictional and the tendency to explain suicide attacks in this way perpetuates the myth that the individual is the 'root of all evil'. Even though attempts to produce a predictive profile of 'the mind of the terrorist' have proved fruitless (see Merari, 1998; Reuter, 2004), many forensic psychologists still see the root of the problem firmly located within the mind of the individual (Canter 2005; Meloy, 2004; Pomerantz, 2001). Others have, however, reported links between the social environment and the formation of the beliefs of a suicide attacker (Valenty, 2004; Crenshaw, 2000; Post, Sprinzak & Denny, 2003), but this has yet to develop into a research paradigm that gives adequate weighting to the social, cultural and historical context of the behaviour. This is a theoretical and cultural blind spot that results from the belief that the individual is self-contained and separate from the 'social', that the individual resides in, but is not a product of, the environment (see Greenwood, 2004; Farr, 1996).

Conceptualising the self as a separate and discrete entity in the West is not surprising given that capitalism was forged on the concept of individualism. Competition for jobs and markets is the lifeblood of the culture and the identification and measurement of psychological constructs, such as intelligence and personality has made it possible to discriminate between those who have capital value and those who do not. Consequently, these constructs have taken on considerable cultural, social and economic significance. Furthermore, performance in business, education and sport is premised on the pursuit of abstract, individualistic objectives, which ultimately dichotomises people into 'winners and losers' so that achievement and success become part of our everyday understanding of the world, the meaning and purpose to life. Social and economic life has thus become an intra- and international battleground in which only the fittest survive, an inhospitable 'dog-eat-dog' world that, despite its material and technological advances, comes to lament the absence of community and the spiralling increase in crime. The psychological isolation induced by individualism thus provides the basis for an approach to human nature that sees the social context as having secondary status—a mere 'add on' to the individual. This is the Western view that celebrates the triumph of the individual over the environment and endorses a world where the agency of the individual reigns supreme. These assumptions are far-reaching since they not only determine how we should act, but they also provide a template for interpreting the actions of others. Hence, individualism has the potential to obscure our understanding of other equally valid cultural perspectives on politics, family, law and order, morality, war, economics, religion and human nature.

The alternative to this approach is a cultural model of human nature that promotes the idea that society is as much in us—determining who we are—as we are in it. Rather than thinking of the individual and society as separate units, it may be more productive to think of them as inseparable components of a system, neither of which can make sense without the other (Burr, 2003). In this model, human nature is not universal across time and place but instead, is constructed by the dominant social, political, religious and economic ideologies of the time. For example, it has been argued that capitalism has altered human nature in the West over the centuries to the extent that it has made us 'more independent, self-reliant and critical and ... more isolated, alone and afraid' (Fromm, 1942, p. 90). Fromm (1957) further argues that the principles of capitalism have infected human relations to the point that people have now become objects for use and consumption. Thus, the social, political and economic system, which we assume to be outside of us, has become part of our internal mechanism for thought and action. This therefore raises as many questions about our own world-view as it does about those of others and because the analysis applies as much to 'us' as it does to 'them', social reality becomes a matter for negotiation. Most importantly, it highlights that there are always two theoretical positions available to us when we study social phenomena. The individual and the collective/cultural both offer plausible accounts of social reality but the latter is rarely given pre-eminence in the West for all sorts of historical, religious and cultural reasons. To ignore it however, or to downplay its significance, only produces a partial view of the world. Indeed, one could argue that to ask psychologists to unravel the mystique of suicide attacks is to presume the nature of the cause in the first place. Anthropologists, sociologists and political analysts would no doubt provide a different level of explanation. Durkheim put it more succinctly: 'Every time a psychological explanation is offered for social phenomena; we may rest assured that the explanation is false' (Durkheim 1895/1982, p. 129). This, in our view, is the first potential pitfall of any analysis—a lack of interdisciplinary research and an uncritical approach to the epistemological assumptions of the discipline of the researcher.

Cherry (1995) illustrates this to powerful effect in her analysis of the murder of Kitty Genovese that took place in New York in 1964. Thirty-eight people witnessed the attack from the comfort of their homes, but no one called the police. Social psychologists later explained the event in terms of an individual psychological state induced by the situation; a 'diffusion of responsibility' to act caused by the number of people observing the event (Darley & Latané, 1968). This proposition, which was empirically tested in a series of experimental trials, is indeed plausible and perhaps resonates with our own experience of public incidents. However, Cherry argues that these conclusions obscured a more critical insight—that Kitty Genovese died because of an implicit cultural and political belief, (what we might now call social representations of gender relations) that violence to certain types of women was an acceptable practice. Cherry also points out that this event—a violent act against a woman—was stripped of its meaning and reconstituted into a theory about the reactions of individual observers in generalised public settings—a theory that has come to be known as 'bystander intervention'. The consequence of this type of theorising was that the culture of the day was not indicted and the status quo was maintained. What is more, the authoritative voice of objective psychological research (reductionist science) had confirmed that the fault lay not within American society but within the mechanism of a universal, omnipresent psychological phenomenon that is simply triggered by the presence of others.

In making such a claim, Darley and Latané transformed a political and cultural artefact (seeing violence against certain types of women as benign) into a scientific phenomenon, which had the effect of absolving the community from blame, inhibiting societal self-reflection and confirming the reassuring myth that 'we the people are good'. Cherry further argues that Darley and Latané's theory was itself a product of culture, politics, time and place since their insights were coloured by their own social demographics and professional training. More importantly, had they exposed the wider cultural discourse existing at the time, they may have also identified the means by which such behaviour could be eradicated. For sure, the solution to the problem of violence against women does not depend on an awareness of a state of 'diffusion of responsibility', since this achieves intervention at best, but it lies in challenging and changing the cultural values that are indifferent to the rights of women. Furthermore, the cultural milieu has greater explanatory power since it not only explains the actions of the passive observer but also of the assailant. Thus, even a monocultural view of social reality is more holographic than photographic—such that a subtle degree of movement that shifts the analysis from the individual to the cultural produces a completely different picture. Cherry's work thus presents a warning to us not to exclude culture from the analysis, not least because the fixed position of the post-dictive observer (as opposed to the predictive observer) is vulnerable to error and oversight. Indeed, the 'sleight of hand' that takes the eye away from the cultural towards the cognitive state of the individual has the effect of transforming a legitimate perspective into an unequivocal reality. It is therefore important to take a critical stance towards any theory that decontextualises the original action even when there is empirical support for it. This cautionary tale concerning the political nature of theorising has a parallel in the analysis of terrorism.

The objective of scholarly research: prevention or understa

Those charged with the responsibility of protecting the public f
motivated violence, including those involved in decision-mak _
development are, by circumstance and social role, locked into a mindset of
prevention where the objective is to deter, detect, enforce and apprehend. In the
'prevention' mindset the criminal is deemed to be 'not like us', but uncivilised
and evil. These absolute categories, which often take root in times of war, allow
us to demonise the opposition, which then moves us to adopt what we consider to
be the appropriate action, i.e. to deter, detect, enforce and apprehend. This
approach, however, has far-reaching consequences because it forces us to theorise
from a fixed position and in one direction only so that an atrocity against *us* is
always assumed to be about '*them*' and because theorising centred on '*them*' is
decontextualised, we are inevitably drawn to a thesis about their irrational, internal
states. The alternative is to think reflexively and consider the interactive position,
that any action *against* us must be *about* us, and therefore we should be generating
a theory about ourselves—our own culture, politics and values rather than focusing
on '*them*'. The dynamics of an interactive model of social behaviour are taken
for granted at the micro level of small groups, but these are ignored at the macro
level of culture. This is because national governments are primarily governed by
what is 'in the national interest', a self-serving principle that often trumps any
argument based on individual or collective ethics or morals and one that is
oblivious to any suggestion that their own stance has been a source of provocation.
What is also characteristic of the prevention mind-set is that it produces a consistent
discourse, i.e. that (alien and irrational) individuals are determined to change our
way of life but they will not prevail. This may appear to be an appropriate response,
but the political nature of this rhetoric is exposed when we consider the alternative
approach, one that focuses on acquiring an understanding[1] of terrorism, and more
specifically, suicide attacks.

Understanding this phenomenon can only be achieved by looking beyond
the level of the individual and examining the nature of cultural discourse (in both
communities). For example, the assumptions embedded in a Western view of
terrorism and the representations propagated by government, media and foreign
policy produce a working contradiction. On the one hand, adversaries are seen as
irrational, fanatical and unpredictable and, on the other, policy is based on the
premise that terrorists are calculating actors who will be deterred by the threat of
punishment (Crenshaw, 1998). However, when we move towards a cultural level
of analysis we see that both assumptions may be wrong. Firstly, suicide attacks
do have a rational objective since they aim to raise awareness and to apply pressure

---

1. This should not be construed as a route that leads to justification any more than condemnation
indicates a lack of understanding. Explanation and moral judgement are independent processes
and there is no logical necessity to conflate them.

...1at will ultimately secure the withdrawal of Western forces from Muslim territories (Crenshaw, 1990; Pape, 2005). Secondly, these attacks are unlikely to be deterred by threats of punishment since they are governed by a sense of religious duty, self-sacrifice and an unremitting belief in the rewards of the afterlife (Oliver & Steinberg, 2005).

Language, constructs, categories and cultural frameworks

Within any community engaged in conflict, constructs, categories and cultural frameworks provide the structure and foundation for action. For example, to describe the enemy as inherently evil is an essentialist position that reduces uncertainty, intensifies emotion and increases commitment to the cause. However, in many cases, the ephemeral nature of these constructions is exposed years later when the humanity of a former enemy becomes apparent, e.g. members of the Argentine military after the Falklands conflict; the people of the former Soviet Union after the end of the Cold War. We learn that they too had the same thoughts and ideals: to have a home and family and to live in peace. To make sense of this situation, either we extol the human capacity for change or we conclude that our former enemy was never so far removed from us in the first place. Either way, the structures of our world are slowly dismantled to the extent that past events can now only be satisfactorily explained by the motivating power of religious, cultural and political discourse or the political landscape of the time. Thus, as we endeavour to understand the situation holistically, the wider political and historical framework becomes of central importance (Hudson, 1999).

The intellectual distinction between an essentialist and a constructivist conception of human nature is important because it determines the way in which we understand others and ourselves. The tension between these two positions is illustrated by the way in which recent British governments have handled the political situation in Northern Ireland. For example, Margaret Thatcher maintained an unambiguous position on the issue of negotiation with the IRA. 'We do not negotiate with terrorists.' was the stated policy. This was the language of absolutism. To the government of John Major, however, the nature of the IRA was a more malleable construction, one that was eventually reformed, much to the discomfort, pain and difficulty of those on the opposing side. The transition from terrorist to statesman is not a new phenomenon; it is one that has also been seen in recent decades in Israel and South Africa. Indeed, once the veil and obfuscation of terrorism and all its rhetorical properties are stripped away, what remains are the actions of an unconventional war, waged by an oppressed and relatively powerless minority limited in economic resource. Consequently, what is deemed a terrorist atrocity carried out by fanatics by one side is seen as legitimate military activity carried out by soldiers on the other.

This therefore calls into question the legitimacy of the term terrorism and its use as a construct within social and political discourse. As we reflect on the mental pictures and emotions that terrorism invokes and the way in which it creates political conceptions, we experience its profound effects. However, from an ontological position, terrorism does not exist at all—it is a construct—one that dates back to the French Revolution and one that is now employed by ruling elites to de-legitimise politically motivated violence against state interests. What really exists is the bloodshed and although there is uncritical acceptance of the construct among political elites of all persuasions across the world, it is noteworthy that the role of the terrorist is always filled by a different group of actors. Thus, 'terrorism' is a marker that is used to distinguish between legitimate and non-legitimate politically motivated violence; it is a linguistic tool that serves the interests of the state and those who wish to maintain the status quo and obscure the political import of the act. The battle to grant or deny legitimacy to politically motivated violence of any sort is fought on a second front in the media by those skilled in political rhetoric. It is here in this public space that social representations are formed, emerging in response to the claims and counterclaims of politicians and the moderating views of political commentators. However, if 'terrorism' were replaced by the term 'politically motivated violence' two things would become explicit: (1) we would be forced to confront the *political* objectives and their legitimacy (which is what is usually done in the long term) and (2) state military action would also fall within this definition, which might reduce its moral capacity to act. Therefore, terrorism, as a construct, exerts enormous rhetorical power within the public sphere to the extent that a cry of 'terrorism' from any government is to claim the moral high ground. Equally, we should be cautious about any claim that suicide attacks are simply acts of destructive rage carried out by gangs of brainwashed religious fanatics. The essence of this rhetorical assertion is that the 'brainwashed' are psychotic, out of touch with the consensus and out of touch with *our* sense of reality. Their reality is one that *we* cannot see or one with which *we* cannot agree. Thus, the rhetoric of everyday life creates a self-deception that enables us to uphold our version of reality and reduce the political, religious and epistemic view of 'the other' to untreatable madness.

On the other side of the ideological fence, bin Laden and other Islamic ideologues represent the Americans and British as crusaders, anchoring them in the familiar setting of Islamic history as religious heretics who have sought to gain control of Palestine from the Muslims (bin Laden, 2001b). This categorisation process, like any other, provides a basis for understanding the world and, in this case, invokes a sense of certainty—a belief in the unchanging nature of the enemy and their longstanding political and religious motivations. However, as the process of labelling and categorisation provides one level of insight, it simultaneously eliminates all other possibilities because everything is construed within the one framework. Political rhetoric in the West does much the same, as it provides its own categories of reference. For example, media reports about the war in Iraq were initially framed within a reference of 'liberation and democracy'—the expressed objectives of the West—rather than 'invasion and occupation'—the experience of those living in the region. Therefore, the specific use of language, the formation of constructs, categorisation and cultural frameworks play a significant part in the construction of social reality. This means that knowledge is not just represented within a culture; it is manufactured *by* the culture. The culture, therefore, determines what is true and false, what is of value and what is not. Furthermore, knowledge that is unobtrusive, taken for granted or deemed to be common sense is unlikely to be challenged, and even when ideas are explicit they will often be oversimplified, distorted or corrupted versions of more complex and ambiguous situations and events. In most cases, people rely on the media to report, interpret and provide meaning to events and these representations are later reconstituted as common-sense knowledge resulting in the dissemination of a 'processed' version of reality. This is the essence of the theory of social representations (Moscovici, 1961/1976).

Social representations of suicide attacks

Social representations theory thus provides a theoretical framework for understanding the structure and dynamics of collective/cultural thinking and this dovetails well with a social constructionist approach since both work on the premise that social reality is a product of time and place. This is where the passive/active assimilation of ideas produces a mosaic of cultural thought and the knowledge (and action) that results ultimately expresses the collective understanding of a community. This fabric of understanding is continually adjusted and filtered by the media, which select events and report them within a specific moral and political framework. These accounts are the fodder of everyday conversation, which comes to fuel debate and structure thinking. Therefore, the subject matter of everyday conversation and the interactive process that takes place between people becomes more theoretically significant than the individuals themselves (see Wagner & Hayes, 2005). Furthermore, the anthropologic principle established by Lévy-Bruhl ([1925]/1926) takes on particular significance—that social representations, whatever their cultural origins, are always rational to the culture that generates them, although 'they need not be so, either in the same sense or according to the same logic, in the eyes of another' (Moscovici & Duveen, 2000, p. 213). Hence, the theory offers a psychological explanation of social, cultural and international conflict, real and imagined; and what we have, in the case of the Middle East and the West, are two civilisations that have generated different social representations of the same set of political circumstances.

The view of the Middle East from the West

From the position of the West, values such as freedom of speech and human rights are paramount and, because these freedoms are equated with democracy, the West thus assumes all other systems to be undesirable or oppressive. To illustrate, former British Foreign Secretary, Jack Straw recently stated that he believed that, 'democracy is within the heart of every human being' (Barron, 2005). This cultural assumption par excellence transforms democracy from a political system into a universal theory of human nature, thus dismissing a whole spectrum of legitimate alternatives including anarchism, monarchy and theocracy. The West also positions itself as the 'civilised world' whose morally unassailable values are currently under threat and underpinning this perspective is the 'War on Terror' in which the enemy is unseen, unknown and undefined. Raising a profile of anonymity not only raises the level of fear among the general public, but conveniently allows governments to make arbitrary identification of those who appear to fit the description of 'those who are against us' and, paradoxically, to act repressively and in a manner contrary to principles of freedom and human rights even within their own territories. The West also sees suicide attacks as something alien, uncivilised and cowardly, carried out by fanatics. There is often reflexive incomprehension about what the assailants achieve for themselves, given that people in the West are largely fixated on this life rather than, what has become for many, the hypothetical or fictitious afterlife. Abhorrence for the deaths of innocent civilians has also led to accusations of moral bankruptcy and individual derangement; concluding by the logic of mutually exclusive categories that *they* are evil and *we* are good. Furthermore, the separation of religion and state in the West allows commentators to make a clear distinction between the aims and objectives of religious and political groups operating within a culture. Therefore, for example, Zionism and Judaism in Israel and Republicanism and Catholicism in Northern Ireland are neither confused nor conflated, whereas there is currently no word or phrase in the English language to distinguish between the actions of politically motivated radical Islamic groups and ordinary Muslims. In the world of labels and categories, they are all Muslims—all adherents of Islam.

The view of the West from the Middle East

The view from the Middle East presents a different picture of the West. Key Islamic ideologues, such as Sayyid Qutb, who was largely responsible for shaping the thinking of bin Laden, have expressed revulsion at the culture (Ruthven, 2004). Decades on, Western culture has not changed; if anything, it has veered even further away from Islamic ideals. This is because, notwithstanding its Christian foundations, the West assumes an evolutionary paradigm in science and promotes sexual liberation, gay rights and feminism. Furthermore, the media provide a staple mental diet of Hollywood violence, game shows, reality TV and soaps, a trivialisation of reality that worships youth, and encourages and elevates the narcissistic pursuit of fame, celebrity and bodily perfection. Add to this the widespread immoderate use of alcohol and the resulting violence among young people, the incessant profanity in public discourse and an endemic disregard for marriage; it is not surprising that the social consequences of liberal democracy are seen as an assault on conservative religious values rather than evidence of a superior culture. Moreover, in the realm of politics, Islamic culture sees no necessity to separate religion and state. Although the armies of the Islamic Ottoman Empire succeeded in conquering vast areas of South-Eastern Europe, the cultural development of Islam remained in a state of fixed orthodoxy and did not go through the equivalent of Europe's Renaissance, the Enlightenment, constitutional reforms or transition to modernity. Islamic religious law therefore provides a comprehensive system for regulating individual, social and political life in accordance with the perceived will of God. Consequently, political consciousness and religious identity converge to the point that the private and the political are indistinguishable (Monroe & Kreidie, 1997).

Radical Islamic movements also contend that a society of good Muslims can only be achieved through an Islamic state where religion is at the apex of power regulating the legitimisation of knowledge and beliefs. Moreover, the belief that all truth is contained in the Qur'an means that there is a 'prescribed programme for action for any political grievance' (Burke, 2004, p. 28). Consequently, Islamic groups, who require moral sanction for their use of violence, but who do not have the approval of an officially recognised government, are able to appeal to a higher source. The integration of religious values and principles into political life makes sense to those who see God as supreme and having such a religious framework also makes it easy to explain political grievances and makes remedial action easier and far more potent (Burke, 2004). Therefore, when conflicts are framed within a discourse of good and evil, believers and unbelievers, it tends to 'transcendentalise disputes, elevating them from the mundane to the cosmic level … rendering them more intractable and less susceptible to negotiation' (Ruthven, 2004, p. 167).

The view from the East also draws us into a historical analysis. Since the British occupation of Palestine in 1917, the region has been a source of contention throughout the world. Bin Laden describes this period as '80 years of humiliation' (bin Laden, 2001a) and further accuses the US of 'occupying the lands of Islam', specifically Lebanon, Saudi Arabia and Iraq—'plundering its riches, dictating to its rulers, humiliating its people, terrorising its neighbours and turning its bases in the peninsula into a spearhead through which to fight the neighbouring Muslim peoples' (bin Laden, 1998).

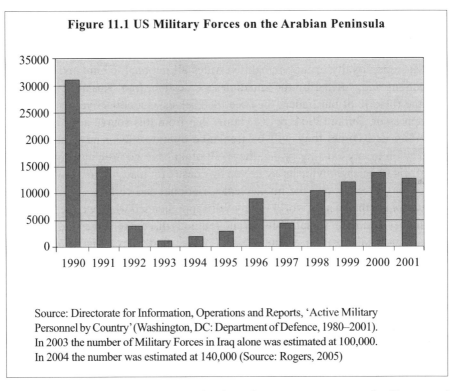

Figure 11.1 US Military Forces on the Arabian Peninsula

Source: Directorate for Information, Operations and Reports, 'Active Military Personnel by Country' (Washington, DC: Department of Defence, 1980–2001). In 2003 the number of Military Forces in Iraq alone was estimated at 100,000. In 2004 the number was estimated at 140,000 (Source: Rogers, 2005)

The Anglo-American alliance is therefore seen as an embodiment of Christendom—a reincarnation of ancient Anglo-Saxon crusaders forming part of a joint venture with Israel to take the Holy Land from Islam. Indeed, the growing ideological harmony between Muslims means that many now see the cause of the Palestinians, along with Kashmir, Chechnya and Iraq, as part of one battle, a global jihad, the root of which can be traced back to the Soviet invasion of Afghanistan in 1979. After the Mujahidin had repelled the Soviet army, the movement grew, based on a belief that God would sponsor further success. Eventually, its attention turned westward and, in 1996, Osama bin Laden declared war on the United States. The events in New York on September 11th 2001 brought the conflict to the fore and radicalised the West. However, it was Europe's failure to protect Bosnian Muslims from the Serbs in 1995 that polarised the views of many Muslims living in the West and their response was to be driven by cultural and religious concepts that are rarely articulated or understood by the West.

Ummah and martyrdom

One of these concepts is the ummah—the Muslim brotherhood. Before 'European colonisation divided the world into discrete territories, Islamic polities were organised communally rather than territorially' (Ruthven, 2002, p. 137). This community of faith, feeling and destiny still prevails today and generates a sense of collective identity within the Islamic world. Secularists, however, find this instinctively difficult to grasp since it has no parallel in the West. Nonetheless, for Muslims, loyalty to the ummah overrides all national, ethnic and linguistic affiliations and, fuelled by the situation in Palestine, Iraq, Kashmir, Chechnya and the rhetoric of bin Laden, they see themselves as a collective ready to face the oppressor. Burke (2004, p. 26) claims that from this source a 'new wave of terrorists will come; they will be freelance operators who have no obvious connection to any existing group; they will often have no previous involvement in terrorism'. Such individuals are driven by a desire for martyrdom—a willingness to die for the cause; and the intellectual, emotional and cultural significance of martyrdom in the Islamic world is only fully apprehended when we see the extent to which it dominates social, political and religious discourse. Given the epistemic and ontological position of the West, the idea that there exists a desire for martyrdom in parts of the Islamic world (Sageman, 2004b) and that it gives status equivalent to stardom perhaps comes as a shock.

Oliver and Steinberg (2005) describe the social environment in Palestine where massive canvases fill public squares; market stalls sell audiocassettes filled with songs of martyrdom and videotapes of the last words of suicide attackers calling for others to follow. Shops sell martyr books containing hagiographies, plays and leaflets, and martyr cards are passed around by children like football cards. Murals in the mosques depict red poppies sprouting from land irrigated with the blood of martyrs, and martyr heroes are depicted, gun in hand, commanding boys to their deaths. Inside the houses, shops and mosques are photographs of martyrs, martyr calendars and martyr shrines while outside walls are covered with the names of those who most recently have given their lives for the cause. According to Islamic teaching, a martyr is afforded six privileges with God; a guaranteed place in paradise, a crown of glory, forgiveness of sins, redemption from the torments of the grave secure from the fear of hell, marriage to 72 virgins and guaranteed intercession for 70 members of his family (Rapoport, 1998). The act also affirms the martyr's faith, courage and bravery; it indicates superiority of faith over the opponent as well as demonstrating strength to those he or she hopes to motivate (Sageman, 2004a, b). For the surviving family, honour is bestowed upon them and their social status is elevated. They receive cash gifts (Hamas pay the surviving family $25,000) and in some cases, a new home. Schools recount the heroic nature of the death and tell children that these are the moral examples to follow. Along with the usual nursery rhymes, children are taught songs and chants about defending their homeland and achieving victory over America and Israel. After school, children parade through the streets, chanting about martyrdom. On public television, the Palestinian Broadcasting Corporation airs videos of men being lured away by the *hur*, the beautiful virgins of paradise promised to martyrs, as if they were commercials. 'By pressing the detonator, you can immediately open the door to Paradise—it is the shortest path to heaven,' reports one suicide attacker whose mission failed (Hassan, 2001). Here the individual, the cultural, the political and the religious merge into one, fuelling a conviction that foments a desire to cross the barrier from life to death to life again. This is the mobilisation culture where meanings attached to actions provide moral certainty and conviction and, given the degree of cultural indoctrination in Palestine, and its example among the Muslim community of resistance to oppression and injustice, it is not surprising that other members of the ummah have chosen to take the fight beyond the borders of Israel.

Conclusions

In this chapter, we argue that the psychology of suicide attacks should be understood in terms of the motivational power of complex cultural and religious belief systems, the historical, political and social milieu and the economics of marginalised groups. Thus, the psychology of the Islamic militant is not pathological but cultural. Their view of the world is rationally constructed on dircct or vicarious experience of oppression and elaborated historical and political discourse that is reinforced through the dynamics of everyday conversation. Moreover, their resistance to oppression is guided by ancient cultural concepts such as ummah, jihad and martyrdom, which give meaning to actions in the 'here and now', hope for the future and moral sanction to acts of violence. Consequently, the main research objective of those who wish to understand these actions should be to identify (1) the ideologies that construct the subjective realities of the perpetrators and (2) the processes by which these are transmitted through the culture, i.e. a research paradigm that gives sufficient weighting to the historical, political and social context. In addition, we argue that social psychological research needs to focus on the *content* of beliefs rather than simply delineating the structure of individual cognition, e.g. attitudes, stereotypes etc. We know that shared beliefs drive all forms of economic and social behaviour, therefore it makes sense to factor these into the analysis and not dismiss them as inconsequential social artefacts. Social representations theory enables us to do this—and with its emphasis on culturally derived knowledge and subjective realities, it explains how and why the West and the Islamic world fail to understand each other. We leave it to others to outline the way in which ideas in the Islamic world and the West have been anchored and objectified through the understanding of history, reporting in the media and other channels of communication. These features should be studied and explicated so that links between key ideologues and the interpretation of historical events provide a detailed and rational account of both positions. Furthermore, because young British Muslims are subject to the contradictions, paradoxes and conflicts of two cultures, it would be helpful to explore the relationship between social representations, discourse and identity, since identity is created from the substance of available cultural discourses (Shotter & Gergen,

1989) and can be construed as the assimilation and internalisation of a social representation (Duveen & Lloyd, 1990).

At the centre of this analysis is the issue of oppression and dominance and since 'dominating and dominated classes do not have a similar representation of the world they share' (Moscovici, 1984, p. 51), it is important to recognise the legitimacy of those who claim to be oppressed if we are to stave off politically motivated violence. However, the greater challenge is perhaps to see our role in the oppression of others. Oppression comes in many forms. To the strictly religious; it is decadence, to the libertine; it is religious orthodoxy; to the capitalist; it is intervention and restricted practice; to the socialist, it is greed and social injustice. Such is the relative nature of the social world. Of course, war, famine, maiming and death are not relative in any sense, but the political, cultural, ideological and epistemic arguments that create and justify them are. Therefore, in a world where there are few absolute realities, we might ponder on whether it is really possible to make a moral distinction between the call to jihad within the Islamic world and Winston Churchill's historic speech to the British people in 1940 that 'we will fight them [the German invaders] on the beaches ...' And if we now believe that suicide attacks are the product of an alien culture how should we explain the actions of Colonel H. Jones, a British army officer during the Falklands war in 1982, who elected to charge the enemy single-handedly in the full range of fire? This action, according to his comrades, was irrational and suicidal. Notwithstanding these views, much was made of this suicide attack by the establishment and the British press at the time. This was not the behaviour of a deranged lunatic or the product of an inferior and barbaric culture; this was valour of the highest order for which he was posthumously awarded the Victoria Cross—the highest award for a British soldier in combat.

CHAPTER 12

A Psychology for Peace?

DAVID HARPER, RON ROBERTS
AND JOHN SLOBODA

Psychology cannot attain the true idea of a science unless it also becomes dangerous. (Moscovici, 2000, p. 119)

The reasonable man adapts himself to the world. The unreasonable persists in trying to adapt the world to himself. Therefore all progress depends on the unreasonable man (Shaw, quoted in Power, 2003, p. 516)

Introduction

In this chapter we wish to pose a number of questions about the possibility of a psychology for peace and what the aims of such an undertaking would or could be. In an earlier chapter it was remarked that the genesis of psychology as a scientific discipline has meant that it lacks any historical roots in projects that have sought to improve the public good or bring radical social change. This is perhaps one reason why there exists no equivalent of the Hippocratic Oath which prevails in medicine. Lacking such a proclamation to 'first do no harm' means that many psychologists still cling steadfastly to the myth of scientific neutrality. Conway, Suedfeld and Tetlock (2001, p.67) for instance write,

> There is a tendency in the psychological literature to assume that war as an outcome is bad and that peace is good. Our own view is that this is a philosophical issue that generally lies beyond the scope of psychology. It may well be that wars are best judged, in the moral sense, as 'good' or 'bad' on a war-by-war basis. Whatever the case, however, the goal of the psychologist is to focus on the processes that lead to particular, predictable outcomes—and not to assign normative values to those outcomes.

So we should not assign normative values to war! With such a stance it is not difficult to understand why psychologists can be, and have been, readily recruited by military authorities to oversee campaigns of propaganda, psychological warfare, torture and mind control with no threat of sanctions from any professional body (see Chapters 1 and 4). Is it pertinent to ask whether psychologists working for the military should abide by ethical guidelines? If so, how would they be set and how would they be policed in a society where the security and state industries pursue their goals largely hidden from public scrutiny? If psychological knowledge is to be enlisted in any drive to enhance the well-being of people in the world, then it is important to recognise that to date it has had a rather dishonourable history, working on behalf of powerful elites to pursue aims which have a damaging effect on enormous numbers of people. With such a history the humanitarian purpose of psychology as an applied discipline remains at best unclear.

One can of course ask whether psychologists should be charged with possessing any greater responsibility than the followers of other intellectual endeavours to pursue peaceful resolutions to conflict or to challenge the philosophy and conduct of war. It is certainly recognised that physicists, chemists and biologists, whose knowledge has been employed in the design and manufacture of specific weapon systems, have a particular responsibility to question the wisdom of warfare. Amongst physicists, Einstein is perhaps the most well known of those who recognised the responsibility which their profession bequeathed to them (Pais, 2005). He considered it a moral duty to take 'an active part in the solution of the problem for peace' (quoted in Krieger, 2005). In this quest for peace he was particularly dismissive of those who pursue warfare as the means to resolve disputes:

How vile and contemptible war seems to me ... I happen to think highly enough of mankind to believe the spectre of war would long have disappeared had the sound common sense of the people not been systematically corrupted by commercial and political interests operating through the schools and the press. (Quoted in Braun & Krieger, 2005, p. 1)

Einstein's championing of the cause of peace encompassed outspoken attacks on militarism, nationalism, nuclear weapons and naked power as a goal in and of itself. Amidst his calls for human rights and social justice, he further argued that conscience supersedes all authority emanating from the state. So wherein lies the conscience of our discipline as our state wages war and destroys the peace of others?

Intrinsic to the question of psychologists' responsibility, in their capacity as psychologists (which stands in addition to their capacity simply as human beings), to question the role of war is the issue of whether there is any intrinsic relationship between war, conflict and psychology in the first place. To answer this one need only be reminded that warfare doesn't simply destroy the physical bodies of people or the environments in which they live. As a result of being in the presence of war and terror—whether as perpetrator, direct victim, witness, bystander or helper—huge numbers of people are traumatised. More diffuse and long-term effects will also ensue—loss of trust between peoples; of different nations or of different sectors of the same societies defined along gender, ethnic, religious or cultural lines. In short, war and international conflict is causing large-scale psychological distress among populations. All this of course, is in addition to the role that professional psychologists have had in supporting the state interests that have pursued violence and the fact that those who prosecute current policies are using psychological means to manipulate public opinion (Sloboda, 2003).

Peace psychology

Undoubtedly a major factor behind the formation of peace psychology came from the Cold War. Indeed the spiralling distrust and antipathy between the two superpowers, which at face value appeared to fuel the arms race and with it the threat of nuclear annihilation, almost of necessity demanded attention to the psychological dimensions of the conflict between East and West (Christie, Wagner & Winter, 2001). The Cold War in fact seemed to characterise a unique psychology of its own and led social psychologists in particular to seek greater understanding of not only the processes which might lead us into nuclear war but also how any survivors might respond to the aftermath. Such phenomena as fear appraisal, threat escalation, crisis management, human fallibility and conflict resolution thereby received due attention (e.g. Thompson, 1985).

A shortcoming of some of this work is that attention is focused narrowly on how the imagined possibilities open to actors and decision makers engaged in specific strategic interactions might lead to specific 'winnable' outcomes. Coleman (1982) for example describes the use of game theory to model the Cuban Missile Crisis. Theorists have been reluctant to consider how the concerns of the civilian populations, who would of course bear the brunt of any outcome, impact on the 'reasoning' featured within these modelled scenarios. Why is it necessary for example for the public to be kept ignorant of what is going on? Why does so much of this decision-making occur in secret, even in societies considered democratic? One can't help but conclude that the parameters within which such research is conducted are restricted to a limited set of assumptions that, intentionally or not, cater to elite interests—a point acknowledged by Pettigrew (1998) in his discussion of the failure of social psychology to impact on public policy. A more interesting application of psychological theorising to nuclear arms possession comes from Hymans (2006) who poses the question of why some states seek to obtain nuclear weapons whilst others do not. In a series of case studies of leaders from France, Argentina, India and Australia over a number of years, he argues that a key variable is the leader's conception of national identity.

Those who see their nation as at odds with an external enemy, to which it is either equal or superior—described by Hyman as 'oppositional nationalists'—are more likely to make the emotional push for nuclear weapons acquisition. Further tests of the theory are eagerly awaited, though further elaboration of the determinants of national identity conception—psychological, sociological, economic, technological and historical—are required. An interesting facet of 'nuclear' psychology is that unusually within the discipline a good deal of research has directed attention toward the behaviour of elites—in this case elite decision makers in military and/or political circles.

Peace psychology: problems

A major difficulty which persists in many of the analyses undertaken by psychologists concerned with peace and conflict is that the psychological nature of conflict situations, for example between different national, ethnic, social or religious groups, is assumed to occupy a fundamental explanatory role ahead of any economic or political considerations that may in fact be the real driving forces behind both the conflict and the psychological realities concomitant with it. Steinhart (2005) for example describes the Iraq War as the outcome of a conflict raging between collectivist, conformist and oral traditions and the individualistic, pluralistic and literate forms in US society. US domination of global energy reserves seems to have been bypassed or forgotten in this analysis.

Certainly political and cultural leaders have regularly co-opted others to their struggle for goods, resources and privileges by invoking the psychological and cultural characteristics of other groups (whether real or imagined) as viable threats to their own existence. Suitably persuaded, the political programs of all manner of demagogues may come to fruition through the violent actions of frightened people. Indeed at the Nuremberg trials Göring famously remarked:

> Of course the people don't want war. But after all, it's the leaders of the country who determine the policy, and it's always a simple matter to drag the people along whether it's a democracy, a fascist dictatorship, or a parliament, or a communist dictatorship. Voice or no voice, the people can always be brought to the bidding of the leaders. That is easy. All you have to do is tell them they are being attacked, and denounce the pacifists for lack of patriotism, and exposing the country to greater danger. (Gilbert, 1947, pp. 278–279)

Giving undue prominence to psychological aspects of conflict however risks feeding prejudices—that the root causes of conflict actually do reside in people's differing characteristics or affiliations—and hence that peaceful coexistence is not possible. A Western focus on individuals or small groups effectively precludes the development of a more comprehensive understanding. So, rather than uncritically inflate the importance of psychological insights above others, what is required is that relevant social psychological insights and perspectives be linked (as mediating variables) to the macro levels of culture, institution, social and economic structure (Druckman, 2001) and political strategy, and to be applicable across both industrialised and non-industrialised societies (Pettigrew, 1998).

We would propose several further requirements before psychological variables and mechanisms can be successfully (and usefully) incorporated into a broader explanatory scheme, one that includes the geopolitical and historical context. Firstly, psychologists must show themselves willing to embrace uncomfortable truths. The wish to refrain from apportioning blame and to maintain the pretence of neutrality in the face of armed conflict makes no sense whatsoever when that conflict is the result of a unprovoked aggressive war waged by one heavily armed party against another poorly armed or defenceless group—such as civilians! One must of course be clear to distinguish the mere attribution of moral responsibility from an explanatory framework in which key actors/agents are identified with specific actions. Agger (2001) provides a telling example. In discussing reconciliation work undertaken in Bosnia she is completely unable to mention in her account that the Bosnian war began when Serbian forces launched a wanton attack upon the civilians of Bosnia, followed later by an attack from the Croatian side. From her account we learn little about the events or circumstances of the war—for example, who the major perpetrators were, or the fact that it was the Bosnian Muslims who were subject to genocide, whilst the international community stood by and watched. Her own account is worth examining in some detail:

> I was ... to ... give a lecture to a group of psychologists, psychiatrists and social workers who were participating in a training program on post-traumatic therapy. I talked about the importance of not using testimonies to increase tensions among ethnic groups, and I said 'Now at a time when Bosnia has been in a process of peace for more than a year, the main issues are related to confidence building, dialogue, and reconciliation among the three ethnic groups who fought each other'. They shouted angrily at me, and I felt the impact of their aggression as a wave coming toward me to silence me ... According to their model of the world, there were not three ethnic groups who had fought each other. There was an aggressor and a victim ... There were 35 people in the room, and maybe 10 of them spoke angrily; the others were silent and looked uncomfortable. (Agger, 2001, p. 242)

During the Bosnian war a frequent excuse offered by the international community (both the European Community and the US government) for not intervening was precisely the point of view, adopted by Agger, which held all sides equally responsible for the fighting. Though abundant information was available to refute this position, nothing was done and a three-year-long bloodbath ensued. No wonder Agger's audience were angry, silent or uncomfortable in the face of an outsider coming to tell them that 'in order to recover' from the trauma of war they had now to adopt the same incorrect model of reality that in part had been responsible for prolonging it. Agger in fact seems determined to sit on the fence and deny the validity of her participants' anger. In pursuit of the 'view from nowhere', Agger is actually going nowhere. She seems continually unhappy with any demonstration of anger from her participants—the expression of which is described in one place (p. 249) as a 'monologue'. Could one imagine the Warsaw uprising described as two ethnic groups—Jews and Germans fighting each other, or Jewish outrage about these events described as a monologue? In a profession wedded to neutrality and a scientific world-view that decries the value of emotion, the question of how to deal with anger is problematic in the extreme—but it is central to addressing the consequences of conflict.

This example illustrates not just the unwillingness to face uncomfortable feelings, or the desire to remain neutral in the face of an uneven conflict—uneven both morally and militarily—it is testimony also to a lack of reflexivity on Agger's part concerning the cultural influences which have shaped her views, and what her position in Bosnia might represent to those who live there. Furthermore, this episode provides a demonstration of the necessity for psychologists to be more fully informed of events occurring in the international arena prior to launching into unbridled speculation about their causes or how to manage their consequences—a particular danger when experts are 'parachuted' into local 'hot spots' purveying an expert discourse ignorant of the local knowledge available. Many other examples can to be found in the psychological literature where unpalatable truths go unspoken—the role of the illegal US bombing of Cambodia in bringing the Khmer Rouge to power is ignored in favour of an approach where 'an ideology of antagonism' (Staub, 2001) between different groups is considered central to their emergence. Staub also appears to adopt a somewhat benevolent approach toward the US when considering the role of leaders in perpetrating violence:

> During the summer of 1990, Saddam Hussein ordered a successful Iraqi invasion of the oil-rich country, surprising the rest of the world. (Staub, 2001, p. 70)

In fact the main causes of Iraq–Kuwait tension prior to the first US Gulf War originated in the policies of Kuwait, which during the Iran–Iraq War had stolen over two billion dollars worth of oil from oilfields within the territorial borders of Iraq, had constructed military installations on Iraq territory, and had been colluding with the United Arab Emirates to exceed production quotas fixed by OPEC, leading to reduced oil prices, which in turn resulted in revenue losses of

14 billion dollars a year to Iraq (Ahmed, 2003). There is ample evidence that US sources had given indications to the Iraqi regime that it would turn a blind eye to any military confrontation with Kuwait.

Far from being a surprise to the rest of the world, the US had in fact been running war-game simulations of an Iraqi invasion of Kuwait since late the previous year and according to 'Stormin' Norman Schwarzkopf who led the US attack, the invasion had been 19 months in the planning (Ahmed, 2003). Not exactly a surprise then. This is not to exonerate the Iraqi regime under Saddam from responsibility for colossal bloodshed, merely to show that psychologists can too easily adopt a position whereby Western complicity in such events is conveniently ignored.

Staub again:

Some leaders have been especially important in creating great violence: Hitler, Stalin, Idi Amin, Saddam Hussein, probably Milosevic in Yugoslavia, and warlords in Africa, like General Aidid in Somalia. (Staub, 2001, p. 80)

One thing of interest in this extract is to notice who has been excluded as well as who has been included. US presidents (Kennedy, Johnson, Nixon) involved in prosecuting the wars in Southeast Asia which saw the slaughter of millions of people for example are excluded, as is the ringleader of the Rwanda genocide (Bagosora), not to mention Mao Tse-tung. On the other hand Milosevic is included, with the qualification that he was only 'probably' instrumental in creating great violence. No doubt hundreds of thousands of people in the Balkans, not to mention the members of the International War Crimes Tribunal in The Hague, would 'probably' disagree with this timid assessment. If further examples of sanitizing brutal realities are required then we can turn to terrorist psychologist John Horgan to provide them. In probing the funding and training of terrorist organisations he is apparently oblivious to the role of US and British security services in arming, funding and training the Mujahidin not only during the Afghan war against the Soviet Union (Ahmed, 2003) but in their participation in the global terror networks which have emerged since then (Ahmed, 2006). Then, in discussing the background of the 9/11 hijackers, he states 'prayer and other normalising activity … may have been an important feature of the hijackers' collective behaviour before and during the attacks' (p. 34). He again seems unaware of a large body of evidence—this time regarding the behaviour of the lead 9/11 hijackers—which shows that they were not all devout Muslims (see Ahmed, 2005). Numerous further examples could be provided, but these should suffice to make the point that too often psychologists' understanding of international events appears tied to the ideological considerations of the Western powers.

Peace psychology: possibilities

Woolf and Hulsizer (2004) have noted that despite the enormous mental and physical suffering that results from it, psychologists have tended to ignore human rights issues and mass violence. They argue that equipped with knowledge of the cognitive, affective, social, cultural and societal roots of mass violence, students will in future be more likely to accept the mantle of social responsibility and become more involved as citizens and psychologists in the global culture. Those who have exercised some of this responsibility to date and pursued a psychological understanding of peace and violence have borrowed conceptual tools from different branches of the discipline. Within the social domain, game theory and identity theory have been employed to examine aspects of strategic decision-making (Snidal, 1985) and the origins of group conflict respectively (Tajfel, 1981). Cognitive, social and biologically oriented psychologists have identified numerous factors underlying human fallibility in decision making and in responding to crises: boredom, habit, routine, familiarity, mindset, isolation, drug and alcohol use, stress, circadian rhythms and group think (Dumas, 2001). Those with a more clinical orientation have contributed to analysing the steps involved in successful conflict resolution (Strasser & Randolph, 2004) and recovery from trauma (Herman, 2001). A benign assumption behind this work is that the knowledge gained may contribute in future to an improvement in the human situation. Not all applications of psychological theory however offer an optimistic vision of human nature or the future possibilities for benevolent change.

In recent years evolutionary psychologists have applied Darwinian principles to the problem of human aggression and begged the question as to whether human aggression is adaptive. Buss (2004) for example has proposed several adaptive problems for which aggression might theoretically have evolved to provide the solution. These include the enhancement of status or power within existing social hierarchies; to inflict costs on sexual rivals (intra-sexual competition); to deter mates from infidelity or rivals from future aggression; to defend against attack; and to co-opt or steal the resources (e.g. land, food, water, tools and weapons) of others to enhance one's own survival and reproduction. These considerations find their apotheosis in and Cosmides' (1988) 'risk contract' theory of warfare and ethnocentric conflict. This proposes that human males have evolved a number of mechanisms, which function to increase their reproductive success, and which render them susceptible to participation in 'coalitional' warfare. They argue several 'characteristics' of males appear consistent with this theory, for example morphological adaptations suited to fighting, being more likely to engage in warfare, increased sexual access to victims of warfare i.e. the rape of victims, and having the capability to spontaneously assess their fighting ability better than women. Evolutionary accounts of contentious areas of human behaviour however have not been without their critics (e.g. Rose & Rose, 2001) and this proposal is no exception.

Ferguson (2000, 2001) has pointed out that Tooby and Cosmides' contentions are not supported by a detailed examination of historical evidence. In documented instances of tribal warfare e.g. the Yanomani people of Brazil, he contends that allegiances do not in fact follow genetic relatedness, that instinctive hostility is not directed to strangers or those who are culturally different and contrary to received opinion (e.g. Pinker, 1998) men do not initiate raids solely to capture women. He further argues that there is little evidence that warfare was ever a regular feature of our ancestral environment, though evolutionary psychologists continue to dispute this (e.g. Gat, 2000). Dawson (1999) meanwhile believes that whilst it is conceivable that warfare may once have been a major agent of (small) group selection in our evolutionary past, since the rise of state-level societies thousands of years ago, it certainly no longer is. The observable rates of extinction amongst human groups are so slow as to render the prospect of group selection through warfare extremely improbable.

So if warfare is not an agent of selection in the modern world, the actions of powerful nations in enforcing economic, political and military dominance to control resources throughout the world should not then be envisaged as part of a Darwinian struggle for survival, explicable in evolutionary-genetic terms. This can be dismissed. In this context it is important to distinguish between those who make the decisions to wage war and those who, in joining the armed forces, are charged with fighting it. Milgram (1974) famously drew attention to the propensity of people to follow the orders of those in authority—a propensity which may well have arisen as a result of natural selection. However the plundering of the resources of other nations is a project repeatedly unleashed by dominant elites to favour their own interests, not their citizens. Economic and material interests, not ethnocentric or biological relatedness, unite such elites, i.e. it is corporate bonds, rather than biological bonds, which motivate them.

The danger with evolutionary explanations of warfare is that they can so easily sound like justifications and imply somewhat fatalistically that it is an inevitable feature of the human landscape. Consequently they may be co-opted by vulgar social Darwinists as vindication for any ethnonational military campaign undertaken for the 'survival' of those who feel their identity is threatened. Evolutionary explanations apply to our past, and only one particular version of our past. Considerations of egalitarianism (Erdal, Whiten, Boehm & Knauft, 1994) and how this might have evolved are still in their infancy. The relationship between these 'instincts' and an older 'drive' for dominance inherited from our primate ancestors is still poorly understood, as are the implications which these have for the future management of our ecosystem. Ultimately the adaptive value of our current behaviour will be left to future generations to judge. As the small print for various financial products regularly informs us—past success is no guarantor of future performance. A reading of current indicators is that the survival of the planet as a habitable ecosystem for humans is under threat. As bearers of human intelligence we have the capacity to shape our own evolution—and because of this, human evolution cannot be understood from a purely natural science perspective. A psychology which takes this as its starting point will be concerned with our ability to effect change—this is one reason why Sloboda and Doherty's work in this volume (Chapters 5 and 6) is important. It turns the lens back onto ourselves and asks how we can be effective in instigating and maintaining change. What works? What doesn't? How can what works be effectively communicated and taken up elsewhere? Research from this perspective has barely begun but the prospects for new questions and new answers, which this begs, warrant our immediate attention. This would be a different kind of peace psychology, one tied to action in the political arena. It could be simultaneously a liberation psychology and a psychology of resistance, one geared toward social transformation and challenging oppression.

Dawes (2001) describes the efforts of a number of psychologists during the apartheid era in South Africa, where liberation and resistance were the clear driving forces behind the work. In one example data was gathered on the effects of police harassment, torture and imprisonment. This was subsequently made available to the general public and publicised amongst communities subject to repression, along with self-help material on how to cope and deal with the psychological aftermath of mistreatment. Robbins' contribution in this book (Chapter 3) has parallels with this work. There is however a danger in publishing accounts of torture and detention since torturers read the literature and go to conferences (see Chapters 1 and 4) and it is important we don't contribute to the improvement of their techniques. Other examples include training local people in trauma work, and combating the internalised effects of oppressive treatment on self-esteem, identity and culture—referred to by some as the colonisation of subjectivity—a concept which owes much to Fanon (2005). Developing our understanding of these coercive public dimensions to private identity and the means to uproot them will be a task that psychologists are well placed to undertake.

Perhaps the greatest challenge for psychologists today is to address the consequences of the current global crisis (Sloboda, 2003). There can be little doubt that globalisation, increasing economic disparities, induced climate changes, destruction of the biosphere, and the coming energy crisis consequent on the depletion of the planet's natural resources will lead to further major conflict. Iraq, Afghanistan and the 'War on Terror' are manifestations of the end of the petroleum age, and the beginning of the battle for control of the world's remaining energy reserves. In this, war will remain a strategy that is profitable for big business.[1] Consequently the future will likely bear witness to further major upheavals throughout the world, upheavals that will most probably result in enormous psychological and physical distress and the disintegration of traditional cultural and social divisions.

---

1. Verkaik (2006) reports that the first three years of the Iraq War have netted British businesses over one billion pounds.

Kaldor (2001) sees these changes as having already produced power struggles embracing new forms of warfare and organised violence—struggles which, though they have taken on the mantle of traditional nationalism or tribalism, should not be mistaken as being rooted in ethnonational conflict. To talk of 'segregation' or 'desegregation' as critical determinants of 'ethnic cleansing' for example is missing the point. Areas of the former Yugoslavia, such as Sarajevo, which were subject to an onslaught by (Serbian) nationalist forces, were extremely well integrated, with many people in the region from mixed backgrounds. The idea of ethnic conflict is of course simple and its 'black-and-white' nature makes fertile ground for convenient psychological speculation. Dislike, enmity, and segregation may be present but they have never been sufficient by themselves to lead to genocide. Of relevance, but rarely discussed by psychologists, is the critical role of economic disintegration, corruption and crime with the undermining of traditional sources of political legitimacy. Whether in the Balkans, Cambodia, Rwanda or Nazi Germany, these have been the precursors of genocide.

This means that the psychological concomitants of social breakdown need to be well understood, and this cannot be done in the laboratory. Psychologists have something valuable to contribute to debates on genocide and ethnic cleansing (see Hewstone et al., in press, for example), but contributions must remain cognisant of the broader context in which enmity develops, otherwise they may end up telling us more about the arrogance of our discipline than about what is happening out in the world.

It would be an act of supreme folly should we choose to ignore these global developments, hanging on desperately instead to an intellectually and morally bankrupt position which asserts the irrelevance of these things to psychology and psychologists. 'Lack of hope in the future', Dallaire (2005, p. 522) observed 'is the root cause of rage'. It is one of our jobs as psychologists to provide a rational basis for hope.

Possibilities for research and action

It is perhaps fair to suggest that peace psychology reached its zenith during the Cold War. Theoretical frameworks developed then are less applicable today as we face a more fragmented picture of global injustice, unfair trade and numerous wars with varied root causes. However, at a time when it is most needed peace psychology lies at the fringes of British psychology. There are some important questions to ask; for example, what is the aim of peace psychology? Is it simply the ending of conflict or might it also embrace structural injustices—frequently found to be the root causes of conflict? Here we present some examples of how psychologists could contribute to these challenges.

Focusing on language and communication

A neglected aspect of peace psychology is how language is used. For example, the September 11th attacks were immediately viewed in some quarters as acts of war (Billig, 2001). Whilst in some ways this can be an understandable emotional reaction to an overwhelming event, it can close down other ways of viewing situations and restrict both the range of positions (warrior, enemy etc.) and of options (attack, surrender etc.). The term 'terrorist' has similar effects. On the one hand it criminalises legitimate liberation movements (Khan, 2006), whilst on the other, it has such a fluid meaning that it can quickly spread to all sorts of people engaged in activities which then come to be seen as 'suspicious' (Lynch, 2006).

How might a focus on language illuminate issues in peace psychology? Mary Boyle's (1997) work is a good example. She investigated how, in debates on abortion, opponents of abortion are presented as 'pro-life'. However, when examining voting patterns, she found that 88% of British MPs who voted for the most restrictive amendments on abortion in 1990 also voted, in 1991, to reinstate the death penalty for certain military offences. This echoed previous research in the 1970s in the US in which it was found:

> a strong positive relationship between opposition to abortion, support for capital punishment ... support for the continued funding of the Vietnam war ... and opposition to gun control. (Boyle, 1997, p. 51)

On the basis of her work, Boyle suggests that the debate about abortion should not be framed as pro-life but, rather, the debate should be about socially sanctioned killing (e.g. in war). This kind of research can move beyond rhetorical justifications for political positions and start to open up more complex and nuanced debates. How might this insight inform political debate and action? It could, for example, help to improve dialogue. In the days of the Cold War, Hamwee (1986) conducted a study of meetings between members of peace groups and civil servants involved in nuclear weapons decision making. He found that the civil servants tended to deny responsibility for their decisions:

> [The decision maker] takes daily and detailed responsibility for one minuscule part of a giant worldwide process ... He [*sic*] concentrates, as he [*sic*] has to, on the technical task, and can only talk about it in technical language. To talk in the (peace) groups' language would be to abandon all the assumptions behind all that he [*sic*] knows and does. (Hamwee, 1986, p. 6)

No doubt similar processes go on today in the giant military-industrial-intelligence bureaucracies. Moreover, if peace psychology has a positive vision of addressing injustice and inequality, rather than the more limited one of ending conflict (though that in itself is hardly a modest task), a focus on language may be of use. For example, the journalist John Pilger has noted that:

> The new order is beset by euphemisms, which can often mean the opposite of the new jargon term. Liberalization—more commonly known as the 'free trade' agenda—sounds reasonable in itself. Much of the language used to describe it suggests that it is a positive trend: the removal of 'restrictions,' 'barriers' and 'obstacles' to what should be 'free' trade. These throw up a smoke screen. The important question: 'Free' for whom? (Carlton Television (2001, p. 3)

Indeed, much of the language of conflict is euphemistic with talk of 'smart bombs', 'surgical strikes' and 'collateral damage', all of which serve to maintain our denial about the reality of war (Grossman, 1996).

As well as understanding how language is used to maintain conflictual stances, it can also be used to reduce conflict. In the US, the *Public Conversations Project* (http://www.publicconversations.org/) has aimed to bring together groups in conflict on topics as wide-ranging as abortion, September 11th and the war in Iraq. The group aim to develop dialogue, which is facilitated and structured along key principles of respect and of deepening understanding of one's own position and that of others.

Peace and justice: building the psychological foundations for peace

In an interesting review of peace psychology, Christie (2006) notes how peace research can be viewed along two dimensions: episodic–structural and violence–peacebuilding. One could argue that much research focuses only on episodic violence (e.g. wars and terrorist acts) and episodic peace building (e.g. conflict resolution). However, the danger here is that attempts to bring peace without justice are shortsighted and likely to fail. Rather, what is needed is an attempt at structural and systemic long-term peace-building. This was one of the insights that led to the Truth and Reconciliation Commission in South Africa. Although it has received criticism for focusing on discovering truth rather than seeking the justice of criminal convictions, it does provide a template for resolving conflict through understanding.

As Christie argues;

> Violent episodes are conceptualized as manifestations of systemic factors, many of which are rooted in structure-based inequalities and destructive cultural narratives that are situated and operate in a particular geohistorical context. From such an analysis, it follows that the prevention and mitigation of violence and the promotion of a sustainable peace require systemic peacebuilding efforts that transform systems of violence into more equitable and cooperative interpersonal and social arrangements. (2006, p. 14)

How might we begin to research structural injustices that so often drive conflicts? Certainly we need to move beyond psychology's focus on the individual. For example, in a recent review of research into explanations of poverty (Harper, 2003) the overwhelming majority of studies focused on the attitudes of the general public who have no control over world economic resources, as opposed to governments and transnational corporations, which do. Indeed, in the review only one study was found which focused on a group that did have some power to change things: politicians (Beck et al., 1999).

Another network with power is the media. A report by the Third World and Environment Broadcasting Project noted that 82% of Britons relied on television as their main source of information on the 'developing world' or the 'Third World'—which we shall refer to as the South (Christian Aid News, 1995; see also Department for International Development, 2000; and Voluntary Service Overseas, 2002). The media use images and explanations to great effect, and they are greatly influenced by a variety of commercial and other interests. With some notable exceptions, most coverage of poverty in the South by the press and broadcasters tends to focus less on any links between the North's wealth and the South's poverty. Instead, they concentrate on poor individuals, the climate or corruption and inefficiency in national governments of the South.

In a fascinating study, Iyengar (1990) has shown that how a question is framed has a significant impact on participants' responses. Between 1981 and 1986 Iyengar studied TV news broadcasts about domestic poverty in the USA and delineated two major categories. One category described poverty primarily as a social or collective outcome (a thematic frame); the other described poverty in terms of particular victims (an episodic frame). Generally, episodic frame news stories outnumbered thematic frame stories by two to one. In an initial experimental study, Iyengar showed a selection of news stories illustrating thematic and episodic frames. The participants' perceived responsibility for poverty was significantly influenced by the way the media framed the story. Thematic frame stories evoked more structural (situational) attributions, and episodic frame stories evoked more individualistic attributions of responsibility. The results reinforced the original finding that beliefs about causal responsibility depended on *how poverty was framed*. From this, Iyengar suggests that the predominance of individualistic explanations of poverty may be due not only to dominant cultural values (individualism) but also to 'news coverage of poverty in which images of poor people predominate' (1990, p. 29). Such research applies equally to coverage of poverty in the South. The news media are the major source of information on poverty for the general public.

A study by Voluntary Service Overseas (2002) found that members of the public were bewildered when presented with information that ran counter to dominant media images and angry with the press and broadcasters for not conveying this complexity. It was argued that the public needed both context for, and an emotional connection with, those portrayed in reports about the South.

What can psychologists offer here? One thing they can do is to intervene in political debates and comment on how the debates are being framed. They can also develop structured interventions, which raise awareness of structural injustice. For example, Lopez et al. (1998) investigated an educational intervention for college students on inter-group relations that covered structural sources of racial or ethnic inequalities. They found that the course led to increases in structural (situational) thinking about racial or ethnic inequality, and that this generalised to other inequalities that had not been explicitly covered in the course, an effect enhanced by the use of active learning strategies.

Building trust

One of the key political and psychological themes of the current era is the need to build trust at micro, meso and macro levels. At the domestic community level, evidence shows that disadvantaged areas typically have increased risks of assault, burglary and theft, greater prevalence of graffiti, vandalism, derelict buildings and street gangs, and are characterised by powerlessness and low levels of trust (Ross et al., 2001). People there are more likely to be unemployed or homeless, to have experienced social isolation, and to have fewer opportunities, more restrictive choices and fewer resources.

Moreover, in the context of the current 'War on Terror', both Muslim and Jewish communities are feeling increasingly threatened (Sheridan & Gillett, 2005; Sivanandan, 2006; Guardian Unlimited, 2006) with young Muslims and Asians in the UK the subject of increased use of stop and search powers: up by 302% between 2002–2003 (Cowan, 2004); with a twelve-fold increase after the July 7th bombings in London (Dodd, 2005). In the US, the problem has been even worse with Mathur (2006) describing the mass arrest of 'thousands of Muslim, South Asian and Middle Eastern men' (p. 31) by the FBI, police and immigration officers, after September 11th, who were held in various prisons in New York and New Jersey. Bernstein (2006) reports the $300,000 settlement of a court case where dozens of Muslim men were arrested in the New York area, 'held for months in a federal detention centre in Brooklyn and deported after being cleared of links to terrorism'.

Indeed, there are signs that at particular moments of raised anxiety mistrust flourishes. For example, following Operation Overt in the UK in August 2006 (where 25 men were arrested for allegedly plotting to blow up transatlantic airliners) there were a number of examples of official and passenger anxiety:

- A young Arab American man was refused entry to a flight because he was wearing a T-shirt with the slogan 'We Will Not Be Silent' in English and Arabic because some passengers were 'apparently concerned at what the Arabic phrase meant' (BBC News Online, 2006g).
- A flight from Luton Airport to Majorca was delayed whilst police inspected it after finding a 'scribbled note' on the back of a safety card (BBC News

Online, 2006h).

- Two men 'of Asian or Middle Eastern appearance' were taken off a Monarch Airlines flight from Malaga because flight attendants thought they were 'acting suspiciously'. They were released without charge after being questioned for several hours (BBC News Online, 2006i).
- A week later a United Airlines flight from the UK to the US was diverted and escorted to Boston by two fighter jets because a 59-year-old female passenger had become claustrophobic and disruptive. She was restrained until the plane landed (BBC News Online, 2006j).
- Perhaps the most shocking case occurred in Miami in December 2005. Rigoberto Alpizar had got up from his seat and said he had to leave the plane. Eye witness Mary Gardner said that his wife ran down the aisle saying he had a diagnosis of bi-polar disorder and had not taken his medication. He was shot dead by two undercover air marshals (BBC News Online, 2006k) who claimed that he had said he had a bomb, though this is disputed by other witnesses—John McAlhany said he did not hear the word 'bomb' (Freeman and agencies, 2005).

Politicians' statements can also raise anxiety. Thus Home Secretary John Reid called for Muslim parents to be vigilant because there were 'fanatics ... [who were] looking to groom and brainwash children, including your children for suicide bombing' (Stanton, 2006). They were to contact the authorities if they saw 'tell-tale signs'.

The issue of how to manage anxiety in a time of broad-ranging but non-specific threats is both a political and psychological one. Some commentators, some of whom are on the political right, have noted that the threat of terrorism is exaggerated (Durodie, 2004; Oborne, 2006). Indeed, Robinson (2005) reports that the number of international terrorist attacks has actually decreased rather than increased—for example a reduction from 200 in the mid-1980s to fewer than 30 in 2004.

Interventions here are likely to be influenced by the cultural context. Thus, in the wake of the July 7th London bombings observers noted that many of the responses reflected a British sense of humour and self-deprecation. For example, as a response to the 'we are not afraid' Internet websites after the September 11th attacks in New York, a British website called www.iamfuckingterrified.com/ was set up:

We're sick of this whole 'courageous London' thing. It's an over-easy media tag that means nothing. People have to live and work in this stinking city, so we get on the trains and we get on the buses and we keep our fingers crossed that the person sitting opposite us isn't about to press the red button in his pocket. (http://www.iamfuckingterrified.com/why)

They also quote from http://www.wereshittingourselves.com/:

> The point we want to make is the futility of the 'We survived the blitz' attitude and point out that recent events such as these don't just happen in a vacuum … They are not the actions of a few religious nutters who hate our way of life, they are a symptom of a bad situation that only our leaders have the power to finish.

One of the symptoms of a lack of trust in the State is the increasing pervasion of conspiracy theories. A review of some of the political setting conditions for conspiracy theories is beyond the scope of this paper but it should be noted that calling someone a 'conspiracy theorist' is one step away from labelling someone 'paranoid' and both these rhetorical devices serve to undermine the legitimacy of the other person's views without actually addressing the content of their argument (Harper, 2000). Moreover, conspiracy theories will always circulate in an age of fast information transfer, where highly complex and fast-moving events involve large numbers of people with only partial or ambiguous information. In the wake of the September 11th attacks many conspiracy theories have developed, for example that the Pentagon was hit by a missile, not a plane (Reynolds, 2006); that the attacks were an 'inside job' (Gillan, 2006) or that the World Trade Centre buildings were brought down by pre-planned controlled explosions (Pope, 2005). These theories have gained ground—Gillan (2006) reports that a recent poll found that 36% of Americans believed it 'very likely' or 'somewhat likely' that their government was involved in allowing the attacks or had carried them out itself. Whilst some of the reasons for believing this may be questionable, there remain some difficult questions for the US authorities to answer (Ahmed, 2005).

These theories have become so widespread that the US State Department has revised its information about misinformation drawn up during the Cold War to include post-9/11 Internet conspiracy theories (State Department, 2005) and detailed rebuttals of claims about the attacks (Popular Mechanics, 2005).

One of the difficulties is that, in a post-Watergate age, the public are much more sceptical of official accounts. This scepticism is increased with the knowledge that security and intelligence agencies have conspired in the past. (Porter, 1992; Blum, 2003). Moreover, bureaucracies tend to cover up their errors and mistakes which can appear as a concealment of conspiracies. Bronner (2006), for example, discusses how the chaos in the North American Aerospace Defense Command (NORAD) was not adequately conveyed in the 9/11 Commission hearings (National Commission on Terrorist Acts upon the United States, 2004). Campbell (2005) discusses how poor communication between Porton Down and the Metropolitan Police meant that later tests of the flat in the London 'ricin plot' which showed that ricin was not present were not passed on to the prosecutors and that so-called al-Qaeda manuals were, in fact, translations of material found on American survivalist websites. It is easy to then adopt the belief that these plots are all fictitious but, Campbell speaking as an expert witness for the defence, says of Kamel Bourgass, the sole convicted defendant: 'I do not doubt that Bourgass would have contemplated causing harm if he was competent to do so. But he is an Islamist yobbo not an Al-Qaida-trained super-terrorist'. Campbell's article itself became the subject of a conspiracy theory when it was withdrawn from the Guardian's website as a result of a Public Interest Immunity certificate. Apparently this was because of the naming of a Porton Down scientist (Mayes, 2005) rather than the content of the article.

In the Internet era, theories can circulate which have very little foundation. This is not helped by political rhetoric which can easily slide from the claim that neoconservatives have benefited from the 'War on Terror' to the claim that therefore they *must* have planned it. It is of interest that some commentators (e.g. Tony Benn and Noam Chomsky) steadfastly argue against conspiratorial explanations on the grounds that they tend to distract from addressing the key issues.

How do we counter the related discourses of fear of terrorism and conspiracy theories? What role might peace psychology play? How might we develop forums where we can engage in mature, open, transparent and honest political debate? One key area for intervention is the media. They have come to play an important role in the way wars are perceived (Glasgow University Media Group, 1985) and in generating fear of terrorism (Bright, 2002).

Of course, media articles about acts of terrorism serve particular interests. In November 2005, the *Sun* newspaper carried a banner headline 'Terror Laws: Tell Tony he's right' with a picture of one of the survivors of the July 7th 2005 bombings. This reporting framed the survivors as a group with a homogenous set of political views in line with that of the newspaper's editorial team. However, uncommonly, the person in the photograph spoke out. As a university professor in media studies, John Tulloch was more aware than most of the power of images:

> It's incredibly ironic that the *Sun*'s rhetoric is as the voice of the people yet they don't actually ask the people involved what they think. If you want to use my image, the words coming out of my mouth would be, 'Not in my name, Tony'. (Coward, 2005)

Perhaps peace psychologists could collaborate with researchers in media studies (e.g. Glasgow University's Mass Media Unit: http://www.gla.ac.uk/departments/sociology/units/media.htm) to understand the impact of the media and how media reporting can be influenced.

Peace psychology: proposals

For peace psychology to function as an effective branch of professional psychology, it needs to have a programme of activity that spans research, education, and practice. Practice is key, because the aim of the enterprise is to contribute to the prevention and reduction of violent conflict, not just to analyse from the sidelines. It would be a contradiction in terms if a psychologist who had never contributed to the well-being of a clinical patient were to describe him or herself as a clinical psychologist. Similarly one could argue that if a psychologist has never applied his or her skills to an actual conflict situation with the aim of preventing or reducing violence it would be hard to take seriously his or her claims to be a 'peace psychologist'. Of course, publishing well-targeted research and analysis may well directly contribute to peacemaking, but only if picked up and used by practitioners. Just 'putting the materials into the public domain' should not be considered as the end goal. There is an obligation to proactively engage those who can use the findings and analyses to make a real difference.

Our first proposal is that psychologists concerned for the promotion and maintenance of peace should *develop and maintain productive and meaningful relationships with specific individuals (or organisations) who are living or working in conflict or post-conflict situations.* There are many possibilities here, from local and national peace groups and NGOs, through press and media, through to government and other statutory agencies. The aims of this are (1) to become knowledgeable in the dynamics and requirements of a specific conflict area, (2) to establish credibility with some of the players, and (3) to locate the best opportunities for mediating psychological knowledge or skills into the area of activity. In addition, interested psychologists with different skills and specialities could group together and form consultancies, possibly with other activists.

Currently it is our guess that, at least in the UK, a considerable number of psychologists who aspire to develop peace psychology are already active as volunteers in organisations working for pro-peace policies and initiatives. It is their activism that motivates their psychological interests. Many of these organisations are not well funded, have few if any paid staff, and obtain their support from small donations given by individuals. On the other hand, at least in the UK, hardly any psychologists regularly work as psychologists on a voluntary basis. One useful strategy might be to work with organisations to secure funding (e.g. through research grants) which would provide a firmer financial footing for the organisations. While it may have to be accepted that, considering the low priority given to peace work in current UK societies, some proportion of this work will have to be done on a *pro bono* basis, it should be a firm aspiration to create a situation where peace psychology work generates income and does so on an equal footing to any other branch of applied psychology.

Our second proposal is, therefore, that peace psychologists should *determine realistic recompense for their work* and communicate these to the constituencies that can make use of their services. If a peace organisation needs a computer, it would not dream of asking the retailer to give the computer to them for nothing. Similarly, it should not expect psychologists to offer valuable services for nothing. This proposal has an important practical corollary, which is that it will force peace psychologists to characterise and describe what they have to offer in an explicit and persuasive way. It will also help psychologists to be clearer about role boundaries and role conflicts. It may, for instance, be difficult to be both a paid and an unpaid worker for the same organisation at the same time.

Our third proposal is that peace psychologists should collaborate to *produce a code of conduct*, assuming the common code shared by all professional psychologists, but adding specific components pertinent to peace psychology. One area of specific concern is the area of ethics and values. The profession of medicine is underpinned by a core value, which is enshrined in the Hippocratic Oath. It is possible that peace psychology would benefit from something similar. A possible suggestion is:

> I undertake to give the utmost priority to using my psychological skills and knowledge to contribute to the reduction, and eventual elimination, of violence at all levels (physical, psychological, structural) as a means of addressing human conflict.

For a professional psychologist (or aspiring professional psychologist) the key to being able to turn such a statement from pious aspiration into action requires the accumulation and refining of the relevant skills and knowledge. This means education, training and continuing skills development. Perhaps this would require institutional recognition. We could learn here from the success of qualitative research or community psychology. Whilst there are some full-time qualitative researchers and community psychologists and a literature, most people do this as part of their jobs. We need to build up this recognition through modules, symposia, conferences, and research grants, books, papers and perhaps a British Psychological Society special interest group. The easiest place to begin this work is probably the undergraduate psychology degree. Institutions in many countries provide opportunities for the introduction of optional short courses (or modules) on the specialist interests of staff members. Our fourth suggestion is, therefore, that peace psychologists should *develop model peace-psychology single-semester courses* and produce resources (e.g. textbooks, reading lists, learning packs, workshops) that would help teachers wishing to mount such courses in their own institutions. A textbook explicitly designed for level 2 or level 3 UK undergraduate courses does not currently exist. The nearest is Christie, Wagner and Winter (2001), but this does not have an explicit pedagogical orientation, being a collection of 30 chapters all by different authors. The discipline would be greatly helped by a 'through-written' textbook designed with students in mind. The recently published book by Blumberg, Hare and Costin (2006) appears promising in this respect.

Any such course would serve a key function of raising awareness among students and faculty. But opportunities would be lost if such courses remained within the traditional academic mould (guided reading with assessment by research-oriented essay and exam). A challenge would be to introduce an applied component into such courses so that the link to real work, in real conflict situations, was established from the start. Some things which could be considered are: (a) relating psychological knowledge to current conflicts (particularly conflicts in which the student's own country is involved); (b) devising case-study opportunities where, instead of a traditional essay, a student might, for example, interview a person or group involved in conflict, trying to apply rigorous psychological thinking to the problem they are facing; (c) supervised work placements with peace and other organisations where the student could do some research useful to the group.

Universities are, at the current time, probably the greatest resource for peace psychologists. As well as offering teaching opportunities for motivated staff, they provide contexts in which professional networking is expected and encouraged (conferences, meetings etc.) and in which research and consultancy activities are supported and encouraged. In addition, they bring together different academic disciplines which impact on peace and conflict. Many universities with psychology departments also have politics and international relations departments (some even have 'Peace Studies' departments or groups) that would welcome psychological input into their work. Yet, typically, psychologists have not been successful at establishing good links with relevant sister departments. The peace psychology enterprise could benefit enormously from the *establishment of strong interdisciplinary groups bringing together psychologists with other relevant disciplines within a single university*. Given the way in which institutions work, such groups are probably best guaranteed by actually making interdisciplinary appointments (e.g. a joint appointment between two departments). Voluntary inter-departmental collaboration is vulnerable—and is often the first casualty of overwork.

A very specific resource available to university-based staff is the research grant. Grant-awarding bodies are responsive to national and international priorities, and conflict is one such priority. Regardless of the ideological framework in which grant-giving programmes are framed, there is always a meaningful chance that imaginative and progressive proposals will get funded. It is probably a responsibility of peace psychologists working in universities to *place grant-getting at a higher priority than their natural inclinations might suggest*. Not only does this allow valuable resource to be diverted from less important intellectual problems onto more important ones, it provides the kind of respect among institutional leaders that encourages further institutional investment. In this respect, the history of the Bradford University Peace Studies Department (O'Connell & Whitby) is one that should command the interest of all peace psychologists. In 20 years it moved from being viewed by many commentators (both within and outside the university) as an ephemeral and highly suspect manifestation of the 'loony left' into being the University's flagship 5-star grant-getting department, whilst losing none of its capacity to promote messages which continue to be deeply challenging to government and to prevailing militaristic norms within the UK. It is a matter of regret that more psychologists have not been involved with this extraordinary success story.

Finally, peace psychology is, at the current time, difficult to sustain. It is not a mainstream area of psychology and its adherents are in a tiny minority. Mutual support is vital. This can take many forms, but a very important aspect, with proven success in other fields, is the *formation of a professional association, which sustains contacts between practitioners* through conferences and publications, and offers outlets for discussion, debate, mutual professional development, and the promotion and dissemination of good work. There are a few models around the world, perhaps the most solid of these is the American Psychological Association's Division 48—'The Society for the Study of Peace, Conflict, and Violence: Peace Psychology Division'. Forming sections or divisions within broader national psychology associations is a good way of mobilising existing resources (often funded largely through member subscriptions), which if not commandeered by peace psychologists would be sucked into other activities. Although this route can encounter a variety of institutional resistances and restrictions, it is probably a strategic necessity. Peace psychology needs to be in the mainstream, rather than a shrill voice on the periphery, if it is to increase its influence and projection in the profession, and increase its share of available resources.

REFERENCES

Abbott, C., Rogers, P.F. & Sloboda, J.A. (2006). Global responses to global threats: Sustainable security for the 21st century. *Oxford Research Group*, June 2006. <http://www.oxfordresearchgroup.org.uk/publications/briefings/globalthreats.htm>, accessed 16 September 2006.

Ackroyd, C., Margolis, K., Shallice, T. & Aitkenhead, T. (1977). *The Technology of Political Control.* Harmondsworth: Penguin.

Agger, I. (2001). Reducing trauma during ethno-political conflict: A personal account of psycho-social work under war conditions in Bosnia. In D.J. Christie, R.V. Wagner and D.D. Winter (Eds.) *Peace, Conflict, and Violence* (pp. 240–250). New Jersey: Prentice Hall.

Ahmed, N.M. (2002). *The War on Freedom: How and why America was attacked.* California: Tree of Life.

Ahmed, N.M. (2003). *Behind the War on Terror: Western secret strategy and the struggle for Iraq.* East Sussex: Clairview.

Ahmed, N.M. (2005). *The War on Truth: 9/11, disinformation, and the anatomy of terrorism.* Northampton, MA: Olive Branch Press.

Ahmed, N.M. (2006). *The London Bombings: An independent inquiry.* London: Duckworth.

Aitkenhead, D. (2006). Hot gossip. *Guardian magazine*, 6 May. <http://www.guardian.co.uk/weekend/story/0,,1767307,00.html>, accessed 28 September 2006.

Al-Ganimee, A.A. (2005). The stain of abuse in psychiatric services in Iraq during the 1980s and 1990s. Presentation at the International Conference 'Resilience, Recovery and Reconciliation', International Society for Health and Human Rights, Vadodara, India, 4 February 2005.

Ali, T. (2002). *The Clash of Fundamentalisms.* London: Pluto.

Ali, T. (2005). *Rough Music*. Blair Bombs Baghdad London Terror. London: Verso.

Allard, J.G. (2004). French prisoners were experimented on at Gitmo. *Granma International.* 25 December.

Allen, K. (2005). Amnesty International to investigate UK's current record on human rights. London: Amnesty International.

American Civil Liberties Union (ACLU) (2004). The matrix: Total Information Awareness Reloaded. <http://www.aclu.org/FilesPDFs/matrix%20report.pdf>, accessed September 2006.

American Medical Association (2006). H-140.870 Physician participation in interrogation. Chicago: AMA. <http://www.ama-assn.org/apps/pf_new/pf_online?f_n=browseanddoc=policyfiles/HnE/H-140.870.HTM>, accessed 28 September 2006.

American Psychiatric Association (2000). *Diagnostic and Statistical Manual of Mental Disorders—text revision* (4th edn). Washington, DC: American Psychiatric Association.

American Psychiatric Association (2006). Psychiatric participation in interrogation of detainees: Position Statement. *Psychiatric News, 41*, 12, 10. <www.psych.org/edu/other_res/lib_archives/archives/200601.pdf>, accessed 20 August 2006.

American Psychological Association (undated). PPO Update for BSA—Featuring Homeland Security Activities. <http://www.apa.org/ppo/issues/sbsaupdate403.html>, accessed 28 September 2006.

American Psychological Association/Federal Bureau of Investigation (2002). Countering Terrorism: Integration of practice and theory: FBI Academy, Quantico, Virginia, 28 February 2002. <http://www.apa.org/ppo/issues/ct.pdf>, accessed 28 September 2006.

American Psychological Association (2005). Report of the American Psychological Association Presidential Task Force on Psychological Ethics and National Security. <www.apa.org/releases/PENSTaskForceReportFinal.pdf>, accessed 12 July 2005.

American Psychological Association (2006). American Psychological Society reaffirms unequivocal position against torture and abuse. APA press release, 10 August. Washington DC: APA <www.apa.org/releases/notorture.html>, accessed 20 August 2006.

Aminzade, R. & McAdam, D. (2001). Emotions and contentious politics. In R.R Aminzade, J.A

Goldstone, D. McAdam, E.J. Perry, W.H. Sewell, S. Tarrow & C. Tilly *Silence and Voice in the Study of Contentious Politics* (pp.14–50). Cambridge: Cambridge University Press.

Amnesty International (1984). *Torture in the Eighties*. London: AI.

Amnesty International (2005). Press Release. 11 November 2005.

Amnesty International (2006a). *Amnesty International Report 2006: The state of the world's human rights*. London: AI.

Amnesty International (2006b). *Les Droits Humains sous Pression. Violations des droits humains au nom de la 'guerre contre la terreur'*. Section Suisse, Berne: AI.

Amnesty International (2006c). Guantánamo: Lives torn apart—the impact of indefinite detention on detainees and their families. <www.amnesty.org/library/print/ENGAMR510072006>, accessed 13 February 2006.

Amnesty International (2006d). Iraq beyond Abu Ghraib: Detention and torture in Iraq. <http://web.amnesty.org/library/Index/ENGMDE140012006>, accessed 6 March 2006.

Amnesty International (2006e). United Kingdom. Human rights: a broken promise. <http://web.amnesty.org/library/Index/ENGEUR450042006?open&of=ENG-GBR>, accessed 6 March 2006.

Amris, K. (2000). Physiotherapy for torture victims (I). Treatment of chronic pain. *Torture, 10*, 73–76.

Anderson, L. (2005). The end of the moon. <http://www.avant-garden.de/more/laurie.html>, accessed 15 October 2005.

Anthony, D. (1990). Religious movements and 'brainwashing' litigation. In D. Anthony and T. Robbins (Eds.) *In Gods We Trust* (pp. 299–344). New Brunswick, NJ: Transaction.

Arendt, H. (1994a). *The Origins of Totalitarianism*. London: Harcourt.

Arendt, H. (1994b). *Eichmann in Jerusalem: A report on the banality of evil*. Harmondsworth: Penguin.

Arrigo, J.M. (2004). A utilitarian argument against torture interrogation of terrorists. *Science and Engineering Ethics, 10*, 3, 1–30.

Austen, I. (2006). Canadians fault US for its role in torture case. *New York Times*, 19 September.

Bailes, G. (2003). Media. *The Psychologist, 16*, 5, 280.

Bamford, J. (2005). The man who sold the war: Meet John Rendon, Bush's general in the propaganda war. *Rolling Stone, 17 November.* <http://www.rollingstone.com/politics/story/8798997/the_man_who_sold_the_war/1>, accessed 28 September 2006.

Banyard, P. (2004). Terrorism asking the right questions. Letters. *The Psychologist, 17*, 11, 624.

Barron, P. (Ed.) (2005, 12 October). *Newsnight*. London: BBC.

Barry, J., Hirsch, M. & Isikoff, M. (2006). The roots of torture. *Newsweek World News*. <http://www.msnbc.msn.com/id/4989422/>, accessed October 2006.

Basoglu, M., Jaranson, J.M., Mollica, R. & Kastrup, M. (2001). Torture and mental health: A research overview. In E. Gerrity, T.M. Keane & F. Tuma (Eds.) *The Mental Health Consequences of Torture* (pp. 35–62). New York: Kluwer Academic/Plenum.

Basoglu, M., Paker, M., Paker, Ö, Özmen, E. & Sahin, D. (1994). Factors related to long term traumatic stress responses in survivors of torture. *Journal of American Medical Association, 272*, 357–363.

Baudrillaud, J. (1994). *Simulacra and Simulation*. Ann Arbor, MI: University of Michigan Press.

Bauer, P. (2006). Statement on Interrogation Practices, 31 July 2006. <www.amnestyusa.org/denounce_torture/statement_on_interrogation.pdf>, accessed 18 August 2006.

Baumeister, R.F. & Zhang, L. (2006). Your money or your self-esteem: Threatened egotism promotes costly entrapment in losing endeavors. *Personality and Social Psychology Bulletin, 32*, 7, 881–893.

BBC News Online (2004a). Interview with Kofi Annan. <http://news.bbc.co.uk/1/hi/world/middle_east/3661640.stm>, accessed 16 September 2004.

BBC News Online (2004b). Red Cross hits out at Iraq abuses. <http://news.bbc.co.uk/1/hi/world/middle_east/4027163.stm>, accessed 19 November 2004.

BBC News Online (2004c). Iraq out of control says Jordan. <http://news.bbc.co.uk/1/hi/world/middle_east/4021803.stm>, accessed 19 November 2004.

BBC News Online (2004d). Britons allege Guantánamo abuse. 4 August. <http://news.bbc.co.uk/1/hi/world/americas/3533804.stm>, accessed 28 September 2006.

BBC News Online (2005a). EU-wide warrant over 'CIA kidnap'. 23 December. <http://news.bbc.co.uk/1/hi/world/europe/4555660.stm>, accessed 28 September 2006.

BBC News Online (2005b). Lords reject torture evidence use. 8 December. <http://news.bbc.co.uk/1/hi/uk_politics/4509530.stm>, accessed 28 September 2006.

BBC News Online (2005c). The police case for 90 days. Letter from Met Police to Home Secretary. <http://news.bbc.co.uk/1/shared/bsp/hi/pdfs/08_11_05_police_letter.pdf>, accessed 7 November 2005.

BBC News Online (2005d). Davis attacks UK multiculturalism. <http://news.bbc.co.uk/1/hi/uk_politics/4740633.stm>, accessed 3 August 2005.

BBC News Online (2006a). MI6 payouts over secret LSD tests. 24 February. <http://news.bbc.co.uk/1/hi/uk/4745748.stm>, accessed 26 September 2006.

BBC News Online (2006b). Q and A: Bush and CIA secret prisons. 6 September. <http://news.bbc.co.uk/1/hi/world/americas/5321986.stm>, accessed 28 September 2006.

BBC News Online (2006c). Guantánamo suicides 'acts of war'. 11 June. <http://news.bbc.co.uk/1/hi/world/americas/5068606.stm>, accessed 28 September 2006.

BBC News Online (2006d). Oyster data is 'new police tool'. 13 March. <http://news.bbc.co.uk/1/hi/england/london/4800490.stm>, accessed 28 September 2006.

BBC News Online (2006e). Passenger profiling: A way forward? 15 August. <http://news.bbc.co.uk/1/hi/uk/4794975.stm>, accessed 28 September 2006.

BBC News Online (2006f). More control orders on suspects. 12 June. <http://news.bbc.co.uk/1/hi/uk_politics/5071384.stm>, accessed 28 September 2006.

BBC News Online (2006g). Arabic T-shirt sparks airport row. 30 August. <http://news.bbc.co.uk/1/hi/world/americas/5297822.stm>, accessed 1 October 2006.

BBC News Online (2006h). Plane note prompts airport alert. 22 August. <http://news.bbc.co.uk/1/hi/england/5275358.stm>, accessed 3rd October 2006.

BBC News Online (2006i). 'Suspicious' pair taken off plane. 20 August. <http://news.bbc.co.uk/1/hi/england/5267884.stm>, accessed 3 October 2006.

BBC News Online (2006j). Woman held over plane diversion. 17 August. <http://news.bbc.co.uk/1/hi/world/americas/4800635.stm>, accessed 3 October 2006.

BBC News Online (2006k). Q and A: Air marshals. 10 August. <http://news.bbc.co.uk/1/hi/world/americas/4780571.stm>, accessed 1 October 2006.

BBC TV (2002). Watching 'subversives'. 17 October. <http://news.bbc.co.uk/1/hi/programmes/true_spies/2326491.stm>, accessed 28 September 2006.

Becirevic, E. (2003). *International Criminal Court: Between ideals and reality*. Sarajevo: Arka Press.

Beaglehole, R. and Bonita, R. (1996). *Public Health at the Crossroads*. Cambridge: Cambridge University Press.

Beck, E.L., Whitley, D.M. & Wolk, J.L. (1999). Legislators' perceptions about poverty: Views from the Georgia General Assembly. *Journal of Sociology & Social Welfare, 26*, 87–104.

Beetham, D. (2003). Political participation, mass protest, and representative democracy. *Parliamentary Affairs, 56*, 597–609.

Begg, M. (2006). *Enemy Combatant: A British Muslim's journey to Guantánamo and back*. London: Free Press

Benjamin, M. (2006). Psychological warfare, salon.com: July 26 2006. <www.salon.com/news/feature/2006/07/26/interrogation/print.html)>, accessed 20 August 2006.

Benjamin, R., Clements, C., McCally, M., Pellett, P.L., Van Rooyen, M.J. & Waldman, R.J. (2003). The humanitarian cost of a war in Iraq. *The Lancet, 361*, 874.

Bennett, D. (2005). The war in the mind. *The Boston Globe*, 27 November 2005. <www.boston.com/news/globe/ideas/articles/2005/11/27/the_war_in_the_mind?>, accessed 12 June 2006.

Bernholz, P. (2000). Democracy and capitalism: Are they compatible in the long-run? *Journal of Evolutionary Economics*, *10*, 1–2, 3–16.

Bernstein, N. (2006). US is settling detainee's suit in 9/11 sweep. *New York Times*, 28 February.

Bhutta, Z.A. (2002). Children of war: The real casualties of the Afghan conflict. *British Medical Journal*, *324*, 349–352.

Biddle, S. (2006). Seeing Baghdad, thinking Saigon. *Foreign Affairs*, *85*, 2, 2–14.

Bilanakis, N., Pappas, E and Dinous, M. (1998). The impact of the political suppression and torture on the second generation—a comparative study. *Torture, 8,* 9–12.

Billig, M. (2001). The language of war. *The Psychologist, 14,* 566.

Bin Laden, O. (1998, 23 February). Declaration of the World Islamic Front for jihad against Jews and crusaders. Al-Quds al-Arabi.

Bin Laden, O. (2001a, 7 October). News broadcast of speech. Qatar: Al Jazeera.

Bin Laden, O. (2001b, 3 November). News broadcast of speech. Qatar: Al Jazeera.

Bloche, M.G. & Marks, J.H. (2005a). When doctors go to war. *New England Journal of Medicine, 352,* 3–6.

Bloche, M.G. & Marks, J.H. (2005b). Doctors and interrogators at Guantánamo Bay. *New England Journal of Medicine, 353, 6–8.*

Blum, W. (2003). *Killing Hope: US military and CIA interventions since World War II.* London: Zed Books.

Blumberg, H.H., Hare, A.P. & Costin, A. (2006). *Peace Psychology: A comprehensive introduction.* Cambridge: Cambridge University.

Bodi, F. (2004). Al Jazeera's war. In D. Miller (Ed.) *Tell Me Lies: Propaganda and media distortion in the attack on Iraq* (pp. 243–250). London: Pluto Press.

Borger, J. (2003). Poindexter forced to resign over terror bet plan. *The Guardian,* 2 August, p. 17.

Born, M., Bridgman, P.W., Einstein, A., Infeld, L., Joliot-Curie, F., Muller, H.J., Pauling, L.J., Powell, C.F., Rotblat, J., Russell, B. & Yukawa, H. *The Russell-Einstein Manifesto.* London: Pugwash. <http://www.pugwash.org/about/manifesto.htm>, accessed 25 June 2006.

Bowers, J. (1990). All hail the great abstraction: Star wars and the politics of cognitive psychology. In I. Parker & J. Shotter (Eds.) *Deconstructing Social Psychology* (pp. 127–140). London: Routledge.

Boyle, M.E. (1997). *Rethinking Abortion: Psychology, gender, power and the law.* London: Routledge.

Bracken, P. & Gorst-Unsworth, C. (1991). The mental state of detained asylum seekers. *Psychiatric Bulletin, 15,* 657–659.

Bracken, P., Giller, J.E. & Summerfield, D. (1995). Psychological responses to war and atrocity: The limitations of current concepts, *Social Science and Medicine, 40,* 8, 1073–82.

Braun, R. & Krieger, D. (2005). Einstein's importance today. In R. Braun & D. Krieger (Eds.) *Einstein— Peace Now* (pp. 1–8). Weinheim: Wiley-VCH.

Braungart, M. M. & Braungart, R.G. (1991). The effects of the 1960s political generation on former left- and right-wing youth activist leaders. *Social Problems, 38,* 3, 297–315.

Briggs, R. (1992). *When the Wind Blows.* London: Penguin.

Bright, M. (2002). Terror, security and the media. *The Observer,* 21 July.

British Medical Association (1986). *The Torture Report: Report of a working party of the BMA investigating the involvement of doctors in torture.* London: BMA.

British Psychological Society (2005). Declaration of the British Psychological Society concerning torture and other cruel, inhuman or degrading treatment or punishment. *The Psychologist, 18,* 4, 190.

British Psychological Society (2006a). *The 2005 Annual Report.* Leicester: British Psychological Society.

British Psychological Society (2006b). *Code of Ethics and Conduct.* Leicester: British Psychological Society.

Broder, J.M. (2006). Contradictions cloud inquiry into 24 Iraqi deaths. *The New York Times,* 17 June.

Brogan, B. (2005). It's time to celebrate the Empire, says Brown. *Daily Mail,* 15 January.

Bronner, M. (2006). 9/11 live: The NORAD tapes. <http://www.vanityfair.com/features/general/060801fege01>, accessed 3 October 2006.

Brooks, R. (2005). Ticking bombs and slippery slopes. *Los Angeles Times,* 29 May.

Brown, C. & Morris, N. (2005). Race-hate crimes surge after bombs. *The Independent,* 3 August.

Brown, K. (2005). President's Column. *The Psychologist, 18,* 2, 59.

Brown, R. (2000). Social identity theory: Past achievements, current problems and future challenges. *European Journal of Social Psychology, 30,* 6, 745–778.

Brownlie, I. (1972). Interrogation in depth: The Compton and Parker reports. *Modern Law Review, 35,* 501–507.

Bruner, J. (2004). Foreword. In S. Milgram *Obedience to Authority* (pp. xi–xv). London: Pinter and Martin.

Bull, R. (2003). Slippery politicians. *The Psychologist*, *16*, 11, 592–595.

Bulletin of Atomic Scientists (2006). Timeline of doomsday clock. <http://www.thebulletin.org/doomsday_clock/timeline.htm>, accessed 25 June 2006.

Bulstein, P. (2004). Agencies say poverty persists despite global efforts. *Washington Post*, 23 April, p. 24.

Bunker, R.J. (Ed.) (1997). Nonlethal weapons: Terms and references. INSS Occasional Paper 15. USAF Institute for National Security Studies. Colorado: USAF Academy. <http://www.thememoryhole.org/mil/nl-weapons_terms/nl-weapons_terms.pdf>, accessed 28 September 2006.

Burke, J. (2004). *Al-Qaeda: The true story of radical Islam*. London: Penguin.

Burkle, Jr, F. & Noji, E.K. (2004). Health and politics in the 2003 War with Iraq: Lessons learned. *The Lancet, 364*, 1371–1375.

Burnham, G., Lafta, R., Doocy, S. & Roberts, L. (2006). Mortality after the 2003 invasion of Iraq: A cross-sectional cluster sample survey. *The Lancet*, DOI:10.1016/S0140-6736(06)69491-9.

Burr, V. (2003). *Social constructionism* (2nd edn). London: Routledge.

Buss, D.M. (2004). *Evolutionary Psychology: The new science of the mind*. London: Pearson.

Byrne P. (1997). *Social Movements in Britain*. London: Routledge.

Cameron, D.E. (1957). Psychic driving: Dynamic implant. *Psychiatric Quarterly, 31*, 703–712.

Campbell, D. 2005). The ricin ring that never was. *The Guardian*, 14 April.

Canter, D. (2005). Bombers had death wish. <http://www.sky.com/skynews/article/0,,30000-13464480,00.html>, accessed 18 November 2005.

Carlton Television (2001). *The New Rulers of the World*. Birmingham, UK: Carlton Television.

Carpenter, T.G. (Ed.) (2000). *NATO's Empty Victory: A post-mortem on the Balkan War*. Washington: Cato Institute.

Carter, A. (1992). *Peace Movements*. Harlow: Longman.

Cash, J.D. (1996). *Identity, Ideology and Conflict. The structuration of politics in Northern Ireland*. Cambridge: Cambridge University Press.

Central Intelligence Agency (1963). *KUBARK Counterintelligence Manual* (July 1963). File: Kubark, Box 1: CIA Training Manuals, National Security Archive, Washington.

Central Intelligence Agency (1983). *Human Resource Exploitation Training Manual* (June 8 1988), Box 1: CIA Training Manuals, Folder: Resources Exploitation Training Manual, National Security Archive, Washington.

Chamberlain, G. (2006). Iraq civilian deaths 'highest since end of war'. *The Scotsman*, Thursday 9 March 2006.

Cheney, D. (2001). The Vice-President appears on 'Meet the Press' with Tim Russert. <http://www.whitehouse.gov/vicepresident/news-speeches/speeches/vp20010916.html>, accessed 29 September 2006.

Cherry, F. (1995). *The Stubborn Particulars of Social Psychology: Essays on the research process*. London: Routledge.

Chomsky, N. (1967). The responsibility of intellectuals. *New York Review of Books*, *8*, 3, 16–26. Supplement. <http://www.nybooks.com/articles/12172>.

Chomsky, N. (1989). *Necessary Illusions: Thought control in democratic societies*. Boston: South End Press.

Chomsky, N. (1992). *Deterring Democracy*. London: Vintage.

Chomsky, N. (1999a). *The New Military Humanism: Lessons from Kosovo*. London: Pluto Press.

Chomsky, N. (1999b). *Fateful Triangle: The United States, Israel and the Palestinians*. London: Pluto Press.

Chomsky, N. (2003a). *Understanding Power*. P.R. Mitchell & J. Schoeffel (Eds.) London: Vintage.

Chomsky, N. (2003b). *Power and Terror: Post 9/11 talks and interviews*. New York: Seven Stories Press.

Chomsky, N. (2004). *Hegemony or Survival: America's quest for global dominance*. London: Penguin.

Chomsky, N. (2005a). Personal communication.

Chomsky, N. (2005b). *Imperial Ambitions: Conversations on the post-9/11 world*. New York: Metropolitan Books.

Christian Aid News (1995). 'Third World' losing out on TV, *Christian Aid News, 87* (April/June), 2.

Christie, D.J. (2006). What is peace psychology the psychology of? *Journal of Social Issues, 62*, 1–17.

Christie, D.J., Wagner, R.V. & Winter, D.D. (Eds.) (2001). *Peace, Conflict, and Violence: Peace psychology for the 21st century*. New Jersey: Prentice Hall.

Chu, B. (2005). The great deception. *The Independent*, 15 February.

Church, A.T. (2005). ISFT Final Report 2005. Executive Summary (unclassified). Medical Issues related to interrogation, p.19. <www.defenselink.mil/news/Mar2005/d20050310exe.pdf>, accessed 16 June 2005.

Clark, J. (2003). Medact report highlights aftermath of Iraq conflict. *British Medical Journal, 327*, 1128.

Clark, W.R. (2004). *Petrodollar Warfare: Oil, Iraq and the future of the dollar*. Gabriola Island: New Society.

Cloud, D.S. & Semple, K. (2006). Ex-GI held in 4 slayings and rape in Iraq. *The New York Times*, 4 July.

Cobain I., Grey, S. & Norton-Taylor, R. (2005). Britain's role in war on terror revealed. *The Guardian*, December 6.

Cockburn, P. (2006). New terror that stalks Iraq's republic of fear. *The Independent*. <http://news.independent.co.uk/world/middle_east/article1696153.ece> Accessed 24 September 2006.

Cohen, N. (2002). Of course it's true. After all, it was MI5 who told us. *The Observer*, 21 July.

Cohen, R. (1998). *Hearts Grown Brutal*. New York: Random House.

Cohen, S. (2001). *States of Denial: Knowing about atrocities and suffering*. London: Polity Press.

Coleman, A. (1982). *Game Theory and Experimental Games: The study of strategic interaction*. Oxford: Pergamon Press.

Committee on Legal Affairs and Human Rights (2006). Alleged secret detentions and unlawful inter-state transfers involving Council of Europe member states. Draft report—Part II (Explanatory memorandum) Rapporteur: Mr Dick Marty, Switzerland, ALDE. Strasbourg: Council of Europe. <http://news.bbc.co.uk/1/shared/bsp/hi/pdfs/07_06_06_renditions_draft.pdf>, accessed 28 September 2006.

Conway, L.C., Suedfeld, P. & Tetlock, P.E. (2001). Integrative complexity and political decisions that lead to war or peace. In D.J. Christie, R.V. Wagner & D.D. Winter (Eds.). *Peace, Conflict, and Violence* (pp. 66–75). New Jersey: Prentice Hall.

Corera, G. (2005). Does UK turn a blind eye to torture? BBC News Online, 5 April. <http://news.bbc.co.uk/1/hi/uk/4414491.stm>, accessed 28 September 2006.

Cotter, L.H. (1967). Operant conditioning in a Vietnamese mental hospital. *American Journal of Psychiatry, 124*, 23–8.

Cowan, R. (2004) Young Muslims 'made scapegoat' in stop and search. *Guardian Unlimited*. 3 July. <http://www.guardian.co.uk/terrorism/story/0,12780,1253114,00.html>.

Coward, R. (2005) 'They have given me somebody else's voice—Blair's voice.' *Guardian Unlimited*. 10 November. <http://www.guardian.co.uk/terrorism/story/0,12780,1638838,00.html>.

Crenshaw, M. (1990). The logic of terrorism: Terrorist behaviour as a product of strategic choice. In W. Reich (Ed.) *Origins of Terrorism: Psychologies, ideologies, theologies, states of mind* (pp. 7–24). Cambridge: Cambridge University Press.

Crenshaw, M. (1998). Questions to be answered, research to be done, knowledge to be applied. In W. Reich (Ed.) *Origins of Terrorism: Psychologies, ideologies, theologies, states of mind*. Washington, NY: Woodrow Wilson Center Press.

Crenshaw, M. (2000). The psychology of terrorism: An agenda for the 21st century. *Political Psychology, 21*, 405–420.

Curtis, A. (2002). *A Century of the Self*. London: BBC.

Curtis, A. (2004). *The Power of Nightmares*. London: BBC.

Curtis, M. (2003). *Web of Deceit. Britain's real role in the world*. London: Random House.

Curtis, M. (2004). *Unpeople. Britain's secret human rights abuses*. London: Random House.

Curtis, P. (2003). School children march for peace. *Guardian Unlimited*, March 5. <http://education.guardian.co.uk/schools/story/0,,908019,00.html>.

Dallaire, R. (2005). *Shake Hands with the Devil: The failure of humanity in Rwanda*. London: Arrow.

Danieli, Y. (Ed.) (1998). *International Handbook of Multigenerational Legacies of Trauma*. New York: Plenum.

Danner, M. (2004). *Torture and Truth: Abu Ghraib and America in Iraq*. London: Granta.

Dardagan, H., Sloboda, J. & Doherty, B. (2006). Speculation is no substitute: A defence of Iraq Body Count. <http://www.iraqbodycount.org/editorial/defended/>, accessed 20 April 2006.

Darley, J.M. & Latané, B. (1968). Bystander intervention in emergencies: Diffusion of responsibility. *Journal of Personality and Social Psychology, 8*, 377–383.

Darling, A.B. (1966). The birth of Central Intelligence. *Studies in Intelligence, 10*, 1–19.

Dawes, A. (2001). Psychologies for liberation: Views from elsewhere. In D.J. Christie, R.V. Wagner & D.D. Winter (Eds.). *Peace, Conflict, and Violence* (pp. 295–306). New Jersey. Prentice Hall.

Dawson, D. (1999). Evolutionary theory and group selection: The question of warfare. *History and Theory, 38*, 4, 77–100.

Department for International Development (2000). *Viewing the World: A study of British Television coverage of developing countries.* London: DfID <www.dfid.gov.uk>.

Dobson, P. (2003). Perinatal mortality in Iraq more than tripled since sanctions. *British Medical Journal, 326*, 520.

Dodd, V. (2005). Two-thirds of Muslims consider leaving UK. *The Guardian*, 26 July. <http://www.guardian.co.uk/attackonlondon/story/0,16132,1536222,00.html>, accessed 12 December 2005.

Donald, M. (2001). *A Mind So Rare.* New York and London: W.W. Norton.

Druckman, D. (2001). Nationalism and war: A social-psychological perspective. In D.J. Christie, R.V. Wagner & D.D. Winter (Eds.). *Peace, Conflict, and Violence* (pp. 49–65). New Jersey. Prentice Hall.

Duckett, P. (2005). Commentary: Globalised violence, community psychology and the bombing and occupation of Afghanistan and Iraq. *Journal of Community and Applied Social Psychology, 15*, 414–423.

Dumas, L.J. (2001). Why mistakes happen even when the stakes are high: The many dimensions of human fallibility. *Medicine and Global Survival, 7*, 1, 12–19.

Durkheim, E. (1982). The rules of sociological method. New York: Macmillan. (Original work published 1895.)

Durodie, N. (2004). Facing the possibility of bioterrorism. *Current Opinion in Biotechnology, 15*, 264–268.

Duveen, G. & Lloyd, B. (Eds.) (1990). *Social Representations and the Development of Knowledge.* Cambridge: Cambridge University Press.

Dyer, O. (2003a). Hundreds die in northern Iraq from land mines and unexploded munitions. *British Medical Journal, 326*, 166.

Dyer, O. (2003b). British Iraqi doctors set up charity to support Iraq's mental health services. *British Medical Journal, 327*, 832.

Dyer, O. (2004). Infectious Diseases in Iraq as public health service deteriorates *British Medical Journal, 329*, 940.

Edwards, D. & Cromwell, D. (2004) Mass deception: How the media helped the government deceive the people. In D. Miller (Ed.) *Tell Me Lies. Propaganda and media distortion in the attack on Iraq* (pp. 210–214). London: Pluto Press.

Eitinger, L. (1961). Pathology of the concentration camp syndrome. *Archives of General Psychiatry, 5*, 371–379.

Engelhardt, T. (2005). The Press in Iraq. November 4. <http://www.zmag.org/content/showarticle.cfm?SectionID=21&ItemID=9053>, accessed 14 November 2005.

Erdal, D., Whiten A., Boehm, C. & Knauft, B. (1994). On human egalitarianism: An evolutionary product of Machiavellian status escalation? *Current Anthropology, 35*, 175–183.

Ericsson, K.A. (Ed.) (1996). *The Road to Excellence: The acquisition of expert performance in the arts and sciences, sports and games.* New Jersey: Lawrence Erlbaum.

European Parliament (2001). Report on the existence of a global system for the interception of private and commercial communications (ECHELON interception system) Rapporteur: Gerhard Schmid. Luxembourg: European Parliament. <http://www.fas.org/irp/program/process/rapport_echelon_en.pdf>, accessed 28 September 2006.

European Union (2003). EU Council Directive on the reception of asylum seekers, 2003/9/EC of 27 January 2003.

Evans, R.I. (1976). *R.D. Laing: The man and his ideas.* New York: Dutton.

Fanon, F. (2005). *The Wretched of the Earth*. New York: Grove Press.

Farr, R.M. (1996). *The Roots of Modern Social Psychology*. Oxford: Blackwell.

Farrell, N. (2004). *Mussolini*. London: Weidenfeld and Nicholson.

Fay, MG G.R. (2004). AR 15-6 Investigation of the Abu Ghraib Detention facility and 205 Military Intelligence Brigade. <www4.army.mil/ocpa/reports/ar15-6/AR15-6.pdf>.

Ferguson, N. (2006). *The War of the World: History's age of hatred*. London: Allen Lane.

Ferguson, R.B. (2000). The causes and origins of 'primitive warfare'. On evolved motivations for war. *Anthropological Quarterley*, *73*, 3, 159–164.

Ferguson, R.B. (2001). 10,000 years of tribal warfare; History, science, ideology and 'the state of nature'. *The Journal of the International Institute*, *8*, 3. Summer. <http://www.umich.edu/~iinet/journal/vol8no3/ferguson.html>, accessed 20 March 2006.

Fest, J.C. (1974). *Hitler*. Harmondsworth: Penguin.

Festinger, L. (1957). *A Theory of Cognitive Dissonance*. Stanford, CA: Stanford University Press.

Fisk, R. (2006). Who knows how many atrocities have been committed? *The Independent*. 3 June.

Fitzpatrick, J. (1994). *Human Rights in Crisis: The international system for protecting rights during states of emergency. Volume 19, Procedural Aspects of International Law Series*. Philadelphia: University of Pennsylvania Press.

Foreign and Commonwealth Office (2002). *Saddam Hussein: Crimes and human rights abuses*. London: Foreign and Commonwealth Office.

Foster, M. (2006). Psychologists adopt anti-torture policy. *Washington Post*, 10 August.

Freedman, D. (2004). Misreporting war has a long history. In D. Miller (Ed.) *Tell Me Lies. Propaganda and media distortion in the attack on Iraq* (pp. 63–69). London: Pluto Press.

Freeman, S. & agencies (2005). Witnesses dispute official line on plane shooting. *The Times*, 9 December.

Fromm, E. (1942). *The Fear of Freedom*. London: Routledge.

Fromm, E. (1957). *The Art of Loving*. London: HarperCollins.

Fyans, T., Stankovich, M. & Paterson, M. (2003). Iraq: The human cost. *Amnesty*, *118*, 16–19.

Garbarino, J. & Kostelny, K. (1996). The effects of political violence on Palestinian children's behavior problems: A risk accumulation model. *Child Development*, *67*, 33–45.

Garrod, A., Beal, C.R., Jaeger, W., Thomas, J., Davis, J., Leiser, N. & Hodzic, A. (2003). Culture, ethnic conflict and moral orientation in Bosnian children. *Journal of Moral Education*, *32*, 2, 131–150.

Gat, A. (2000). The causes and origins of 'primitive warfare'. Reply to Ferguson. *Anthropological Quarterley*, *73*, 3, 165–168.

Gergen, K.J. (1999). *An Invitation to Social Construction*. London: Sage.

Gibbon, G. (2005) Law of the war. <http://www.channel4.com/news/2005/03/week_4/23_letter.html>, accessed 15 December 2005.

Gilbert, G.M. (1947) *Nuremberg Diary*. New York: Farrar, Straus & Company.

Gillan, A. (2006). Full house as leading 9/11 conspiracy theorist has his say. *The Guardian*, 9 September.

Gittings, J. (Ed.) (1991). *Beyond the Gulf War. The Middle East and the new world order*. London: Catholic Institute for International Relations.

Glasgow University Media Group (1985). *War and Peace News*. Buckingham: Open University Press.

Glover, J. (2005). Two-thirds believes London bombings are linked to Iraq war. *The Guardian*, 19 July. <http://www.guardian.co.uk/attackonlondon/story/0,16132,1531387,00.html>, accessed 19 July 2005.

Gobodo-Madikizela, P. (2003). *A Human Being Died that Night: A story of forgiveness*. Claremont, South Africa: David Philip.

Goldenberg, S. (2002). Big Brother will be watching America. *The Guardian*, 23 November, p. 16.

Goldhagen, D.J. (1997). *Hitler's Willing Executioners: Ordinary Germans and the Holocaust*. Little Brown & Company.

Goldstein, R.D., Wampler, N.S. & Wise, P.H. (2005). War experiences and distress symptoms of Bosnian children. *Pediatrics*, *100*, 873–878.

Goldston, J. (2006). Ethnic profiling and counter-terrorism trends, dangers and alternatives. Anti-Racism and Diversity Intergroup, European Parliament. <http://www.soros.org/resources/articles_publications/articles/counterterrorism_20060606/goldston_20060606.pdf>, accessed 28 September 2006.

Gordon, A.F. (2006). Abu Ghraib: Imprisonment and the War on Terror. *Race and Class, 48,* 42–59.

Granovetter, M. (1973). The strength of weak ties. *American Journal of Sociology, 68,* 1360–1380.

Gray, J. (2002). *False Dawn: The delusions of global capitalism.* London: Granta.

Gray, J. (2005). Power and vainglory. *The Independent Review,* 19 May, p. 3.

Gray, G. & Zielinski, A. (2006). Psychology and US psychologists in torture and war in the Middle East. *Torture, 16,* 2, 128–133.

Greenfield, P. (1977). CIA's behavior caper. *APA Monitor, 1,* (December) 10–11. <http://www.cia-on-campus.org/social/behavior.html>, accessed 26 September 2006.

Greenwood, J.D. (2004). *The disappearance of the social in American social psychology.* Cambridge: Cambridge University Press.

Gregory, F. & Wilkinson, P. (2005). Riding pillion for tackling terrorism is a high-risk policy. *In Security, Terrorism and the UK.* Chatham House ISP/NSC Briefing Paper 05/01.

Grice, A. (2004). Chirac speaks out on differences over Iraq ahead of Blair meeting. *The Independent.* 18 November, p. 2.

Grose, P.M. (2005). Iraq—Should the BPS have a view? Letters. *The Psychologist, 18,* 4, 199.

Grossman, D. (1996). *On Killing: The psychological cost of learning to kill in war and society.* New York: Back Bay Books.

Guardian (2003). Awe from the air. The aim is to show resistance is futile. 23 March. *The Guardian.*

Gudjonsson, G.H. (1999). *The Psychology of Interrogations, Confessions, and Testimony.* New York: Wiley.

Gudjonsson, G.H. (2003). *The Psychology of Interrogations and Confessions: A handbook.* Chichester: Wiley.

Hakvoort, I. & Hägglund, S. (2001). Giving voice to children's perspectives on peace. In D.J. Christie, R.V. Wagner & D.D. Winter (Eds.). *Peace, Conflict, and Violence.* New Jersey. Prentice Hall.

Hakvoort, I., Hägglund, S. & Oppenheimer, L. (1998). Dutch and Swedish adolescents' understanding of peace and war. In J.-E. Nurmi (Ed.) *Adolescents, Cultures and Conflicts: Growing up in contemporary Europe* (pp. 75–105). MSU Series on Children, Youth and Family. New York: Garland.

Hall, B. (1994). *The Impossible Country.* Harmondsworth: Penguin.

Halpin, E.F. & Wright, S. (2002). The hidden dimensions of global information networks. What price privacy? <http://www.lmu.ac.uk/ies/im/2002-4.pdf>, accessed 29 September 2006.

Hamwee, J. (1986). Dialogue with decision makers. Paper presented at the London conference of the British Psychological Society, December, London, UK.

Hamwee, J., Miall, H. & Elworthy, S. (1990). The assumptions of British nuclear weapons decision makers. *Journal of Peace Research, 27,* 359–372.

Hardy, R. (2005). Multi-culturalism under spotlight. <http://news.bbc.co.uk/1/hi/uk/4681615.stm>, accessed 14 July 2005.

Hargreaves, S. (2003). Questions remain over lack of UN role in humanitarian aid in Iraq. *British Medical Journal, 326,* 729.

Harper, D.J. (2000). Some effects of conspiracy thinking and paranoid labelling. *Clio's Psyche* [Special issue: The Psychology of Conspiracy Theories], *7,* 112–113.

Harper, D.J. (2003). Poverty and discourse. In S.C. Carr & T.S. Sloan (Eds.) *Poverty & Psychology: From global perspective to local practice* (pp. 185–204). New York: Kluwer-Plenum.

Harper, D.J. (2004). Psychology and the 'War on Terror'. *Journal of Critical Psychology, Counselling and Psychotherapy, 4,* 1–10.

Harris, P. & Beaumont, P. (2006). Iraq war created a terrorist flood, American spymasters warn Bush. *The Observer.* <http://www.guardian.co.uk/Iraq/Story/0,,1879940,00.html>, accessed 24 September 2006.

Hasanovic, M., Sinanoviæ. O. & Pavloviæ, S. (2005). Acculturation and psychological problems of adolescents from Bosnia and Herzegovina during exile and repatriation. *Croatian Medical Journal, 46,* 1, 105–115.

Haslam, S.A. & Reicher, S.D. (2005). The psychology of tyranny. *Scientific American Mind, 16,* 3, 44–51.

Hassan, N. (2001). An arsenal of believers: Talking to the 'human bombs'. *The New Yorker.* November 19 <http://www.newyorker.com/fact/content/?011119fa_FACT1>, accessed 24 May 2005.

Hausman, K. (2006) Military looks to psychologists for advice on interrogations. *Psychiatric News*, (7 July), *41*, 3, 4.

Hayes, B. (2006). *Arming Big Brother: The EU's Security Research Programme*. Amsterdam: Transnational Institute/Statewatch. <http://www.statewatch.org/news/2006/apr/bigbrother.pdf>, accessed 28 September 2006.

Herman, J.L. (2001). *Trauma and Recovery. From domestic violence to political terror*. London: Pandora.

Herman, E. S. & Chomsky, N. (1994). *Manufacturing Consent: The political economy of the mass media*. London: Vintage.

Hewstone, M., Tausch, N., Voci, A., Hughes, J., Kenworthy, J. & Cairns, E. (in press). Prior intergroup contact and killing of ethnic out-group neighbours. In V. Esses & R. Vernon (Eds.) *Why Neighbours Kill*. Montreal, Canada: McGill University Press.

Hinkle Jr, L.E. & Wolff, H.G. (1956). Communist interrogation and indoctrination of 'enemies of the States': Analysis of methods used by the Communist State police (a Special Report). *Archives of Neurology and Psychiatry*, *76*, 115–174.

Hinton, J. (1988). *Protests and Visions*. London: Hutchinson.

Hitchens, C. (1995). Minority report. *The Nation*, *261*, 21. 18 December. <http://www.barnsdle.demon.co.uk/bosnia/nowin.html>, accessed December 2005.

Hodge, J. & Cooper, L. (2004). Roots of Abu Ghraib in CIA techniques—50 years of refining and teaching torture found in interrogation manuals. *National Catholic Reporter,* 5 November 2004. <www.NCRonline.org/29>, accessed 2 February 2005.

Hoffman, M.A. & Bizman, A. (1976). Attributions and responses to the Arab–Israeli conflict: A developmental analysis. *Child Development, 67*, 117–128.

Hoffman, P. (2004). Human rights and terrorism. *Human Rights Quarterly, 26*, 932–955.

Hogg, A. (2003). Lessons from Britain's War on Terror 1971–1972. *The Supporter*, 24 March, p. 2.

Home Office (2006). The New Asylum Model: Swifter decisions—faster removals. <http://www.ind.homeoffice.gov.uk/aboutus/newsarchive/nam>, accessed December 2006.

Horgan, J. (2005). *The Psychology of Terrorism*. London: Frank Cass.

Horowitz, M. (1998) *Psychodynamics and Cognition*. London: University of Chicago.

Horowitz, M. & Arthur, R. (1988) Narcissistic rage in leaders: The intersection of individual dynamics and group process. *International Journal of Social Psychiatry 34*, 2, 135–141.

Horton, R. (2004). The war in Iraq: Civilian casualties, political responsibilities. *The Lancet*, *364*, 1831.

House of Commons (2005/2006) Legislative and Regulatory Reform Bill. <http://www.publications.parliament.uk/pa/cm200506/cmbills/141/06141.i-ii.html>, accessed 2 May 2006.

House of Lords (2004). Judgments—A(FC) and others (FC) (Appellants) v Secretary of State for the Home Department (Respondent) House of Lords UKHL 56. Thursday 16 December.

Hudson, K. (2005). *CND: Now More than Ever. The story of a peace movement*. London: Vision Paperbacks.

Hudson, R.A. (1999). *The Sociology and Psychology of Terrorism: Who becomes a terrorist and why?* Washington, DC: Federal Research Division, Library of Congress.

Human Rights Watch (2003). Rwanda lasting wounds: Consequences of genocide and war for Rwanda's children. <http://hrw.org/reports/2003/rwanda0403/>, accessed 6 September 2006.

Human Rights Watch (2004). United States: Guantánamo two years on. <http://hrw.org/english/docs/2004/01/09/usdom6917.htm> Accessed 6 September 2006.

Hunt, S. (2004). *This Was Not Our War. Bosnian women reclaiming the peace*. Durham and London: Duke University Press.

Hunter, E. (1956). *Brainwashing: The story of the men who defied it*. New York: Pyramid Books.

Hutton. J.B.E. (2004). Report of the inquiry into the circumstances surrounding the death of Dr David Kelly CMG. <http://www.the-hutton-inquiry.org.uk/content/report/index.htm>, accessed 28 January 2004.

Hymans, J.E.C. (2006). *The Psychology of Nuclear Proliferation*. Cambridge: Cambridge University Press.

ICHRP (2000). *The Persistence and Mutation of Racism*. Geneva: International Council of Human Rights Policy.

ICHRP (2002). *Human Rights after September 11*. Versoix, Switzerland: International Council on Human Rights Policy.

ICRC (2004). Report of the International Committee of the Red Cross (ICRC) on the treatment by the coalition forces of prisoners of war and other protected persons by the Geneva Conventions in Iraq during arrest, internment and interrogation. ICRC. Geneva <www.redress.btinternet.co.uk/icrc_iraq.pdf>, accessed 2 June 2006.

Ignatieff, M. (2004). Mirage in the desert. *New York Times Magazine*, 27 June, 13–15.

Indemyer, J. (2001). Iraqi Sanctions: Myth and Fact. *Swans Commentary*. <http://www.swans.com/library/art7/jlind002.html>. 3 September.

Intelligence and Security Committee (2005). *The Handling of Detainees by UK Intelligence Personnel in Afghanistan, Guantánamo Bay and Iraq*. Norwich: HMSO.

Iyengar, S. (1990). Framing responsibility for political issues: The case of poverty. *Political Behavior, 12*, 19–40.

Jarret, C. (2006a). London bombings trauma victims still being found. News. *The Psychologist, 19*, 3, 132.

Jarrett, C. (2006b) Controversy over psychologists' role in national security. 24 August. <www.bps.org.uk/publications/thepsychologist/extras/pages$/2006-news/controversy-over-psychologists-role-in-national-security.cfm>, accessed 2 September 2006.

Jasper, J. (1997) *The Art of Moral Protest*. Chicago: University of Chicago Press.

Jenkins, S. (2005) Bush and Blair have brilliantly done bin Laden's work for him. *The Sunday Times,* 19 February.

Jensen, P.S. & Shaw, J. (1993). Children as victims of war: Current knowledge and future research needs. *Journal of the American Academy of Child and Adolescent Psychiatry, 32*, 4, 697–708.

Jiad, A.H. (2004). The BBC: A personal account. In D. Miller (Ed.) *Tell Me Lies. Propaganda and media distortion in the attack on Iraq*. London: Pluto Press.

Johnston, D. (2006). At a secret interrogation, dispute flared over tactics. *New York Times*, 10 September.

Joinson, A. (2003) Time to make love not war, *The Psychologist, 16*, 4, 224.

Joint Committee on Human Rights (2006). The UN Convention Against Torture (UNCAT). Nineteenth Report of Session 2005–6. Volume 1—Report and formal minutes. <www.parliament.uk/commons/selcom/hrhome.htm>, accessed 8 June 2006.

Jolly, S. (2001). Wearing the Stag's Head badge: British combat propaganda since 1945. *Falling Leaf: The Journal of the Psywar Society*, March. <http://www.kcl.ac.uk/orgs/icsa/Old/jolly-stag.html>.

Judd, T. (2006). For the women of Iraq, the war is just beginning. *The Independent*. 8 June.

Justo, L. (2006). Doctors, interrogation, and torture. *British Medical Journal, 332*, 1462–1463.

Kaldor, M. (2001). *New and Old Wars: Organized violence in a global era*. Cambridge: Polity Press.

Kassin, S.M. & Gudjonsson, G.H. (2004). The psychology of confessions: A review of the literature and issues. *Psychological Science in the Public Interest, 5*, 33–67.

Keefe, P.R. (2006). Can network theory thwart terrorists? *New York Times*, 12 March.

Keller, A.S., Rosenfeld, B., Trinh-Sevrin, C. et al. (2003). Mental health of detained asylum seekers. *The Lancet, 362*, 1721–23.

Kent, B. (1992). *Undiscovered Ends: An autobiography*. London: HarperCollins.

Kershaw, I. (1987). *The Hitler Myth: Image and reality in the Third Reich*. Oxford: Oxford University Press.

Khan, I. (2006). Best of the web: Us and them. *The Guardian*, 26 August.

Kirkup, B. (2004). Battle hospital: Medics at war. *British Medical Journal, 328*, 530.

Kirkup, J. (2005). MI5 calls on Chancellor for more cash to fund fight against terror. *The Scotsman*, 21 November.

Klaehn, J. (Ed.) (2005). *Filtering the News. Essays on Herman and Chomsky's propaganda model*. London: Black Rose Books.

Klandermans, P.B. (1990). Linking the 'Old' and 'New' Social Movement networks in the Netherlands. In R. Dalton & M. Kuechler (Eds.) *Challenging the Political Order* (pp. 122–136). Cambridge: Polity.

Koocher, G.P. (2006). Speaking against torture. *APA Monitor, 3*, 2, 5.

Koppl, R. (2005). Epistemic systems: Episteme. *Journal of Social Epistemology, 2*, 2, 91–106.

Kos, A.M. & Derviškadiæ-Jovanoviæ, S. (1998). What can we do to support children who have been through war? *Forced Migration Review, 5*, 4–7.

Kovel, J. (1986) *Against the State of Nuclear Terror*. London: Free Association.

Krähenbühl, P. (2004). Iraq: ICRC calls for greater respect for basic tenets of humanity. *ICRC news 04/ 138*. 19 November.

Krebs, V. (2002–2006). Connecting the dots: Tracking two identified terrorists. <http://www.orgnet.com/ prevent.html>, accessed 28 September 2006.

Krieger, D. (2005). Einstein—Man of peace. In R. Braun & D .Krieger (Eds.) *Einstein—Peace now* (pp. 49–61). Weinheim: Wiley-VCH.

Kruglanski, A.W. & Fishman, S. (2006). Terrorism between 'syndrome' and 'tool'. *Current Directions in Psychological Science*, *15*, 1, 45–48.

Kuterovac, G., Dyregrov, A. & Stuvland, R. (1994). Children in war: a silent majority under stress. *British Journal of Medical Psychology*, *67*, 4, 363–377.

Laing, R.D. (1965a). *The Divided Self*. Harmondsworth: Penguin.

Laing, R.D. (1965b). Mystification confusion and conflict. In I. Boszormenyinagi & J.L. Framo (Eds.) *Intensive Family Therapy: Theoretical and practical aspects* (pp. 343–363). New York: Harper and Row.

Laing, R.D. (1967). *The Politics of Experience*. Harmondsworth: Penguin.

Laing, R.D. (1968). The obvious. In D. Cooper (Ed.) *The Dialectics of Liberation (*pp. 13–33). Harmondsworth: Penguin.

Laing, R.D. (1971). *The Politics of the Family and Other Essays*. London: Tavistock.

Laing, R.D. & Esterson, A.E. (1964). *Sanity, Madness and the Family*. London: Tavistock.

Langley, C. (2005). *Soldiers in the Laboratory: Military involvement in science and technology—and some alternatives*. London: Scientists for Global Responsibility. <http://www.sgr.org.uk/ ArmsControl/Soldiers_in_Lab_Report.pdf>, accessed 28 September 2006.

Laor, N., Wolmer, L. & Cohen, D.J. (2001). Mothers' functioning and children's symptoms 5 years after a SCUD missile attack. *American Journal of Psychiatry*, *158*, 1020–1026.

Leiman, M. (1997) Procedures as dialogical sequences: A revised version of the fundamental concept in cognitive analytic therapy. *British Journal of Medical Psychology*, *70*, 193–207.

Le Carré, J. (2003). The United States of America has gone mad. *The Times*, 15 January, p. 20.

Lee, M.A. & Shlain, B. (1992). *Acid Dreams: The complete social history of LSD: The CIA, the Sixties and beyond*. New York: Grove Press.

Leigh, D. (2004). UK forces taught torture methods. *The Guardian*, 8 May.

Leiman, M. (1997). Procedures as dialogical sequences: A revised version of the fundamental concept in cognitive analytic therapy. *British Journal of Medical Psychology*, *70*, 193–207.

Lévy-Bruhl, L. ([1925]/1926). *How Natives Think*. (Trans. Lilian Clare). London: George Allen and Unwin.

Lewis, N.A. (2004). Red Cross finds detainee abuse in Guantánamo. *New York Times*, 30 November (quoting leaked summary of ICRC report, 2004).

Lewis, N.A. (2005a). Interrogators cite doctors' aid at Guantánamo. *New York Times*, 24 June.

Lewis, N.A. (2005b). Guantánamo tour focuses on medical ethics. *New York Times*, 13 November.

Lewis, N.A. (2006). Military alters the makeup of interrogation advisers. *New York Times*, 7 June.

Lifton, R.J. (1967). *Thought Reform and the Psychology of Totalism: A study of brainwashing in China*. Harmondsworth: Penguin.

Lifton, R.J. (1986). *The Nazi Doctors: Medical killing and the nature of genocide*. New York: Basic Books.

Lifton, R.J. (2004). Doctors and torture. *New England Journal of Medicine*, *351*, 415–416.

Lopez, G.E., Gurin, P. & Nagda, B.A. (1998). Education and understanding structural causes for group inequalities. *Political Psychology, 19*, 305–329.

López, M.M. (1991). Hegemonic regulation and the text of fear in Puerto Rico: Towards a restructuring of common sense. Paper presented at Second Discourse Analysis Workshop/Conference, Manchester, UK.

López, M.M., Rueda, D. & Suárez, D. (1996). Colombia, the United States, drugs, terror and social control: Interview with Noam Chomsky. *Justicia y Paz*, *1*, 8–14.

Lynch, T. (2006) Doublespeak and the war on terrorism. Cato Institute. Briefing Paper no. 98. <http:// www.cato.org/pubs/bp/bp98.pdf>, accessed September 2006.

McAdam, D. (1988). *Freedom Summer*. New York: Oxford University Press.

McCoy, A.W. (2006). *A Question of Torture: CIA Interrogation, from the Cold War to the War on Terror*. New York: Metropolitan Books.

McDermott, M.R. (2004). Blame and responsibility in Abu Ghraib. *The Psychologist, 17*, 7, 424.

McFate, M. (2005). Anthropology and counterinsurgency: The strange story of their curious relationship. *Military Review*, March–April. <http://www.army.mil/professionalwriting/volumes/volume3/august_2005/7_05_2_pf.html>, accessed 28 September 2006.

Mack, A. & Nilezen, Z. (Eds.) (2005). *Human Security Report 2005: War and peace in the 21st century*. New York: Oxford University Press.

Mackey, C. & Miller, G. (2004). *The Interrogator's War: Inside the secret war against Al Queda*. London: John Murray.

Madood, T. (2005). Remaking multiculturalism after 7/7. <http://www.opendemocracy.net/conflict-terrorism/multiculturalism_2879.jsp#>, accessed 11 October 2006.

Maguire, D. (1992). When the streets began to empty. *West European Politics, 15*, 4, 75–94.

Maksoud, M.S. & Aber, J.L. (1996). The war experiences and psychosocial development of children in Lebanon. *Child Development, 67*, 70–88.

Malik, K. (2005). Multiculturalism fans the flames of Islamic extremism. *The Times,* 16 July.

Manchin, R., Kury, H., Van Dijk, J. & Schaber, G. (2006). *The EU ICS 2005: Highlights and policy implications*. The European Commission.

Manningham-Buller, E. (2005). The international terrorist threat and the dilemmas in countering it. <http://www.mi5.gov.uk/output/Page387.html>, accessed 10 September 2005.

Marsden, P. & Attia, S. (2005). A deadly contagion? *The Psychologist, 18*, 3, 152–155.

Mathur, S. (2006). Surviving the dragnet: 'Special interest' detainees in the US after 9/11. *Race and Class, 47*, 31–46.

Mayer, J. (2005). The experiment. *The New Yorker*, 11 and 18 July. <http://www.newyorker.com/fact/content/articles/060227fa_fact>, accessed 28 September 2006.

Mayer, J. (2006). Outsourcing torture: The secret history of America's 'extraordinary rendition' program. *The New Yorker*, 14 February.

Mayes, I. (2005). Open door. *The Guardian*, 24 October.

Medact (2003) *Continuing Collateral Damage: The health and environmental costs of war on Iraq 2003*. London: Medact.

Medical Foundation (2004). Torture on the map. *The Supporter*, issue 29. London: Medical Foundation for the Care of Victims of Torture.

Meek, J. (2005). Nobody is talking. *The Guardian*, 18 February.

Meerloo, J.A.M. (1956). *The Rape of the Mind: The psychology of thought control, menticide and brainwashing*. New York: The Universal Library, Grosset & Dunlap.

Meloy, J. (2004). Indirect personality assessment of the violent true believer. *Journal of Personality Assessment, 82*, 138–146.

Merari, A. (1998). The readiness to kill and die: Suicidal terrorism in the Middle East. In W. Reich, (Ed.) *Origins of Terrorism: Psychologies, ideologies, theologies, states of mind* (pp. 192–207). Washington, NY: Woodrow Wilson Center Press.

Michael, G. & Wahba, K. (2001, 13 December). Transcript of bin Laden Videotape. Los Angeles Times. <http://www.rickross.com/reference/alqaeda/alqaeda34.html>, accessed 26 May 2005.

Miles, S.H. (2004). Abu Ghraib: Its legacy for military medicine. *The Lancet, 364*, 725–729.

Milgram, S. (1967). The small world problem. *Psychology Today, 2*, 60–67.

Milgram, S. (1974). *Obedience to Authority*. New York: HarperCollins.

Miller, D. (Ed.) (2004). *Tell Me Lies. Propaganda and media distortion in the attack on Iraq*. London: Pluto Press.

Mollard, C. (2001). Asylum: The truth behind the headlines. Oxfam. <http://www.oxfam.org.uk/what_we_do/issues/conflict_disasters/downloads/asylum_truth.pdf>, accessed 10 October 2005.

Monroe, K. R. & Kreidie, L. (1997). The perspective of Islamic fundamentalists and the limits of rational choice theory, *Political Psychology, 18*, 19–43.

Moran, M. (2005). Terrorist-suspect questioning prompts APA Ethics Review. *Psychiatric News*, 19 August, *40*, 16, 1.

Moran, M, (2006). AMA interrogation policy similar to APA's position. *Psychiatric News*, 7 July, *41*, 13, 1–4.

Moscovici, S. (1961/1976). *La Psychanalyse, Son image et son public*. Paris: PUF.

Moscovici, S. (1984). The phenomenon of social representation. In R. Farr & S. Moscovici (Eds.) *Social Representations* (pp. 3–69). Cambridge: Cambridge University Press.

Moscovici, S. & Duveen, G. (Eds.) (2000). *Social Representations: Explorations in social psychology*. Cambridge: Polity.

Moszynski, P. (2003). Deadly radiation ignored in Iraq. *British Medical Journal*, *327*, 11. Moszynski, P. (2004). A quarter of young children in Iraq are chronically malnourished. *British Medical Journal*, *329*, 819.

Mueller, J. (2005). Six rather unusual propositions about terrorism. *Terrorism and Political Violence*, *17*, 487–505.

Muldoon, O. (2003). The psychological impact of protracted campaigns of political violence on societies. In A. Silke (Ed.) *Terrorists, Victims and Society: Psychological perspectives on terrorism and its consequences* (pp. 161–174). Chichester: Wiley.

Mullan, B. (1995). *Mad to be Normal: Conversations with R.D. Laing*. London: Free Association.

Murray, A. & German, L. (2005). *Stop the War: The story of Britain's biggest mass movement*. London: Bookmarks.

Murray, C. (2005). Damning documentary evidence unveiled. Dissident bloggers in coordinated exposé of UK government lies over torture. 29 December: <http://www.craigmurray.co.uk/archives/2005/12/damning_documen.html>, accessed 11 January 2006.

Murray, C. (2006). *Murder in Samarkand*. Edinburgh. Mainstream.

National Commission on Terrorist Acts upon the United States (2004). *The 9/11 Commission Report: Final Report of the National Commission on Terrorist Acts upon the United States*. Authorized edition. London: W.W. Norton and Company. <www.9-11commission.gov/report/911Report.pdf>, accessed 3 October 2006.

Nie, N.H. (2001). Sociability, interpersonal relations, and the Internet: Reconciling conflicting findings. *American Behavioral Scientist*, *45*, 3, 420–435.

Nilson, K.A. (2004). 102,000 killed in Bosnia. *Norwegian News Agency*. <http://www.nrk.no/nyheter/utenriks/4260912.html>, accessed 15 November 2005.

Norton-Taylor, R. (1993). The spies who came in from the cold war. *The Guardian*, 17 July, p. 3.

Norton-Taylor, R. (2003). Law unto themselves. *The Guardian*, 14 March. <http://www.guardian.co.uk/Iraq/Story/0,2763,914020,00.html>, accessed 15 November 2004.

Norton-Taylor, R. (2005). Revealed: The rush to war. *The Guardian*, 23 February. <http://politics.guardian.co.uk/iraq/story/0,12956,1423304,00.html>, accessed 4 December 2005.

Norton-Taylor, R. & White, M. (2005). Secrecy gag prompted by fear of new Blair–Bush revelations. *The Guardian*, 24 November.

Osborne, P. (2006). *The Use and Abuse of Terror: The construction of a false narrative on the domestic terror threat*. London: Centre for Policy Studies.

O'Brien, L.S. (1998). *Traumatic Events and Mental Health*. Cambridge: Cambridge University Press.

O'Connell, J. & Whitby, S. (2001). Constructing and operating a Department of Peace Studies at the University of Bradford: A reflection on experience between 1973 and 1995. Bradford University Department of Peace Studies. <http://www.brad.ac.uk/acad/peace/tmp/about/history.pdf >, accessed 15 July 2006.

Office of the High Commissioner for Human Rights (OHCHR) (1966). International Covenant on Civil and Political Rights. <http://www.ohchr.org/english/law/ccpr.htm>. Accessed October 2006.

Office of the High Commissioner for Human Rights (OHCHR) (1984) Convention against Torture and Other Cruel, Inhuman or Degrading Treatment or Punishment. <http://www.unhchr.ch/html/menu3/b/h_cat39.htm>, accessed October 2006.

Office of Surveillance Commissioners (2006). Annual Report of the Chief Surveillance Commissioner to the Prime Minister and to Scottish Ministers for 2005–2006. London: The Stationery Office. <http://www.official-documents.co.uk/document/hc0506/hc12/1298/1298.pdf >, accessed 28 September 2006.

Oliver, A.M. & Steinberg, P.F. (2005). *The Road to Martyrs' Square*. Oxford: Oxford University Press.

Oliver, L.M. (2005). Iraq—Should the BPS have a view? Letters. *The Psychologist*, *18*, 4, 198.

O'Neil, S. (2002). The extremist network that sprang from 'Londonistan'. *News.Telegraph*. <http://www.news.telegraph.co.uk/news/main.jhtml?xml=/news/2002/01/03/whij103.xml>, accessed 25 November 2005.

Orwell, G. (1970). *Nineteen Eighty-Four*. London: Penguin Books.

Otunnu, O. (2002). Protecting children from war. *SGI quarterly*, 30 October. <http://www.sgi.org/english/Features/quarterly/0210/feature1.htm>, accessed 4 September 2006.

Padel, R. (2005) *Tigers in Red Weather*. London: Little, Brown.

Pais, A. (2005). *Subtle is the Lord: The science and the life of Albert Einstein*. Oxford: Oxford University Press.

Palmer, I. (2002). Psychosocial costs of war in Rwanda. *Advances in Psychiatric Treatment*, *8*, 17–25.

Pape, R.A. (2005). *Dying to Win: The strategic logic of suicide terrorism*. New York: Random House.

Patel, N. (2003). Clinical psychology: Reinforcing inequalities or facilitating empowerment? *International Journal of Human Rights*, *7*, 1, 16–39.

Patel, N. (2007). 'What are my human rights if I am not even human to others?' Developing psychological health services for refugee survivors of torture. In S. Fernando & F. Keating (Eds.) *Mental Health in Multiethnic Society*. London: Brunner-Routledge.

Patel, N. & Granville-Chapman, C. (2006). *Assessment of Vulnerable Survivors of Torture: Good practice guidelines*. London: Medical Foundation for the Care of Victims of Torture & Department of Health.

Patel, N. & Mahtani, A. (2004). Psychological approaches to working with political rape. In M. Peel (Ed.) *Rape as Torture* (pp. 21–41). London: Medical Foundation for the Care of Victims of Torture.

Patel, N., Saviæ, B., Pen a, C. & Williams, A. (2006). *Clinical Audit Report 2005*. London: Medical Foundation for the Care of Victims of Torture.

Perks, N. (2005). *Money for Peace: A study of income of UK peace organisations*. York. Joseph Rowntree Charitable Trust. November. <http://www.jrct.org.uk/documents.asp?section=00010006>, accessed 25 June 2006.

Perry, W.J. (1995). US Policy on Bosnia remains consistent. *Defence Issues*, *10*, 60. <http://www.defenselink.mil/speeches/1995/t19950607-perry.html>, accessed 8 November 2005.

Petersen, C., Maier, S.F. & Seligman, M.E.P. (1995). *Learned Helplessness: A theory for the age of personal control*. New York: Oxford University Press.

Pettigrew, T.F. (1998). Applying social psychology to international social issues. *Journal of Social Issues*, *54*, 4, 663–675.

Pfaff, W. (2005). A monster of our own making. *The Observer*, 21 August.

Pfefferbaum, B., Seale, T.W., Brandt, E.N. Jr., Pfefferbaum, R.L., Doughty, D.E. & Rainwater, S.M. (2003). Media exposure in children one hundred miles from a terrorist bombing. *Annals of Clinical Psychiatry*, *15*, 1–8.

Phillips, T. (2005). Sleepwalking to segregation. Speech given at the Manchester Council for Community Relations. 22 September 2005. <http://www.cre.gov.uk/Default.aspx.LocID-0hgnew07s.RefLocID-0hg00900c002.Lang-EN.htm>, accessed 11 December 2005.

Philo, G. & Berry, M. (2004). *Bad News from Israel*. London: Pluto Press.

PHR (2002). *Dual Loyalty and Human Rights in Health Professional Practice: Proposed guidelines and institutional mechanisms*. Cape Town: Physicians for Human Rights & School of Public Health and Primary Health Care, University of Cape Town.

PHR (2005). *Break Them Down: Systematic use of psychological torture by US Forces*. Cambridge, MA: Physicians for Human Rights.

Pilger, J. (2003a). Foreword. In M. Curtis *Web of Deceit. Britain's real role in the world* (pp. ix–xv). London: Random House.

Pilger, J. (2003b). John Pilger reveals WMDs were just a pretext for planned war on Iraq. *Daily Mirror*, 22 September.

Pinker, S. (1998). *How the Mind Works*. London: Allen Lane.

Pomerantz, J. (2001). Analyzing the terrorist mind. *Drug Benefit Trends*, *13*, 2–3.

Pope, J. (2005). 9/11 conspiracy theorists thriving. *ABC News*, 5 October. http://abcnews.go.com/US/

wireStory?id=2279929>, accessed October 4 2006.

Popular Mechanics (2005). Debunking the 9/11 myths. *Popular Mechanics*, March. <http://www.popularmechanics.com/technology/military_law/1227842.html?page=2>, accessed 3 October.

Porter, B. (1992). *Plots and Paranoia: A history of political espionage in Britain 1790–1988*. London: Routledge.

Portillo, M. (2005). Does Britain need nuclear weapons? No. Scrap them. *Sunday Times*, June 19. <http://www.timesonline.co.uk/article/0,,2088-1660237,00.html>, accessed 25 June 2006.

Post, J.E., Sprinzak, E. & Denny, L.M. (2003). The terrorists in their own words: Interviews with 35 incarcerated Middle Eastern terrorists. *Terrorism and Political Violence, 15*, 171–184.

Potter, S. & Lloyd, J. (2005). With war in mind: A dialogical analysis of the mindset underlying Blair's case for war with Iraq in 2003. *Medicine Conflict and Society, 21*, 4, 283–298.

Pourgourides, C., Sashidharan, S. & Bracken, P. (1995). *A Second Exile: The mental health implications of detention of asylum seekers in the United Kingdom*. Birmingham: North Birmingham Mental Health Trust.

The Power Enquiry (2006). *Power to the People: An independent enquiry into Britain's democracy*. York: York Publishing Distribution. <http://www.powerinquiry.org/report/documents/PowertothePeople_002.pdf >.

Power, S. (2003). *A Problem from Hell*. London: Flamingo.

Preston, P. (1995). *Franco: A biography*. London: Fontana.

Priest, D. & Gellman, B. (2002). US decries abuse but defends interrogations. *Washington Post*, 26 December.

Pruit, D.G. & Kim, S.H. (2004). *Social Conflict: Escalation, stalemate, and settlement* (3rd edn). London: McGraw-Hill.

Punamaki, R.L. (1996). Can ideological commitment protect children's psychosocial well-being in situations of political violence? *Child Development, 67*, 55–69.

Punamaki, R.L. & Suleiman, R. (1990). Predictors and effectiveness of coping with political violence among Palestinian children. *British Journal of Social Psychology, 29*, 1, 67–77.

Quiroga, J. & Jaranson, J.M. (2005). Politically motivated torture and its survivors: A desk study review of the literature. *Torture, 15*, 2–3, 1–111.

Rai, M. (2002). Children against the war demonstration. Justice not vengeance. <http://www.j-n-v.org/ARCHIVE/children.htm>, accessed 3 September 2006.

Rampton, S. (2003). Transcript of interview conducted on 19 July 2003. <www.firethistime.org/ramptoninterview.htm>, accessed 4 November 2003.

Rampton, S. & Stauber, J. (2003). *Weapons of Mass Deception: The uses of propaganda in Bush's war on Iraq*. London: Robinson.

Rangwala, G. (2002). *Iraq and the West: The politics of confrontation*. Cheltenham: Understanding Global Issues Ltd.

Rapoport, D.C. (1998). Sacred terror: A contemporary example from Islam. In W. Reich (Ed.) *Origins of Terrorism: Psychologies, ideologies, theologies, states of mind* (pp. 103–130). Washington, NY: Woodrow Wilson Center Press.

Rasmussen, O.V., Amris, S., Blaauw, M. & Danielsen, L. (2005). Medical physical examination in connection with torture. *Torture, 15*, 1, 37–45.

Rasmussen, O.V., Amris, S., Blaauw, M. & Danielsen, L. (2006). Medical physical examination in connection with torture. *Torture, 16*, 1, 48–55.

Rasul, Iqbal & Ahmed (2004). Statement of Rasul, Iqbal and Ahmed on their detention in Guantánamo Bay. London: Birnberg Peirce.

Ray, P. (2006). New AMA ethical policy opposes direct physician participation in interrogation. Press release, 12 June. AMA. <www.ama-assn.org/ama/pub/category/16446.html>, accessed 20 August 2006.

Rees, L. (1997). *The Nazis: A warning from history*. London: BBC.

Reich, W. (1975). *The Mass Psychology of Fascism*. London: Pelican.

Reich, W. (1998). Understanding terrorist behavior: The limits and opportunities of psychological inquiry. In W. Reich (Ed.) *Origins of Terrorism: Psychologies, ideologies, theologies, states of mind* (pp.

261–279). Washington, NY: Woodrow Wilson Center Press.

Reuter, C. (2004). *My Life is a Weapon: A modern history of suicide bombing*. Princeton, NJ: Princeton University Press.

Reyes, H. (1995). Torture and its consequences. *Torture, 5*, 4, 72–76.

Reynolds, P. (2006). Conspiracy theorists down but not out. *BBC News Online*, 17 May. <http://news.bbc.co.uk/1/hi/world/americas/4990686.stm>, accessed 3 October 2006.

Richards, G. (2002). *Putting Psychology in its Place* (2nd edn). Sussex: Psychology Press.

Richmond, O. (2005). Understanding the Liberal Peace. Conference Paper, Society for Conflict Resolution. Presented March 2005. Goldsmith College, London University.

Rimmington, S. (1994). Security and democracy: Is there a conflict? The Richard Dimbleby Lecture. BBC Television, 12 June.

Robbins, I. (2004). Interrogation. *New Scientist, 184*, 2474, 44–45.

Robbins, I., MacKeith, J., Davison, S., Kopelman, M., Meux, C., Ratnam, S., Somekh, D. & Taylor, R. (2005). Psychiatric problems of detainees under the Anti-Terrorism Crime and Security Act 2001. Psychiatric Bulletin, *29*, 407–409.

Roberts, L., Rafta, R., Garfield, R., Khudhairi, J. & Burnham, G. (2004). Mortality before and after the 2003 invasion of Iraq. Cluster sample survey. *The Lancet*. Published online 29 October 2004. <http://image.thelancet.com/extras/04art10342web.pdf>.

Roberts, R. (2001). Science and experience. In R. Roberts & D.Groome (Eds.) *Parapsychology* (pp. 7–18). London: Arnold.

Roberts, R. (2005). The response of British Psychology to the Iraq War 2003–2004. *Journal of Critical Psychology, Counselling and Psychotherapy, 5*, 1, 1–9.

Roberts, R. & Esgate, A. (2005). Don't mention the war. Letters. *The Psychologist, 18*, 2, 64.

Robinson, P. (2005). The good news about terrorism. *The Spectator*, 2 April.

Rochon, T. (1990). The West European Peace Movement and NSM Theory. In R. Dalton & M. Kuechler (Eds.) *Challenging the Political Order* (pp. 105–121). Cambridge: Polity.

Rockefeller, N.A. et al. (1975). Report to the President by the Commission on CIA Activities within the United States (the Rockefeller Commission). Washington, DC: Government Printing Office.

Rogers, P. (2005). *Iraq and the War on Terror: Twelve months of insurgency 2004/2005*. London: I.B. Taurus.

Rome Statute of the International Criminal Court (1998). A/conf.183/9. <http://www.un.org/law/icc/statute/english/rome_statute(e).pdf>, accessed September 2006.

Ronson, J. (2004). *The Men who Stare at Goats*. London: Picador.

Rose, D. (2004). *Guántanamo: America's war on human rights*. London: Faber & Faber.

Rose, H. & Rose, S. (2001). *Alas Poor Darwin: Escaping evolutionary psychology*. London: Vintage.

Roseneil, S. (1995). *Disarming Patriarchy: Feminism and political action at Greenham*. Buckingham: Open University Press.

Roseneil S. (2000). *Common Women: Uncommon practices: The queer feminisms of Greenham*. London: Cassell.

Ross, C.E., Mirowsky, J. & Pribesh, S. (2001). Powerlessness and the amplification of threat: Neighbourhood disadvantage, disorder and mistrust. *American Sociological Review, 66*, 568–591.

Ross, L. (1977). The intuitive psychologist and his shortcomings: Distortions in the attribution process. In L. Berkowitz (Ed.) *Advances in Experimental Social Psychology (*vol. 10, pp. 174–220). New York: Academic Press.

Royal College of Psychiatrists (2006). Press release: Royal College of Psychiatrists passes resolution condemning psychiatric participation psychiatric participation in the interrogation of detainees. 12 July. <http://www.rcpsych.ac.uk/pressparliament/pressreleases2006/pr825.aspx>, accessed 28 September 2006.

Rubenstein, L.S. (2003). The medical community's response to torture. *The Lancet, 361*, 1556.

Rubenstein, L.S. (2005). Letter to Ronald F. Levant and Stephen Benke. July 15.

Ruthven, M. (2002). *A Fury for God: The Islamist attack on America*. London: Granta Publications.

Ruthven, M. (2004). *Fundamentalism: The search for meaning*. Oxford: Oxford University Press.

Ryle, A. & Kerr, I. (2002). *Introducing Cognitive Analytic Therapy: Principles and practice*. Chichester:

John Wiley and Sons.

Sack, W.H., Him, C. & Dickason, D. (1999). Twelve-year follow-up study of Khmer Youths who suffered massive war trauma as children. *Journal of the American Academy of Child and Adolescent Psychiatry, 38*, 9, 1173–1179.

Sageman, M. (2004a). Understanding terror networks. Foreign Policy Research Institute E-notes. 1 November. <http://www.fpri.org/enotes/20041101.middleeast.sageman.understandingterrornetworks.html>, accessed 28 September 2006.

Sageman, M. (2004b). *Understanding Terror Networks*. Pennsylvania: University of Pennsylvania Press.

Sampson, A. (2004). *Who Runs this Place? The anatomy of Britain in the 21st century*. London: John Murray.

Savage, C. (2005). Split seen on interrogation techniques. Navy official says many back stance against coercion. *The Boston Globe*, 31 March.

Save the Children Norway (2005). *Regional/Countries Situation Analysis. Sarajevo*. Save the Children Norway.

Scatamburlo-D'Annibale,V. (2005). In 'sync': Bush's war propaganda machine and the American mainstream media. In J. Klaehn (Ed.) *Filtering the News* (pp. 21–62). London: Black Rose Books.

Schatzman, M. (1973). *Soul Murder: Persecution in the family*. London: Allen Lane.

Schein, E.H., Schneier, I. & Barker, C.H. (1961). *Coercive Persuasion: A socio-psychological analysis of the 'brainwashing' of American civilian prisoners by the Chinese Communists*. New York: Norton.

Schlesinger, J.R., Brown, H., Fowler, T.F. & Horner, C.A. (2004). Final Report of the Independent Panel to Review DoD Detention Operations. The Schlesinger Report. August 24 <www.news.findlaw.com/cnn/docs/dod/abughraibrpt.pdf>, accessed 14 June 2006.

Schlesinger, P. (1991). *Media, State and Nation*. London: Sage.

Schmitt, E. (2005). In new manual, Army limits tactics in interrogation. *New York Times*, April 28.

Schmitt, E. (2006). Pentagon study describes abuse by units in Iraq. *The New York Times*, 17 June.

Scottish Bishops (2006). Statement on the Trident Nuclear Weapons System. <http://www.scmo.org/_titles/view.asp?id=460>, accessed 25 June 2006.

Seabrooke J. (1988). *The Myth of the Market*. London: Black Rose Books.

Sereny, G. (1974). *Into that Darkness*. London: Pimlico.

Sereny, G. (1995). *Albert Speer: His battle with truth*. London: Picador.

Shallice, T. (1972). The Ulster depth interrogation techniques and their relation to sensory deprivation research. *Cognition, 1*, 385–405.

Shallice, T. (1984). *Psychology and social control*. Cognition, *17, 29–48*.

Sheridan, L.P. & Gillett, R. (2005). Major world events and discrimination. *Asian Journal of Social Psychology, 8*, 191–197.

Sherrard, C. (1991). Letter: Facing up to social control. *The Psychologist, 4*, 463–464.

Shiner, P. (2005). Blind to Britain's torture. Letters, *The Guardian*, 13 March.

Shinn, B. (2006). Psychologists and torture: APA, PENS, SPSSI, and DSJ. Forward. *Society for the Psychological Study of Social Issues, 229*, April, 1–3.

Shotter, J. & Gergen, K.J. (Eds.) (1989). *Texts of Identity*. London: Sage.

Shue, H. (1978). Torture. *Philosophy and Public Affairs, 7*, 124–143.

Silke, A. (2004). Terrorism, 9/11 and psychology. *The Psychologist, 17*, 9, 518–521.

Silove, D., Steel, Z., McGorry, P. et al. (1998). Trauma exposure, post migration stressors and symptoms of anxiety, depression and post traumatic stress in Tamil asylum seekers: Comparisons with refugees and immigrants. *Acta Psychiatrica Scand, 97*, 3, 175–181.

Simonowitz, S. (2003). The Human Shield Movement. *Z Magazine online*, November 2003, Vol 16, 11. <http://zmagsite.zmag.org/Nov2003/simanowitzpr1103.html>.

Singh, R. (2003). Equality: The neglected virtue. Paper presented at London School of Economics, November.

Sivanandan, A. (2006). Race, terror and civil society. *Race & Class, 47*, 1–8.

Skons, E., Omitoogun, W., Perdomo, C. & Stalenhem, P. (2005). Military expenditure. In A. Bailes (Ed.) *SIPRI Yearbook 2005: Armaments, Disarmament and International Security* (pp. 307–344).

Stockholm. Stockholm International Peace Research Institute.

Sloboda, J.A. (2003). The war, what war? Psychology in Denial. *DECP Debate*, *107*, 5–11.

Sloboda, J.A. & Abbott, C. (2004). The 'Blair Doctrine' and after: 5 years of humanitarian intervention. *OpenDemocracy.net*, 22 April. <http://www.oxfordresearchgroup.org.uk/publications/briefings/blairdoctrine.pdf>. Accessed 25 June 2006.

Sloboda, J.A. & 16 others (2006). PTSD in Iraq. Letters. *The Psychologist*, *19*, 4, 205.

Snidal, D. (1985). The game theory of international politics. World Politics, *38*, 1, 25–57.

Soldz, S. (2005). To heal or to patch? Military mental health workers in Iraq. *Znet*, 29 November. <http://www.zmag.org/content/showarticle.cfm?ItemID=9221>, accessed 31 January 2006.

Staff and Agencies (2006). Prejudice against Jews and Muslims on the rise. *Guardian Unlimited*, 7 September. <http://www.guardian.co.uk/religion/Story/0,,1867065,00.html>, accessed 1 October 2006.

Stanley, J. (2004). The surveillance-industrial complex: How the American government is conscripting businesses and individuals in the construction of a surveillance society. New York: American Civil Liberties Union. <http://www.aclu.org/FilesPDFs/surveillance_report.pdf>, accessed 28 September 2006.

Stanton, M. (2006). Reid's Muslim advice. *Yellow Advertiser Walthamstow, Leyton & Chingford*, 27 September.

State Department (2005). How to identify misinformation. <http://usinfo.state.gov/media/Archive/2005/Jul/27-595713.html>, accessed 3 October 2006.

Statewatch (2003). Special Branch more than doubles in size. <http://www.statewatch.org/news/2003/sep/SB.pdf>, accessed 28 September 2006.

Staub, E. (2001). Genocide and mass killing: Their roots and prevention. In D.J. Christie, R.V. Wagner & D.D. Winter (Eds.) *Peace, Conflict, and Violence* (pp. 76–86). New Jersey: Prentice Hall.

Steel, Z., Momartin, S., Bateman, C., Hafshejani, A., Silove, D.M. et al. (2004). Psychiatric status of asylum seeker families held for a protracted period in a remote detention centre in Australia. *Australian and New Zealand Journal of Public Health, 28*, 6, 23–32.

Steinhart, N. (2005). Group psychology, sacrifice, and war. *Peace Review: A Journal of Social Justice, 17*, 9–16.

Sterba, J. (2003). Terrorism and international justice. In J. Sterba (Ed.) *Terrorism and International Justice* (pp. 206–228). Oxford: Oxford University Press.

Stevens, J. (1987). *Storming Heaven: LSD and the American Dream*. New York: Grove Press.

Strasser, F. & Randolph, P. (2004). *Mediation: A psychological insight into conflict resolution*. London: Continuum International Publishing Group.

Such, E., Walker, O. & Walker, R. (2005). Anti-war children: Representation of youth protests against the Second Iraq War in the British national press. *Childhood*, *12*, 301–326.

Suedfeld, P. (1990). Psychologists as victims, administrators, and designers of torture. In P. Suedfeld (Ed.) *Psychology and Torture* (pp. 101–115). New York: Hemisphere.

Sultan, A. (2001). Testimony. *The Lancet*, *357*, 1426.

Sultan, A. & O'Sullivan, K. (2001). Psychological disturbance in asylum seekers held in long term detention: A participant–observer account. *Medical Journal of Australia, 175*, 593–596.

Summerfield, D. (1995). Addressing human response to war and atrocity: Major challenges in research and practices and the limitations of Western psychiatric models. In R. Kleber, C. Figley & B. Gersons (Eds.) *Beyond Trauma: Cultural and societal dynamics* (pp. 17–29). New York: Plenum.

Tajfel, H. (1981). *Human Groups and Social Categories: Studies in social psychology*. Cambridge: Cambridge University Press.

Tajfel, H. & Turner, J.C. (1986). The social identity theory of inter-group behavior. In S. Worchel & L.W. Austin (Eds.) *Psychology of Intergroup Relations* (pp. 7–24). Chicago. Nelson-Hall.

Taleb, B.A. (2004). *The Bewildered Herd. Media coverage of international conflicts and public opinion*. New York: iUniverse.

Tarifa, F. & Kloep, M. (1996). War versus ghosts: Children's fear in different societies. *Childhood, 3*, 1, 67–76.

Tarrow, S. (2000). Mad cows and social activists: Contentious politics in the trilateral democracies. In S.J. Pharr & R.D. Putnam (Eds.) *Disaffected Democracies* (pp. 270–289). Princeton, NJ: Princeton University Press.

Tayal, U. (2003). Public health at risk as aid agencies pull out of Iraq. *British Medical Journal, 327,* 522.

Taylor, P. (2006). The jihadi who turned 'supergrass'. *BBC News Online,* 13 September. <http://news.bbc.co.uk/1/hi/programmes/5334594.stm>, accessed 29 September 2006.

Thabet, A.A.M. (2006). Trauma exposure in pre-school children in a war-zone. *British Journal of Psychiatry, 188,* 154–158.

Thompson, J. (1985). *Psychological Aspects of Nuclear War.* Leicester: British Psychological Society.

Thomsen, A.B., Eriksen, J. & Smidt-Nielsen, K. (2000). Chronic pain in torture survivors. *Forensic Science International, 108,* 155–163.

Tipton Three (2004). Detention in Afghanistan and Guantánamo Bay: Statement of Shaifiq Rasul, Asif Iqbal and Rhuhel Ahmed, 26 July. <www.ccr-ny.org/v2/legal/september_11th/docs/Guantánamo_composite_statement_FINAL.pdf>, accessed 26 August 2006.

Todorov, T. (2003). *Hope and Memory. Reflections on the twentieth century.* London: Atlantic Books.

Tooby, J. & Cosmides, L. (1988). The evolution of war and its cognitive foundations. Institute for Evolutionary Studies, Technical report #88-1.

Unicef (2003). The situation of children in Iraq. <http://www.unicef.org/publications/pub_children_of_iraq_en.pdf>, accessed 4 March 2006.

United Nations (1982). UN Principles of Medical Ethics relevant to the role of health personnel, particularly physicians, in the protection of prisoners and detainees against torture and other cruel, inhuman or degrading treatment or punishment. UN: Geneva.

United Nations (2006). United Nations Human Rights experts request urgent closure of Guantánamo detention centre. Press release, 14 June. <www.unhcr.ch/hurricane/hurricane.nsf/view01/D916F2EB424D1588C1257188>, accessed 18 June 2006.

United Nations Development Programme (2005). Iraq Living Conditions Survey. <http://www.iq.undp.org/ILCS/overview.htm>, accessed 10 April 2006.

US Congress (1976). The Select Committee to Study Governmental Operations with Respect to Intelligence Activities, Foreign and Military Intelligence (the Church Committee), report no. 94-755, 94th Congress, Second Session. Washington, DC: Government Printing Office.

US Department of State (2000). *Patterns of Global Terrorism.* Washington, DC: US Department of State.

United States Senate Select Committee on Intelligence (2006). Report on Post War findings about Iraq's WMD programs and links to terrorism and how they compare with prewar assessments. <http://intelligence.senate.gov/phaseiiaccuracy.pdf>, accessed 8 September 2006.

Valenty, L.O. (2004). Organizational behavior theory and the socialization of the suicide terrorist. Paper presented at the Society of Political Psychology, Twenty-seventh Annual Scientific Meeting, July 15–18, 2004 in Lund, Sweden.

van Dijk, T.A. (1996). Discourse, opinions and ideologies. In C. Schäffner & H. Kelly-Holmes (Eds.) *Discourse and Ideologies* (pp. 7–37). Philadelphia: Multilingual Matters.

van Dijk, T.A. (2006). Discourse and manipulation. *Discourse & Society, 17,* 3, 359–383.

Verkaik, R. (2006). The war dividend. *The Independent,* 13 March.

Vernon, J. (1966). *Inside the Black Room: Studies of sensory deprivation.* London: Penguin.

Victorian, A. (1996). United States, Canada, Britain: Partners in mind control operations. <www.elfis.net/elfo10/mkconsp/mkuscan.txt>, accessed 16 March 2005.

Victorian Foundation for Survivors of Torture (1998). The East Timorese: Clinical and social assessments of applicants for asylum. In D. Silove & Z. Steel (1998) *The Mental Health and Well Being of Onshore Asylum Seekers in Australia* (pp. 23–27). Sydney: The University of New South Wales Research and Teaching Unit.

Voluntary Service Overseas (2002). The Live Aid legacy: The developing world through British eyes—A research report. London: VSO <www.vso.org.uk>.

Vulliamy, E. (1994). *Seasons in Hell: Understanding Bosnia's War.* London: Simon and Schuster.

Wagner, W. & Hayes, N. (2005). *Everyday Discourse and Common Sense: The theory of social representations.* Basingstoke: Palgrave Macmillan.

Waldron, J. (2003). Security and liberty: The image of balance. *Journal of Political Philosophy, 11,* 5–35.

Watson, P. (1978) *War on the Mind: The military uses and abuses of psychology.* New York: Basic Books.

Weizman, E. (2006). The art of war. <http://www.frieze.com/feature_single.asp?f=1165,>, accessed 28 September 2006.

Westermeyer, J. & Williams, M. (1998). Three categories of victimisation among refugees in a psychiatric clinic. In J. Jaranson & M. Popkin (Eds.) *Caring for Victims of Torture* (pp. 61–86). Washington, DC: American Psychiatric Press.

White, J. & Higham, S. (2004). Use of dogs to scare prisoners was authorised. *Washington Post*, 11 June.

Whittier, N. (1997). Political generations, micro-cohorts, and the transformation of social movements. American Sociological Review, *62*, 5, 760–778.

Whyte, J. & Schermbrucker, I. (2004). Young people and political involvement in Northern Ireland. *Journal of Social Issues, 60*, 603–627.

Wilks, M. (2005). A stain on medical ethics. *The Lancet, 366*, 429–431.

Williams, AC de C., Amris, K. & Van der Merwe, J. (2003). Pain in survivors of torture and organised violence. In J.O. Dostrovsky, D.B. Carr & M. Koltzenburg (Eds.) *Proceedings of the 10th World Congress on Pain* (pp. 791–802). Seattle: IASP Press.

Williams, R. (2006). The psychosocial consequences for children and young people who are exposed to terrorism, war, conflict and natural disasters. *Current Opinion in Psychiatry, 19*, 4, 337–349.

Wintour, P. (2006). 'Cross-dressing' on political policy is here to stay, says PM. *The Guardian*, 31 July, p. 6.

WMA (2006). World Medical Association Declaration of Tokyo: Guidelines for physicians concerning torture and other cruel, inhuman or degrading treatment or punishment in relation to detention and imprisonment. Adopted by the 29 World Medical Assembly, Tokyo, Japan, October 1975, and editorially revised at the 170 Council Session, Divonnes-les Bains, France, May 2005 and the 173rd Council session, Divonnes-les Bains, May 2006. <www.wma.net/e/policy/c18.htm>, accessed 23 July 2006.

Wood, N. (2005). *War Crime or Just War? The Iraq War 2003–2005*. London: South Hill Press.

Woodcock, A. & Ross T. (2005). Ex-MI5 boss criticises 'useless' ID cards. *The Independent*, 17 November.

Woodward, S. (1995). *Balkan Tragedy. Chaos and dissolution after the Cold War*. Washington: The Brookings Institution.

Woolf, L.M. & Hulsizer, M.R. (2004). Psychology of peace and mass violence. Genocide, torture, and human rights: Informational resources. <http://www.lemoyne.edu/OTRP/otrpresources/woolf_hulsizer0401.pdf>, accessed 16 March 2006.

Wright, S. (1998). An appraisal of technologies for political control. Luxembourg: European Parliament: Scientific And Technological Options Assessment. <http://www.statewatch.org/news/2005/may/steve-wright-stoa-rep.pdf>, accessed 28 September 2006.

Wright, S. (2002). Future sub-lethal, incapacitating and paralysing technologies: Their coming role in the mass production of torture, cruel, inhumane and degrading treatment. A draft paper presented to The Expert Seminar on Security Equipment and the Prevention of Torture, 25–26 October 2002. London, UK. <http://www.statewatch.org/news/2002/nov/torture.pdf>, accessed 28 September 2006.

Wright, S. (2005). The Echelon trail: An illegal vision. *Surveillance and Society 3*, 2/3, 198–215. <http://www.surveillance-and-society.org/Articles3(2)/echelon.pdf >, accessed 28 September 2006.

Yergin, D. (2006). Ensuring energy security. *Foreign Affairs, 85*, 2, 69–82.

Zivcic, I. (1993). Emotional reactions of children to war stress in Croatia. *Journal of the American Academy of Child and Adolescent Psychiatry, 32*, 4, 709–713.

Zizek, S. (2006). The depraved heroes of 24 are the Himmlers of Hollywood. *The Guardian*, 10 January.

Useful Addresses

Below we suggest a number of useful links where readers can find further information, connect to groups and organizations etc.

Aljazeera: http://www.aljazeera.com
Amnesty International: http://www.amnesty.org/
BBC TV True Spies website: http://news.bbc.co.uk/1/hi/programmes/true_spies/default.stm
Campaign against the Arms Trade: http://www.caat.org.uk/
Craig Murray Weblog (Former Ambassador to Uzbekistan): http://www.craigmurray.co.uk/
Disinfopedia: http://www.disinfopedia.org/
Electronic Lebanon: http://www.electronicintifada.net/lebanon/
The Fire this Time: http://www.firethistime.org/
Human Rights Watch: http://www.hrw.org
Information Warfare Site: http://www.iwar.org.uk/psyops/
Institute for Policy Research and Development: http://www.globalresearch.org/
International Committee of the Red Cross: http://www.icrc.org/
Iraq Body Count: http://www.iraqbodycount.net/
London Bombings Independent Inquiry: http://www.independentinquiry.co.uk/
Medical Foundation for the Care of Victims of Torture: http://www.torturecare.org.uk/
Oxford Research Group: http://www.oxfordresearchgroup.org.uk/welcome.htm
PR Watch: http://www.prwatch.org/
Privacy International: http://www.privacyinternational.org/
Psychologists Acting with Conscience Together (PsyAct): http://www.vanderbilt.edu/community/psyact/
Psychologists for Social Responsibility (PsySR): http://www.psysr.org/
Scientists for Global Responsibility: http://www.sgr.org.uk/
Statewatch: http://www.poptel.org.uk/statewatch/

INDEX

270 JUST WAR

Snidal, D. 220, 253
social
    breakdown, psychological concomitants of
        223
    constructionism 199
    Darwinists 221
    Identity Theory (SIT) 129
    network analysis 39
    different approach to 39
    reality 201
    representations
        of suicide attacks 206
        contemporary
    sciences involved in military 41
socialism as a political force 111
society
    dominated by suspicion 44
    for the Investigation of Human Ecology
        18, 19
    for the Study of Peace, Conflict, and Viol
        234
soldiers
    brutalisation of 26
    and court-martials 22
    resigned commissions 111
Soldz, S. 56, 253
South Vietnam 163
Southeast Asia 161
Special Immigration Appeals Commission
    (SIAC) 65
Speer, Albert 28, 184
spiked drinks 17
Stalin, Joseph 219
Stanley, J. 253
Stanton, M. 228, 253
State
    Department 253
    lack of trust in the 229
    terrorism 60
Statewatch 37, 44, 253
Staub, E. 218, 219, 253
Steel, Z. 69, 253
Steinhart, N. 216, 253
Sterba, J. 75, 253
Stevens, J. 17, 253
Stop the War Coalition (STWC) 119
Storr, Anthony 21
Strasser, F. 220, 253
Straw, Jack 49, 122, 207
Stress Positions 87
Such, E. 180, 253
Suedfeld, P. 86, 88, 254
Suharto. Mohammed 163
suicidal ideation 69
suicide

attacks
    psychology of 211
    social representations of 206
    bombings in London 195
    by detainees 28
    mass attempt 64
Sultan, A. 69, 254
Summerfield, D. 254
superpower, public opinion of 168
surveillance 15, 190
    face recognition 36
    new technologies 35
    from space platforms 36
    techniques, electronic 36
Survival, Evasion, Resistance and Escape
        training 85
survivors of torture, services for 103
Sutton, Jon 57
Syria 26
Tajfel, H. 129, 220, 254
Taleb, B.A. 47, 254
Tamil asylum seekers 69
Tarifa, F. 173, 254
Tarrow, S. 131, 254
Tayal, U. 54, 254
Taylor, P. 33, 254
terror 181
    state 197
terrorism 34, 52, 204, 205
    as construct 205
    deconstructing 199
    definition of 60, 75
    fear of 230
    Information Awareness 37
    laws to combat 192
    media coverage 230
    stopping 165
    Western view of 203
terrorists, predict potential 37
Thabet, A.A.M. 171, 254
Thatcher, Margaret 113, 115, 133, 204
'them' and 'us' 162
Third World and Environment Broadcasting
        Project 226
Thompson, J. 215, 254
Thomsen, A.B. 98, 254
thought control 167
TIA 38
ticking bomb scenario 29, 98
    flawed assumptions of 30
Tipton Three, the 100, 254
Tizard, Henry 17
Todorov, T. 189, 198, 254
Tokyo Declaration (1975) 71
Tooby, J. 221, 254